C000128506

Monkeys in My Garden

Valerie Pixley

Published in 2014 by FeedARead.com Publishing

Copyright © Valerie Pixley.

First Edition

The author has asserted their moral right under the
Copyright, Designs and Patents Act, 1988, to be identified
as the author of this work.

All Rights reserved. No part of this publication may be reproduced,
copied, stored in a retrieval system, or transmitted, in any form or by
any means, without the prior written consent of the copyright holder,
nor be otherwise circulated in any form of binding or cover other than
that in which it is published and without a similar condition being
imposed on the subsequent purchaser.

A CIP catalogue record for this title is available from the British
Library.

PROLOGUE

THE NIGHT THE BANDITS CAME

Saturday, 4th December, 2010

We were happy that day, I remember. It was a day of sunshine, of laughter, and perfect for filming. The sky was a pure, pure blue and light danced and sparkled all over the leaves of the Nhamacoa forest around us.

I remember the simple pleasure on Douglas′ face when he spotted the female bushbuck in the trees right in front of our house and came to call us. "Quick, quick, get the camera before she goes back into the forest!" I remember our laughter while we were filming the little Mupupu tree and the hundreds of insects feeding on its beautiful mauve-pink flowers rained their water down all over us. "Don′t let them pee on O'D's camera, Lee," I had told him. "It′s the only one we′ve got!"

How innocent and carefree life had seemed … and how naive we had been. Completely unaware of the danger that was on its way to our secluded little forest … completely unaware that in a few short hours our lives were going to be turned upside down.

Actually, Lee had sensed the danger but had been side-tracked by something very strange and almost supernatural that had happened to him.

One evening, earlier in the week, he had been overcome with a premonition that something terrible was about to happen. The premonition had been so dark, so powerful that he had even phoned his mother in Zimbabwe to tell her about it.

Then, a few evenings later, when he had been opening the gate to his rented cottage in Chimoio, he had felt something moving under his right foot, something wriggling and struggling under his shoe. He had looked down and had got the shock of his life. He had been standing on the head of a black mamba!

Leaping high up in the air with terror, he had made a wild dash for his cottage and had locked himself in. Peering through the window he had seen the snake coming after him, as if hunting him down, but then his landlord's cat had appeared on the scene and launching a series of attacks, had sent the snake slithering off.

"I don't think that snake could have been a black mamba, Lee," O'D had told him.

"It *was* a black mamba," Lee had insisted stubbornly. "I know what a black mamba looks like. I saw one in the Harare Snake Park."

Overwhelmed by his narrow escape from death and convinced that the snake, a symbol of the devil, had been sent to take him out, Lee had relaxed, thinking that the danger was all over. But he had been wrong.

His premonition hadn't been about the snake. It had been about a dark blue Toyota Mark II that was about to set off from Chimoio that very afternoon for the drive down to our forest and whose occupants were to prove just as deadly as a poisonous snake.

It was late afternoon when Lee and I finished editing the last of O'D's films about the little genet he had raised. We were working at the table in the sitting room and the chairs were hard.

"We need a break," I said, standing up and stretching my stiff back. "What about a Coke, Lee?"

"Thanks, Val," he said. His eyes were bloodshot from the long hours we had spent working at his computer. "But I think I'll go for a walk first."

We didn't know that the dark blue Toyota had been cruising around the area asking questions about us and that while Lee was walking around under the trees, it was pulling up next to the ramshackle little bancas at the entrance to our forest.

A big man climbed out of the Toyota. "I'm a friend of the foreigner who lives here," he told the staring locals. "How do I get to his house?"

After he and his companions had walked off along the path to our shop, the locals examined the shiny Toyota with wonder. Cars like this never drove around rural areas.

"It's a Mercedes," they decided. "It's foreign. Look at the number plate. It's not Mozambican. AAM 201 MC. It must be from Alemanha, Germany."

In the shop, Douglas was busy setting up the television, DVD player and speakers. Saturday nights were the nights we showed free films to the local people and tonight he had chosen 'Special Forces

U.S.A.' It was an exciting film, full of action. Just the kind of film the locals enjoyed.

He didn't know that the big man who walked up the steps into the shop had been asking questions about him and had come to look him over.

"Four GTs," the big man ordered, handing over a 200 meticais note, "and a Fanta."

Everyone stared while the big man lit a cigarette and then drank some Fanta. No one in the rural areas bought four cigarettes and a drink with a 200 meticais note!

The staring made the big man uneasy. Halfway through the Fanta, he put the bottle down on the counter and abruptly left the shop. Douglas and the locals stared after his retreating back. No one bought a drink and then left half of it to go to waste!

When dusk fell, I plugged in a lamp and put it close to Lee's computer so that he could see his keyboard. Douglas had turned on the generator to show the film so we had electricity.

"Look at this, Val," Lee said, "look at what I've done to Amelia in Images of How We Live."

He had speeded up the film of Amelia ironing with the charcoal iron and now she ironed away furiously, flipping O'D's socks down one by one onto the ironing table in what looked like a very petulant manner. At the end, there was a shot of me holding up the ironing blanket which was full of iron-shaped burn holes.

I burst out laughing. "Oh, I like that. Let's see it again, Lee."

Suddenly, the cats began to growl. They had been lying all over the chairs, the sofa and the carpet but now they ran out of the room in a small bunched herd, growling and milling around uneasily in the corridor.

"That's strange," I said. I stood up and walked to the door. There was nothing to see and nothing to hear. "It must have been the male buck," I told Lee. "They always growl when they hear it bark. For some reason they don't like the sound."

We didn't know that while we had been bending over the computer laughing at Amelia, men had crept silently up the back stairs and had been watching us through the window. Watching and making a note of Lee's computer, O'D's camera, the solar inverter and the batteries.

We went to bed around about half past ten. As I drifted off to sleep, Douglas turned off the generator and I heard the large crowd of filmgoers making their way down the path through the forest to their huts. They were talking and laughing at the top of their voices … loud … always so loud. My eyelids closed and I fell into a deep and dreamless sleep … until about three o´clock in the morning …

BANG!

O´D and I started awake.

"What the …" he said.

The loud bang was followed by smashing, crashing, cracking sounds as our back door shattered.

O´D jumped out of bed, and grabbing his torch, ran to the door. He opened it and stepped into the corridor. The light of his torch picked out a horrifying sight and his heart quailed.

Men, armed men, were storming down the corridor towards him!

Running back into our bedroom, he slammed the door shut and locked it.

"Four of them," he told me grimly. "Armed with an AK-47, a pistol and machetes! Bandits!"

Aah! Icy dark terror flooded through every fibre of my being and my heart speeded up wildly, thumping erratically and painfully in my chest. Bandits! Everyone´s worst nightmare in Mozambique! They were going to kill us! We were going to die!

I scrambled out of bed and fumbled around in the dark for my pepper spray I had so carelessly left on top of my dressing table.

The bandits began to attack our door and while they smashed and hacked and kicked at it, I could hear more of them in the bedroom next to ours where Lee had been sleeping. There was the sound of a gunshot and then the acrid smell of cordite.

"Where is the computer?" they shouted at Lee, hitting him with a machete. "Where is the camera?" They kicked him in the face.

Our bedroom door lock suddenly splintered out of the wooden frame and the door burst open. I froze, all thoughts of my pepper spray forgotten. The bandits were in! But … no! O´D threw his weight against the door and slammed it shut. The bandits kicked it open again. Again he threw his weight against it. Open! Shut! Open! Shut! The struggle went on until finally the bandits kicked the door open with such vicious violence that it slammed into O´D´s face and hurled him back against the wall.

6

I dropped to the floor and slid under the bed.

Mistake! Mistake! a voice in my head told me. They're going to find you. Why didn't you jump out of the window? You had the time.

A strange and sudden hush fell over the house. A stillness filled with menace, with evil.

Under the bed, I watched the feet of a bandit walking into the room. Watched his feet walking over to my dressing table, heard him opening drawers, pulling things out and throwing them onto the floor.

Hardly daring to breathe, I lay still, feeling tremors of terror vibrating through my body from head to foot.

"Jesus," I prayed silently, "Jesus, please don't let them find me …"

The bandit walked over to the cupboard and opened the doors, pulling clothes out, throwing them onto the floor, searching for hidden money, hidden valuables.

"Jesus," I prayed, "please make me invisible, hide me …"

"What's this?" the bandit asked, his feet turning away from the cupboard and the beam of his torch lighting up the floor under the bed. "Come out of there!"

I slid out from under the bed as far away as I could get from him and stood up, wrapping my capulana more tightly around me. He was tall and wore a shirt the colour of blood. A white cap was pulled down low, shadowing his face.

I backed away from him and as I backed away, he lunged across the room and dug his hand into my hair. Twisting me around against him, he half dragged and half pushed me down the corridor towards the sitting room.

The sitting room was a mess. They had ransacked it, overturning bookcases and smashing lamps. Books and papers and files from O'D's desk lay scattered all over the floor. They had broken the sofa and it sagged on one end, the end where they had thrown O'D.

O'D …

As Red-shirt manhandled me towards the sofa, I stared at O'D with shock. What had they DONE to him? His face was a mask of blood. Blood streamed down from a deep wound in his forehead and dripped steadily down onto his shirt, drenching it. He looked dazed, out of it.

Red-shirt let go of my hair and shoved me down onto the sofa, at the other end from O'D. Numbly, my eyes took in the scene. They had turned on the light of the solar inverter. Two bandits stood in front of the dresser, sifting through the contents of the drawers and throwing the things they didn't want onto the floor. One of them was wearing a dark jacket and trousers. Chillingly, the other was dressed in police uniform. As I watched, the one wearing the jacket found my memory sticks and put them into his jacket pocket.

Another bandit, who appeared to be the leader, prowled restlessly around the room. Armed with a pistol, his off-white shirt strained too tightly around his short and stocky body. His shaven head gleamed in the light from the solar inverter and his eyes in his round face were the eyes of a dead fish.

The blow when it came surprised me. "WHERE. IS. THE. MONEY!" Red –shirt shouted, punctuating each word with a hard blow on my left shoulder with the flat of his machete. "WHERE. IS. THE. MONEY!"

"I don´t know," I said.

The leader walked over to us. "Take the Senhora back to the bedroom," he told Red-shirt, "and rape her."

Red-shirt hauled me roughly up from the sofa and holding me tightly around the ribs, began to push me forward, at the same time trying to tear my capulana off me.

A terrible black despair engulfed me at this new and hideous turn of events. Rape! I would rather die than this! "No!" I screamed. "No!" I began to struggle, desperately digging my bare feet into the floor and letting my legs cave in so that I became a dead weight. "O´D! Help me! Help me, O´D! O´D!"

The leader came over to help Red-shirt and grabbed me from the front and together, pushing and pulling, they began to drag me towards the corridor.

O´D stood up slowly. "Deixe a Senhora! Leave the Senhora! Deixe! There´s some money in a cupboard."

While Red-shirt went off with O´D, the leader pointed his pistol into my face at point blank range. "Shut up," he ordered, "or I will kill you!" He shoved me back down onto the sofa and put a cushion over my face, pressing the barrel of his pistol into it. I pushed the cushion away. If he was going to shoot me, he could look into my face when he pulled the trigger.

The bandits who had been with Lee came into the room, carrying the safe. It had been well hidden in the bathroom cupboard, but they had found it all the same.

"The key!" the leader called to O'D. "Bring the key ... and if we find money in this box," he added illogically, "we're going to kill you!"

O'D brought the key and opened the safe while the six bandits stood around him, hardly able to contain their excitement. Then, like pigs at a trough, they bent over it and began to fight each other with their fingers for the treasures they found inside.

While I sat on the sofa watching them scrabbling greedily around in the safe, I had the dreadful feeling that when they left they were going to take me along with them as a hostage. The thought was terrifying, horrifying.

Without even thinking about it, I stood up, and as if in a dream, began to walk across the room. My bare feet were silent on the cement floor and the bandits' greed made me invisible.

As they tore at the delicate gold and diamond pendant Marion had given me, grabbed at my wedding ring, snatched at the Pixley bracelet, made up of ancient 24 carat gold Greek coins that were stamped with the heads of Alexander the Great and Philip of Macedonia, I walked past their bent backs. My right arm inadvertently brushed against Red-shirt's back but he didn't notice. Down the corridor and into the front room, out of the front door and into the night.

Douglas ... I had to get to the shop and Douglas. He had a phone I could use to call for help.

It had turned into a very dark night, cloudy and rainy and without moon or stars to light the way and so I and the seventh bandit who was walking up from the Nhamacoa River didn't meet each other.

Hidden by the night but not able to see anything either, I used my bare feet to find my way. O'D's Toyota pickup had made two wheel tracks down to the shop and as long as I walked in the tracks and not on grass, I wouldn't lose my direction.

Light was shining from Douglas' windows but when I crept quietly up to his room, I saw that it was eerily empty. The green double doors had been flung wide open. His small paraffin lamp glowed orange. "Douglas?" I called out softly. "Douglas?"

There was no answer. Had he heard the noise and run away? Or ... had the bandits killed him and dragged his body into the bushes? I turned away from the shop. There was no help to be had here after all. I would have to hide.

Making my way past the borehole, I walked into the forest, deeper and deeper into the trees. When I thought I had gone far enough, I sat down. I pulled my legs up to my chest and wrapping my arms around them, rested my head on my knees. Soft rain began to fall. I closed my eyes. I was safe now. Safe in the leafy arms of the forest that O´D and I had saved. I would stay here until dawn, until daylight, and then I would go back to the house to find out what had happened to O´D ... to Douglas ... to Lee ...

CHAPTER ONE

HOW IT ALL BEGAN

There's some speculation in the little town of Chimoio as to why someone like O'D would be living in Mozambique and in a place like the Nhamacoa.

Bob Manser, who owns the company ProSol and provides gas cylinders for our cookers, fridges and freezers, is equally puzzled. One morning, while he was slipping an overdue bill for gas bottles across the counter towards O'D, he set out to satisfy his curiosity.

"Where did you go to school, O'D?" he asked.

Surprised at a question concerning a school he'd left decades ago, O'D replied, "Er … England, of course."

"No, no," Bob said impatiently. "WHICH school? WHICH school did you go to?"

When O'D admitted that he'd gone to Eton, Bob rubbed his chin thoughtfully and came up with some ideas that were far from flattering. "Hmmm … you're too young to be that Lucan fellow … Are you a Remittance Man then, by any chance, O'D? The black sheep of a family who're paying you to live in Mozambique, to keep you out of their hair?"

Others think O'D is a wanderer or working for the British Government and spying on the Mozambicans, but this also isn't true. You don't spend seventeen long years in one spot if you're a rambling man and what on earth would anyone want to spy on the Mozambicans for?

I, of course, know the answer to this mystery, having been married to O'D now for far too many years than I care to reveal. The reasons why we came to Mozambique in the first place are quite complex but why we continue to live here after all we've been through can be put down solely to O'D's character. A character that becomes quite clear to anyone who reads the third chapter of my story, which I've called "An English Jailbird" and which is a hair-raising account of O'D's incarceration in the vile-smelling Primeira Esquadra jail in Chimoio.

As I've already mentioned, O'D and I first met many years ago. O'D, by the way, is short for O'Donnel and pronounced Oh

DEE. He was named after his great-uncle O'D, who was Cornish. Well, anyway, O'D and I actually met in a bar, but this was no ordinary bar. It was a thatch-roofed and white-painted little bar and it was set in the beautiful and enchanting Victoria Falls, on the banks of that great river, the Zambezi.

It happened during the dying days of the Rhodesian bush war, when terrorists (or freedom fighters, depending on which side you were on) paddled canoes across the wide river at night from Zambia to infiltrate the country or, every now and then, entertained themselves by using this safe-haven across the border to shoot mortars at the tiny town. There were notices on the mirrors in the hotel bedrooms, telling you to lie down on the carpet between the wall and your bed when you heard the explosions of these mortars. And when you got on the airport bus to travel to or from the small airport in the bush, young sunburnt soldiers dressed in faded camouflage and armed with FN machine guns, drove dusty Land Rovers in front of you and behind you to protect you from an ambush.

It was the time when few tourists visited the country and only the intrepid made their way to Victoria Falls. It was the time when a terrorist rocket was aimed at a small plane flying some of these intrepid tourists over the spray and the rainbows and the water thundering down into the gorges of the Falls; a rocket that missed the plane and hit the original Elephant Hills Hotel instead, burning it down to the ground.

It was the time when one of these intrepid visitors was sitting in the bar at the A'Zambezi River Lodge, when I wandered inside out of the sunshine on a hot, steamy December afternoon and asked for a Coke to quench my thirst.

The bar had been empty that afternoon, except for the African barman and a young man with grey eyes and a thick mop of silky dark hair who had been sitting disconsolately on a bar stool in front of the bar counter. Dressed in shorts and a white T-shirt with a green cartoon crocodile printed on its front, the young man had been nursing a beer and ruminating over the loss of dozens of his cousin Strath Brown's crocodiles. Crocodiles that had disappeared during the night while he, O'D, was supposed to have been in charge of them!

Out from England on a working holiday, O'D had spent about six months on his cousin John Brown's farm in Mangura when, suddenly, he'd found himself being bundled onto a plane one morning and whisked out to his other cousin Strath's crocodile ranch at Victoria

Falls. No sooner had he arrived at the Falls, than Rob Gee (Strath's partner who managed the croc ranch) had decided to go off for a holiday, leaving O'D in control.

With the casual wave of a hand and a nonchalant "See you in a week's time, O'D!" Rob had jumped into his old Land Rover and had disappeared in a cloud of dust in the direction of Salisbury (Harare).

The day after Rob's departure, David Blake, the National Parks' Vet, had arrived at the croc ranch to check on the gender of some of the larger crocodiles. There had been fighting among the reptiles and he'd been asked to sort out male from female so they could be separated and put into different pens. As the scaly creatures all look horribly alike and there's no external indication to show what gender they might be, the only way to find out was through an internal investigation, by putting a finger up their cloacae. This, as you can imagine, is a rather strenuous procedure, especially when it involves crocodiles measuring between six to ten feet in length!

Together with O'D and five other men, David Blake had entered the first of the crocs' pens.

"Right," the Vet had said to them, pointing a finger at random in the direction of an inert crocodile, lying with its mouth open to the sunshine. "Let's get on with it."

One of the men had approached the unsuspecting crocodile and, taking it by surprise, had thrown a hessian bag over its head. This, O'D had told me, made crocodiles docile. Then, making sure they all worked in unison, because crocodiles are powerful and dangerous creatures and could inflict a great deal of damage if a tail or a leg was unsecured, the other men had each grabbed hold of the croc's legs and tail and bagged head at the same time. At a signal, they had heaved the reptile over onto its back and then had quickly thrown their weight down on the bits they were holding, pinning the croc firmly onto the ground while David Blake had made his examination.

"Male" the Vet had muttered. "Okay, let it go and bring on the next one."

Everything had gone well and to plan but the following morning, to O'D's consternation, he had woken up to discover that the crocs had had plans of their own!

The invasion of their personal privacy by David Blake had upset the crocodiles and had made them irritable and they had decided to run away. During the night they had somehow managed to lift up the gates of their pens with the use of their snouts and when the gates had come out of their hinges and fallen over, the crocs had escaped, fleeing en masse into the bush. Some of them had splashed their way back home into the Zambezi River, others had wandered around village huts and given the Africans terrible frights and there had even been reports from two elderly intrepid American tourists that they had hit a crocodile on the head with one of their golf balls while playing on the golf course of the burnt down Elephant Hills Hotel.

The crocodiles' disappearance had worried O'D for three reasons. The first was that they were valuable. The second was that they were difficult to catch. And the third reason was the reaction of their owner when he found out that they had gone.

I had understood why O'D was worried. His cousins, the Browns, were originally from Scotland and, as everyone knows, people from Scotland are very tight with their money and Strath was no exception. After all, there's that old riddle that says it all. "Do you know how to make copper wire? Just give two Scotsmen a penny!"

Settling in Rhodesia in 1928, Jim Brown had worked hard to turn virgin bush into future cotton, coffee and tobacco farms. Later, the Browns had also started up an engineering works and after President Mugabe took over the country, they grew roses for export to Europe as well and built the Ilala Lodge at the Falls.

I had met O'D's cousin Strath. A member of a family that was not only large in number but large in physique as well, Strath was the largest of the lot at that time, although his nephew Philip would later supplant him as the biggest Brown. A man with arms like hams and legs like tree trunks, cousin Strath had a voice to match his size. It was loud and booming and could crack your eardrums.

"What are you going to do?" I had asked O'D.

"I'm going to have another beer," he had replied, "and then I'm going to go gambling at the Casino."

Although O'D came from a race of people who had put my Dutch great grandmother, Heiletje Borstlap, into one of their concentration camps during the Boer War, I hadn't held this against him. After all, the past was past and from all accounts, even though she'd been their prisoner, my great grandmother had still managed to show the British a thing or two!

Heiletje and her family (on my mother's side of the family tree) had come from Rotterdam and had settled down to farm in South Africa. When gold was discovered in the Transvaal, the British had

14

annexed the territory. Naturally, the Boers who lived there had objected to this high-handed behaviour and war had broken out. At first, things had gone badly for the British Army and to prevent any further humiliation by a bunch of bearded farmers on horseback, General Kitchener had come up with a rather fiendish plan. Knowing that their families on the farms kept the elusive Boer fighters going with food and supplies, Kitchener had ordered his soldiers to burn all the Boer farms and to imprison all the women and their children in camps on the veld.

To avoid being captured and taken to one of these camps, Heiletje and her sister had spent the days lying in hiding among the reeds of a river flowing through their farm. Then, one evening, just as the sun was going down, disaster had struck.

Preparing to go back to the farmhouse as usual for the night, Heiletje had cautiously parted the reeds in front of her for a careful look to see if it was safe to emerge from their hiding place. To her absolute horror, the first thing she had seen were two British army boots, planted in the mud only inches from her nose. The game was up!

At the camp, my great grandmother's fiery temper had soon landed her in trouble. When the women had been handed large lumps of green and stinking rotten meat to cook for their meals, my great grandmother had lost it, completely. Grabbing hold of one of these putrid lumps of meat, she had stormed over to the Camp Commander and had hit him over the head with it!

Outraged by this attack and the loss of his dignity, the Camp Commander had put my great grandmother into solitary confinement.

Now, you wouldn't think that romance would blossom in a prison camp in the African bush during a war, would you, but that's just what happened.

One of the soldiers guarding the camp had been a young South African born Scotsman called Peter John Christie and - unlike the Camp Commander - he'd been greatly impressed by this slip of a girl with her flashing dark eyes and the way she had taken on the might of the British Empire by battering it over the head with bad meat! What spirit! What courage! Suppressing his laughter and keeping a straight face at the remarkable sight, he had thought that this was just the sort of girl for him. By the time the Boer war had ended, Heiletje and Peter Christie had come to know each other rather well and some time after she had been freed, they had married. Leaving South Africa and the British behind, they had travelled to South West Africa (a German colony at that time and now called Namibia) where they had bought a farm, learned to speak German and settled down to raise a family.

One year after our meeting, also during a war in Africa, O'D and I got married in Guildford, in Surrey, England.

At first, we lived in cold and drizzly London. We rented a bed-sit in Rosary Gardens, Kensington and I can't say that our new life was full of fun. While I worked for some architects in Victoria, O'D went to work for old Mr. Copping, the owner of one of the last independent silversmiths in London and the most irascible man in England.

Although he was English, O'D didn't take too well to a nine-to-five lifestyle or to wearing a suit every day and a long grey Tweedy coat to ward off the wet, icy winds.

Things looked up when we bought a flat in Kingston and he left Mr. Copping and went to work for George Bush Senior instead, on one of his Zapata exploration oil rigs in the sea off Abu Dhabi. Instead of nine to five every day, it was one month on the rig and one month at home. Here, he exchanged his suits for red overalls and worked twelve hour shifts with tough old Texans, like the rig tool pusher who was called Double L and Norman, a laconic Australian who was tall and fair and an excellent mechanic.

He liked being in the company of men like these and listening to the stories they had to tell. As Norman's assistant, he helped to maintain the Caterpillar engines down in the motor room, as well as the desalination plant, and soon he also had stories of his own to tell.

Once, during a changeover in shifts, a young and fairly inexperienced driller made a mistake and before they knew it, the smell of rotten eggs began to fill the atmosphere and swirl around the rig. H2S … deadly hydrogen sulphide!

Leaving a driller and thirteen of the crew behind to try to cap the killer gas, the rig was hurriedly evacuated. Rig workers jumped into the basket, which a crane lowered into one of the boats that continually circled the rig in the interest of safety.

It was a short sea that day, O'D told me, and as the boat rode the choppy waves around the rig, a noxious vapour of another type began to fill the atmosphere as a tightly-packed crowd of about eighty men consisting of Pakistanis, Indians, Arabs, Americans, Australians, New Zealanders, Scotsmen and Dutchmen all began to throw up. The

16

American Medic had begun to vomit as soon as his feet had touched the deck and as a result hadn't been of help to anyone.

Crushed in the midst of this great mass of groaning, heaving, spewing men, even O'D who never suffered from seasickness began to feel a touch of nausea, a certain lurching queasiness, as the boat relentlessly circled around the rig … on and on and on … for the next twenty four torture-filled hours …

And then there'd been the time when O'D had been helping Norman to clean out the rig's drains.

They'd closed off all the taps (or so they'd thought) and Norman had been leaning over the side of the rig platform, watching for the spout of filthy water to begin gushing into the sea when O'D turned on the high pressure in the noisy motor room ...

There'd just been a changeover in shifts and the kitchen and galley (which resembled a fast food restaurant) had been busy with chefs cooking behind a counter and tired, hungry men eating at tables, when without any warning at all, all hell had broken loose.

Fountains of water, filled with the greasy filth and garbage of years, had suddenly erupted all over the kitchen and with high velocity had hurled stinking, slimy sludge all over the ceiling and walls of the kitchen and had splattered onto the hot plates and fridges and food and cooks. Taken by surprise and overcome with the horror of it all, tough roustabouts and tool pushers and drillers had reacted with screams and shouts and by overturning their chairs in panic.

It had been these loud screams and shouts that had alerted Norman to the fact that something had gone wrong. Tracking the noise down to the kitchen and galley, he had walked into a scene of chaos.

Unflappable whatever happened, he had thoughtfully surveyed the shambles in the room and had drawled laconically in his dry Aussie twang, "Been thinking for some time that the kitchen needed a good clean out."

As Zapata paid for its employees' airfares to and from the rig no matter where they lived, O'D and I took this as an opportunity and began to look for a home in a warmer part of Europe. Leaving England behind, we went off to the lovely pine-scented Greek island of Samos for a year.

Here, we stayed in a tiny house in a fishing village with the tongue-twisting name of Ormos Marathakambos and learnt even more tongue-twisting phrases like 'logharyasmo, parakalo!' (the bill, please!) Life was fairly pleasant amongst the Greeks until summer arrived and something very disturbing occurred. When the last grey wintry cloud blew away and the sun burned down on the island's long sandy beaches, all traces of Greece suddenly vanished ... and we discovered we were living in a GERMAN colony ... which, even more alarming, appeared to be populated by large crowds of enormous, pink and NAKED Germans!

Black-garbed Greek women grew grim and slitty-eyed at the sight of naked Germans sitting and reading books, standing and windsurfing, striding around eating ice cream cones and lying down on their towels on the beaches. Greek men, of course, weren't the least little bit concerned about this blatant disregard Germans showed towards Greek culture. They left their fishing nets and sat perched goggle-eyed on top of the cliffs overlooking the beaches, sharing a couple of binoculars and laughing.

When we'd had enough of island life, O'D and I packed our suitcases and drove off to France.

As I'd been a Francophile since the age of four, the prospect of living permanently in France was a delightful one. While African Americans go on about finding their roots in Africa, my earliest roots as a White African lay in the France of my Huguenot ancestors (on my father's side of the family) who centuries ago had fled to the Cape of Good Hope in South Africa to escape religious persecution.

While O'D worked away on the rig, I lived in the comfortable little apartment Madame Faure had rented to us in the village of Mazan, in wine-drenched and lavender-scented Provence. Every Monday, Wednesday and Friday, I caught a bus and travelled to the town of Cavaillon where Patrice, a young schoolteacher, would be waiting for me.

I was brushing up my school French and Patrice, who was charming and wore a pink chiffon scarf rakishly tied around his neck, was supplementing his income by giving me lessons at five pounds a lesson.

My lessons took place in Patrice's house where he still lived with his parents. His mother, a woman with sharp black eyes, black hair and an olive complexion, viewed me with an equally black and deep suspicion, convinced that I had intentions towards her son and that these intentions were not good.

No doubt her suspicions had been fuelled by Patrice's choice of a location for my tuition. In the house for my first lesson, he had

18

waved a hand towards some dark wooden stairs and had tried out his French-accented English on me. "Pleeze climb zeese banisters up to my bedrrroom," he had told me.

As we had climbed the stairs, I had pointed out the difference between banisters and stairs. If Patrice had been embarrassed by his faux pas, he had hidden it well. "My English girlfriend from Kent went into an electrical shop the other day to buy a fuse," he had informed me with a laugh. "Instead of asking the assistant for a 'fusible', she mispronounced the word and asked him for a 'fusil bleu' – a blue gun!"

In his bedroom, we sat demurely side by side on two hard wooden chairs in front of a desk facing a blank wall. Books on grammar lay open in front of us, full of the conjugations of the verbs Patrice was drumming into my head. Although learning all these verbs was extremely tedious, my lessons were enjoyably enlivened from time to time by sudden and unexpected interruptions.

These interruptions took place when Patrice's mother could no longer contain all the suspicions she was harbouring in her breast and rushed wildly into the room, flinging the closed door open so violently that it would bounce against the wall. Always hoping to catch us out by the unexpectedness of her appearance and always foiled when she found us doing nothing except sitting innocently in front of a desk, she would saunter around the room, trying to think up flimsy excuses for her explosive entry. Had Patrice remembered to put his white shirt into the laundry? Did he have any idea where she had left her car keys?

I was settling down nicely in France when our ordered lives began to slip out of our control and we began to take our first steps towards Mozambique.

It was a chance remark, or so I thought, that brought us to Arrojela in Portugal. Arrojela, which was to be our training ground where we would be taught to do certain things to prepare us for what was to come, a sort of halfway house to gently ease us out of the comfort and safety of the developed part of the world and into the primitive, dangerous lifestyle that was waiting for us in an African forest.

But although many of the things that happened to us at Arrojela were foreshadows of our future, there was nothing that could really prepare us for all the shocks and hair-raising experiences we went through in the Nhamacoa Forest. After all, who in England would

19

ever see a woman turn into a demon in front of their eyes, who, even in Portugal, would open their car bonnet and find a Spitting Cobra coiled up on the engine and waiting to shoot its venom into their face, and who in the West would ever find themselves threatened by a fat, corrupt Judge wearing a pale pistachio green suit?

No, nothing could prepare anyone for that sort of thing!

And nothing could ever have prepared us for the truly dreadful experience of having to watch a lovely indigenous hardwood forest, filled with the most beautiful birds and butterflies, tree orchids, buck and monkeys, being completely destroyed all around us and being absolutely powerless to stop it from happening. The Nhamacoa wasn't the Amazon and so nobody out there in the Western World cared.

Our journey towards Mozambique began one day when we were back in London. One afternoon, during a conversation with my sister-in-law, Caroline, she told us about her recent holiday in the Algarve. Her description of the people and the countryside was so glowing that it caught our imagination and O'D and I decided to go and have a look for ourselves. This was in 1985, before Portugal became part of the EU and lost its charm.

Arriving in the Algarve on a sunshiny summer's day, we were enchanted by what we found and when we chanced upon Arrojela, we were lost.

We bought Arrojela because there was something about it that reminded me of Africa. Perhaps it was because the sky was the same blue as the blue of the African skies or perhaps it was the stillness, broken only by the sound of the hot October breeze rustling silkily through the leaves of the enormous cork oak tree that stood not far from the dilapidated old mud brick house. But whatever it was, when I first saw Arrojela, I felt as if I had finally come home.

Arrojela was seven hectares of two hills and a valley, set conveniently only 19 kilometres from the bustling little town of Portimao and halfway between the sea and the Monchique Mountains. There was a stream and springs, orange orchards and olive groves. The air was fresh and clean and scented with the wild herbs that grew on the hillsides. It was beautiful, very beautiful.

It was this very beauty that blinded us to the fact that there were certain important and necessary things that were missing from the old mud brick house, such as electricity, running water, plumbing, a bathroom, a lavatory and a telephone. There were large empty spaces on the ancient tiled roof and the floors in every room were hard-packed dirt. Plaster crumbled off the walls, there was no glass in the windows and the doors and wooden shutters hung askew on their hinges. The house was a wreck! Were we nuts?

Fortunately, Remy Bongarde, the gorgeously good looking Swiss Estate Agent who had sold Arrojela to us, had also had the foresight to introduce us to Jan and Lia Kosterman, the Dutch couple who lived at the beginning of the dirt track leading up to our house.

They overwhelmed us with warmth and took us under their wing. Jan, who was already old and in his seventies, became our mentor, strengthening and reviving us with numerous 'slokkies' of brandy and giving us the benefit of his expert advice and experience when it came to providing our own electricity and water with generators and pumps.

To begin with, he told us, we should build a temporary tower next to the house, with a water tank on top and then fill the tank by pumping water up from the stream. Once we had done this, we could fill a large drum with water and heat it up over a wood fire. This would give us hot water for bathing every day.

When O'D had built the tower and wrapped it in huge sheets of black plastic for privacy, it became our rather dark and murky bathroom. Here, I bathed in a small tin tub and O'D washed his workday dust away under an Algarvean shower.

This shower was a remarkable piece of equipment and showed the ingenuity of the Algarveans in their slow advancement towards modern plumbing technology. It consisted of a large galvanised bucket with a plug in the bottom and dozens of holes sprouting out everywhere! With the addition of hot water and a pull on the plug, this delightful contraption gave such luxurious showers and worked so well that all these years later I wish we had one right now, here in Mozambique.

Finding people to help renovate the house wasn't difficult. Jan brought Francisco, his strong and stocky old gardener and a bricklayer called Dominge.

Dominge was tall and swarthy and looked a bit like Lucky Luke, the French cartoon cowboy. He didn't speak a word of English and so, at lunchtime, when we sat around the table eating bread and cheese and olives in our tumbledown kitchen, he taught us to speak Portuguese. He did this by picking up a fork and saying "garfo!" and expecting us to repeat the word perfectly. Pointing to a knife, "faca!" A plate, "prato!"

21

Dominge was the only Algarvean we ever met who didn't drink any alcohol at all. This, we discovered later on from his mother, was because she had become so fed up with his drunken binges that she secretly put a certain herb into his black morning coffee that made him throw up instantly whenever a drop of alcohol passed his lips.

This secret herb not only had a physical affect on him but, it seemed to us, it may also have been responsible for some of Dominge's other habits, which were more than a little quirky to say the least.

Once, while we were eating our usual lunchtime meal of bread and cheese and olives, Dominge noticed that his wristwatch had stopped working. In an attempt to get it going again, he took the watch off and shook it around violently in the air by its strap for a few minutes. When this still didn't do the trick, he opened it up and began to tinker around among its small parts with his penknife. Finally, with a face darkening like a thundercloud and his black moustache quivering, he pushed back his chair and stood up.

"I'm going outside to fix this watch," he told us, grittily.

Wondering how Dominge was going to repair his watch outside when he couldn't repair it inside, O'D followed him.

Outside, Dominge put the watch down on top of a large boulder and picked up a hammer ... raised the hammer up in the air ... brought it down ... again and again ... until he had smashed his watch to smithereens.

Back in his chair in the kitchen again, O'D said, "Remind me never to leave my watch lying around when Dominge is here."

Francisco also enlivened our lunches. Apart from teaching us how to plant tomatoes, fava beans and potatoes and flood-irrigate them with little canals, he also taught us Algarvean poetry and Algarvean history, with himself as the main character. The poems were very short because Algarveans don't like anything involving a lot of effort and were about a subject very dear to their hearts – food and drink.

"Laranja na guela," (Orange in the throat,) Francisco would declaim, popping an orange segment into his mouth and chewing it ...

"Vinho depois dela!" (Wine after this!) he would end, throwing an entire tumbler of dark red wine down his throat.

Our history lessons centred on the period of the dastardly despotic ruler, Salazar, because this was the time when Francisco had been young. Life had been harsh and in order to earn a bit of money, he had laboured on the estate of a rich landowner in the Alentejo for the mere pittance of six escudos a month. Imagine, SIX escudos! Here, cruel Overseers with whips had stood over Francisco and his fellow labourers, giving them a lash every now and then, to make sure that the rich got richer while the poor got poorer.

Still, there had been time for fun. He remembered dancing in the big main room in this very house we were busy fixing up - it was seventy five years old, ten years older than he was - and after the dance, stumbling along on his way home in the black night, he had fallen head first into a well! Of course, this would never have happened if he hadn't drunk so much of that local aguadente, medronho ... and talking about medronho ... had he ever told us about the time he had mistakenly donned his wife's cuecas? (knickers?) No? Well, this had happened one night when, in the dark, he had got out of bed and struggled into a pair of underpants for a hasty trip to a bush (Algarvean peasant houses didn't have lavatories). He had hazily wondered why the underpants had been so strangely tight all of a sudden but it was only after he'd jumped out of the bedroom window and almost broken his neck because of the way they had tangled and constrained his leg movements that he'd realised what he'd put on!

We'd been working on the house for about two months when a very peculiar thing happened. It occurred after O'D and Dominge had just finished putting new red terracotta tiles on the front half of the roof and although we naturally didn't know it then, it was to be our introduction to ... something ... that we would meet again in the Nhamacoa Forest, that would be waiting for us there almost exactly ten years later.

When the last tile was laid, O'D and Dominge climbed off the roof and down the ladder, leaving behind the long plank they had used to stand on while they worked. Down on the ground, we all stood looking up at the roof, examining the straightness of the tiles and admiring the house's new look. And then, out of nowhere on this hot, still, windless day, there was a furious rushing sound and a strong gust of wind lifted the plank up, swept it off the roof and sent it hurtling through the air straight at O'D!

It happened so fast that he only had time to put his left arm up in front of his face to ward off the flying wooden missile. The plank hit his wrist with a glancing blow and then fell to the ground.

Not a sound came out from between O'D's lips but his face turned paper-white with the pain from the blow.

"Are you alright?" I asked, shocked.

"I think so," he said, supporting his wrist with his right hand. "I don't think anything's broken."

"Strange. That was so strange," I said. "It was almost as if … something … picked up that plank and *aimed* it straight at YOU!"

O'D flexed his fingers gingerly, and dismissed the incident. "Strange, yes. But freak accidents do happen."

I didn't dismiss it. For one thing, apart from that solitary strong gust of wind, the day had gone back to being still, without even a hint of a breeze. Another thing that made me uneasy was that as the plank had flown off the roof towards O'D, I had, for a split second, sensed a shimmer of malevolence, of hatred, in the air. I was sure I hadn't imagined it. And then, there had been plenty of open space for the plank to travel but it had headed directly towards O'D. If he hadn't put his arm up to protect himself and it had hit him in the face, he would have been terribly injured, or even killed … Could the old mud-brick house be haunted? Oh, what a ghastly thought!

"Of course it's not haunted," O'D laughed later at my fears. "This house has got a lovely feel about it."

It took us two years to finish the work on the old mud-brick house and during this time we had quite a few visits from family and friends. They were remarkable people. They slept in rubble-filled rooms and used our murky bathroom in the black tower. They were fascinated by our Algarvean shower and made us photograph it at work while they stood under it with cascades of soapy water tumbling over their heads and shoulders. They picked oranges straight off our trees and ate so many of them that they got bad diarrhoea from overdosing on Vitamin C. They fell into the stream. They even spent some time in the grim-faced, black-clad Mrs. Ventura Pinto's blue-painted bar at the end of our track, eating Tremocos (Lupins) and drinking Cristal and Sagres beer with sun-wrinkled Algarvean men wearing old felt hats.

Although the interior of Mrs. Pinto's blue bar was as stark and as unwelcoming as herself, when you got to know the place, it was where unusual and sometimes even heart-stopping events took place. This was where Rui had once had an argument with Luis and in the heat of the moment, when passions had run high and the blood had boiled in their veins, Rui had pulled out a pistol and had shot Luis right in the groin – the groin, of all spots to be shot! The shooting and wounding had been hushed up, of course. No need to call the police

24

and to have them poking their interfering noses into things that didn't concern them.

O'D, too, often had a few surprises when he stopped off at the blue bar for a beer and a chat. One evening, after a bibulous couple of hours, he climbed into his Land Rover, which he had left parked under the trees not far from Mrs. Pinto's front door, and started off on the drive along the track back home. During the drive, the Land Rover's performance was uncharacteristically sluggish and this puzzled him. He wondered what on earth could be wrong. It was almost, he thought, as if the brakes were binding, as if some heavy weight was dragging on the vehicle. As he turned a corner on the track, the Land Rover slewed to one side and in the rear view mirror he caught a glimpse in the moonlight of a large dark shape with long pointy ears that appeared to be following him!

"What the …?" he asked himself.

Startled, and with his heart pounding, he put his head out of the window for a better look and discovered that the dark shape was not following the Land Rover but was in fact attached to it, attached to it and resisting this attachment by digging its heels into the ground! Slowing to a halt, O'D steeled himself to get out and there, tied to the back of the vehicle by its reins was a plump grey donkey.

Although all donkeys look the same to everyone except their owners, O'D immediately recognised this donkey when he put his hand out to give it a calming pat and it bared its big dirty yellow teeth and gnashed them irritably at him. He recognised it because he had on several occasions watched the donkey walking along a narrow path behind its owner, Old Manel, and baring these very same teeth to impatiently give Old Manel's skinny bottom a couple of nips to hurry him along. Besides all this, he had only a few minutes before bought Old Manel a glass of Mr. Pinto's homemade medronho in the blue bar. Obviously Old Manel had now taken up the new habit of carelessly using the back of the Land Rover as a hitching post at the blue bar and unaware of this, O'D had accelerated away from the bar, dragging his reluctant donkey half way home with him.

Old Manel was our nearest Algarvean neighbour and lived at the bottom of our hill in a tiny, crumbling mud-brick house. At night, he slept wrapped up in a dirty grey blanket on a bed made out of twigs and branches and during the day, he worked in his fields, growing sweet potatoes and looking after his small flock of sheep. He was

25

poor, as poor as any poverty-stricken African but despite this, he was surprisingly happy.

Our visitors liked Old Manel. They smiled back at the enchanting toothless smile on his impish face and when he held it out, they shook his outstretched friendly hand. They were also pretty darn quick though, I can tell you, to rush off as soon as they decently could to wash their hands after touching his. I didn't blame them at all for doing this, because I used to do the very same thing. The state of Old Manel's two grimy hands deeply ingrained with the earth of his fields and his ten dirt-encrusted black fingernails was a shocking sight to people who lived in cities.

Although our visitors put up with all sorts of things, their courage failed when it came to O Doido, 'The Crazy One'.

Doido was another of our nearest Algarvean neighbours and he was a lumbering, blocky, middle-aged man who looked after his brother Antonio's cows and goats. During the day, he wandered around the hills and valleys while the animals grazed; at night, he slept amongst them in an old barn, and from the strong noxious odour of manure that hung ripely around his large figure, I would say that his ideas of hygiene were on a par with Old Manel's. In fact, I might even go further to say that from the state of Doido's spiky, greasy, brown hair (which, now I come to think of it, appears to be the height of Western fashion) I also had the feeling that Doido didn't even own a bar of soap and thought that water was only for drinking.

"Doido is completely harmless," Dominge assured us the first time we breathed in the terrible scent of manure wafting up our hill and realised it was emanating from a blocky figure lumbering towards us. "Even little children are safe with Doido."

Dominge's reassuring words had no effect on me. One look at Doido's crafty little pale blue eyes told me that I wouldn't even leave myself alone with him, let alone a little child.

O'D, on the other hand, was very impressed with the Algarvean way of treating people who weren't all there. He went on and on about how humane they were to allow Doido to wander harmlessly around in the fresh country air, caring for his brother Antonio's animals instead of being incarcerated in an asylum. Even when Doido came onto our land and let his goats eat some of our orange trees right down to a stump, O'D spoke kindly to him at first, explaining that this wasn't a neighbourly thing to do. Yes, O'D was patient with Doido, very patient until the day we were in the kitchen, drinking tea with O'D's brother Willy (who, incidentally, at this time looked a lot like the actor Jeremy Irons) when the sound of cowbells alerted us to the fact that something wasn't quite right.

Outside, we stood looking down the hill and there was Doido, once again wandering across the stream that divided our land from his brother Antonio's. This time he was accompanied by about a dozen large black cows and while we watched, he stood idly by as his animals ambled through our bean fields, knocking over the cane supports Francisco had driven into the ground, trampling and squashing tomatoes which were almost ready to pick and crushing and flattening our crisp green Cos lettuce.

Outraged, O'D ran down the hill and Willy and I saw him talking to Doido and waving his arms around and gesticulating. Then O'D grabbed a cow by the bell hanging around its neck and started walking back across the stream with the animal.

The sight of O'D walking off with one of his cows was too much for Doido and he raised the thick and heavy wooden staff he always carried with him - raised it high up in the air with both his hands - and brought it down with a powerful blow across O'D's back. O'D staggered under the blow and then turned around and wrenched the staff out of Doido's hands and hit him across the legs with it. And Doido threw himself flat on his back on the ground and screamed and kicked his big chunky legs up and down in the air like a child having a tantrum.

Thinking that Doido had finally got the idea, O'D turned to walk back up to the house, taking Doido's staff with him. Doido, however, had some ideas of his own and clambered to his feet. He gave O'D's back a baleful glare and bereft of his staff, bent down to pick up a large rock ...

"Go and help O'D!" I cried, sensing more violence in the air and looking around for Willy, who had suddenly left my side and for some reason appeared to be sheltering behind a large medronho bush.

Willy shot an incredulous look at me from his bush. "He's old enough to look after himself," he drawled.

... the rock flew through the air, bowled at O'D with an underarm movement so skilful and forceful that it would definitely have secured Doido a place in the Pakistani cricket team.

"Look out!" I shouted at O'D.

My warning came just in time. O'D managed to duck his head but not before the rock skimmed through his hair and scraped his

27

scalp, drawing blood. Completely enraged now, O'D turned towards Doido and Doido, knowing he had gone too far this time, fled across the stream and down the valley until his blocky figure was swallowed up by the cystis bushes.

"What I can't understand," O'D said afterwards, blotting his bloody scalp with a handkerchief, "is how the Algarvean authorities can allow someone as unstable and dangerous as Doido to run around the countryside. Someone like him should be kept locked up in an asylum!"

News travels fast around the world and Doido's infamy soon spread far and wide to England, Switzerland, Australia, South Africa and even Zimbabwe. Now, when visitors arrived, they were wary. The snap of a twig or the chirp of a bird in a tree made them jump. "Is that … the Doido?" they would whisper.

My brother David (who now looks remarkably like the actor Brian Blessed, only shorter) also came to visit and he was nervous too. At bedtime, he closed his windows tight, drew the curtains shut and double-locked himself into his room by not only turning the key in the door but also by pushing a heavy chest of drawers across the floor to reinforce the door and prevent any unauthorised entry.

"I don't fancy the thought of being woken up in the middle of the night by a madman hovering over me with an axe," he told us from behind the door.

Despite the eccentricities of our neighbours, it was easy to fall into the Algarvean lifestyle and to settle into its slow and relaxing rhythm. Here, time seemed to stand still and everyone did exactly what they wanted to do; drinking wine at any hour of the day and night and sometimes eating restaurant lunches that stretched far into the star-studded evenings with their guitars and fado. There was a certain delightful freedom in living without the social constraints that chained your actions down to what hour of the day it was ... surely this was how humans were supposed to live?

As O'D had given up working for Zapata when the rig had been decommissioned and towed off to Singapore in 1986, we started a small tourist business on Arrojela to earn a living. It was the obvious thing to do and for a while it looked as if this was going to turn out to be a success.   But although we didn't know it then, of course, our idyllic life in the Algarve was about to end. We had learnt what we were supposed to learn at Arrojela and graduation day was already looming on the horizon.

One hot summer's day in June 1991, O'D and I drove over to Faro to visit various tour companies in order to promote our business. Their response was fairly satisfying and after lunch, we made our way back home.

The afternoon was sweltering and the drive was tedious. We crawled along, caught up in traffic jams and were forced to stop every few minutes. To combat the boredom, I idly flipped through a copy of 'The Algarve News' and read the gossip and scandal about the activities of the local ex-pats out aloud to O'D. When our slow progress came to a halt again, just before the bridge over the Portimao River, I looked up from the paper towards the Monchique Mountains and noticed something rather alarming. Enormous and ominous clouds of smoke were billowing up high in the sky, seemingly right over … Arrojela!

I threw the paper down on the seat. "O'D, look!" I cried, pointing at the smoke. "I hope that's not our house burning down!"

"I don't think so," he said slowly, examining the sky. "It looks as if that fire's quite a distance away, beyond the house."

Despite his words, as soon as we were able to extricate ourselves from the traffic, O'D put his foot down on the accelerator and we raced home.

We found Arrojela as calm and peaceful as ever, although the clouds of smoke in the sky seemed much larger and nearer. Later on in the evening, O'D climbed the hill in front of the house to have a better look and when he came back he told me not to worry, as the fire was quite far away from us and in the region of Rasmalho. Even so, I stayed awake late that night, long after O'D had gone to bed and made my last check on the fire at about one o'clock. At that time there was nothing much to see in the black night sky, just a dim red glow behind our hill and I went to sleep, thinking that the danger was past and we were safe.

It was still dark when I felt O'D shaking my shoulder. I opened my eyes and saw his dim shape standing over me. "Why are you waking me up in the middle of the night?" I mumbled crossly.

"Get up and go and look out of the front door."

Groggily, I climbed out of bed and walked into the sitting room. A weird flickering orange light lit up the room brightly and something outside was making a loud crackling, sizzling, roaring sound. The front door was open and the sight I saw through it was so shocking that my brain stopped working and my mouth went completely dry, leaving my tongue as parched as the Kalahari Desert.

Fire! The fire I had seen the day before had come to us!

Speechless, I stood in the open doorway and tried to take in the spectacle of this inferno that was so greedily devouring everything in its path and roaring towards us.   A massive sheet of flame had engulfed the entire hill!   Hot sap in the trees boiled and spurted. Explosions caused showers of sparks to fly up like fireworks. And although the fire had not yet jumped the stream, fingers of flame were already creeping across from the trees on one side of the stream bank and over into the trees on the land near our house. Soon we would be encircled and cut off from escape!

Numbly, I assessed our prospects for survival. They appeared to be bleak. Even from the doorway I could feel the fierce heat from the burning hillside blasting my face and body. There was little doubt in my mind as to what was going to happen to us over the next few hours. We were going to be ... FRIZZLED!

I opened my mouth and tried to speak. A hoarse croak like the sound of a frog came out. I tried again.

"We're going to die ..."

O'D didn't even attempt to reassure me or to deny my words.

As I turned away from the awful sight, I suddenly remembered something that could just possibly bring help to rescue us. The telephone!

Although the EDP, the Electricity Department of Portugal, had never given us electricity at Arrojela, the TDP, the Telecommunications Department of Portugal, had recently installed a glossy white telephone in our kitchen. This apparently had been a mistake on their part, the disgruntled telephone engineer had told us. A serious bureaucratic blunder, leading to great expense. They had had no idea that they would have to dig 39 holes in the ground in order to plant 39 wooden poles and string three and a half kilometres of telephone line across the hills and valleys to Arrojela, just for one mud brick house in the middle of nowhere. And a house not even boasting the ubiquitous swimming pool!

I turned back to O'D. "The Fire Brigade ... phone the Fire Brigade!"

The Portimao Fire Brigade told us they knew all about the fire and assured us that the Bombeiros (firemen) were already on their way to us. Amazed but relieved by this unexpected efficiency from a race of people who were not known for their efficiency, we waited for their arrival.

They never arrived.

Fortunately, I was married to a man of action and while my mind had been numbed with horrifying visions of everything, including ourselves, being burnt to a crisp, O'D's mind had made a quick recovery and was now racing with ideas on how to avert this fate.

Just minutes before the fire consumed the expensive 39 telephone poles and cut Arrojela off from the rest of the country, he made two more phone calls. One call was to his brother, Willy, who was now also living in the Algarve not far from us. The other phone call was to Eddie, a friend who lived in Portimao. When he put the receiver down, he went outside to the workshop and started up the Allen. This was a ferocious petrol powered heavy-duty grass and vegetation mower. He mowed down all the grass and bushes around the house and then he went and sat on top of the water tank and while the fire boiled towards him, he worked frantically, joining water pipes together to make a very long hose.

Willy was the first to arrive. Clad in his black leathers and black crash helmet, he roared along the burning track to our house on his motorbike. Although he had balked at the thought of tackling the bulky Doido, driving down a dirt road ablaze with a huge fire didn't faze him one bit.

Eddie arrived a little while later, on foot and with Stuart, another friend. They had met the Bombeiros at Mrs. Pinto's blue bar and had been forbidden to drive up to our house in their car. Not only had the Bombeiros no intention at all of coming to our rescue but they had also even closed the road up to our house, telling people it was too dangerous. When Eddie and Stuart heard this, they decided to leave the car at the blue bar and walk up to Arrojela.

What a welcome sight they were … and how brave!

The fire rampaged through the hills and valleys of Arrojela all that day. Finally, when it seemed that everything that was going to burn had been burned, we sat down at the table on the verandah. Tired and streaked with black, we drank cold beers to wash out smoke polluted throats and idly watched two small planes in the distance, dumping water on the fire which was now heading off to the north of us.

"What's the time?" Willy asked, draining his bottle of Sagres.

"Almost half past four."

He picked up his helmet. "Time I went home."

After Willy had roared off on his motorbike, O'D drove Eddie and Stuart down to their car at the blue bar. When he came back, we sat on at the table on the verandah and drank down some more beers. What else was there to do now?

"When I dropped Ed off at the blue bar, Mrs. Pinto told us that a wood lorry overheated in the Monchique Mountains and started this fire," O'D told me.

I stared at the black sooty desolation around us, hideous with the charred, smoking skeletons of leafless trees and the tangled remains of vegetation. It looked as if a bomb had been dropped on top of us. The air smelled sour, acrid. A gust of wind swept across a terrace, turning the hot black ash into a small black whirlwind. There was a tiny explosion nearby and a heap of manure belonging to Old Manel's plump grey donkey burst into flames.

"Well," I said, "this fire has just ruined our business."

"It looks like it," O'D replied.

"What are we going to do now?" I asked. As well as being ruined, there was a recession going on in the world.

"I don't know," he said.

"What a pity you saved the house," I went on. "If it had burnt down, we would at least have had the insurance money."

Another heap of donkey manure exploded and burst into flames ... and then another ... and another. Unbeknown to us until now, Old Manel's donkey had been sneaking onto our land under cover of night and trespassing all over it while we slept.

"I don't suppose there's any chance of all this exploding donkey manure setting the house on fire ... is there?" I asked, hopefully.

"No," O'D told me. "No chance at all."

As if one shock wasn't enough, there were still more shocks in store for me. The first of these happened one evening a couple of weeks after the fire. I opened the telephone book to look for a number and discovered I was completely unable to read the tiny print on its pages! What was going on here?

A trip to the Opticians in Portimao soon told me what was going on. Inside a huge room, its walls smothered with hundreds of frames for spectacles, a bored, white-coated woman led me over to a grey machine. Ordering me to sit down next to the machine, she told

32

me to look into it and to describe the image I saw. Obediently, I peered into the machine.

"I see a fat Portuguese farmer with black hair," I told the woman. "He's wearing a bright red sweater … he's sitting on a bright blue tractor … in the middle of a bright green field."

Pleased with myself and with the clarity of the image I had seen, I looked up from the machine. There was obviously nothing wrong with my eyesight after all.

"Wait over there," the woman told me, pointing to a counter at one end of the room.

While I waited for the verdict, I examined the large, colourful, advertising posters placed strategically here and there among the frames to persuade us that wearing their brand of glasses would beautify us. These were all giant-sized photographs of beautiful blonde young women wearing glasses and looking thrilled about having bad eyesight and fashionable spectacles attached to their faces. As usual, glamour was being used to sell a product that was far from being glamorous.

"Who do you think you're kidding?" I muttered at the larger than life faces, so smoothed and perfected by air-brushing that they hardly looked like real people anymore.

When the white-coated woman returned, she handed me a slip of paper. It had some writing on it and when I read it, I could not believe what it said.

My eyesight had deteriorated, it seemed, and I needed reading glasses. I had old age eyes!

How was this possible? I'd seen the test picture so clearly. Was there something wrong with the machine?

"This must be a mistake," I told the woman.

She gave me a cold look. "We don't make mistakes."

With plummeting spirits, I let a young man lead me over to a frame-covered wall to choose my new glasses.

What I didn't know then and what no one ever told me, was that there was a very simple and inexpensive cure for the deterioration of my eyesight. A cure discovered as long ago as the beginning of the 20th century and which Ophthalmologists and Opticians had totally disregarded and almost, but not quite, buried. The reason for this, of course, is plainly obvious. We live in a money-mad world and the spectacle and lens industry is worth billions.

Unaware that I was being sent down a path that would almost lead me to blindness, I chose a pair of frames. Frames for the reading glasses I would use for the next ten years until an extraordinary set of circumstances in a Mozambican forest (set in train by a Vervet monkey and the Zimbabwean President, Robert Mugabe!) introduced me to a long-dead old American Ophthalmologist. Yes, it's true. Real life IS stranger than fiction.

Well, it took me quite a while to get adjusted to my new reading glasses. I hated them, of course, and oh, what a nuisance they were! I was always losing them and leaving them in supermarkets or sitting on them or dropping them on the tiled floor.

Apart from the nuisance factor of having to wear glasses for reading, I soon began to notice something else which was far more disturbing. Within a few months of using my new reading glasses, I discovered that I now not only had a problem reading small print without glasses but I was also finding it difficult to read the normal print in books, magazines and newspapers without glasses. An uneasy suspicion began to form in my mind that the glasses were actually causing my normal eyesight to deteriorate even faster than it had been doing naturally. Something was wrong but I couldn't find out what this was and anyway, there were far more serious things to think about.

Now that the fire had ruined our tourist business on Arrojela, we soon realised that we had no alternative but to leave Portugal and to look elsewhere for work. Despite our efforts, every door we tried was closed. Eventually, we decided that the only thing to do would be to rent Arrojela out for a nominal rent, considering the dreadful state it was in, and try our luck in South Africa, where I had been born and where what remained of my small family was still living.

It was a sad decision to make but I consoled myself that it wouldn't be for long, maybe just for a year or two. It was also sad saying goodbye to the friends we had made in the Algarve, especially as I knew that some of them like our dear old Dutch friend Jan wouldn't be alive when we came back. Jan had emphysema from all the cigarettes he'd smoked all his life and died in 1992, not long after I left.

When we had a last farewell supper with our friends Rev and Merryl who owned the beautiful Casa Meranka Guest House in Figueira, near Villa do Bishpo, Rev tried his best to cheer us up with jokes and riddles.

"Do you know how to make a small fortune in Portugal, O'D?" Rev asked, while he filled our glasses with the rough Algarvean wine he liked to drink and which always stained our tongues a virulent deep purple. Rev was tough and lean and had once been a British paratrooper.

No," O'D said glumly. "If I knew how, I would have done it."

"But you DO know how," Rev said with his loud, cackling laugh, "because you've just done it!"

"What are you talking about?" O'D asked.

Rev gulped down some wine and gave another cackling laugh. "How do you make a small fortune in Portugal? You bring a big one with you when you come here!"

"I don't think that's funny at all, Rev," I said.

CHAPTER TWO

AFRICA!

I left the Algarve for South Africa a few months later, in November. O'D stayed behind to find homes for our two dogs, Genghis and Attila, and to look for someone to rent Arrojela. I was still numb and in something of a state of shock from being so unexpectedly uprooted from the home I loved. I had planned to grow old at Arrojela and now here I was, on a plane heading towards Africa! I was someone who liked to know what I was doing and now I didn't have a clue where I was going to end up and I had no ideas at all for the future.

At Jan Smuts Airport (later called Johannesburg International and later still, renamed O.R. Tambo Airport) a sunburnt, blonde Immigration Officer stamped my British passport (courtesy of being married to O'D) and gave me a cheery grin. "Aaah ... born in Port Elizabeth," he said. "Welcome back to South Africa!"

"Thank you," I said gloomily.

I went off to find my luggage, which fortunately had arrived at the same destination as I had, and made my way over to the Domestic Terminal. Although I was now in South Africa, my journey still wasn't over. I had to catch a flight to George, the small town in the Cape, where my sister Jennifer and her husband Paul would be waiting at the tiny airport to drive me off to their house, not far from Mossel Bay.

On the plane, I sat surrounded by chattering, camera laden and bespectacled Asian tourists and it appeared that, except for the flight attendants and the pilot, I was the only Caucasian passenger.

Where were these talkative travellers from the Far East going? To the lagoons of Knysna or the Tsitsikamma forest? I looked out of my window. We were flying over jagged ranges of mountains and harsh scenery that was completely unfamiliar to me. Not a good place to crash, I thought and wondered how on earth the Voortrekkers had ever managed to get over this terrain with their heavy, creaking wagons and their oxen.

With a sigh, I looked away from the window. I was back in the land of my birth, back in Africa, a turbulent continent that had never brought anything but turmoil to my ancestors' lives ever since they had first set foot on its soil.

As the sunburnt Immigration Officer had noticed from my passport, I'd been born in Port Elizabeth, in the Cape. My first ancestors who had come to Africa had been Huguenots, making their escape from France in the 18th century and when I'd been very young, my grandmother had given me an extremely colourful version of this escape.

Until I was five, my mother, father and I had lived with my grandparents (my father's parents) in their big old house overlooking a leafy park. We had lived downstairs, while Gran and Gramps had lived upstairs.

Here, the best part of the day for me always came first thing in the morning. When I woke up, I would creep up the stairs and tap on my grandparents' bedroom door to be let in. They would still be in bed and while they drank coffee and ate sweet biscuits, Gran, who was something of a socialite and very fashionable, would give me the tremendous treat of allowing me to try on her huge and gorgeous collection of hats.

Oh, what a thrill it was to open hat box after hat box and to feast my eyes on wonderful confections of organza, velvet and straw, felt and fur; feathers dyed the colour of jewels and flowers and fruit fashioned out of delicate silken fabrics and wax.

While I occupied myself with my favourite morning occupation, sitting in front of the mirror and admiring myself in a variety of delectable hats, Gran occupied herself with her favourite occupation … which was talking.

Usually, this involved real life stories about our ancestors and the way Gran told them, they were certainly much more exciting than the bedtime fairy stories my mother read to me in the evenings.

"My family, the Duvinage, was originally from France, you know, Valry," my grandmother would begin. She always called me Valry, much to my mother's annoyance. She even spelled my name that way on letters and birthday and Christmas cards. "We were called Huguenots and we had to flee for our lives from France because the Roman Catholic Church was after us. We escaped in wine barrels … sailing off across the ocean all the way from France until we landed at the Cape of Good Hope."

Unaware that my grandmother had omitted a vital piece of information, which was something she often did, the bygone antics of these remarkable ancestors of mine filled me with admiration. How daring they had all been! Imagine … sailing away across the ocean in BARRELS!

Picturing the scene quite clearly, my childish mind imagined dozens of men and women, hair in ringlets and clad in silk and velvet, bobbing along bravely in their big wine barrels over the sparkling, white-tipped blue waves of the sea and unerringly making their way straight to the shores of South Africa.

It was only later when I learnt to read that I discovered what my grandmother had forgotten to tell me. Disappointingly, my Huguenot ancestors had not barrelled their way to Africa. To avoid detection while boarding ship in France, they had merely hidden themselves inside some empty barrels, pretending to be part of a consignment of wine being loaded for South Africa.

After their arrival in the Cape, it had been downhill all the way for my ancestors. Except for short periods of peace, which allowed them to prosper temporarily and which gave them a false sense of optimism that everything was going to turn out alright, they seemed to have spent most of their time involved in some life and death struggle or other. They battled with the inhospitable bush, they fought malaria and blackwater fever and rinderpest; they ran away from the British during the Great Trek and somehow found themselves on the losing side of every war, except for World War One and Two.

Over a period of more than three centuries in Africa, we moved around in a great and slow circle from the Cape to Johannesburg and then, before the apartheid era came into being, we left Johannesburg for South West Africa. From South West Africa we went to Rhodesia, where another war caught up with us and when this was over, most of us who were young decided to leave Africa for good. Enough was enough!

And now here I was - back in Africa and in the Cape again, thanks to a fire! Hopefully, it wouldn't be for long.

At this time, my family were living a short fifteen-minute drive away from Mossel Bay in a deadly boring place called Kleinbrak, where the monotony of life was only broken by the weekly arrival of the garbage men to collect the rubbish. Their house was situated in a peaceful rural spot, very close to the river and although it was quite an old house, it was comfortable and spacious with the biggest kitchen I've ever seen. In the garden at the back of the house, there were two small cottages and I rented one of them.

After living in Arrojela, it was a bit difficult adjusting to life in a tiny cottage. It was even more difficult adjusting to life in a small, mainly Afrikaans coastal town. Although I enjoyed being with my family after so many years of separation, I found the atmosphere in South Africa rather off-putting and inhibiting, stifling even, especially where safety was concerned. In Europe, I'd grown used to living amongst people who were fairly law-abiding. Now, back in a country where mugging, car-hijacking and handbag snatching were national pastimes, I would have to re-learn the old safety habits I'd been so glad to discard when I'd gone to live in England.

With nothing to do except wait for O'D, I gratefully accepted Paul's offer of a temporary Girl-Friday job at his boatworks in Mossel Bay. It made the time pass more quickly and gave me some pocket money.

My brother-in-law, who was tall and lean and who sported an enormously wild and bristly beard on his face, was passionate about boat engines. They appeared to be his first love, even supplanting my blonde and blue-eyed sister, and he often talked about them to me for hours on end. Chained to my chair out of politeness, I would listen to Paul explaining how he had gone about repairing his latest engine and describing the size, shape and number of every nut, bolt and screw he had used, even down to the spanners and screwdrivers. On and on he would talk, in his slow and drawling voice, while I listened until my eyes glazed over … like a Zombie's … from having to endure this most dreadful mental torture a man could ever inflict on a woman.

Despite this downside to Paul's character, he did have other more interesting things to talk about, and these were often to do with his own personal experiences with the Afrikaners in Apartheid South Africa.

One of his anecdotes that I found particularly hilarious was about the time when Paul had been living in a lighthouse.

The weather, Paul told me, had been exceptionally wet, miserable and stormy even for the Cape and this had kept him cooped up in his lighthouse for several days and nights. One Sunday afternoon, unable to take it anymore, he had decided to clear the cobwebs out of his head with some fresh air by going for a ride on his motorbike. As temperatures had plummeted and the day was freezing, he had thought that the best way to combat the excessive cold was to wear his form-fitting black wetsuit for the ride, and putting on his black safety-helmet, black gloves and black boots, he had sped off down the road.

After a few miles of exhilarating speed, he had heard the unwelcome sound of howling sirens and had been overtaken by some police cars with flashing lights. "Now what do these Turkeys want?" he had asked himself. Slowing down to a halt behind them, he had watched several beefy and very grim Afrikaans policemen climb out of their vehicles and begin to walk towards him. From the looks on their large, square faces and the way their stubby fingers had twitched over the triggers of the revolvers in their holsters, it had seemed to Paul that his misdemeanor, whatever it had been, was an extremely serious one!

"Howzit! What's the problem?" he had drawled a greeting, and removed his helmet.

At this point in his story, Paul always snickered with enjoyment into his big beard when he remembered how the Afrikaner policemen's beefy jaws had dropped when he had revealed his face to them and they had seen the colour of it.

"Magtig, man!" one of the Afrikaans policeman had cried. "What a terrrrible shock you've jist given us! When you flashed past us at high speed in that black wetsuit, we jist couldn't believe our eyes. We thought we was seeing a NAKED AFRICAN riding a motorbike! A NAKED AFRICAN!"

This seemingly outrageous contempt for all social conventions by an AFRICAN in SOUTH AFRICA had rendered the policemen almost speechless for several long minutes before they had managed to pull themselves together. Then they had scrambled for their cars, to hit the road in hot pursuit after the perverted black biker.

Another of Paul's loves was Pluto, his African grey parrot. Pluto had been born in captivity and had been given to Paul as a present. She adored him with all her little parrot heart, jealously treating Jenny and their two daughters, Danielle and Andrea, as rivals for his affection and flying at them to furiously peck at their feet to warn them off. When Paul fell asleep on the sofa in the sitting room, as he sometimes did on a Sunday afternoon, she would hop onto his chest, snuggle up into the curve of his neck and also go to sleep in the nest-like comfort of his great and bushy beard.

The little town of Mossel Bay was a trifle livelier than Kleinbrak. It was pretty and immaculately clean and had banks and shops and traffic in its streets. The sandy coves and beaches looked inviting but lost their allure for me one morning on a drive along the coastal road to the town with Paul.

"This part of the coast, you know," Paul told me, "is the breeding ground of the Great White. The sea teems with sharks." He removed a hand from the steering wheel and pointed a finger at the sparkling blue waves of the Indian Ocean. "There's an island called Dyer Island further along the coast. It's like a shark supermarket. The water around it is full of Great Whites because about 50 to 60 thousand seals live on the island and the Great Whites feed on the seal pups."

The Great White!

"Wow," I said.

"If you're interested," Paul, who was a man of the wild African outdoors and the wilder the better, went on, "I can contact one of the shark tour companies and arrange for you to spend some time underwater, in a cage, watching the sharks up close while they circle around the cage."

A menacing and well-known film theme tune came into my mind ... dada dada dada dada ... and the picture of a girl struggling and screaming in a moonlit sea while her boyfriend slept, snoring and oblivious, on top of a sand dune ... JAWS ...

Another picture came into my mind, this time of myself in a cage while a Great White swam towards me with its blank cold eyes and its enormous cavern of a mouth gaping open wide, to crunch the cage ...

I gave Paul a look. "Thanks, but I'll give it a miss."

Later on, when my sister Jennifer told me about my father's recent stay in the tiny Mossel Bay hospital, I realised that danger wasn't only confined to the sea in this somnolent little spot on the South African map. It lurked above ground as well, and in places you certainly wouldn't expect to find it.

My father, who had been suffering from a heart problem for many years, had fallen ill and had had to spend some time in hospital. He'd been put in a room by himself until, one night, another patient, an African man, had been brought into the room and put into the empty bed next to his.

Dad had talked to the man for a while and had asked him what was wrong with him. The man had replied that he had been at a beer drink with some of his friends and that during the evening he had drunk down a bottle of DIESEL by mistake!

After a few more minutes of conversation, my father and the man had gone to sleep. Then, at about two o'clock in the morning, they had both been rudely awakened when some extremely drunk men had noisily burst into their room. Brandishing knives, the intruders had for some inexplicable reason rushed over to my father's bed and grabbed hold of him, shouting that they were going to kill him!

Fortunately for my father, the drunks had turned out to be the diesel- drinking man's companions and he'd been able to calm the men down by telling them that my father was his friend and persuading them not to harm him. In the end, the drunks had staggered out of the room, calm had returned and my father had eventually fallen asleep again.

However, as if being attacked in his hospital bed hadn't been bad enough, there had been still more to follow.

In the morning, when my father had woken up, he had greeted his companion in the next bed but had received no reply. On closer scrutiny of the still form lying under its hospital blanket, he had noticed that the man's open eyes staring fixedly up at the ceiling had been sightless and that there had been no up and down movement of his chest. Sometime during the night, the poison had done its work and without even a sound, the diesel-drinking man had breathed his last breath and died.

My father had informed the hospital staff of his companion's demise but they had made no effort to remove the dead body out of the room. As the day had progressed, the hospital staff had served Dad his breakfast of milky tea and soggy scrambled eggs on soggy toast and at lunchtime had given him another meal, behaving as if it was quite normal for a man to eat in the presence of a corpse mouldering away in the bed next to his. With this kind of attitude, who knows how long the dead man might have been left in that bed.

Luckily, my sister had paid a visit to my father at three o'clock that afternoon. She'd been shocked by the hospital staff's lack of respect toward the dead as well as their insensitivity towards the sick. She'd also been aghast at the sight of the long trail of ants soldiering down the wall, marching across the floor, climbing up onto the dead man's bed and walking all over his face, into his eyes, into his nostrils and into his mouth.

Jenny hadn't minced her words with the hospital staff and within a few seconds of her arrival, they had come with a trolley and had taken the dead man away.

42

While I was getting to grips with some of the grim realities of life in Africa, O'D was still busy sorting everything out at Arrojela. It took him four months to pack our possessions into boxes and to store them in his mother, Marion's, attic in her house in Montes da Cima and to find a home for Genghis and Atilla. He also rented Arrojela to a German who appeared out of the blue and offered to pay 198 pounds a month to live there with his family while we were away.

The German was called Uwe Heitkamp and his hair was long and pulled back from his head in a ponytail. He was a journalist, he told O'D, and owned a small yacht that he intended to use to take tourists on boating trips along the Algarvean coast.

A legal contract was drawn up for the rental of Arrojela. It was a contract that had to be renewed every year and when O'D warned Uwe that Arrojela might have to be sold and that he wasn't interested in renting to people who became 'sitting tenants', Uwe gave O'D his word that we didn't have to worry about this sort of thing because he wasn't one of these people.

It was already going on for May when O'D arrived in Mossel Bay. Unlike me, he had to apply for a Work Permit and not being one to enjoy sitting around idle while he was waiting for permission to work, he decided to travel to Zimbabwe to visit his cousins, the Browns.

As O'D's proposed visit would have to be done on a shoestring, he decided to travel economically to Zimbabwe on a long distance bus, breaking up the more than 2,000 kilometre journey with a short rest in Johannesburg. Paula, my brother David's first wife, lived in Roodepoort with her husband Menno and she offered to put O'D up for a few days.

The bus O'D travelled on stopped at Johannesburg Railway Station and it was here, in the cavernous Station's murky gloom, that he received a welcome from the local residents in the traditional South African way.

Wandering from dimly lit platform to dimly lit platform in his search for the train to Roodepoort, O'D lost his way and ended up in the wrong place at the wrong time. Six sharp dark eyes had been following his progress and when they judged that the time was right, three men appeared out of the murk and surrounded him.

"Give us your wallet," one of the muggers hissed viciously at O'D, waving a glinting knife at the outline of his old crocodile skin wallet they could see in his buttoned up shirt pocket.

Instead of obeying, O'D crossed his arms firmly across his chest, standing his ground and staring at the men in silence. This course of passive resistance wasn't because O'D had nerves of steel and was preparing to overcome his attackers with a karate kick or two, it was a course he embarked on through necessity. His passport and driver's licence were in the same pocket with his wallet and the wallet contained the only money he possessed in the world. If the muggers had their way, he would be stranded in Johannesburg without any identity or travel documents and completely penniless, without even the means to make a phone call for help.

O'D's behaviour in the face of attack didn't deter the muggers. The moment he crossed his arms, the men went through his trouser pockets as quick as a flash and divested him of his penknife and all his change. Then they closed in and the mugger wielding the knife raised his weapon.

Still keeping one hand protectively clamped over his shirt pocket, O'D tried to grab at the man's arm with his free hand in an attempt to force him to drop the knife, and in the struggle the man slashed and ripped away at O'D's shirt.

O'D was never sure what saved him or caused the muggers to give up - perhaps they lost their nerve because his continued resistance was prolonging the attack - but all of a sudden, and quite inexplicably, they turned tail and slipped away back into the gloom.

Hardly able to believe his luck, O'D drew in a deep breath to steady himself and then, with legs that trembled, he began to walk back the way he had come. An African man stopped him. "I saw what happened to you," he told O'D. "Are you okay, man?"

"Yes," O'D said. "Yes."

He must have looked an odd sight as he sat in the train while it clanked its way towards Roodepoort. A white man, dishevelled and wearing a blue and white checked shirt that had once looked good but now hung in tatters around his body, with one torn sleeve dangling by a thread from his shoulder.

On the short walk from Roodepoort Station to Paula's house, he got some looks. A white man, walking around the neighbourhood in a shredded shirt. Was he a down-and-out? A tramp?

When O'D finally arrived at Paula's house, she was naturally concerned but not surprised. After all, this was Johannesburg where everyone got mugged sooner or later.

"You were lucky, O'D!" she exclaimed. "Your guardian angel must have been looking after you!"

"I have the feeling the muggers were amateurs," O'D replied. "Just starting out on their careers."

"Well, you can't walk around looking like that," Paula told him. "Take off your shirt and I'll sew it up for you."

The stress of the day finally overcame O'D. His shaky legs gave way and he collapsed wearily down onto the sofa. "I'd rather have a beer, if you don't mind," he said.

Apart from a brief phone call telling me he'd arrived safely in Harare, I knew nothing of O'D's adventures until he phoned one evening about three weeks after he'd left South Africa.

I was sitting on the verandah, eating a supper of crispy roast chicken wings with my family, when the phone rang. Paul answered it with a loud 'HOWZIT O'D!' and handed the receiver over to me.

Although the line was faint and crackly, I was able to make out that O'D was now employed as an Administration Manager on a tobacco farm ... in MOZAMBIQUE!

"How ... how did this happen?" I asked O'D. Although South Africa wasn't an ideal country in which to live, Mozambique was even further down my list.

"While I was staying with John Brown, Kath Gamble asked me if I'd like to drive down to Beira with her. She's got a sawmill there. We'd just arrived in Beira, when someone told us that Tabex, a tobacco company in Chimoio, about an hour's drive from the Zimbabwe border, was looking for an Administration Manager. So I applied for the job and they asked me to start right away." There was silence on the line and then O'D added modestly, "I think this was only because I spoke fluent Portuguese."

"But you always told me you never liked this kind of work," I exclaimed. "You said you detested being cooped up in an office, sitting behind a desk and shuffling papers around!"

"Actually, this isn't too bad," O'D went on, sounding surprisingly enthusiastic. "My work often takes me out of the office and Mozambique's quite an interesting country. Much more interesting than South Africa. Or Zimbabwe."

When I put the phone down, my mother asked, "How is O'D enjoying himself with the Browns?"

45

"He went fishing in Kariba with them," I told her, "and then he went horse-riding with cousin Jeffrey at Nyanga. Now he's working on a tobacco farm as an Administration Manager."

"Oh, that's nice," my mother said, pleased to hear O'D had found a job. "And when are you going to Zimbabwe?"

"I'm not going to Zimbabwe. He's working in Mozambique."

As Mozambique was a country still at war in 1992, my family's reactions to the last piece of my news were predictable.

"MO ZAM BIQUE!" my mother cried, appalled. "There's a war going on there! Why is O'D working in a country where there's a war when he could be working in South Africa, where it's safe?"

Considering that O'D had just told me he'd almost been mugged and knifed in Johannesburg I thought this was going a bit far. "Mom," I said, "more people die from violence every day right here in South Africa than anywhere else in the world – and this country isn't even at war!"

"I read in the paper the other day that everyone in Mozambique is starving and eating roots," my father said. "Did O'D tell you what he's eating?

I helped myself to another chicken wing. This might just be the last chicken I would be eating for a while. "Dad," I replied, in an attempt to reassure myself as well as to reassure my father, "you know that O'D is not only a gourmet but a gourmand as well. I'm quite sure that someone like him would never live in a country where he hasn't got access to food."

Paul stopped crunching on a chicken wing for a second. "Bandits all over the place in Mozambique," he drawled. "I've heard that the road to Maputo is full of the wrecks of burnt-out cars with the charred skeletons of the drivers still propped up against the steering wheels."

"Oh, thanks, Paul," I said.

I arrived in Zimbabwe in June. It had been cold and stormy in Mossel Bay and freezing in Johannesburg and so I'd dressed in jeans and a thick, hand-knitted Algarvean sweater. June was winter in Africa but you wouldn't have thought so when I stepped off the plane at Harare airport. It was hot, as hot as a sweltering October day and I just couldn't wait to open my suitcase, rip off my sweater and put on something cooler. The terrible 1992 drought had Southern Africa in its grip.

Although he'd been out of my care and on his own for about a month, O'D looked surprisingly well and fit, proving that he was either more than capable of looking after himself - or that someone else had been taking on that responsibility. He was also obviously not suffering any ill effects from living in a war-torn, drought-stricken country where everyone was living on a diet of roots.

During the four-hour drive to the border, I questioned O'D closely about what to expect in Mozambique. The phone line between Mozambique and South Africa had been so bad, we had never been able to talk for long.

Now I asked, " How many people live on this farm with you and what do you do for food?"

There were three white farmers, O'D told me, and a white mechanic. Maciel, one of the farmers, was originally from Angola while Clive and Tim were both from Zimbabwe. The mechanic was called Jake Jackson and he was Zimbabwean too.

As it was quite true that there was nothing to eat in the country, the farmers working for Tabex drove across the Zimbabwean border to the small town of Mutare to stock up their larders. Fresh vegetables weren't a problem, though, as Maciel grew them. Despite the drought, water was plentiful because the farm had several good boreholes.

O'D had also heard that the road to Maputo was littered with charred skeletons still sitting in their charred vehicles but Maputo was a long way away and there really wasn't much to worry about in Manica Province. The Tabex farm was very safe and very comfortable and he was sure I would enjoy living there …

The drive from Harare to the border was boring and monotonous and the few little towns we passed were nothing to get excited about. To while away some time, I opened a copy of 'The Herald', Zimbabwe's government newspaper. Its scanty pages were filled with bad news – all about the worst drought in decades Southern Africa was experiencing. Oblivious of incongruity, the headlines cried, "We are starving!" not far from a bad photograph of the 200 kg dark bulk of Moven Mahachi, the Minister of Home Affairs. Apart from the whites of his eyes and a white smile in the shape of a slice of watermelon, the Minister's face was a featureless dark blob. The Government photographer had forgotten the most basic aspect of photography - illumination.

After reading a few pages about the ravages the drought was also having on the wildlife, where hippo and elephant were dying

47

around waterless dams, pans and rivers, I folded the newspaper and put it down on the seat again and turned my attention back to the road.

For most of the journey, we had the road to ourselves except for the ancient buses that roared past us, breaking the speed and safety limits and belching out thick clouds of foul smelling and sulphurous black smoke. They were overloaded with passengers and top-heavy with bundles, baskets, bicycles, chickens and the occasional goat. Trapped for a while behind one of these buses as we crossed the bridge over the dry Odzi riverbed, I idly wandered how the chickens and goats felt about being tied by a leg to the roof rack of a speeding bus, but then, these were African chickens and goats and were, no doubt, probably used to travelling on buses. Perhaps they even enjoyed the wind that roared through their feathers and hair at 120 kilometres an hour.

At last we began our steep ascent up Christmas Pass and when we reached the top and looked down, the lovely little town of Mutare lay below us, nestling amongst trees and flowers. On our way down, we passed the large "Welcome to Mutare" sign, with its words planted out in flowers and took the road into the town. A beauty of a place, Mutare was forgotten and neglected by the rest of the country and probably, because of this, life was still lived at a deliciously slow pace and everyone still had time for a smile and a chat.

We took the turning at the Beira signpost and drove down the narrow, winding road to Forbes Border Post. The road was in a bad state of repair and riddled with potholes. A few cars travelled towards us slowly, swerving and weaving all over the road to avoid the holes, as if their drivers had spent too much time at a pub and were staggeringly drunk in charge of their vehicles.

And then, just as we were approaching the sign by the side of the road that warned of landmines, something happened which neither O'D nor I expected to happen on the Zimbabwean side of the border and it disorientated me completely.

Suddenly, and out of nowhere, there was the dry, loud crack of rifle shots. O'D braked sharply, whiplashing our necks a little and brought our car to a standstill just as several people burst out of the bush and ran wildly across the road right in front of us. They were barefoot and dressed in rags, the colourless and dirty remnants of what had once been shirts and trousers hanging in tatters on their bodies and they were pursued hotly and closely by two men wearing dark blue uniforms and armed with rifles.

Taken aback by the violence being acted out in front of our eyes, we watched with astonishment as one of the uniformed men dropped down onto one knee right in front of our car bonnet and took aim. He fired more shots at the fleeing band of people and then jumped up and pounded after them.

For a while, O'D and I sat still and listened to the crashing sounds of people running through the bush. There were still more rifle shots and then the sounds of flight and pursuit faded.

I'd expected to see this sort of thing in Mozambique, not in Zimbabwe, and now the incident muddled me up. My mind went completely blank and for a moment I didn't have a clue where I was!

"Are we in Mozambique now?" I asked O'D.

He gave me a surprised look. "Of course not. We haven't gone through the border yet."

"Oh. Who do you think those people were?"

"Probably Mozambican border jumpers. They come looking for jobs. Or food. They use a path through the mountains. The Zimbabweans don't want them over here."

Shooting at people who were jobless and starving seemed a rather harsh way of dealing with border jumpers. I ruminated on this for a while until another thought entered my mind. Imagine shooting at people ACROSS A PUBLIC ROAD!

"How irresponsible, how careless!" I fumed to O'D. "They could have shot *us*. They could even have KILLED us with a stray bullet by mistake!"

O'D turned on the ignition. "I never think of things like that," he said.

At Forbes Border Post, we parked the car under trees that were filled with black-faced Vervet monkeys and walked inside the small white building. Here, too, the Zimbabwean Immigration and Customs officials didn't seem to be suffering much from lack of food. Dressed in smart white shirts and navy blue trousers or skirts, teamed with navy blue jackets, their clothes strained at the seams. As they dealt with us plumply and efficiently, I looked out through the windows and watched the Vervets. Several were busy rummaging among the pile of empty potato crisp packets, Coca-Cola cans and the other rubbish littering the ground under the trees. One Vervet, more daring than the others, cheekily jumped into the open back of our vehicle and tried to prise open a cardboard box with its tiny black hands.

I walked out through the open doorway, towards the car. "Hey! What do you think you're doing?"

Caught in the act, the Vervet looked guiltily at me with its bright, brown, round eyes and then scampered up into the trees again.

Back in the car, we drove down the steep hill and across the bridge over the empty Munene River that separated Forbes Border Post from Machipanda Border Post.

Compared to Forbes, Machipanda was decidedly rundown and shabby. With nothing to do, three Mozambican officials lounged at a counter in the empty room and I felt a pang of compassion for them when I noticed how threadbare their brown uniforms were and saw how terribly thin they were. This feeling of compassion didn't last long, though. As O'D and I approached the counter, the officials quickly straightened up and vanished through a doorway!

Their disappearance surprised me, especially as it lasted for more than twenty long minutes.

"What can they be doing?" I asked O'D irritably. After all, we were the only people at Machipanda.

"Heaven knows," he replied. "They often do this. I think it's something to do with showing us who is in charge. A type of power play."

While we waited, I stared out of the windows. They were smeared with dust and there weren't any little monkeys here. There was no rubbish either. Without thinking, I began to drum my fingers to the tune of' 'chopsticks' on the wooden counter top.

"You'd better stop doing that," O'D warned me. "If they hear you they'll make us wait even longer."

I stopped drumming immediately. "Don't they like chopsticks?"

Eventually, the door opened and the officials came over to us.

"Boa tarde," O'D said politely.

"Boa tarde," they replied.

When our passports were stamped and all the paperwork was done, we climbed back into our car and drove towards the exit. A thin guard in a frayed uniform raised the barrier - a long, rough wooden pole – that was blocking the road and we went through.

I was now in Mozambique - a country still at war - in June 1992.

Bob Dylan wrote a song about Mozambique in the 1970's. It had a fast, rolling rhythm and I'd liked it a lot. I'd played it over and over again until my mother had come into the sitting room and had told me that if I didn't stop, she was going to smash my Dylan LP into hundreds of little pieces.

Dylan's song gave you the idea that Mozambique was a happy and romantic place. It made you want to go there right away, but now, driving into it some decades later, I could see that there was nothing to sing about this country, unless it was a lament.

It may have been my imagination but as O'D and I drove along the road, hearing nothing but the thrumming of tyres on tar and seeing nothing but dry countryside and the ruins of small houses dotted around on top of hills, it seemed to me as if an air of menace hung over us.

Not a blade of grass grew on the sides of the road for several metres and although we passed large clusters of huts, there was no sign of people, animals or any other vehicles driving towards us or coming up behind us. There was just the vast emptiness of blue sky, yellow grass and some purple mountains in the distance.

The abnormal silence and lack of activity was eerie. Already rattled by the border jumper incident we had witnessed, I sat tensely on the seat, scarcely breathing and clenched my hands in my lap. If people were running around shooting rifles in a peaceful country like Zimbabwe, what was a warring country like Mozambique going to throw at us?

"Are you sure we're not going to be ambushed?" I asked O'D when the grassy scenery began to change into bush and trees.

"Look over there," he told me, pointing into the trees. "It's full of soldiers. Zimbabwean soldiers. They're camped all along this road – which is called the Beira Corridor - in order to guard the oil pipeline from Beira to Mutare. It's costing the Zimbabwean government millions of dollars. That's why there are all these huts along this road as well. This is the only place where the people feel safe."

I stared into the trees and saw what I hadn't noticed before. Soldiers, dressed in camouflage that blended in with the trees, were sitting or moving around dark green tents. Relief flooded through me and I relaxed back against the seat, even unclenching my hands.

"The soldiers are based at the farm as well," O'D continued. "There's a camp not far from our houses. They're using water from the farm boreholes so I've arranged a trade with their Commander. In

51

exchange for our water, the Zimbabwe Army gives us some of their rations. Bread, milk, meat and eggs."

Our journey to the farm was uneventful until we drove towards a place called Antennas. In the distance, two men walked along the road towards us. Dressed in the 1992 Mozambican fashion of dirty rags and bare feet, they carried AKs as a must-have accessory. I tensed up immediately at the sight of the rifles and clenched my hands again. This was it, I knew! O'D also tensed up, I noticed, and tightened his hands on the steering wheel.

"Are they bandits?" I asked fearfully.

"It's hard to say who they are," he murmured thoughtfully. "They could be Frelimo, Renamo or just ordinary Mozambicans out for a stroll. Everyone has a gun in this country."

We kept our eyes fixed on the men but they barely glanced at us as we went by and they plodded along to wherever they were going. Their faces were gaunt and expressionless and there was an awful air of hopelessness about them.

Fourteen kilometres away from the town of Chimoio (once called Vila Pery in Portuguese Colonial days) I saw a sign on the right hand side of the road that read Tabacos da Manica. Here, O'D turned off the tar and for a while we bumped along a dirt road, past a small dam filled with muddy brown water, until we came to fields planted with rows and rows of small green plants.

"Tobacco," O'D told me, waving a hand at the plants.

"Oh," I said, trying to sound enthusiastic. "Tobacco …"

A kilometre or so later, we drove around a bend in the road and approached a small guardhouse with a barrier in the form of a long pole blocking our way. An armed and uniformed guard appeared and greeted O'D with a salute and a "Boa tarde" and raised the pole. Further along the road, we travelled past tall tobacco barns, with high thatched roofs and workshops, with tractors and trailers and then finally, as O'D drove towards a small complex of houses, he slowed the pickup and said, "This is it."

After what I'd seen so far in Mozambique, I must say I was very relieved and pleasantly surprised when I climbed out of the pickup and surveyed my new home. It was pretty, picturesque, a pleasant blend of lush green lawns, shady trees and vibrant flowerbeds. In the midst of all of this, three old houses were set in a semi-circle around a pool shelter and a rectangular swimming pool sparkling with clear, cool, pale blue water.

Inside the house furthest away from the pool, I met the person who had been looking after O'D so well. This was the skinniest little man I had ever seen, naturally skinny, I learnt later. His name was Biasse and for the next nine years or so, his small presence was to loom large in my life.

It wasn't easy to settle down to life on the Tabex farm. For one thing, O'D had forgotten to tell me that the house didn't come with a radio or a television. There weren't any books or magazines to read either and I couldn't even occupy myself in the kitchen because this was the domain of our skinny little cook.

When O'D went off to work at the Tabex office in Chimoio the next day, I sat in an armchair in a silent house and wondered what on earth I was going to do with myself.

I hadn't thought to bring any writing paper, so I couldn't write any letters and as the farm didn't have a phone, I couldn't enliven the long empty hours by chatting away to my family or friends.

Apart from drinking coffee under the thatched pool shelter and talking about Portugal to Conceicao, Maciel's wife, there was absolutely nothing I could think of doing to fill the long empty hours that lay in front of me.

One afternoon a few days later, while I was sitting on the verandah idly watching some ants carting off the remains of a dead grasshopper - you couldn't get any lower than this where entertainment was concerned - Jake Jackson came to my rescue.

He was a nice man, Jake, tall and bearded and lean. He arrived with O'D and was carrying a large cardboard box which he dumped down on the verandah. "Magazines," he told me with a grin, "and," he handed me a red and white can of Coca-Cola, "you can borrow this until you get to Zimbabwe to buy your own radio."

It's amazing how a tinny-sounding radio masquerading as a can of Coke can brighten up a house. It's equally amazing how the more than ten year old South African 'Fair Lady' magazines and the ancient 'Time' and 'News Weeks' can hold your interest and absorb you when you've got nothing else to read. And when Jake managed to unearth a television and a video player from one of the storerooms, life on the farm really took an upturn!

After lunch one afternoon about ten days after my arrival, O'D took me on a tour of the town of Chimoio, as well as the Tabex factory.

"Here," he said kindly, handing me a large plastic carrier bag bulging with dirty, small denomination meticais notes worth about five U.S. dollars. "You can do a bit of shopping as well, when we get into town". The plastic bag was far too big to squash into my shoulder bag and so I had to carry it in my hand.

Although O'D had taken me out to a restaurant in Chimoio one evening for a dinner of rice and prawns, this was the first time I had seen Chimoio in daylight.

The entrance into the town was not - and still is not - a pretty sight. It had once been a light industrial area but now it was scruffy with broken-down unoccupied warehouses and fenced-off areas full of rusty scrap. Most of it appeared to belong to Aderita, a small bearded man with dancing, sparkling eyes who was a member of the little band of Portuguese residents in Chimoio who had ignored a man called Guebuza's famous 20 – 24 command and had stayed on all through the war in Mozambique. The 20 –24, by the way, had been an order to the Portuguese to get out of Mozambique within 24 hours, or else - and had only allowed them to take 20kgs of a lifetime's possessions with them.

The Tabex factory was also in this area, and so O'D drove through its gates to show me his office and the tobacco grading shed.

His office was a spartan grey cement room, furnished simply with a couple of desks and chairs, a telephone and a computer and printer. A small man was sitting behind one of the desks and O'D introduced me to him.

"This is Zefferino," he told me, "my assistant. He's also the Tabex 'Fixer' because he's an expert at knowing how to get around the Mozambican maze of bureaucratic red tape. This expertise consists mainly of knowing who is the right person to bribe."

We left O'D's office and walked a short distance over to the tobacco grading shed. The room was large and dimly lit by the daylight that came in through windows high up in the walls. It was full of men and women who were sitting on benches in front of long tables. The tables were covered in masses of dry yellow-brown tobacco leaves and as they sorted the leaves out into different piles and grades, thousands of tiny shreds of tobacco floated up and filled the air around them.

Although the air was full of these minute particles of tobacco, which they were no doubt inhaling deeply into their lungs, not one of these men or women were using the white nose masks they'd been given to protect themselves. They had all pushed the masks casually up onto the top of their heads and were wearing them like some kind of fashion accessory on their crinkly African hair.

On the way back to the car, I wondered how they could endure working in the grading room without the use of their nose masks. Didn't they care about their health?

"I've told them over and over again to wear their nose masks to protect themselves," O'D told me. "But they just refuse to listen."

We left the factory and drove on towards the town. There was little traffic on the road because very few Mozambicans had vehicles or even a bicycle.

At the second roundabout on the way into town, I made O'D stop the pick up while I examined a long and colourful curved board which told the story of how the Mozambicans had won their war of liberation against the Portuguese. It was painted in a sort of cartoon-style and it was obvious that the artist had had great fun and had enjoyed himself immensely in depicting the Portuguese as cowardly little twits and the Mozambicans as brave and fearsome.

There were scenes of sallow-skinned Portuguese soldiers with big drooping noses trudging through the bush, while helicopters soared overhead. The soldiers all wore over-large, clumsy black boots and their eyes peered shiftily sideways out of the picture at you. They were scared out of their wits.

The Mozambicans, on the other hand, were painted as strong and fearless hawk-faced warriors, dressed in camouflage and scaring the hell out of their soft, weak European enemy.

In the town, O'D drove around the deserted streets pointing out various shops he thought might be of interest to me. Within no time at all, it became clear to me that if you were someone who liked to shop till you dropped, the shops in Chimoio would definitely have given you a nervous breakdown when you tried to cope with withdrawal symptoms.

Large empty expanses of dusty pane glass looked blankly out onto the streets, with a display or two of an ancient yellowed comic book, a can of tomatoes long past its sell by date, an old Barbie doll, its plastic blotched white by the sun as if it had a virulent skin disease.

"I managed to buy a screwdriver at this shop here," O'D told me, pointing to a building streaked with black mould. "It was Chinese. It bent as soon as I tried to screw in a screw because the steel was too soft."

We drove on.

"And this is where I found some ballpoint pens for the office. They were also Chinese. Zeff and I couldn't get them to write a word until we hit on the idea of soaking them in a jar of boiling water for three or four hours to liquefy the ink."

"Mmm ..." I said. So much for Made in China.

We turned down into some small streets, drove past the railway station where no trains had run for years and where a small, dark, dusty shop sold carafes of wine from Portugal. Dotted here and there in the streets were beautiful examples of Portuguese architecture that made my fingers itch to renovate. Although these houses were badly maintained and streaked with black, the Portuguese had built well and to last. It wouldn't take much, I knew, to restore them to their former glory.

"This is just like a ghost town," I said to O'D. Chimoio looked as if a neutron bomb had been dropped on it, leaving all the buildings intact but killing all the people. There was no evidence of the destructiveness of war here; there were no bullet-riddled buildings or bombed out piles of rubble. The only sign of strife was to be found in a quiet, lovely tree-lined street. Here lay the blackened and charred remains of a house a Mozambican government official had once bought for his mistress. His wife, in a fit of jealous rage, had set the house alight one night and burned it to the ground.

We turned another corner, into the main road and drove past a large and well-guarded building that O'D told me was where the Governor of Manica Province was sometimes to be found in his office.

A man walked down the centre of this road towards us. He was completely naked and his hair was long, down to his shoulders in Rastafarian dreadlocks and incredibly matted. He shouted as he walked along, and waved his arms around in the air.

"Mad," O'D told me. "I often see him about town."

I was beginning to wonder why O'D had bothered to give me a carrier bag full of money, when he pulled up in front of a shop called Mar Azul. It was a Chinese shop and its shelves were full.

Inside the shop, I strolled down three or four short aisles. There was a lot of food here but it was all in cans; canned fruit, canned vegetables, canned meat, canned fish. There wasn't any fresh or frozen meat or bread, milk or eggs. Everything was imported from Portugal and South Africa and it was all so very expensive, even for us.

Eventually, just to buy something, I picked up a small bottle of olives and then noticed a counter with a couple of bolts of cloth. This I discovered was material for the capulanas (sarongs) the Mozambican women wore. I chose a length of thin red cotton, with blue fish swimming all over it. It was to be the first of the many capulanas I bought over the years and wore instead of my European clothes. Not only were the capulanas pretty and colourful, they were also comfortable and wonderfully cool and casual in a country much too hot and damp for Western fashions.

Life on the Tabex farm was unexpectedly peaceful and for the next two years we led a placid and almost, but not quite, normal existence. To get out and about a bit and to stock up with supplies, we often drove across the border to Mutare to shop. Mugabe was loosening up Zimbabwe's economy and the shelves in the shops were full, the roads crammed with expensive cars and the towns bustled with activity. Compared to Mozambique, Zimbabwe was a land of plenty, of milk and honey.

Shopping in Mutare was a pleasure, especially in places like Kingstons and the Book Centre, which were something of a paradise for people as starved of books as we were in a bookless society like Mozambique. Our greatest treat of all, though, was to drive out of the town and up the twisting road in the hills to lunch at the Inn on the Vumba. Here, in the small and homely hotel's tranquil and rather old-fashioned English surroundings, we ate delicious meals brought to us by ancient white-haired and slow-moving waiters and drank a delightful drink called a "Glog".

This drink was introduced to us one lunch-time when O'D asked a portly and grizzled waiter if the hotel had any imported gin. After some thought, the waiter went off to make enquiries at the bar and on his return, told us that they did, indeed, have imported gin. This gin was from Scotland and it was called "Glog."

"Glog ..." O'D repeated thoughtfully, never having heard of a gin called "Glog" and as a result suspicious of its origins. Was this another attempt by the Chinese, those great imitators of Western products, to trick consumers into thinking they were drinking genuine, bona fide Scottish-distilled juniper berries? "Bring the bottle," O'D told the waiter. "I'd like to see the label."

The waiter ambled off to the bar again and came back with a bottle. With a shaky old finger, he pointed at the label on which was printed the word 'GLOAG'. "You see, Sir, "he said, "it is Glog, from Scotland."

"Mmm …," O'D muttered. "It looks authentic but it's not from Scotland, it's from England. We'd better try it out. Bring us two of these … er … Glogs … and some tonic."

With Zimbabwe on the rise, some of the people who had left in 1980 when Mugabe had taken over, began to return. When my cousin Arlene and her husband Horst who lived in London, decided to open a clothing factory in Harare, they asked my brother David to help manage it and soon he and Caroline, with my niece Olivia and my baby nephew Tom, arrived back in Southern Africa. Unfortunately, their fortunes were to fluctuate with the caprices of President Mugabe and rose and fell with the country. But all this was still in the unknown future and at the time everything looked quite rosy. Olivia was chosen for a part in the film "Thinking of Africa" and Caroline began to think of starting up her own business. With the return of some of my family, our visits to Zimbabwe now included Harare.

Zimbabwe wasn't the only country that saw an influx of new residents. In Mozambique too, things were on the move.

When the Rome Peace Accord was signed, the Zimbabwean soldiers moved out and ONUMOZ, the United Nations Peacekeepers, moved in. A large contingent of Italians set up camp on the Tabex farm and although they mostly kept to themselves, some of their officers sometimes came over to our house to talk to O'D about various things.

Compared to the Zimbabweans, I thought the Italians looked - and behaved - more like social workers than battle hardened soldiers. They were young, with soft, smooth, olive-skinned faces and when they talked of the destruction the war had caused to the country and to the people, their emotions overwhelmed them and their brown eyes glistened with moisture. Even the sight of African huts upset them.

"This is terrible … terrible!" they exclaimed one day on my verandah. "To live in a hut made out of mud and grass! We thought they all lived in proper houses, like us!"

Their reactions didn't inspire me with confidence. Surely even European soldiers who had had no experience of war for fifty years were aware that wars maimed and killed and destroyed? And as for the huts, didn't they know that this was traditional Southern African architecture, as well as being environmentally friendly?

"If we're attacked," I said, giving O'D my gloomy assessment of the Italians' military prowess, "it's my opinion that they'll all cut and run. Or hoist a white flag of surrender above their tents."

"Oh, don't be ridiculous!" he told me. "They're the Alpini, the best mountain fighting unit in Italy."

"Is that so …" I said thoughtfully. "Now why do you think they sent the Alpini to a country that's mostly flat?"

Although the UN soldiers were upset by the state of the Mozambicans, their compassionate feelings towards the people were mixed with another emotion as well … fear. Tensely holding their rifles at the ready in case of attack, they patrolled up and down the Beira Corridor Road in their white UN vehicles.

When no attacks came from the war-weary Mozambicans, the soldiers stopped worrying about their safety and began to grow bored. To keep them occupied during the long, hot, dusty days. their officers thought up things for them to do. Some of these things included setting up roadblocks on the Tabex farm's little dirt roads without telling anybody and as these roadblocks were set up around corners and out of sight without any warning signs at all, they were quite dangerous, as O'D and I found out one early morning.

O'D has always been a fast driver and so we were bowling along at quite a pace when we rounded a corner and unexpectedly found ourselves about to smash straight into several white UN vehicles which had been parked in a zigzag pattern on the narrow road to close it.

As if it wasn't enough that O'D and I were a split second away from being mangled in a mess of metal, the sight of our pickup heading straight towards them shocked the young UN soldiers and they reacted by raising their rifles and pointing them at us as if about to shoot!

Unable to stop, the only thing O'D could think of doing to avoid a disaster was to swerve our pickup in a violent chicane-like manoeuvre in and out between the UN vehicles. This manoeuvre was so sharp and in such a tight space that at one stage the pickup almost overturned, lifting up in the air on the driver's side while we drove along on the left front and back wheels on my side. Just as I thought the car was going to roll, it thumped back onto all four wheels again in a cloud of dust and we were out of the tangle of vehicles and away. We didn't stop because we really didn't have anything to say to the UN at their roadblock but from that day on and until the UN left

Mozambique, O'D drove warily and at a much-reduced speed along the farm roads.

After practising their road blocking abilities on all of us, the UN decided to give an airing to some of the equipment they had brought with them and hadn't had the occasion to use.

Having prepared themselves for all contingencies – sending mountain fighters to a flat country - they now decided to test the performance of the amphibious personnel carrier they had brought to Mozambique during the worst drought in decades. As all the rivers were bone dry and even Lake Chicamba's water level was running low, the UN's eyes alighted on a small stretch of water conveniently close to home ... the Tabex farm dam.

Clive, one of the Tabex farmers, was driving past the dam when he saw the crowd of UN soldiers who had gathered to watch the carrier's trial run on top of the muddy water and he stopped his pickup to watch.

The personnel carrier started up and moved towards the water. Then, instead of driving buoyantly over the surface, it took a slow downward plunge and ploughed towards the muddy bottom of the dam until only its antennas were visible. While the brown water bubbled and gurgled, the submerged carrier's occupants shot to the surface, muddy and gasping and entwined with long, slimy weeds.

Clive knew the UN were embarrassed because when he drove home laughing his head off to get his camera and returned five minutes later to click off some pictures, soldiers shouted at him quite rudely - "No photo! No photo! Gettaway from here!" This was UN business and he had no authority to take photographs of their efforts to retrieve an amphibious personnel carrier out of its watery grave.

In April 1994, the Italians based on the Tabex farm pulled out their tent pegs and prepared to go back home to Europe. Colonel Zambelli, their charming commander, sent out invitations to a farewell lunch at Chimoio Airport and we all went along to say goodbye to them.

O'D and I sat at a table with Alfredo, an Italian game hunter who wore his blonde hair long, down to his shoulders, and some government officials, one of whom was Weng San, the large and burly Commandant of the Manica Province Police.

The food was far from memorable and when the wine ran out halfway through the meal, we all looked forward to the tropical exotic fruit salad, which the menu promised was drenched in rum. Alas, the fruit salad never made its appearance and for the next two hours we were all forced to listen in complete sobriety to interminable and identical self-congratulatory speeches from the UN and Mozambican government officials, first in English, then in Portuguese and finally in Italian. The whole room fidgeted with the tedium and boredom of it all. In desperation, Commandant Weng San grabbed an empty bottle of wine and shook the few remaining drops into his empty wine glass. He raised the glass to his lips and gave us a doleful look. The drops weren't even enough to wet his tongue.

Mozambique had been a success story for the UN, although this was due more to the country's war-weariness and desire for peace than anything else. With their departure, we were left without foreign military protection. We were all on our own now. At first, this was a little scary but as the peace looked as if it was going to hold, everyone began to think of the future.

I also began to think of the future and of returning to Arrojela. We had saved quite a bit of money working for Tabex, enough to start all over again in Portugal, and Arrojela by this time had recovered from the fire and had regained its beauty during the years of our absence. Mozambique meant nothing to me and I yearned to go back to my own home.

Unbeknown to me, however, O'D had been making some plans of his own and they didn't include returning to Arrojela.

He had met a man called Caetano Martins and they had spent many evenings at the Sports Clube, talking about Mozambique and its opportunities now that the country was no longer at war.

Caetano had been a Captain in the Mozambican Army during the civil war and had travelled to North Korea, where they had trained him in various forms of fighting, including karate. When he had left the Army, he had got a job at Tabex as their General Foreman.

From a surprisingly small family consisting merely of a mother, a father and a sister, Caetano had been very well educated. His father, who had worked for the Administration Department at Catandica during Portuguese Colonial days, had seen to it that both Caetano and his sister Romana had received the best of the schooling available to them at the time. With the war now at an end, Caetano's enthusiasm for the future knew no bounds.

When Caetano told O'D that the timber business was definitely something to look into, O'D's imagination was caught. Already fascinated by the country and its customs, he decided to go into partnership with Caetano. They would fell trees, set up a sawmill, turn the planks and beams into fine furniture for export AND grow small hardwood saplings from seed to replace the trees they felled.

The first I knew of this, was the day we were driving into town to choose some films from Chimoio's tiny video shop. We were just approaching the roundabout with the mural celebrating the Mozambican's victory over the Portuguese when O'D suddenly said "There's Caetano!" and pulled the pickup over to the side of the road.

"Who's Caetano?" I asked.

"My partner," O'D told me, watching a tall, neatly dressed young Mozambican of about thirty lope across the road towards us on long legs.

"Partner? You never told me anything about this!" I was horrified. Since we'd been in Mozambique, we had met several foreigners whose Mozambican partners had tricked them out of the businesses they had financed and taken them over for themselves.

"Of course I told you," O'D insisted.

"O'D Pixley," I cried, "you did not!"

"I'm sure I did."

"We're going to lose everything we've got!"

"Caetano's different," O'D replied.

"Oh, yes?" I asked tartly.

But when Caetano greeted me, with a funny little bow, and I looked into his open face, I could see that there was something very unusual about him. Here was a man who wore his heart on his face and it shone with intelligence and humour, kindness and another quality rarely found in our fellow humans - integrity. O'D was right about Caetano. He *was* different.

It was Caetano who found the old Magalhaes sawmill in the Nhamacoa. When the Portuguese owners had left sometime in the 1970's, a Frelimo co-operative had taken it over for a while. Then, there had been some kind of gun battle with Renamo and the co-operative had fled, leaving Renamo in control of this part of the country.

For the next fifteen years or so, the sawmill had lain silent and the forest in the Nhamacoa had been left untouched by humans. Left to itself, nature had flourished.

Small black-faced Vervets with powder-blue bums swung through the trees, baboons barked and Night Apes screeched their horrible cries after the sun had gone down.

62

In the enormous red mahogany trees on the banks of the Nhamacoa River, Turacos feathered in olive green or blue, with a breathtaking satiny sheen of red under their wings, purred their breathy purrs and Kingfishers flashed blue and orange. The secretive Green Coucals nested in the thick undergrowth and hornbills, heavy with enormous casques on top of their bills, crash-landed clumsily onto branches. This was home to the Green Woodhoopoe with its wild, maniacal laughter, the aptly named Gorgeous Bush Shrike and the golden voiced Oriole. The Wattle-eyed flycatcher made its nests in the mango trees and the black and red Paradise flycatcher trailed its long tail across the sky. Lizard Buzzards with their stripy chests swooped down on their prey and the rare Vanga flitted through the Umbila trees.

A birdwatcher's delight, the Nhamacoa was also filled with other creatures which were more threatening. Pythons wended their majestic way through the long grass and there were the deadly black and green mambas, the Gaboon adders, the puff-adders and the Mozambican Spitting Cobras that flared out their hoods and shot their poisonous venom straight into your eyes ... as O'D was to find out for himself one day.

There were large hairy spiders, emerald green caterpillars with little scarlet horns and black circles on their backs, lovely dusky pink moths and revolting shiny blue-black centipedes, scorpions and the ubiquitous green stink bugs.

Although the Nhamacoa teemed with life, all this was hidden from me the first time I saw it. It revealed its enchantment only to those who made their home in it.

On one blisteringly hot Saturday afternoon, O'D and I went with Caetano to see the old Magalhaes sawmill. We went in the Tabex pickup and drove along forty kilometres of dreadful dirt road. The road was so corrugated and bone-rattling that I had to hang on to the handle above my window with both hands to stop myself from being thrown around.

Leaving a swirling cloud of choking red dust behind us, we travelled through sparsely populated bush until Caetano, who was in the back, hammered on the roof of the pickup. O'D slowed to a stop and Caetano leaned down towards his open window.

"This is Lica," he said and pointed to the left, where there was just a suggestion of a track leading into a mass of grass. "Turn down here and go on for about another six kilometres."

O'D turned into the track and the pickup disappeared right into what seemed like a vast ocean of tall thick yellow elephant grass. Claustrophobia immediately overwhelmed me. We were drowning ... drowning in a suffocating, smothering, sea of grass. The stuff rose high up over our heads, crashed against our windscreen, began to clog up our radiator and whipped in through our open windows. Despite the heat and the feeling of being boxed in, I wound up my window just in case other things besides grass made their way into the car.

O'D drove slowly, forcing the pickup along the narrow track that hadn't seen a vehicle for years. When the track petered out at a small clearing, we stopped. Here, a man wearing a torn shirt and ragged shorts was sitting under a tree, patiently waiting for us. This was Joaquim, our Renamo guide whom Caetano had told us knew the Nhamacoa like the back of his hand. We needed someone who knew the area well because landmines had been planted here during the civil war.

Caetano jumped off the back of the pickup, his hair no longer black but thickly coated with the red dust of the road. O'D and I got out of the front, also dusty but not as much as Caetano. Our tattered guide stood up and came towards us.

"Boa tarde, Joaquim. Como esta?"

"Aah ... Boa tarde," he replied, holding out a hand in greeting to Caetano and then to O'D. "Estou bem".

Joaquim led us down a tiny footpath through the long grass and we followed in close single file. Fearful of treading on a mine and getting blown to bits, Caetano carefully put his size twelve feet exactly where Joaquim's hard, dusty bare feet had trodden. O'D followed Caetano, placing his size eight feet in Caetano's footprints and I brought up the rear, with my size five feet walking in O'D's prints. The sun blazed down on us and the only sound to be heard was the sound of our breathing and the dry rustling of the long grass as our bodies brushed against it ... swish ... swish ... swish ...

Without warning, Joaquim stopped abruptly and we all bumped into each other, like a row of falling dominos.

Caetano turned around towards us, with a great beam of excitement on his face. "The old sawmill of Magalhaes!" he announced triumphantly.

I looked around, with disbelief. "Is this it?"

Once, the Magalhaes sawmill had been the largest and busiest sawmill in Manica Province but after years of war there wasn't much evidence of this and now it could only be described as more than derelict.

"Look at that old steam boiler!" O'D exclaimed with awe, walking over to examine a monstrously large and rusty contraption made out of thick steel plates and huge bolts that had been built in England sometime in the 1920's or 30's. "Getting that thing down here through the bush all those years ago must have taken some doing!"

From the state of the place, it was obvious that the only reason the old boiler was still intact was because it had been too heavy to move and impossible to dismantle. Everything else that could have been unbolted, taken apart, torn down, stripped and carted away, had long since vanished.

All that was left of the saws were their heavy metal tables and all that remained of the four houses just faintly visible through the long grass were their walls, blackened with the smoke of forest fires and the mould of rain. Wooden doorframes and window frames had been hacked out of the plaster and electrical cable and plumbing pipes had been chopped out of the walls.

"Why …" I wondered aloud, "why didn't the people just live in these houses instead of taking them apart and leaving them in ruins?"

"Because they're superstitious country people," Caetano, who lived in town in Chimoio and who was superstitious himself, explained. "They were afraid the houses were still inhabited by the spirits of the mzungu Portuguese who once lived in them."

"We'll have to start all over again," I said, already feeling burdened by the immensity of the task, "right from rock bottom."

"Don't worry about it," O'D told me. "We'll employ people. And the first person we're going to need is a mechanic. Someone who is used to the bush and not very fussy about how he lives." He exchanged a thoughtful look with Caetano.

"Someone like … Chuck?" Caetano asked.

"Yes," O'D agreed. "Chuck."

"Oh no, not Chuck!" I exclaimed. "Not him! He's the reason we're standing here in this wilderness … in the middle of nowhere … the back of beyond!"

Chuck was a Zimbabwean who could have played a bum in a Spaghetti Western without even having to take acting lessons, someone who didn't know the difference between right and wrong, and as for his table manners … eating a meal with Chuck was like dining with a prehistoric cave man. And as if that wasn't enough, he was indeed the reason we were starting off our new venture in the Nhamacoa.

Some months before, O'D and Caetano had set their hearts on another sawmill conveniently very close to Chimoio. This was the Matsinho sawmill, which came complete with working machinery and was already operating. However, while O'D and Caetano had been negotiating with the government department IAC for the lease of Matsinho, Chuck had interfered and the deal, which had been almost in the bag, had fallen through.

Oh, no, not Chuck … not him!

"We really haven't got any choice," O'D told me. "Chuck's the only half decent mechanic in the whole of Manica Province."

While O'D stayed on at the Tabex farm for the next few months, Chuck, our new manager/mechanic set to work to prepare the old Magalhaes sawmill for its new lease of life.

And it was while Chuck was cutting eucalypt poles and grass to make a roof for the main house and uncovering ancient septic tanks, that O'D got into trouble in Mozambique … big trouble!

CHAPTER THREE

AN ENGLISH JAILBIRD
November 1994

We were sitting at the table in our house on the Tabex farm on a hot Friday night and eating one of Biasse's fiery curries, a dish more suitable for the icy Novembers of northern Europe than for the steamy, sweltering Novembers of a Mozambican summer, when O'D broke his news. "I'm driving down to the sawmill in the Nhamacoa tomorrow," he told me. "I'll be leaving very early in the morning."

His words had a strange effect on me. A dart of foreboding, so dark that it made me lose my appetite, flashed through me. I put down my knife and fork.

"O'D," I said, "don't go tomorrow. Something bad is going to happen to you. I can feel it! Put it off until next week."

"I can't put it off," O'D told me, unperturbed at hearing that something bad was going to happen to him and ladling another helping of curry onto his plate. "Chuck's expecting me to bring some equipment to him and there's no way of letting him know if I decide not to go."

Although I had a very well developed sixth sense, which often warned me of things to come, you didn't have to be psychic to realise that driving around Mozambique at the moment wasn't a very good idea. Police and soldiers swarmed all over Manica Province, the province in which we lived. They bristled with rifles; their jittery fingers hovered dangerously over their triggers and the menacing and suspicious glare in their eyes told you quite plainly that they were looking for trouble and would uncaringly riddle you with bullets first and ask questions afterwards.

The reason for this excess of security was that Mozambique had recently held elections for the first time in its history and the day that O'D had chosen for his trip was the very day the election results were to come out. No one knew what the outcome would be and there were fears that the losing party might not accept defeat. The country was in such a state of extreme tension that anything could cause the two year old and newborn peace to snap and the civil war to start all over again. As far as I was concerned, the best place to be on such a day was to be indoors and to keep your head down and away from the windows.

The next morning, very early, a movement on the other side of the bed woke me up. I opened my eyes and in the dim, grey, pre-dawn light, saw O'D, already dressed in a blue cotton shirt and khaki trousers, sitting on the edge of the bed and tying his shoelaces. He stood up, walked quickly over to the door and disappeared down the corridor.

"Wait!" I cried, and raising the mosquito net, got out of bed and ran after him. "Wait!"

I caught up with him in the sitting room, just as he pulled open the screen door leading out onto the verandah. "I still think you should change your mind. I just KNOW something is going to happen to you," I told him.

Ignoring me, he ran down the verandah steps towards his old and very battered white Toyota pickup. This was the company car Tony Taberer, the silver-haired, rich and non-smoking Zimbabwean owner of the Tabex tobacco farm had given O'D to drive. The Toyota's windscreen was starred and cracked, the headlights were tied on with wire and the bonnet was lumpy with dents and tied down with rope. Inside, the stuffing erupted out of the sun-cracked seat like lava out of a volcano. It was not a car that made me feel proud to ride around in but its dilapidated appearance had quite a few benefits, the most important of which was that no car hijacker in his right mind would be interested in it. O'D had driven it now for two years and had become very fond of it. "She goes like the clappers," he had once told me, patting the Toyota's dented bonnet affectionately and, like most men, giving both human and feminine qualities to an inanimate, mechanical, metal object.

O'D ran his eyes over the equipment tied down in the back of the pickup, checking he hadn't forgotten anything. Satisfied, he opened the pickup's door and climbed inside. He closed the door with a clang and wound the driver's window down.

"Don't worry," he told me reassuringly, "nothing is going to happen to me. Nothing." He gave me a pitying smile. "I'll be back no later than seven tonight. Promise."

I stood on the verandah and watched O'D drive off along the short farm driveway, past tractors and barns and then, when he turned a corner and disappeared from sight, I went back inside the house and closed the screen door. This was not a man who listened to his wife.

Although O'D had always been adventurous and drawn to danger like a moth to a candle flame, this hadn't been much of a problem when we'd lived in Europe. There, the only trouble he'd got into was from the traffic police, who had given him a few tickets for speeding and from me, for spending too long in a bar. In Mozambique, however, it had been quite a different story.

Here, he had taken to life in a broken-down, war-torn and primitive African country like a duck to water. He had gone where few people, even the Mozambicans, had cared to go. He had made friends with all sorts of unsuitable people and had become a fount of knowledge on Mozambican colonial history, Mozambican culture, Mozambican religion, Mozambican politics and Mozambican food and drink …

Once, his curiosity about Mozambican culture had had such an adverse effect on him that it had turned the whites of his eyes and the skin on his face as yellow as a paw paw and he had had to take to his bed for more than a month. This had occurred after he had driven down to Macate and had visited a banana plantation belonging to Mr. Mabeleza, a witch doctor. The witch doctor had offered him something called NIPPA to drink and he had accepted this offer – even though it had come out of a very grimy and unhygienic bottle that would have been condemned in England. The consequences of this had been a trip across the border to Zimbabwe. Hepatitis, Dr. Featherstone had told us.

Another time, O'D had ignored my warnings to keep the windows of his ancient Toyota closed at night. "You'll be sorry," I had warned him, "when you find yourself driving down the road with a deadly poisonous green mamba in the car with you."

While no snake had deigned to enter the Toyota's interior in the dark of the night, other creatures had explored it and taken up residence. One morning, O'D had driven off surrounded by a cloud of mosquitoes and with his hands on a steering wheel which had a pungent and particularly unpleasant fragrance. It had taken him several minutes to identify the scent but eventually it had dawned on him that his steering wheel had been liberally sprayed by one of the 27 cats belonging to our neighbour, Maciel.

Marion, O'D's mother, who lived in the Algarve, had once told me to control O'D. I had thought that this was a bit much coming from someone like Marion, who in her youth had been equally adventurous and quite uncontrollable herself.

This was a woman who had been something of a female James Bond in her time and had set an example as a role model that her eldest son had been only too happy to emulate. Before the Second World War, Marion had driven fast cars very fast and had been selected to represent England in the Olympic skiing championships. And then, after the Second World War, she had smoked SIXTY CIGARETTES A DAY (!) while she had been helping Allied Agents to look for all the gold bullion the Nazis had looted. Meeting O'D's father, Ti, she had married him and they had run off for a honeymoon in Paris where they had stayed in the most expensive hotel without having the money to pay for their room! The only thing that had saved them from endless weeks of washing dishes in the hotel kitchen had been a hasty telegram to Ti's father for funds. With a mother like this ...

At eight o'clock, Biasse, dressed in his immaculate white cook's uniform and the veldskoens he had begged me to buy for him from Zimbabwe, called out "Scoff's ready, Madam!" and I emerged from the bedroom, showered and dressed for a long day on my own.

I sat down at the table in the dining room and began to eat toast, scrambled eggs and the pile of hard and dried-out little bits of bacon that Biasse thought was the way to cook bacon. The bacon was impossible to eat with a knife and fork and as Biasse had the usual Mozambican obduracy when it came to changing his ways, O'D and I had had to eat bacon with our fingers for two years.

Biasse had come with the house we were living in on the Tabex farm and had learnt to speak English the Zimbabwean way, hence the "Scoff's ready, Madam!" Regrettably, he had also been taught to cook by white male Zimbabweans, and as white male Zimbabweans only ate meat (preferably steak) and chips and had a horror of vegetables and salads, his range of recipes was very narrow. However, over the years I had managed to introduce two new and simple additions to his repertoire; spaghetti bolognaise, and fish cakes made from tinned tuna. This had required a lot of patience on my part and had made Biasse tremble with anxiety, as if he was taking an examination. The fish cakes had proved such a success with various officials from the Department of Labour that we had all started calling him 'The King of Fish Cakes'. This title had pleased him so much that sometimes, and on his own initiative, he daringly experimented by adding a tablespoon of fresh parsley to the fish cake mixture.

70

I drank the last of my coffee and put down my cup. "Thank you, Biasse. You can clear the table, now."

While Biasse busied himself tidying up, I sat down in the sitting room and began to put the finishing touches to the large charcoal portrait I had drawn of a zebra. "Looking good ... you're looking good," I told the Zebra.

When a loud crash in the kitchen disturbed my concentration, I looked up from my drawing and saw Biasse's small and skinny figure in the doorway. In each hand, he held one half of a mustard coloured plate.

"This plate, Madam," he told me with a mournful look on his wrinkled little face, "it has broken itself!"

Biasse had the Mozambican habit, which I had come to know well, of never admitting personal guilt for anything but always blaming someone or even something else.

"Oh, Biasse," I sighed. Biasse was fumble fingered in the kitchen and since our arrival had sent 6 Tabex plates, 3 soup bowls, one teapot, 2 teapot lids, 5 cups and 2 saucers smashing into smithereens on the grey cement kitchen floor. "I hope we've still got enough plates to eat off until the boss and I get a chance to go across the border to buy some more!"

"I think so, Madam."

I looked down at my drawing again. The heat and humidity of the day had made my fingers grow sweaty and black around my stick of charcoal and my damp hands had smudged one edge of the paper. Still, I was pleased with my efforts and got up to prop the board and its attached drawing against the mantelpiece over the fireplace so that I could admire it every now and then as the day wore on. I wiped my hands on a piece of loo paper - there were no tissues in Mozambique – and decided that the next best thing to do to pass the time was to go for a swim.

Arming myself with an icy Coca-Cola, a glass and a book, I wandered down the brick path to the swimming pool and sat down under the thatched pool shelter for a while.

The sun blazed down out of a pure blue sky. There was not a wisp of a cloud. Except for the cool splashing sound of the small waterfall cascading out of the mouth of the stone fish at the edge of the pool and the drone of the bumble bees browsing fatly in the flower beds and shrubs, there was silence.

Clive, the Zimbabwean farmer and his girlfriend, Trish, who lived in a house only a couple of metres away from ours, had gone across the border into Zimbabwe. Conceicao, who lived in the house at the other end of the swimming pool with her husband Maciel, had flown off to Portugal. I idly wondered where Maciel was. I had forgotten to ask.

Suddenly, the silence seemed eerie and I felt a prickle of apprehension. Was I completely alone on the farm, except for Biasse? Perhaps my feelings of foreboding hadn't been for O'D after all, but for … ME! What would happen if there was trouble and men came to the farm with guns? What would I do? I didn't have a car and there were no telephones.

I ran my eyes over the sparkling swimming pool and the green lawn and flowerbeds, lush with water from all the boreholes. Visitors to the farm often remarked on its resemblance to a resort, and so it was in a way. It was a tiny oasis of beauty and normality in a desolate wasteland still very wild and very, very dangerous even though the civil war had ended.

I remembered what had happened to Clive not so long ago, while the United Nations Peacekeepers and the Italian Alpini had been camped on the farm. One evening, he had driven off with two South African road engineers to Peter Thornycroft's small fishing lodge on Lake Chicamba. On the return drive, they had been ambushed. An obstruction, bags of charcoal or something, had been placed in the road to block it and when Clive had slowed down, men lying hidden in the grass by the side of the road had opened fire with AK-47's. Clive had been shot through both his arms, making them completely useless. Despite this, they had still been able to keep their heads, to turn the car around and make a mad dash for safety. One of the South Africans had taken control of the steering wheel and gears, while Clive had used his feet on the clutch and accelerator. There had been blood all over the inside of the car. Clive was lucky to be alive. They were all lucky to be alive.

The U.N. Peacekeepers had been shocked and had tried to investigate the attack. But the men had never been found.

I pushed these thoughts away and opened my book. It was called 'The Shell Seekers' and had been given to me to read by Frances, the Tabex mechanic's wife. The thought of Frances made me smile as I remembered our recent encounter with a Zimbabwean police superintendent on the other side of the border.

About a week after Frances and Jake Jackson had come back from their short honeymoon, she had asked me if I wanted to go shopping with her in Mutare. Of course, I had jumped at the offer.

We had arrived in Mutare quite early in the morning, about nine o'clock, and Frances had parked Jake's shiny white new pick-up in front of the Holiday Inn. It was only after she had locked and alarmed the car and we were standing on the pavement under the trees that she had revealed that there was another purpose to our trip.

"I have to go to the police to get some papers for Jake's car so we can import it into Mozambique," she had told me. She and Jake were Zimbabwean citizens. "Police clearance papers, stating that Jake bought the pick-up in Zimbabwe and that it isn't a stolen car. Shall we do this now or later, Val?"

"Let's do it now," I had said. Both the Zimbabwean and Mozambican border posts closed at six in the evening. "We don't want to find it takes longer than we thought and end up having to spend the night on this side of the border."

The police station was just across the road from us and so we had gone inside and after being escorted from one person to another, had finally found ourselves in the starkly furnished office of a burly, khaki-clad Zimbabwean Police Superintendent.

He had listened to Frances' request. He had told us to sit down on some hard wooden chairs in front of his desk. He had turned two dark basilisk eyes towards Frances and had examined her ...

She was large and plump and had looked particularly attractive this day. Her long, red-gold hair had hung down to her waist in a thick plait and she had been dressed in a low-cut silvery grey top (which I had recognised as being from Marks and Spencers because I possessed an identical one, in beige - thank goodness I hadn't worn mine!) and wide black silky trousers with big red and green and purple polka dots all over them.

... And then, he had dropped his bombshell.

"You are not allowed to drive Mr. Jackson's car," he had told Frances sternly.

Frances' mouth had fallen open in astonishment. "But ... I'm his wife!" she had exclaimed.

"How do I know this?" The Superintendent had asked. "You could have stolen Mr. Jackson's car. Show me proof that you are Mrs. Jackson. Show me your passport."

Frances' fair skin had turned a dark red. "We've only been married for a few days," she had replied. "My passport's still in my maiden name."

"You see!" the Superintendent had exclaimed, his police instincts now working overtime. "We have to be careful," he had gone on "because people are stealing cars all over the place ... and you ..." he had paused thoughtfully " ... and you have no proof that you are Mrs. Jackson."

"But I AM Mrs. Jackson!"

The Superintendent had picked up the receiver of the old-fashioned black Bakelite telephone on his empty desk and narrowed his eyes at Frances, preparing to call her bluff once and for all. "What is Mr. Jackson's phone number so that I can speak to him and confirm that you are who you say you are?"

Little beads of sweat had popped out on Frances' face at this relentless grilling and the way her simple request was leading into more and more complications, compounding her supposed guilt. "He hasn't got a telephone! We live on a farm in the bush in Mozambique. There's no way I can contact him!"

Satisfied that his suspicions concerning Frances had been confirmed, the Superintendent had given a nod and dropped the receiver back onto the handset. "Well, in that case," he had told her, "we'll have to CONFIS TI CATE Mr. Jackson's car until you can prove that you are who you say you are."

Frances had fallen back in her chair with shock and, close to tears, her voice had risen up in a loud and despairing squawk. "CONFIS TI ...? But how will we get back home to Mozambique, now?"

No one had answered Frances' question and for a short time we had all sat in silence and pondered. It had seemed strange to me that the Superintendent should have thought that a member of a gang of car thieves - and one as flamboyant and unforgettable as Frances - would have gone anywhere near a police station and asked for papers for a stolen car. However, this was Africa ...

I had been ruminating on the probability that the Superintendent no doubt considered me to be Frances' accomplice, when she had rallied.

Pointing a trembling finger at me, she had said, "This lady ... this lady also lives in Mozambique. Her husband, who is THE

74

ADMINISTRATOR of the TABEX FARM at Chimoio, will be very worried when she doesn't come back home."

"Ah! Administrator ... " the Superintendent had said. He had turned towards me and, picking up his telephone receiver again, had asked, "What is your husband's telephone number?"

A sudden and almost uncontrollable laugh had threatened to burst out of me at his question but I had managed to control myself and to suppress it. Laughing, I had known, was the worst thing I could have done in a police station ... especially in Africa, and especially in this one.

"He's not at the office in Chimoio, today," I had told him, struggling to keep a straight face. "He's in the bush - with Mr. Jackson!"

The solution to our problems had eventually come when Frances had remembered that she and Jake were well known by the owner and staff of a local Mutare company called Peter Genari. Fortunately, the Superintendent had been happy to accompany Frances (chauffeured by Frances in Jake's car) and to accept their personal testimony that she was, indeed, who she had claimed to be.

Afterwards and outside Holiday Inn again, Frances had asked me what I wanted to do next.

"I want a drink, Frances," I had told her. "A very, very stiff drink!"

Under the pool shelter, I sat up and closed Frances' book. It was a charming and non-violent story about an old Englishwoman, her flashbacks to her younger days and her three spoilt and selfish children. Reading it in a country like Mozambique made me feel as if I was reading about people who were living not in another country but on another planet.

After a refreshing swim and a light lunch of bread and cheese and a salad, I curled up on the sofa in the sitting room to watch a video. Although the sofa was as comfortable as a cloud, it was perfectly hideous in appearance. Covered in pale brown dralon, the colour matched the rest of the weird décor in the sitting room, which had obviously been planned by a tobacco-mad farmer. The walls were painted a sort of pale Virginia tobacco brown. The floor tiles were darker squares of Burley tobacco brown, intermingled with cigarette paper white squares. On top of this, lay an even darker, tar brown carpet. The curtains, limply framing the windows, were a nicotine khaki colour – with a surprisingly adventurous little touch of red in the form of a stripe. At night, the thirty watt light bulb added to the murky look of the room and gave our complexions a jaded, sallow appearance.

I started the video and settled back to watch Humphrey Bogart in black and white. Biasse wandered in from the kitchen, suddenly finding some dusting to do in the sitting room. I always watched innocuous old black and white videos if I wanted to see a film during the afternoons because I didn't want to pollute Biasse's mind with the Western world's ideas of entertainment and morals. He thought that what he was seeing in a film was real life and I was fed up with having to sit with the remote control in my hand in order to stop the film whenever the characters were suddenly and inexplicably overcome with Hollywood passion and ripped clothes off each other in lifts, on park benches, in taxis, on top of mountains, under water in the sea ...

"Better to get the other one, Madam," Biassse told me, comparing his favourite video with the Bogart one and finding the smart-aleck dialogue and lack of action boring.

"Next time, Biasse," I said.

Biasse's favourite video was Tarzan. He'd been unable to believe his eyes when he had first seen it and had discovered that there was a scantily clad white man somewhere in Africa who was not only living in trees like a monkey but also living WITH a bunch of monkeys. The film thrilled him, fascinated him and he joyously discussed it often with Jacques, Conceicao and Maciel's one-eyed cook who had lost an eye in a drunken brawl.

"Is true, Madam?" he had asked me.

"It's possible, Biasse," I had told him, not wanting to disillusion and disappoint him. "Maybe there is someone ... white ... in a tree somewhere ... in the Congo, perhaps."

At six o'clock, I sprayed myself all over with Autan mosquito repellent and filled a glass with red wine from a carafe all the way from Portugal. There was no food in the country but there was alcohol. I turned on the old-fashioned shortwave radio we had bought in Harare and sat down on the verandah to wait for O'D, and watched the sun set. The terrible drought was still going strong and during the day, hot winds swept across the sun-baked countryside, sending clouds of dust swirling high up into the sky. Now, the dust in the atmosphere turned the sinking sun into an enormous blood-red globe, which loomed alarmingly over me like an alien planet out of a science fiction film.

I sat waiting outside until mauve twilight took the place of the day, until the sun had gone and I was enveloped in damp, velvety blackness. Thousands of stars filled the sky. Gladys Knight and the Pips sang 'Midnight train to Georgia' on Zimbabwe Radio One. An owl in a nearby tree exclaimed "Whoo! WHOO!" as if it had just seen a particularly succulent mouse.

Gladys stopped singing and was replaced by someone pounding urgently on drums, to tell the listeners that the Zimbabwe news was about to begin.

Seven o'clock ...

"This afternoon," the newsreader told us importantly, "President Comrade Robert Gabriel Mugabe opened the new chewing gum factory built by Denmark ...

In Mrewa district, the construction of 36 Blair toilets has been successfully completed and there are plans ..."

When the news ended, I sat on outside, on the verandah, and waited for a glimpse of headlights shining around the corner in the road, bouncing off the walls of the barns and coming towards me. Mosquitoes whined around me but I ignored them. Where was O'D?

Eight o'clock ...

I stood up and went back inside the house. The aroma of a Zimbabwean roast chicken wafted into the sitting room and I suddenly remembered Biasse. I walked into the kitchen. He was sitting patiently and sleepily on the white metal dustbin.

"Oh, Biasse. I'm so sorry. Please go home. I don't feel like eating anything. Just leave the food in the warming drawer."

He stood up. "Oh, thank you, Madam. Goodnight."

"Goodnight, Biasse."

Twenty past nine ...

I stopped pacing around the sitting room and went into the bathroom to run a cool bath. After my bath, I wrapped myself in my red capulana and lay down on the bed. Worrying. In my mind I heard an echo of O'D's voice from the morning again. "I'll be back no later than seven tonight. Seven tonight. Promise ... Promise ... Promise ...

Half past ten ...

Oh, O'D, where ARE you?

Oh, if only there was someone to talk to! Oh, if only there was a phone I could use, to speak to my family, a friend. To tell them that O'D was missing ... missing in MOZAMBIQUE ... and what should I do, do, DO?

There was nothing worse than waiting ... and waiting ... for someone to come home when you lived in a dangerous country.

ELEVEN O'CLOCK!

Sound carries clearly at night in the countryside and I heard Maciel opening his front door and talking to someone in his gruff, rumbling voice. A pang of pure fear knifed through me. I knew Maciel was hearing news of O'D. I remembered what had happened to Clive and my heart seemed to stop beating. Sitting slowly up on the bed, I listened to footsteps walking along the brick path towards my house ... and then up the steps and onto the verandah ... listened to someone tapping softly on my screen door ...

So ... my premonition had come true after all!

I threw myself off the bed and ran to open the door.

An ancient and wizened man stood under the dim yellow verandah light bulb. "Boa noite, Senhora," he greeted me, and handed me a tiny, square, scrap of paper.

I took the note from him and strained my eyes to read the even tinier handwriting in the dim light.

'19 November 1994,' I read. '22.00 hrs.'

'Val, I have been arrested by the police - they are keeping me overnight. In the Primeira Esquadra - maybe Maciel can come and get me out tomorrow - I am fine. O'D.'

The blood drained out of my face and for a moment my legs lost their strength. Jail! I leaned numbly, weakly, against the doorframe for support. Help, I needed help from someone. Then I pulled myself together and ran down the path to Maciel, who was dressed and standing in the dim light on his verandah.

"Maciel! Oh, Maciel! O'D's in JAIL!"

"Yes. We go to the jail now, Vaal. I have U.S. dollar if you need."

Bail. Of course!

"Thank you, Maciel, but it's alright. I have some. I'll be back in a minute."

I ran back into the house and into the bedroom. Threw on a dress. Stepped into shoes. Rummaged in the cupboard for the U.S. dollars we kept in a suitcase for times of need. I stuffed one thousand U.S. dollars into my shoulder bag, a small fortune to the Mozambicans living in a poverty-stricken country. Surely more than enough to bail O'D out of prison?

78

I ran back to Maciel's house again. He was waiting in his Nissan pickup, the engine already running, and leaned over to open the passenger door for me. I climbed in and we drove off along the farm dirt road towards the main tar road to Chimoio.

"What do you think O'D did, Maciel? What do you think happened?"

Maciel's face was grim in the starlit night. Somewhere in his fifties, he was still a handsome man. His strong, clear-cut features and his dark hair and neat beard always made me think of a Spanish conquistador. His English was minimal, as was my Portuguese. He shook his head.

"O'D is not careful here in Africa, Vaal. He should take more care. He is not in Inglaterra now."

Although I knew O'D was careless – reckless - there was a certain tone to Maciel's voice that made me think he knew something about O'D that I didn't know.

"What do you mean, Maciel?"

But he just shook his head again and as we turned off the dirt road and our wheels bumped up onto the rough edge of the main tar road, he warned me.

"Now listen very carefully to me, Vaal. Africa is very dangerous place for white peoples. Near Chimoio is roadblock. They will stop us. You must keep your lips like so." He took a hand off the steering wheel and put his fingers onto his own lips and held them closed. "Whatever happens with police at roadblock, you must say nothing. NOTHING."

"Yes. Yes. I understand."

The road was empty of traffic. As our lone vehicle approached Chimoio, I saw lanterns and the shadowy shapes of several police and soldiers with rifles standing near some drums and a barrier, blocking the road into town. Maciel slowed down and stopped the car at the barrier and soldiers walked up to my side of the pickup. They wrenched open my door and shouted "GET OUT! GET OUT!"

I grabbed my money-filled shoulder bag and got out.

We stood at the side of the road while the soldiers searched the vehicle. After some minutes and finding nothing except a Zimbabwean loo roll in the cubbyhole, they ordered us to get back into the car. Maciel began to obey but then, forgetting his own advice to me to say nothing, NOTHING, he turned to them.

"Are you the ones who arrested Senhor O'D Pixley?" he asked.

79

A soldier moved menacingly up close to him. "Yes," he said, "and if you don't SHUT YOUR MOUTH WE WILL ARREST YOU TOO!"

Maciel clamped his mouth shut and climbed back into the pickup. He turned on the ignition and we slowly drove off, without speaking.

The atmosphere in the town was chilling. It was now well past midnight and the streets were deserted, like those of a ghost town, with no sign of life, human or animal. Not a light showed in any of the houses and not a sound could be heard. The meager lights from the few street lamps threw a dingy, sickly yellow glow here and there in the streets until finally, we arrived at the Primeira Esquadra.

Maciel parked the pickup in front of the jail and we climbed out and walked up the stairs into the building. Immediately, a powerful and nauseating stench of urine filled our nostrils, so strong and sharp I choked and almost gagged.

Maciel said something to a chubby policeman standing idly just inside the doorway and he showed us up more stairs to a room where a man sat alone behind a small desk. "We have come about Senhor Pixley," Maciel said. "We would like to know if there is a possibility of paying bail for his release."

"No. No bail. Only the Head of the Traffic Police has the authority to release him."

"I have the money here," I told the man, taking out the bundle of U.S. dollars and showing it to him.

He glanced briefly at the money. "No."

"But surely ...."

"Can you tell us why Senhor Pixley was arrested?" Maciel asked. "Is there anyone in authority we can talk to about this now?"

The man ignored the questions and sullenly shrugged his shoulders. We realised we were wasting our time.

"Come, Vaal," Maciel said.

We turned away and walked back down the stairs. As we were about to go outside, the chubby policeman stopped us and said to me "Don't worry, Senhora. Senhor Pix didn't commit a serious crime. He only made jokes to us in his usual English way."

Jokes?

"Then why is he in JAIL?" I asked, my voice rising. "If he didn't do anything serious, why is he in here? And what did he DO? Tell me!"

80

The chubby policeman gave me no answer. Just a smile and a shrug.

"We cannot do any more tonight, Vaal," Maciel told me, as we drove away from the Primeira Esquadra and left O'D still securely held in its foul-smelling embrace. "Tomorrow we will try and see the Head of the Traffic Police. Be ready to leave the farm at six o'clock."

Back at the farm, I fell asleep as soon as my head hit the pillow. I slept well now that I knew O'D was alive, although in a spot of mysterious trouble. It was just as well I woke up rested because the day ahead of me turned into a gruelling one with some strange little aspects Maciel and I didn't expect.

In the morning, we drove to the Primeira Esquadra and asked to see the Head of the Traffic Police. He wasn't there, they told us, but in another building across town. At this other building, they told us he was at a meeting - somewhere else – and gave us directions. From there, we were told we would find him at his house. At his house, his wife told us he was at the Primeira Esquadra.

For more than three hours we drove fruitlessly around Chimoio from building to building, following a false trail. Every now and then, we stopped at the Primeira Esquadra to ask if he had arrived, only to be sent away again.

The sun burned down on us ferociously and glittered off the windscreen into our eyes, turning the interior of the pickup into a sauna. Large dark wet patches developed across Maciel's khaki shirt until his back was completely soaked. My cotton dress clung to me, wrinkling and crinkling until it looked as if it had just come out of a dirty laundry basket. I mopped at my face and neck with a long strip of Maciel's loo paper.

"Maciel," I asked, hot and thirsty and weary, "have you ever read a book about someone called the Scarlet Pimpernel?"

Maciel took his eyes off the road for a second and looked at me blankly. "What?" he asked. "What is scarlet pimp …?"

"It's a man no one can find. They seek him here … they seek him there … they seek him everywhere. This Head of Traffic is giving a good impersonation of him."

We turned a corner. Maciel slowed the pickup and pulled up in front of a bar. "I think now we drink a Coca here, Vaal."

The small bar was fractionally cooler than the pickup and fairly clean. Four men sat on stools around the bar counter and drank tiny cups of sugarless black coffee. There was no milk or sugar in the country. "Bom dia," they greeted us.

I leaned limply against the counter and gulped down a glass of Zimbabwean Coca Cola. The Coke was warm but it was liquid and full of energy-giving sugar. "There's nothing bom about this dia," I told them. "My husband's in jail and no one will tell us anything except that he's in there because he told jokes!"

They perked up at my news.

"The police don't like jokes," one man said.

"They're the real criminals," another man said. "They're the ones who should be behind the bars."

"Perhaps your husband told some bad jokes," a third man said.

Maciel gulped down the last of his Coke. "Now," he said, "we try Primeira Esquadra again."

This time, at the Primeira Esquadra, the Police allowed us to see O'D. They waved us curtly over to a barrier and pulled open a large metal door. They shouted his name.

When he walked out of the cell, I stared at him. Oh, O'D …

His dark hair was wild and his grey eyes looked pale against his dirty face. Dust and earth stained his clothes. He was filthy and looked as if he had been rolling around on the ground.

A feeling of outrage filled me. "Did they hit you?"

"Only once."

"What do you need, O'D?" Maciel interrupted, more knowledgeable about African jails than I was.

"Something to drink. The jail hasn't got any water to drink."

"Enough!" A policeman shouted at us. "You go now!"

He shoved O'D back into the cell and clanged its metal door shut again.

Ordered to leave, Maciel and I walked back to his pickup. We hadn't even been given a chance to ask O'D why he'd been arrested.

Inside the pickup, Maciel turned on the ignition. He looked worried. Very worried. "This seems more serious than we think," he said. "First, they don't accept bail money, and now, the Head of Traffic is avoiding us."

"What are we going to do?" I asked, beginning to panic. "What are we going to do, Maciel?"

"Perhaps," Maciel said thoughtfully, "it is necessary I arrange to speak to Pedro Paulino, of D.P.A. But first, we go to the Sports Clube."

At the Sports Clube, Maciel arranged for food to be taken to O'D at mealtimes while he was held in the jail. As well as not having any water for its inmates to drink, the jail, naturally enough, didn't provide them with food either. We bought several Fantas and Cokes and stopped off again at the Primeira Esquadra where we handed the bottles over to a policeman to give to O'D. And then Maciel drove me back to the farm.

While Maciel spent the afternoon in his house talking about O'D with Pedro Paulino, the Director of Agriculture, I spent the afternoon drinking cup after cup of coffee and walking up and down the sitting room, asking myself questions.

If Pedro Paulino couldn't - or wouldn't - help us, how were we going to get O'D out of jail? There were no lawyers in Chimoio. What crime had he committed? Why would no one tell us what he had done? And why was the Head of Traffic avoiding us? What if this all went on for weeks or months … What if they never let him go …

My mind reeled with these unanswered questions. Perhaps if I managed to contact the Browns, O'D's large Zimbabwean cousins, they would be able to help … perhaps even help me to organise a jailbreak … O'D and I would have to flee the country, of course, but who cared!

The afternoon wore on. There was no word from Maciel. The sun began to sink down below the horizon. Dusk fell. And then …

A dilapidated Toyota pickup drove around the corner, past barns and tractors and pulled up next to the house. A door clanged.

A wild haired and filthy man with staring eyes walked up the verandah steps and into the sitting room.

I flung myself at him and burst into tears.

In the morning, Biasse put breakfast on the table. "Good morning, Master," he said, placing a dish of sliced paw paw down next to the toast. He always called O'D 'Master' as if O'D was a slave owner on a plantation in the American Deep South. His wrinkled face was inscrutable and he seemed unaffected by the fact that he was now working for an ex-convict.

O'D's crime was still a mystery to me. Immediately on his arrival back home, he had washed off the prison dirt and germs in a hot bath, which I had lavishly filled with half a bottle of Dettol as a disinfectant. Then while I had taken his discarded clothes, including his handkerchief, to Biasse and told him to burn them in the boiler fire,

O'D had dried himself and had fallen into a deep sleep on the bed until morning.

"So," I said, while O'D spread Zimbabwe's Gold Star Original Syrup over a slice of toast. "What jokes did you tell the police that made them put you in jail?"

At the mention of the word 'jail', O'D looked up from his toast and his eyes glazed over with the thousand-yard stare again. I made a mental note not to use that word for a while.

"There were roadblocks all the way back from Lica," he began slowly, "and I got a bit fed up with having to stop and start and get out of the car over and over again. When I was stopped just after Chimoio, the police made me get out of the pickup again and asked me what I had in the open back. As it was plainly obvious to anyone who wasn't blind that I only had five tyres in the back, I said to them 'What does it look like I've got? Hand grenades? Bombs? Rockets? "

"Oh, dear," I said.

"Yes," O'D agreed. "They didn't like that. They were grim to begin with but now they became grimmer."

He chewed on his toast for a while, reflecting on his next bad move.

"It got worse when I noticed that one of the policemen had very red, blood-shot eyes and asked him if he was drunk. All hell broke lose then and they arrested me."

"Gosh," I said, not knowing what else to say.

"Yes," O'D agreed again, and drank some coffee before continuing.

"The red-eyed policeman I accused of being drunk turned out to be the Head of Traffic. He was furious. Claimed to be a teetotaller."

I was incredulous. A teetotal policeman in Mozambique? How was this possible? They all drank like fish.

"Anyway," O'D went on, 'they hauled me off to the Primeira Esquadra where the Head of Traffic ordered the other police to beat me until I had to be taken to hospital. He told them he would take full responsibility for this."

"Ah!" I said, shocked, as images of blows and broken skin and splintered bone rose up in my mind.

"The police didn't want to hit me, so one just gave me a token blow across the kidneys with his truncheon." O'D gave a rueful smile. "It hurt like hell, so I can imagine what it would have been like if they'd all joined in! Then they put me in a small room, took away my belt and shoelaces and interrogated me. After that, they threw me into a cell."

"What was it like?" I asked.

O'D was silent for a while. "If they had jail cells like this in Europe, they wouldn't have any criminals. It was completely dark, because there weren't any lights. There was a foul smell of shit. I couldn't see what was on the floor and because I didn't want to sit on some excrement, I spent the night standing up and leaning against a wall. In the morning, I discovered there were some holes in the floor for lavatories and that some of the stink was coming from another cell, which they were using as a rubbish dump. The rubbish attracted flies and my cell was full of them. The floor was also crawling with fat white maggots."

"Oough …" I said, disgusted. "Thank goodness you never sat down."

"I wasn't alone in the cell," O'D went on. "There were truck drivers and even a soldier, who had been shot at and then arrested because they had all driven through the barriers. They said they had thought that bandits were manning the roadblocks."

"They weren't wrong," I muttered.

O'D ignored me. "There was even a man there who had been arrested and jailed for stealing an egg." He shook his head in amazement. "Imagine! One egg! I gave him 10 000 meticais (about one U.S. dollar) so that he could get out of there. He was out before I was."

"That was good of you." I said.

"During the night, more and more people were thrown into the cell until it was jam-packed. The cell was so full, that some young boys, who had been arrested for not having Identity papers, leaned against the door and it opened … because the police had forgotten to lock it! Then, in the morning, when the police discovered the open door, they gave all the boys the 'tatu' as punishment for attempting to escape."

"The tatu? What's that?"

O'D raised a hand and showed me, by rapping the first set of his knuckles against the top of my head a couple of times.

"OW!"

"That wasn't hard," he told me. "Imagine how painful that feels when the police use their full force."

After breakfast, O'D got into the Toyota to go off to work in Chimoio. "Oh," he said, leaning out of the window. "I forgot to tell you. Chuck and Eileen are coming over tonight for a shower and a meal."

"Okay." I said. "I'll tell Biasse to roast the leg of lamb. We can celebrate your release from jail. What a relief it's all over!"

"It's not all over," O'D told me, as he accelerated away.

"What? What did you say?" I shouted after him.

But he was gone.

Back in the house, I walked into the sitting room and glanced at my charcoal portrait of the zebra on the mantelpiece. I did a double take, and then let out an anguished cry. The zebra appeared to have evaporated overnight, leaving only a faint grey zebra outline on the white paper!

My cry alerted Biassse and he hurried into the sitting room. "What's wrong, Madam?" he asked anxiously.

"My drawing, Biasse. Look! It's gone!"

Biasse examined the faint zebra outline and a guilty look bloomed all over his face. He tore his eyes off the paper and shot a quick downward look at one end of a yellow duster that was hanging out of the pocket of his spotlessly white apron.

"It was the duster, Madam," he finally and reluctantly admitted. "The duster did it."

"Aaah …" I said.

"Yes," he said, and went on to tell me how, during his dusting duties, the yellow duster had suddenly taken on a life of its own and had flicked all over my drawing, obliterating it.

"I'm sorry, Madam."

"That's all right, Biasse," I said, forcing myself to be calm and kind, although it wasn't all right at all and I felt more like jumping up and down and having a tantrum. That zebra had been the best drawing I'd ever done of an animal! "Never mind. Just be more careful with that duster in future."

"Yes, Madam."

"Oh, and before I forget, take the leg of lamb out of the deep freeze and defrost it. Mr. Chuck is coming for supper and we'll eat it tonight."

CHAPTER FOUR

CHUCK AND EILEEN, AND MITZI OF COURSE

Biasse was basting the lamb in the oven and dusk was falling, when a delightful and chunky little blue Russian lorry called a Gaz, drove slowly up to the house and jerked to a stop by the side of the verandah.

"No brakes!" Chuck's cheerful face looked down at us from the window. "We were speeding around that roundabout - you know the one with the mural of the Mozambicans giving the Portuguese Army a thrashing - when I put my foot down on the brake pedal and … yikes … nothing!" He leaned over towards Eileen in the passenger seat and with a hearty laugh, gave her a poke in the ribs. "Old bag of bones, here, almost went flying out of her window!"

Eileen opened her door, ignoring Chuck's ungallant endearment. She was used to it. She picked up the small snuffling Pekinese dog that had been lying on her ample lap during the trip from the sawmill and kissed it several times on top of its furry head, accompanying this shockingly unhygienic action with loud kissing sounds. "Mmptch! Mmptch! Mmptch! Mitzi wasn't afraid at all, not with her Mum to look after her, were you Meetee-Meetee-Mitzi?" She held the dog out to O'D. "Please take Mitzi, O'D, so I can get out."

Chuck jumped down from the lorry and when Eileen's dumpy figure dangled down out of her door, gave her a steadying hand and eased her to the ground.

They were an odd couple. Chuck was tanned and pleasant-looking, with sandy hair and pale blue eyes. He was fairly tall, well built and very fit for a man of his age, which was on the brink of fifty. Eileen, on the other hand, looked like Chuck's mother and at the age of 74, could quite easily have been his mother. Although they'd been together since Chuck was eighteen and he called her his "sort of wife", they had never married. They doted on Mitzi and like most animal lovers who had never had children of their own, undoubtedly thought of her as their "sort of child."

We all trooped inside the house. Biasse came out of the kitchen and beamed at Chuck and Eileen.

"Oh, manheru, manheru!" he greeted them good evening in Shona.

"Oh, manheru, Biasse!" Chuck replied. Having grown up in the Zimbabwean bush, he spoke Shona fluently. "Bought any more new wives lately, madhala?"

Polygamy was common in Mozambique and Biasse had three wives and twenty two children. Although having an abundance of children in Africa was regarded as having an old age pension, Biasse's huge family was draining him financially.

"Ah, no," Biasse looked a trifle sorrowful. "No money for lobola. I think three is enough now."

"One is enough for me!" Chuck said, with a guffaw.

While Chuck bantered with Biassse, Eileen looked down at her shapeless cotton shift dress and ran a plump hand through her short grey hair. Both her dress and her hair were streaked with red dust. "I'd like to shower before supper," she said. "That road from the sawmill really is terrible. It's nothing but potholes and corrugations. And the dust!"

After they had washed the dust off themselves, O'D poured creamy Amarula into a wine glass for Eileen and Chuck helped himself to a large glassful of what most of us in Southern Africa consider to be the best orange juice ever produced in the world - Zimbabwe's Mazoe Orange Juice.

Chuck noisily gulped down most of his orange juice in one go. "Aaah," he sighed, "this is the way to wash away the dust!" He poured himself a refill and sat down on the sofa. "So, you're a free man now, O'D?"

"Not quite." O'D said. "I had to see Weng San today. He's the Head of the Provincial Police. Apparently, if it hadn't been for Pedro Paulino, I'd still be in jail, with no charges brought against me. It seems that the Head of Traffic wants to turn this into an international incident by ..."

Chuck, Eileen and I all gaped at him.

"International incident!" Chuck exclaimed.

"... by complaining to the British High Commissioner in Maputo and ..." O'D continued.

"British High Commissioner!" Eileen exclaimed.

"... and claiming that I made racist remarks ..."

'RACIST REMARKS!" I exclaimed.

O"D gave us an annoyed look. "I wish you would all stop repeating everything I say like a bunch of parrots," he said irritably.

"Sorry, " I said. "It's just that we're all so amazed."

"That's what Weng San thought too. He told me that when he heard I'd been arrested for making 'racist remarks' he hadn't believed it, and had driven to the Primeira Esquadra in the middle of the night and looked through a hole in my cell door to confirm that it WAS me the Head of Traffic had arrested."

"What now?" I asked. Would this silly incident never come to an end?

"Well," O'D went on, "while I was sitting in Weng San's office, he opened up this massive tome on Mozambican law and, flipping through the pages, told me that the punishment for those who offend, abuse or insult anyone of authority in the State is a jail term of eight years."

"Jeepers!" Chuck gasped.

Eileen echoed his gasp. "Oh, my good grief!"

"EIGHT YEARS!" I cried.

"Weng San told me to write an abject letter of apology to the Head of Traffic and said he'll try to persuade him to accept it. If he does, the case – whatever it is – will be closed."

Biasse came into the sitting room with a welcome interruption. "Scoff's on the table, Madam, Master!"

"I don't know if I can eat now, after hearing that," I said. "I mean about the eight year jail term."

Chuck moved over to the dining room table with alacrity. "I can," he said, and gave an uncaring laugh. "Nothing stops me when it comes to food!"

We all sat down around the table. O'D picked up a carving knife and sliced into the lamb. We had bought it from Tim's Butchery in Mutare and it was perfectly, exquisitely, cooked. To accompany the lamb, Biasse had made Portuguese tomato rice and green beans and carrots from Maciel's vegetable garden.

While Eileen sifted through the lamb on her plate with her fingers for the best titbits to give to Mitzi, who was sitting on the floor by her feet, Chuck piled his plate high and then set to with gusto. He ate ravenously and fast, overloading his fork with lamb and rice and thrusting his next forkful of food into his mouth before swallowing down the first. He chewed with his mouth open, he spoke with his mouth full of food and because of all of this activity, breathed heavily through his nose as if he was running up a hill.

Chuck's awful eating habits always reminded me of a Bud Spencer and Terence Hill Spaghetti Western I had once seen. They had ridden through the desert until they had arrived at a little shack. This was home to their parents, a rather rough couple. They had sat down at the table for a meal and had ALL chewed loudly with their mouths open, talked with food in their mouths, grunted, belched, and thrown bones over their shoulders onto the floor.

Chuck loaded his fork with another piece of lamb and added green beans, carrots and rice to it. He put the load into his mouth. "You know," he began, spraying rice grains up into the air, "it's funny how everything seems to have gone wrong since Caetano arranged that good-luck ceremony with that witch doctor down at the sawmill." Two green beans and a half chewed carrot fell out of his mouth and back onto his plate. "You get thrown into jail, O'D, your lawyer, that woman Carmen Andrade whatsit in Portugal, sends you a fax full of abuse and the Gaz brakes fail."

"Caetano thinks he was conned," O'D said, "and that the witch doctor wasn't a real witch doctor."

"Well, I did think it was a bit strange," Eileen said, "that the ceremony was all over before we arrived. You would think that it was important for *us* to be there, but by the time we got there, the witch doctor and his people had eaten the entire goat and they were all lying around on the ground, dead drunk. You know what I think …"

We never knew what Eileen thought, because she suddenly gave a frightening wheeze and clutched at her throat with both hands. Her face turned deep purple and she started to choke and splutter and cough loudly. Chuck sprang up from his chair, almost knocking it over, and ran to Eileen to help her. While he pounded her on her back, she went on and on but eventually, the purple faded into pink, the spluttering subsided and her breathing returned to normal.

"Oh dear, oh dear, I'm sorry about that!" Eileen gasped weakly, and reached for a glass of water with a shaky hand.

Back in his chair again, Chuck picked up his discarded fork. "She's been like this ever since we lived in Atlantis," he told us.

"Atlanta?" I asked, thinking I had misheard the name. "I didn't know you and Eileen had been to America, Chuck."

Eileen gave a laugh, which ended in a cough and another strangled splutter that made Chuck glance up from his plate for a second. "Oh, no, no, no! Not Atlanta," she corrected me, "ATLANTIS. The Lost City of ATLANTIS. Chuck and I were both drowned there when the city sank beneath the ocean."

"We've been together ever since then," Chuck said, "throughout the centuries."

Although we had come to know quite a lot about Chuck and Eileen during the past year, these were new things they were now revealing about themselves - new and even more alarming things than we already knew. I shot a quick look at O'D and caught his eye. This was the man he had employed to manage our sawmill! O'D's face was impassive and gave me no hint of what he was thinking. He poured some more ruby-red Portuguese Dao into his wine glass.

"How ... extraordinary!" I said. "How did you find all this out?"

"Well," Eileen began, with another series of little splutters, "when we first met, Chuck and I had this very strong feeling that we had known each other before. So one day we went to see a Spirit Medium in Harare, a very nice woman. She was amazing ... she knew everything about us, didn't she, Chuck?"

"Yes," Chuck agreed, wiping his plate clean with a slice of bread and somehow managing to cram the whole piece into his mouth. "She was the one who told us that we've been together since Atlantis and that these choking, spluttering fits Eileen has are from that time, when she was drowning."

"Another thing we learnt from her," Eileen went on, "was that Chuck had been guillotined during the French Revolution. He was a woman at the time."

I shot another look at O'D. His face was still impassive and now he was busy helping himself to more slices of lamb.

"A ... woman," I said.

"I often come back as a woman," Chuck told us, as if this was the most natural thing in the world. He held his plate out to O'D and, with a guffaw said, "I'd better have some more of that lamb too, O'D, before you scoff the lot! And more of that rice, if there's any left."

"Are you interested in reincarnation," Eileen asked me.

"I've read quite a bit about it, "I said. "It's an interesting subject."

"Then I'll introduce you to Penny one day."

"Penny? Is this your Spirit Medium?" I asked. I had no intention, of course, of ever taking Eileen up on her offer.

"Oh no," Eileen smiled conspiratorially. "Penny's my pendulum."

Chuck leaned back in his chair with a sigh and surveyed his empty plate with satisfaction. "I've always been a very fast eater," he told us unnecessarily and without a trace of embarrassment, punctuated his words with an explosive belch of appreciation.

We had met Chuck and Eileen in 1992, through Arthur Slater. Arthur was a tall, white-haired Zimbabwean who usually wore a bush hat with a leopard-skin band around it and who looked a bit like the old movie star, Stewart Grainger. At that time, Arthur had been renting the Matsinho sawmill from the government department IAC, the Instituto de Agricultura de Chimoio.

Arthur's sawmill had fascinated O'D. He had always had a love for wood and fine furniture and so he often went over to see Arthur and to watch the ancient German cross cut saws slowly slicing up logs and turning them into planks. The German saws were more than sixty years old and had broken down sometime in the 1970's, after the Portuguese had been expelled and the Mozambicans had taken over.

When Arthur had first told the Mozambicans that he could repair the saws and get the sawmill working again, they had thought this hilarious and had laughed at the crazy muzungu (white man). Being laughed at hadn't bothered Arthur because he had known something the Mozambicans hadn't known, and it was this. The saws had been manufactured around 1930, in an age before big business had built defects into their machinery and products in order to encourage rampant consumerism and the throwaway society. If the saws were fixed up and given maintenance from time to time, they would still have years of work left in them.

Soon, Arthur had begun to export his sawn timber to Zimbabwe, where it was turned into furniture and then sold to Europe.

Trouble started, however, as soon as Arthur decided to employ a manager to run the sawmill for him when he returned to Harare in Zimbabwe where he had a boiler manufacturing business.

In Mozambique, honesty was (and still is!) a rare commodity. The first manager Arthur employed, a Dutchman, ran off with a large quantity of his timber. The second one disappeared with his money from the sale of his timber. Eventually, he employed a third manager and on the spur of the moment brought him over to our house while O'D and I were in the middle of eating our supper. Luckily, Biasse had cooked more than enough for us all.

During the meal, Chuck had told us that he liked nothing more than living in the bush and that before coming to work for Arthur, he had worked for Blair Laboratories, helping to contain the spread of malaria. In charge of teams of masked workers, he had travelled from village to village in the bush, spraying DDT on the walls of the villagers' huts. His employment with the Laboratories had come to an end when it had been suspected that DDT caused cancer.

"Unfortunately," he had said with a shrug, "since we stopped spraying, the mosquito population has exploded and instead of dying in twenty or thirty years' time of cancer, people are dying in droves, right now, from malaria."

Chuck had, naturally, cleaned his plate while O'D, Arthur and I had still been eating and so he had taken this opportunity to entertain us with some jokes which had amused O'D and Arthur immensely. They had especially enjoyed Chuck's account of a practical joke he had once played on one of his Blair workers. He had given the man a jar of Nair hair removal cream and had helped him to rub this in all over his head, telling him that it was a hair invigorator. When Chuck had got to the part where the man's hair had fallen out until not a strand had been left, O'D, Arthur and Chuck had all laughed uproariously.

We had seen quite a lot of Chuck after Arthur had brought him around to us that evening. Apart from coming to O'D for help when he had to deal with the mountain of paperwork the Mozambican bureaucracy demanded from all of us, he had often dropped in for a chat and a meal in the evenings, or to use our shower as Arthur's house at the Matsinho sawmill was still in the process of being renovated. Sometimes, he'd even come to our house when O'D and I had gone off to Zimbabwe and then he would sit down in our sitting room and Biasse would bring him tea and they would talk for a while in Shona.

Chuck's use of our hospitality had been lavish and so when his betrayal had come, it had taken us completely by surprise. It had never even entered our heads that he would repay us by sneaking around behind our backs and ruining our plans for the future.

It had happened when Arthur had decided that trying to operate a business in Mozambique just wasn't worth the trouble. He'd had a long running dispute with IAC about the rent he paid to them for the Matsinho sawmill, as well as a lot of fines and had finally decided to quit. He'd gone back to Zimbabwe, taking his blue van with him but leaving Chuck behind. We never discovered whether this had been his decision or Chuck's. Probably Chuck's.

Arthur's departure had given O'D and Caetano the idea that an opportunity had come their way and they had started negotiations with Nelson at IAC to take over the lease for the sawmill.

One afternoon, when Nelson had arrived at our house on the farm for a final talk about the sawmill, Chuck had dropped by unexpectedly. He had sat quietly and thoughtfully on one of the dralon-covered armchairs in the sitting room, sipping at a cup of tea while O'D and Nelson had talked away in Portuguese. I don't know how much of the conversation Chuck had understood as his knowledge of the language had been minimal, but I do remember at one point noticing the faraway look that had come into his pale blue eyes. As if he had just thought of something ...

A day or so later, O'D and Caetano had been astounded to hear the news that Nelson had reneged on the agreement he had signed with them to rent Matsinho and that he had gone into partnership ... with Chuck!

We hadn't heard about this new development from Chuck himself because his frequent visits to our house had suddenly come to an abrupt stop and he had dropped completely out of sight.

After Chuck had scuppered the Matsinho deal, Caetano had scoured Manica Province for another sawmill or felling area. This had been quite difficult because every time he had found something that he thought might do, someone else had managed to get hold of it, ahead of us. Eventually, he had come across the old Magalhaes sawmill in the Nhamacoa. He and O'D had applied for it and Dona Ana Paula, the tall and capable woman who had been the Head of the Department of Forestry at that time, had given them permission to rehabilitate the sawmill and to operate in that area. Even then, two other foresters had tried to wrench it out of their grasp.

Just as the Governor of the Province had been about to pick up his Chinese ballpoint pen and put his signature of approval onto the relevant papers, an objection had come from a wealthy Indian called Bika. Bika, who already owned a sawmill and wanted to increase his area, had told the Governor that O'D and Caetano knew nothing about the timber business and had no experience, not enough money and very little equipment to make a success of the venture.

The other objection had come from Giancarlo Bertuzzi, an Italian with long, wild, grey hair. He had been operating in an area adjoining the one we had been granted and had also wanted to possess it in order to increase his felling area.

Knowing that Bika had been right in his claims about them, O'D and Caetano had been on tenterhooks for a while, certain that they were going to lose out on yet another area again. However, as it turned out, they needn't have worried.

Irate that both Bika and Bertuzzi had ignored her and had gone straight over her head to the Governor to overturn her decision, Dona Ana Paula had made sure that they had got nowhere. She had, though, imposed a condition. O'D and Caetano would have to set up a saw and start operating in the Nhamacoa before the end of the year - otherwise they would lose it.

Now that O'D and Caetano had overcome the problem of finding a felling area, they'd been faced with another of the negative effects that Chuck's double-dealing had had on their plans. Although we'd had more than enough money to take over the operation of a sawmill such as Matsinho, which already had a certain amount of infrastructure, we had now found ourselves in the position of having to buy all sorts of equipment we hadn't planned on buying. And then there had also been other important factors which had made Matsinho so attractive and which the old Magalhaes sawmill was without.

Matsinho was close to the main tar road and only a short fourteen kilometre drive to Chimoio. There was ample water from a borehole and electricity from a generator. There was also quite a comfortable house Arthur had been living in and which he'd been in the process of renovating.

In the Nhamacoa, on the other hand, we would have to start off from scratch and this would cost more money than we had. We would have to have a borehole drilled, buy a saw from somewhere, get hold of a tractor, a lorry and trailers, and, most importantly, a generator. These were all major expenses and we had no idea how to find the extra finance. Borrowing from a Mozambique bank had been out of the question. At that time and for many years afterwards, they charged a killer interest rate of 44 % on loans!

What were O'D and Caetano to do? They were entrepreneurs - entrepreneurs without money or access to money!

"Arrojela," O'D had said finally. "We'll just have to take out a mortgage on Arrojela, otherwise we're going to lose our area."

"What?" I had been horrified. Arrojela was totally unencumbered and belonged to us completely.

Our bank, the Midland Bank in Guernsey, had been just as horrified as I had been when O'D had asked for a mortgage on Arrojela. Although Portugal was a member of the EU, the Midland had told us in no uncertain terms that lending money on a property in Europe was not something they would do.

In the end, it had been my brother David who had come up with a solution. Through various channels, he had found someone in England who had been prepared to lend us money privately against Arrojela and although the interest he had wanted had also been high at 25%, O'D had accepted it. There had been no other alternatives.

I had felt a twinge of anxiety at the news that an Englishman I had never met and who was called John Phillips was about to become co-owner of Arrojela.

"But what if something goes terribly wrong," I had asked O'D, "and we end up losing Arrojela?"

David, who had been spending a few days with us on the Tabex farm, had spread some large sheets of paper out over the dining room table. The papers had been a viability and financial study he had drawn up on the proposed Nhamacoa sawmill for O'D and had been filled with columns of figures. "Look at this," David had told me excitedly, tapping his fingers over the columns. "These figures are incredible! You can't lose! Don't worry, you're going to make so much money you'll be able to pay John Phillips back in a matter of months!"

Things had started to go wrong almost immediately, when John Phillips had insisted we use an English-speaking lawyer in the Algarve to deal with the legalities of the Deed of Loan. Although this had been an understandable request from someone who didn't know any Portuguese, it had unfortunately meant that we hadn't been able to use our own lawyer, the nice Mr. Brito.

Stumped by John Phillips' request, O'D had turned to Willy for help. Willy's lawyer had also only spoken Portuguese and so he had been forced to look around for someone else for us. This had taken some time until in August an English ex-patriot (who, I am now certain, had been a secret enemy of Willy's) had recommended an English-speaking lawyer to him. This had been a woman called Carmen Andrade e Silva who had a practice in Lagos and who, apparently, had quite a high profile.

Pleased that he had been able to fulfill John Phillips' wish and completely unaware that he was about to put our future into the hands of a Lawyer from Hell, Willy had set up a meeting with Carmen and John Phillips for the 12th September.

O'D and Caetano now had a mere three and a half months left to get everything up and running before Dona Ana Paula's deadline on the Nhamacoa sawmill ran out.

The meeting with Carmen had gone off smoothly. Willy had told her of the urgency of it all and she had assured him that the Deed of Loan on Arrojela would be through within thirty working days. After all, it was a simple matter. Arrojela was completely free of debts and John Phillips had the cash.

During their meeting with Carmen, though, both John Phillips and Willy had noticed two rather unusual things about her; that she had made little attempt to take notes and that she also appeared to have had "a few bevvies" (as John Phillips would later put it) prior to the meeting. However, this hadn't deterred them from going ahead with her lawyerly services. Leaving our future in Mozambique in the care of a non note-taking and pickled Algarvean lawyer, Willy had waved John Phillips off at Faro Airport and had returned home to send us a fax that all was well and that Carmen would contact us soon.

Now that finance had seemed certain for the larger and more expensive items they would have to buy, O'D and Caetano had begun the search for equipment for their new venture, a difficult task in a country that had nothing.

Forced to cross the border into Zimbabwe for his purchases, O'D had bought tools and machinery in Harare.

In Chimoio, Caetano's search had turned up three 20 foot shipping containers and O'D had bought them, transporting them down to the old Magalhaes sawmill on the back of a hired lorry with a crane. Not only would the containers make excellent storerooms for all their tools and equipment, they would also be theft proof and keep everything safe while the sawmill was uninhabited.

It was at this time also that O'D and Caetano had heard some rather disturbing news on the Chimoio grape-vine about Chuck and Eileen.

It appeared that Chuck's venture with Nelson at Matsinho had turned into something of a disaster. One of the reasons for this had been that Chuck had tempted Nelson away from our agreement by conning him into believing that he had money to put into Matsinho when, in fact, he had had none. When Nelson had discovered the true state of Chuck's finances – or rather, the lack of them – he had begun to treat Chuck and Eileen very badly.

As it had seemed that Chuck needed a new job and O'D and Caetano were going to need a mechanic in the Nhamacoa, they had decided to pay a visit to Chuck.

Amazed, I had questioned the wisdom of employing a man who had had no qualms about stabbing us in the back when it had suited him, but O'D had said, "He's the only fairly good mechanic in Chimoio, there's no one else. And at least we know what he's like now. If we employ someone new, we won't know what we're getting."

The visit to Matsinho had shocked O'D and Caetano. Chuck had looked extremely ill and had lost so much weight that his normally well-built frame had been incredibly emaciated. Eileen hadn't looked too good, either. It turned out that they had, in fact, been starving! What little money the sawmill had made, Nelson had taken and put into his own personal pocket. With no money to buy food, the only way Chuck, Eileen and Mitzi had managed to survive had been with the help of their drunken old cook, Sixpence. He had occasionally managed to scavenge or steal a handful of mealie meal for them and they had all existed on a diet of nothing but sadza.

Naturally, Chuck and Eileen had been only too pleased to see O'D and it had been decided that as soon as we were able to find a lorry, they would leave Matsinho and drive down to the Nhamacoa.

Until then, however, there had been the question of food. Before he had come back home to the farm, O'D had driven into Chimoio to buy some supplies to stock up the empty Matsinho larder and, in order to give them some independence, had handed Chuck some money to keep himself and Eileen going.

While Chuck had recuperated at Matsinho until the end of September, trouble had been brewing elsewhere for O'D and Caetano and in a quite unexpected quarter about six thousand miles away from Mozambique, on another continent.

Despite Willy's optimism – and assurance - that Carmen had understood the urgency of the Deed of Loan on Arrojela, it hadn't taken very long before O'D and I had begun to suspect that she did not, in fact, have our interests at heart.

Although she had received a hundred thousand escudos (half her fee) up front from us to begin the legal process, she had dragged her heels, made numerous errors that forced us to travel back and forth across the Zimbabwean border to get Powers of Attorney from the Portuguese Embassy in Harare and succeeded in turning a simple legal process into a monumental debacle.

With time passing by and nothing to show for it, O'D's frazzled nerves had finally given way and he had cracked under the strain of it all.

In a state of incandescent fury, he had picked up the phone in his office at Tabex and dialled Carmen's number in Lagos to vent his feelings at her incompetence. Unfortunately, she had been out of her office at the time and so, foiled by her absence, he had vented his feelings instead on the woman who had answered his call and then had dashed off an angry fax to Carmen as well.

Carmen's reaction had been predictable. Taking umbrage at O'D's accusations, she had gone on the attack. Unless O'D sent her a letter of apology, she would refuse to do anymore work on his behalf!

Fuming at her threat, O'D had driven back to the farm for lunch and had slammed Carmen's fax down on the dark panga panga dining room table so hard that the plates had all rattled. "Blackmail, as well now!" he had stormed at me. "The woman's been paid half her fee and she knows it's too late to change lawyers!"

Later on that evening, when he and Caetano had met at the Sports Clube to talk about the mess Carmen was making of their plans, O'D had said, "I'd like to wring that bloody woman's neck!"

Nodding his head in agreement, Caetano had thought for a moment. "We can get a Hit Man from Maputo to do it. They're very cheap. Only fifty U.S," he had said, "although there would also be the added expense of the airfare to Portugal and back."

Ignoring Caetano's suggestion, O'D had gone on, gloomily, "She thinks she's safe because I'm thousands of miles away … and she's right!"

In the end, he had bowed to the inevitable. Thanks to Carmen, we were rapidly running out of time. Gritting his teeth, he had written the letter of apology she had demanded.

It was while our lawyer had been behaving more like our enemy than our lawyer, that O'D had made himself unpopular with someone else closer to home and had found himself in the Primeira Esquadra.

On his release from jail, he'd been kept hanging on tenterhooks for some time. Would Carmen do the honourable and finish the job she'd been paid to do before time ran out? And what would happen if he was thrown back into jail again? With our future no longer in his hands but dependant on the whims and caprices of a Portuguese lawyer and a Mozambican policeman, his nerves had been stretched to the limit.

We'd been spending the weekend with David and Caroline in Harare when Willy had phoned. With the help of a Notary called Dona Louisa and no thanks at all to Carmen, Willy had been instrumental in the drawing up of a correct Deed of Loan and it had finally been signed on the 6th December - a marathon twelve and a half weeks for what should have been a very simple legal matter.

Although we had all drunk a celebratory bottle of wine, Carmen had put us through such a long and drawn out and stressful ordeal that none of us had really felt as if we'd had anything to celebrate at all. Especially as O'D and Caetano now had only a mere 25 days in which to buy the larger and more expensive items of equipment in Zimbabwe, not to mention also having to arrange for the necessary customs documents involving their export out of Zimbabwe and import into Mozambique and then their transportation down to the Magalhaes sawmill in the Nhamacoa as well.

More worrying, though, was the fact that they now also only had 25 days in which to fell timber before the cutting season ended.

In Mozambique, foresters aren't allowed to cut down any timber at all in the months of January, February and March, because these are the months when it normally rains the most and as a result, these three months are considered to be the growing season.

Uneasy questions filled our minds. Would we be able to fell enough timber before the 31st December in order to start paying off our loan to John Phillips?

And would we even be able to cut enough timber to help us financially to get through those three months when we were forced to be inactive?

Or would Carmen's procrastination cause us to fail … and to lose Arrojela and our investment … before we even had a chance to begin?

CHAPTER FIVE

BIASSE

O'D's misdemeanour concerning the Head of Traffic hung over his head like a dark cloud for some time. Like a dog with a bone, the Head of Traffic just wouldn't let the matter rest and kept us dangling while we waited to see whether he was going to haul O'D off to jail again or not. Then, a week or so after the Deed of Loan had been signed, the man had finally come to a decision.

One afternoon, while I was lying on the sofa and reading a book, I heard the sound of O'D's pickup pulling up next to the house. As he'd come home earlier than usual, my heart gave an anxious jump. What now? I wondered. Expecting trouble, I closed my book and stood up.

"Biasse! Biasse!" I heard O'D shout. "Come and help me with these boxes!"

"Coming, Master!" Biasse's voice shouted from the back of the house.

"What's up?" I asked, opening the screen door for them as they walked across the verandah carrying two cardboard boxes. The boxes clinked with a familiar and festive sound. "Are we having a party?"

"No," O'D said, dumping his box down on the floor in a corner of the sitting room. "Put that one down here too, Biasse," he ordered. "The Head of Traffic's finally agreed to forget about me. These are gifts for the people who've been keeping me out of jail. Twelve bottles of Johnny Walker Red for Commandant Weng San and another twelve bottles of Johnny Walker Red for Pedro Paulino."

"Oh, great!" I said, relieved to hear that it really was all over now. "And what are you going to give to the Head of Traffic? As he's supposed to be teetotal you can't very well give *him* whisky, can you? Oh, I know! What about giving him twelve Tanganda tea bags?"

"Not likely!" O'D said, and sitting down at the dining room table, he opened his briefcase and pulled out a sheet of white paper. "That would be like waving a red rag in front of a bull. I don't want to spend eight years in a Mozambican hellhole just because I sent some tea bags to a policeman! What he wants is an abject, grovelling, letter of apology."

He uncapped the maroon Waterman pen I had given him for one of his birthdays in England some years ago and while I looked over his shoulder, began to write his second insincere letter of apology in a month.

"Your Excellency," he scribbled in Portuguese, "I would appreciate it very much if you would accept my apology ..."

"Your Excellency?" I interrupted. This seemed to be taking grovelling to the extreme. What would civil servants in England think if you addressed them like this?

"You always have to address Mozambican bureaucrats this way," O'D explained, "even if they're only minor government officials. They have a strong sense of their own importance. It's a hang-over from Portuguese Colonial days."

With all the obstacles now out of his way, O'D prepared for the future by handing in his resignation. We would be leaving Tabex at the end of January, 1995.

Although we'd lived on the farm for two and a half years, I hadn't grown attached to it. The only thing I was going to miss when I went off to my new life, I knew, would be the company of a skinny little old Mozambican man.

I'd grown very fond of Biasse and it was this fondness that caused me to leave him behind when we went to live in the Nhamacoa forest. It had been a self-sacrificing act on my part and later on when I found myself slaving over pots and pans on a mud-brick stove in a smoky makeshift kitchen of poles and grass, I could have given myself a kick for being such an idiot!

Biasse, it seemed, was going to miss us as well. While we packed our few possessions into cardboard boxes, he wandered around the house like a lost soul.

"Please take me with you, Madam."

I looked up from a box. He was very upset, his wrinkled face wore an anxious expression and there was a frightened look in his dark brown eyes. No doubt he was afraid that the new Tabex Administrator wouldn't be as easy-going to work for as we had been. Especially when he started dropping things on the kitchen floor and breaking them!

"No, Biasse, you must stay here," I said, and added, "it's for your own good, Biasse. If you leave your job here on the farm to come with us and then our business doesn't work out, you'll end up with no job at all. What will you do then?" Jobs were hard to find in Mozambique at this time.

"It doesn't matter, Madam."

"Of course it matters, Biasse." I decided once and for all to allay his fears. "And you don't have to worry about the new people who are coming to take our place. The boss has met them. They're from Zimbabwe and he says they're very nice. They'll be kind to you, you'll see."

"No," Biasse told me stubbornly. "They won't be kind. They won't be good people. I know it, Madam!"

O'D was also nervous and a bit strung out. He was cutting all his ties with a multi-national company that had provided a certain security for us in a wild African country, as well as also giving us a regular, guaranteed income every month. Now that the time had finally come for the start of his great adventure with Caetano, the full impact of what he was about to do was making itself felt.

Looking for reassurance, he wandered into the sitting room where I was packing up our books. "Do you remember what my father said when he came for a visit and saw Arrojela for the first time?" he asked me.

"Mmm," I said, remembering the expression on Ti's face as he had taken in the tumbledown mud-brick house and rubble-filled rooms. "He said … My word, O'D, THIS time I really do think you've bitten off too much to chew!"

"I wonder what he'd say now if he knew I was going to rehabilitate an old sawmill in a Mozambican forest?" O'D mused.

"He knows what you're capable of doing now," I said, picturing the beautifully restored Arrojela in my mind's eye. "If he was younger, he'd probably come out to Mozambique to help you."

Although O'D was leaving Tabex to go and live in the Nhamacoa, I wasn't going with him at this time. O'D had decided that conditions at the sawmill were still too basic and primitive for someone like me to endure in silence.

"I don't want you getting in our hair and complaining all the time and distracting us," O'D had told me. "You know what you're like when you're uncomfortable."

I didn't argue. I didn't like basic. I didn't like primitive. I'd seen the awful long-drop hole-in-the-ground lavatory Chuck had constructed for Eileen and himself. It was outside, at the back of the house they were living in and although it was closed in on the sides with hessian bags, it was open to the sky and if you stood at the top of the back stairs of the house, you could actually look down on the person in there, sitting with their knickers around their knees. What had Chuck been thinking of? Hopefully, by the time I came back to Mozambique, it would be gone.

No, I would be much better off staying with my family in Mossel Bay for the next couple of months … just as Biasse would be much better off staying on at the Tabex farm with the new people.

I would miss Biasse, of course. Except for a couple of occasions when forgetfulness on his part had given me some unwanted new experiences – such as the time he had mixed up the bottles of vinegar and boiled water in the fridge and I had thirstily gulped down half a tumbler of pure vinegar all in one go! - he was the perfect cook and housekeeper.

He flitted around the house in his immaculate white uniform and his veldskoens dusting, sweeping and mopping. When he wasn't doing this, he was busy in the kitchen, chopping up vegetables or washing our clothes in the bath and then ironing them impeccably when they were dry.

He kept our house clean and neat and was so unobtrusive that often we were quite unaware of his presence   - until we heard the crash of a plate or a cup on the floor.

I knew a lot about Biasse because sometimes, while he worked away in the kitchen preparing our meals, I leaned against the wall next to his worktable and we chatted about his life before Tabex.

Already old for a Mozambican at fifty six, Biasse had never learnt to read or write and when the end of the month came around and it was time for him to receive his wages, he signed for his money with a big, wavering cross. Despite this lack of education, however, he'd had an adventurous and chequered career.

"When I was young, very young," Biasse told me once, while he chopped up some purple-skinned onions for one of his delicious and fiery curries, "my father took me to work in Rhodesia. At the custard-making factory. You know Willards? Willards custard-making factory in Salisbury … now Harare?"

I nodded my head, eyes smarting a little from the strong-smelling onions. "Yes, I know Willards," I said, and knowing Biasse's love for sugar and all sweet things, added "that must have been a very nice job for you, Biasse."

"No," Biasse replied with some force, surprising me. "I not like this custard-making! I cry, cry, cry, all time! In the end, the foreman tell my father, "Alright! You better send your boy home again!"

"Oh," I said. "So what did you do after that?"

Biasse's little wrinkled face grew grim. Obviously, leaving the custard-making factory had been a bad move. "I go back home to Mozambique, Madam, and one day the Portuguese come for me. Come for ALL young men in my village. Catch us and tie our wrists together, like so," Biasse dropped his knife down on the chopping board and held his arms out in front of him, as if they were tightly bound. "Then they push us in lorries and take us to work on farms." He picked up his knife and began chopping at the onions again. "Here they beat the workers with palmatoria." His knife chopped in time with his words. "Beat, beat, beat!"

Catching sight of the puzzled frown on my face, he asked, "You know palmatoria?"

I shook my head. "No, I've never heard of such a thing, Biasse. What is it?"

The palmatoria, it turned out, was an instrument of Portuguese punishment resembling a ping pong bat but with several round holes in the bat. According to Biasse, it was used often and lavishly to beat the palms of innocent Mozambicans who had done absolutely nothing to warrant such cruel treatment.

The foremen on the Portuguese farms and plantations were the ones who used the palmatoria, at the command of a Portuguese superior, of course, and the beatings would always begin when the Portuguese lit up a cigarette as a signal and started smoking it.

While the Portuguese took a casual puff or two on the cigarette, the foreman repeatedly hit the labourer on the palms of his hands until the holes in the bat raised welts in the soft flesh and the skin broke and turned into a mushy and bloody and excruciatingly painful wound.

The beating only ended when the cigarette burned away to the filter and the Portuguese threw the stub down onto the ground.

"Beat the hands forty, fifty, sixty times!" Biasse told me. "Very much pain. And then worker told 'Go back to work in fields now-now!' With hands full of blood!"

"Did you also get beaten like this, Biasse?"

"Ah no, Madam. Never. But Master Aubrey, HE hit me!" Biasse lunged forward over the chopping board, clenching his thin,

105

small hands into two fists. "Hit me like so … Whap! Whap! Whap!" A carrot and half a green pepper fell down onto the floor from Biasse's violent movements.

I was aghast. Aubrey, a Zimbabwean, had been the Tabex Administrator before O'D had arrived to take his place. "That's terrible, Biasse!" I bent down and picked up the carrot and green pepper and rinsed them off under the cold tap before putting them back on his chopping board. "Terrible! Why did he do that?"

"I dunno, Madam. Just hit me. Hit me for nothing! I go to police and police put Aubrey in jail."

During supper that night, I repeated Biasse's story to O'D. "Apparently, Aubrey was a nasty big fat man who used to hit Biasse," I told him. "Imagine hitting a skinny old man like Biasse."

"I can imagine it," O'D said, a somewhat grim smile flickering across his face as he took stock of all the breakages we had sustained in the kitchen. "Biasse probably broke Aubrey's favourite beer mug."

After the Portuguese had released and then tied Biasse up twice more and taken him off to work on their farms, he had decided that enough was enough and had run away from Mozambique, crossing the border into Rhodesia.

This time he'd gone to work for a Chinese woman who owned the Bamboo Inn restaurant in Salisbury. He'd been the chip cook and he'd enjoyed working there, even though his Chinese employer hadn't been able to pronounce his name and had decided for some reason to call him "Fred" – a shorter name but which, Biasse told me, she also had trouble pronouncing.

To show me what he meant, he put on a high-pitched womanly voice and imitated his Chinese employer's cries for me. "Fled! Fled!" he cried in a Chinese-sounding falsetto that made me laugh. "Come here, Fled! Go there, Fled! Are flied chips ledy, Fled?"

When civil war broke out in Mozambique, Biasse left the Bamboo Inn and came back to look after his ever-growing family.

"Samora no good," Biasse told me grimly, criticising Mozambique's President Samora Machel who had been killed in a plane crash in suspicious circumstances during the civil war. "There was nothing to eat, Madam, and no jobs. No clothes, no shoes, no NOTHING! When I wanted seep - you know seep?" - I raised an enquiring eyebrow and he picked up a bar of green Zimbabwean Sunlight soap on the sink - "Seep!" - and brandished it at me. "When I want seep I have to go over the mountains into Zimbabwe."

As he had no passport, his trips to Mutare were along steep paths through the mountains under cover of night. It was during one of these journeys that he'd been caught by the Zimbabwean Army but on hearing that he was only going to buy soap, they had let him continue on his way, warning him not to forget to return to Mozambique. On his return, he'd been caught again, this time by the Mozambican officials at Machipanda Border Post. Although they had helped themselves to his money, they had been charitable enough to leave him just enough to get back home to his family. This theft, however, rankled with Biasse forever more. "They are tsotsies! Tsotsies, Madam!"

Biasse's English wasn't too good but I soon got used to the unusual way he pronounced some of his words. The same couldn't always be said of O'D, who, although he was a linguist of note - speaking Portuguese, Spanish, French and Italian - was hopeless when it came to Pigeon English.

One Friday morning, unusually mindful of Biasse's habit of only discovering that we had run out of something after O'D had driven off into the distance, O'D asked "Have we got enough milk in the house for the weekend, Biasse?"

Biasse looked at him blankly. "Milk? What is this milk, Master?"

Biasse's sudden ignorance annoyed O'D. "Oh come on, Biasse," he said irritably, "you know perfectly well what milk is. We use it all the time!"

Biasse stood his ground. "I dunno what this milk is, Master," he insisted stubbornly.

O'D's voice rose with exasperation. "Biasse! That white stuff in the blue box. We keep it in the fridge. It comes from cows. COWS!"

A worried look now replaced the blank look on Biasse's face. It seemed O'D's interrogation was getting him deeper and deeper into trouble.

"Cows? I dunno what ..."

Thunderstruck by this new denial, especially of an animal that ambled all over the African continent and one that everyone living in Africa knew, O'D opened his mouth. He looked like a volcano about to explode, especially when he caught sight of my grinning face.

Smothering my laughter, I came to the rescue. "Mombes, Biasse," I explained. "Millick from mombes. The Master wants to know if we have enough millick for the weekend."

A smile of relief lit up Biasse's wrinkled face as understanding dawned. "Aaah ... millick from mombes! Yes, Madam. We have plenty millick."

I left the farm at the end of January for Zimbabwe and the plane at Harare Airport that would take me to South Africa. As we drove away from the house in the pickup, I glanced out of the back window and caught a glimpse of Biasse standing forlornly on the verandah. He made a lonely little figure in spotless white.

Yes, I was going to miss him ... and the easy life I had lived on the Tabex farm.

CHAPTER SIX

A GHASTLY AND A GHOSTLY EXPERIENCE
February 1995

There was no friendly welcome to South Africa this time when I arrived at Jan Smuts Airport. I was last off the plane and last in the queue and when I finally stood in front of the counter where a fair young Immigration Officer was sitting, I made a mistake. Fumbling in my bag, I inadvertently pulled out my South African Identity Document as well as my British passport and handed them both over to him. I could tell I had done something wrong by the theatrical start he gave when he saw the little green South African book.

"Where did you get this?" he asked, looking at me with a stern, cold Afrikaner eye.

It was a long story and I wondered how to cut it short. Thinking that O'D and I would be living in South Africa in 1992, I'd gone about organising the right papers for myself to live and work there. I had filled in all the forms I'd been told to fill in and then I'd been told to pay a visit to the Mossel Bay police. At the Police Station, some constables had divested me of my British Driving Licence and had told me that a South African one would be issued to me instead, inside the new little green book I'd been given by the Home Office. Then, O'D had gone to work and live in Mozambique. Caught in a bureaucratic tangle that would have been impossible to untangle from Mozambique and not wanting to be stuck without a driving licence, I'd left it all to be dealt with later. And now, it seemed that later had arrived.

"It was issued to me by the Home Office," I began, "when I thought I was going to live in South Africa. But then I went to live in Mozambique ..."

Abruptly, the young man swivelled around in his chair and turned his back on me, cutting me short. He'd heard enough. Now facing his computer, he tapped something out on his keyboard. He waited for a while to see what would appear on the screen and then turned back to me, grim-faced.

"You are not allowed to have South African documents if you have a British passport!" he told me.

"Oh, I'm sorry," I said. "I didn't know that." This was true. Nobody at the Home Office in George had said anything to me about passports at all when I had submitted my application to them for a Residence Permit.

"You have committed an offence," he went on, "an offence against the South African government!"

His words made me blanch. There were worse crimes, I knew, than owning a South African I.D. as well as a British passport but he was, I could see, gearing himself up into turning a molehill into a great big bureaucratic mountain. If this went on for much longer I was going to miss my plane to George! I only had half an hour in which to get through Immigration, collect my suitcase from the baggage room and check in at the Domestic Terminal. I began to panic.

"I'm going to miss my next plane!" I cried, "Look, if I'm not allowed to have a South African Identity Document, why don't you just take it. Just take it … and give me your name … and I'll contact the Home Office and explain everything to them."

A glitter came into his eyes and he glared at me. There was no name tag on his uniform and it seemed I had made another blunder by asking him to tell me who he was.

"Now you've done it!" he said threateningly. Snatching up my two offending documents, he jumped off his stool behind the counter and rushed across the floor of the vast and empty Arrivals Hall towards a room. He disappeared into the room and I heard voices, raised and incredulous.

When he reappeared, he had a companion with him. This was an older, brown haired man with a face as hard as flint. They both looked furious as they strode towards me, heels hammering ominously on the floor.

The brown haired man waved my little green book in front of my face.

"What makes you think you have a right to South African citizenship?" he barked.

"Well," I said, taken aback by his aggressive manner, "I was born here, and so were my …" but before I could go on to say "and so were my parents and grandparents and great grandparents and so on," he interrupted me with a sneer, repeating my words and mangling them with his guttural Afrikaans accent.

"Because you were BORN here!" His voice rose up higher with incredulity. "Because you were BORN here! I don't think Dr.

110

Buthelezi, the Minister of Home Affairs, will think you have a right to South African citizenship just because you were BORN here!"

He opened my passport, angrily scribbled something on one of the pages with a pen and then thrust it and the little green book out towards me. "You have committed a very serious crime and because you have been ECKSTREEMELY aggressive ... ECKSTREEMELY ... you are not allowed, you are FORBIDDEN, to leave this country until you have reported to the Home Office!"

Aghast by this unexpected turn of events, I stared at him for a second, taking in his dead reptilian eyes and his close-cropped hair on his bullet shaped head and feeling very much as if I was in the grip of a Nazi Gestapo rightwing fascist. I wondered what he would do if I said something to him in his own language. That would shake him! I racked my brains for some appropriately rude remark in Afrikaans - I was already in so much trouble that a little more really wouldn't matter - but the only Afrikaans word my dim memory could dredge up was "totsiens!" (goodbye!) and so, without saying anything at all, I grabbed my passport and my South African Identity Document from him and ran out of Arrivals, down the corridor and into the baggage hall. I had ten minutes to catch my flight.

On the plane to George, I sat next to a plump, middle-aged Afrikaans woman with blonde hair piled up on top of her head. We didn't talk until I surprised her, as well as myself, by suddenly bursting into tears.

"Ag, what is this now?" the woman asked, looking up from her 'Rooi Rose' magazine and turning to me with concern all over her motherly face. "Why are you crying? What is the matter?"

I pulled a long strip of Mozambican loo paper out of my bag and sobbed into it. "I'm crying because those Immigration Officers have just told me I've no right to be South African ... even though I was born in Port Elizabeth ... and my parents were born here ... and my grandparents and ..."

The woman looked indignant. "They had no right to tell you that, no right at all!" she cried. "Born here, your parents, grandparents ... you should report them to the newspapers! Imagine telling someone who was BORN here that they have no right to be South African! I've never heard of such a thing in my life!"

Although I had recovered a little from my encounter with Afrikaner bureaucracy, I was still smarting when the plane landed at

George. On the drive to Kleinbrak, I gave Jenny and Paul a detailed description of the ill treatment I had endured at Jan Smuts Airport.

"I've told you before never to volunteer any information to those turkeys," Paul drawled. "Only tell them things if they pull your nails out."

"I didn't volunteer anything," I said gloomily. " The S.A. I.D. somehow got stuck in the middle of my Brit passport in my handbag. "

Jenny and Paul also had some news for me - and rather unsettling news it was. Apparently, Paul's partner in the boat works had become addicted to gambling and had frittered all their profits away by playing roulette and black jack in Casinos all along the coast. The boat works had gone bankrupt and Paul and Jenny would be moving to Cape Town to look for work. My mother and father would be staying on at Kleinbrak and if someone could be found to rent the house, my parents would live in one of the cottages in the back garden.

It soon became apparent that the timing of my visit had been quite fortuitous for my parents.

My father had looked well when I had arrived, but a few weeks later there was a sudden deterioration in his health.

On the morning he drove my mother and me to the Home Office in George to sort out my passport problems, he seemed fine, although very quiet. He sat in the car outside the small building and waited while Mom and I went inside and explained everything to the two plump and middle-aged Afrikaans women manning the counter.

We didn't keep him waiting for long. Soothed by my mother's South African accent and reassured by her presence that it had all been a bureaucratic muddle on my part and not a terrible crime, they issued me with a temporary document allowing me to leave South Africa.

Back at the car, my father's complexion had turned grey with tiredness and so we all crossed the road and sat at a café with refreshing cups of tea.

"You drive home," my father told me and pushed his car keys across the café table towards me.

A few days later, he took to his bed, telling us that he felt too weak to move around or to drive the car. From that day on, he lay in bed reading, listening to the radio, watching television or sleeping. He spent a lot of time sleeping.

As he wasn't able to drive anymore, he depended on Jenny and Paul or me to take him to the hospital for his visits to the doctor and for the prescriptions he needed.

This dependence worried me. How were my parents going to manage when Jenny and Paul moved to Cape Town and I returned to Mozambique? How would they shop for food, go to the bank for money or visit the doctor? There was no public transport from Kleinbrak to Mossel Bay and my mother, unfortunately, had never learnt to drive.

I would not, I knew, be able to leave them alone in the house in Kleinbrak when Jenny and Paul left.

My quandary concerning my parents was solved temporarily when O'D telephoned on a crackly line from Mozambique. He told me that conditions at the sawmill were still rough and that it would be better for everyone if I stayed on in Mossel Bay and out of their way.

"Okay," I said. "And how is David getting on there with you?"

Arlene and Horst's clothing company had run into trouble in Zimbabwe and had had to close down. While David was trying to work out his next move, he had come down to the Nhamacoa to help O'D.

"Everything broke down," O'D told me, "almost as soon as David arrived."

"Uh oh," I replied. My brother had deep psychological hang-ups about the African bush and it didn't take much to bring these to the surface. His bad bush experiences had started early in his life on my grandfather's farm in Namibia. When he'd still been a little baby, a mad Herero woman had snatched him out of his pram, thinking that he was her own dead baby. Fortunately, he'd been rescued pretty quickly but then, a few years later, he had given himself another fright by wandering off from the rest of us during a walk and getting lost in my grandfather's mealie field. Even more traumatic had been the time an Ovambo, with teeth filed into points, had playfully picked him up like a chicken by his neck and told him that he ate little white boys like my brother. Was it any wonder that being trapped in the Nhamacoa had sent David fleeing back to the safety of the city?

"So, what happened?" I asked O'D.

"Well, first of all," he replied, "Chuck blew up the Gaz engine when he was driving it because he didn't notice an oil leak. I had to find a replacement engine. Then, while Chuck was repairing the Gaz, the tractor developed a fault and stopped working and then the Land Rover decided to break down as well. So, without any transport at all, we were all imprisoned in the forest for twelve days."

"How did David take this?"

113

"As soon we got a vehicle working, he hot-footed it back to Harare."

It was just as well that I stayed on in Mossel Bay because in April, the end came for my father.

One early morning, Dad was overcome with a terrible coughing fit and then began to vomit.

"We've got to get him to the hospital right away," my mother told me. "Bring the car to the front door and help me to put him into it."

"No, Mom," I said, remembering all those long hours my father had had to sit in a queue, waiting to be attended to by a doctor. "I'm going to phone for an ambulance and that way he'll get to see a doctor immediately."

The ambulance arrived within minutes. The driver got out and helped my father to walk slowly over to the vehicle and to get into it and to lie down on a stretcher. Then the driver shut the door and drove off, very fast, with the siren screaming. In our car, my mother and I followed, more slowly.

By the time we arrived at the hospital, my father was already in a small room with a young Afrikaans doctor and a nurse. They were bustling around him urgently and at one stage, when the doctor left the room to get something and my father began to vomit again, the nurse thrust a bowl into my hands and also ran out of the room. I wondered what they could possibly be doing, but I helped my father as best as I could.

When they returned, the doctor told us he was going to keep Dad in the hospital and that it would be best if we came back the following day.

On Saturday afternoon, we drove over to the hospital again to visit my father. We found him in a ward with several other people and were relieved to see how much better he was looking. Pink in the face and complaining that his hair looked a mess, he joked that the nurses were refusing to comb it.

While we were sitting with him, two coloured men came into the ward and asked us if they could say a prayer for my father. They told us that they came every weekend to the hospital to pray for the patients at their bedside and as we thought it was a kind thing for them to do, my mother and I agreed. Even my father, who always said he was an atheist, seemed grateful that someone was praying to God for him.

When visiting hours ended, we said goodbye to my father. We kissed him on one of his healthy looking pink cheeks and told him we would come and see him the next day.

My mother and I were just on the point of locking the front door and driving off to the hospital on Sunday, after lunch, when the phone rang.

My mother answered it. It was someone from the hospital. They didn't talk for long and when my mother slowly put the phone down, there was a stunned expression on her pale face.

"Your father's … just died," she told me.

"Oh, Mom," I said, and put my arms around her and held her close.

"I can't believe it," she said, over and over again. "I can't believe he's dead."

At the little hospital, a nurse showed us into what appeared to be a storeroom. The room was filled with a jumble of medical equipment and in the middle of all of this we saw a trolley. The trolley was covered with a drab green sheet and underneath this sheet lay the shape of a body.

"I'll leave you alone with him now," the nurse told us.

She left the room and my mother and I stared at the trolley. Finally, my mother spoke. "I still can't believe he's dead," she said. "I want to see for myself." She walked over to the trolley and slowly pulled the sheet off my father's face and chest.

Completely unprepared for what she had revealed, we both started back with shock.

My father's skin was the colour of grey blue metal and it made me think of the horror movies I had seen where mouldering dead people with greeny blue skin had climbed out of their graves and frightened living people half to death.

We were still standing and gazing numbly at this terrible looking corpse, which had once been my father, when the nurse came back into the room. "Lack of oxygen," she explained, noticing the expression on our faces. She glanced down at my father and noticed something else, something we had completely overlooked. "Oh," she said, "you'll want these, won't you," and grasping hold of his limp greeny blue right hand, she removed his signet ring from his finger and his watch from his wrist and gave them to my mother.

The nurse briskly pulled the sheet back over my father's face again and asked us when we were going to remove his body from the hospital. They didn't have a morgue, you know.

Shaken by the suddenness of his death and the sight of him, this new development overwhelmed me. I hadn't even had time to get to grips with everything that had happened and now I was expected to take my father's body away! "But ... what are we going to do with him?" I asked, appalled. I looked at my mother for some ideas. She was at a loss as well. "I don't know what to do! I've never dealt with a death before!"

"Speak to the hospital receptionist," the nurse told us, "and she'll give you the Undertaker's phone number. Arrange with him to come and collect the body. As soon as possible."

Back at the house in Kleinbrak, I picked up the phone and dialled the Undertaker's number. His line was busy and so I had to try over and over again. I began to panic. What if I couldn't get hold of him today? What if he'd gone away for the weekend? Or away on holiday! What was I going to do with my father's body ... his decomposing body?

At last, a young Afrikaans girl answered my call. She told me she was the Undertaker's receptionist and had no idea whatsoever where he was. I told her that my father had just died and there was no morgue and please, could she try her very best to get hold of the Undertaker as soon as possible. It was urgent!

"Oh, really," she said in a tone of voice that suggested she had rolled her eyes at the ceiling at my idiocy, " what do you expect me to do? Get out a ouija board and call up the spirits to find him for you?" She gave a loud cackle of laughter at her joke. "I don't know the spirits THAT well!"

I was taken aback by her insensitivity. Did she expect me to join her in her laughter when my father had just died?

Undaunted by my silence, the Undertaker's receptionist gave another callous cackle of laughter. "Give me your phone number," she told me, "I've just had an idea. I'll try and find him for you by using some ... TELEPATHY!"

I put the phone down. Unfortunately, there was no alcohol in the house otherwise I would have given myself a stiff, strengthening tot of whisky or two. If this was what his receptionist was like, what kind of man was the Undertaker going to be?

Fortunately, the Undertaker was nothing at all like his receptionist. He was down to earth and didn't make one joke – at least not in our hearing - and even arranged for a non-denominational Pastor to say a few words to us at the Crematorium. None of us had set foot in a church for years.

The cremation service in the small chapel in George was a simple one and a small one. Jenny and Paul drove up from Cape Town with their two small daughters, Danielle and Andrea, and David flew down from Harare.

A few days later, when we collected my father's ashes from the Undertaker, we decided to scatter them in the sea, in the Indian Ocean. When he'd still been well enough to drive, my father had often gone down to the shore where he'd sit in his favourite peaceful spot. Here, on a bench by himself and with only his thoughts for company, he'd watched the waves and the sea birds and the occasional ship sailing by in the distance.

At my father's favourite spot, we all walked down to the water's edge and stood on the wet sand while David took off his shoes.

I glanced at my mother and although I hadn't been around at the time, a picture came into my mind of my parents' romantic meeting so many years ago now. It had taken place during the Second World War when my mother, who had joined the South African Army, had been billeted in my father's parents' house in Port Elizabeth.

She'd been playing a waltz on the piano when my tall, good looking father had come back home from the North African deserts where he'd spent a lot of time in sandy fox holes, living on bully beef and biscuits filled with weevils.

Nineteen at the time, my mother had had soft brown eyes, the tiniest of freckles scattered across her pretty face and long curly brown hair floating around her shoulders and, as my father had once told me, he'd been quite bowled over by the sight of her.

Now, my father was gone and although my mother's hair was still curly, it was cut short and had turned silver. She wasn't slender anymore either.

I wondered what memories were going through her mind. Was she also remembering their beginning and thinking how quickly the years flew by?

David waded into the sea with the box of Dad's ashes and started scattering the white grains into the water. Unfortunately, benumbed with sadness, none of us had given a thought to the direction of tides and winds, and so the ashes floated towards the beach and granules blew against my brother's wet bare legs in his shorts and clung there, coating the front of his legs in white. He bent down and washed off these little white grains ... all that was left of Dad.

Jenny and Paul returned to Cape Town and David flew back to Harare, leaving my mother and me to pack up all her possessions. She would be leaving Mossel Bay and going to live in Cape Town with my sister.

On the sixteenth day after my father's death, my mother and I were still busy packing all her things away into large cardboard boxes. Alone in the house except for her small tan and white dog, Bucksie, we went to bed early that night. We were tired.

Despite my tiredness, sleep was impossible and I tossed and turned until I became more and more irritable. Every now and then, I thumped my pillow with frustration, turned on the bedside lamp and glared at the clock. Oh, how slowly the hours were passing!

And then, at around about half past twelve in the morning, it happened.

Moonlight was shining through my windows, as I always open the curtains before I go to sleep and I was lying on my back, still wide awake and staring up at the ceiling. I'd left my bedroom door open and now I heard something just outside the open doorway that grabbed at my attention. A sound that chilled my blood and made my hair stand on end. The quite unmistakeable sound of two heavy footsteps dragging across the carpet, as if someone was forcing himself to walk ...

Aaaah ....

I lay still, hardly daring to breathe. Who ... or what ... was this?

An unwelcome picture came into my mind of a body lying on a trolley in a storeroom in the little Mossel Bay hospital and my imagination took flight.

Was it ... could it be ... my father? Dragging his greeny blue and mouldering self towards me?

No! Oh, no, no, no!

And THEN, a few seconds later, I heard MUSIC just by my door! The tune was a familiar one to me but it was made eerie and unearthly by the instruments, which appeared to be delicate, tinkling little bells.

Pinned rigid to my bed with fainting fearful terror, I listened to the tune of 'Happy Birthday' being played from its beginning to its tinkling end.

When the music finally stopped and there was silence, I still didn't move a muscle but continued to lie motionless on my bed. For the first time in my life I understood what the phrase 'scared stiff' really meant.

In the room next to mine, I heard my mother getting out of bed. She walked into my room and switched on the ceiling light. The flood of light did nothing to dispel the awfulness of what had just happened.

"Did you hear that, Mom?" I asked from my prone position in bed.

"Yes, I did," she said. "And so did Bucksie. She jumped off my bed and ran out of the room, wagging her tail."

Wagging her tail?

"What do you think ... it ... was, Mom?"

"I don't know."

I pulled myself together and sat up, suddenly hopeful. "Perhaps we left the television on ... or the radio!" I threw my sheet and blanket off and got out of bed. "Let's check."

My mother and I walked through every room in the house, turning on every light. All the windows were tightly closed and the back and front doors were firmly locked. The television and radio were off. Brave now that my mother was by my side, I opened cupboards and looked inside them and peered under beds.

"If it had been someone outside the house," I said, "Bucksie would have barked, wouldn't she?"

"Oh, yes," my mother agreed. "She's quite a ferocious little watchdog. No one can get into the garden without her making a noise."

"But instead," I went on thoughtfully, "she wagged her tail."

My search turned up nothing and so, as everything looked completely normal, we went back to our beds. Strangely enough, as soon as my head hit my pillow, I fell asleep.

In the morning, after breakfast, while my mother and I were packing her books into boxes, a sudden thought struck me.

"The doorbell, Mom! That's where the music came from last night. Someone must have rung the doorbell!"

The house had come with a doorbell which, when pressed, had played the most hideous collection of tunes I had ever heard. One of these tunes, I was sure, had been 'Happy Birthday.'

My mother looked up from a box with a strange expression on her face. "That's impossible," she replied. "No one could have rung the bell because Paul got so fed up with the children forever pressing it, that he removed the batteries."

"Perhaps he put them back and forgot to tell you." Eager to solve the mystery and to put the blame on a human, I walked out of the house and pressed my finger down firmly on the doorbell several times. Nothing happened.

"I told you it wouldn't work," my mother said. "Come and have a look for yourself." She walked back into the hall and over to a small cupboard set in the wall. She pulled open the tiny door and I saw for myself that it was completely empty.

"Oh, well," I said.

As the morning went by, I thought about the unearthly music my mother and I had heard in the night and wondered what had been the significance of it. Happy Birthday … it had obviously been some kind of horrible message because almost everyone in my family, including my father, had been born in May.

We were eating a light lunch of my mother's chicken pie when I said gloomily, "It's Dad, isn't it, Mom? It's his ghost. That's why Bucksie ran out of the room last night, wagging her tail."

"No," my mother shook her head. "It's not him. It's not him at all." She gave a shudder. "I'm glad I'm going to Cape Town and leaving this house … this spook house."

My mother's denial that the creepy, ghostly events had anything to do with my father was so definite that I wondered how she knew. Had she seen something I hadn't seen or heard something I hadn't heard? I didn't ask because I really didn't want to know any more. I would also be glad to get out of a house that had suddenly lost its friendly homely warmth and become haunted by … something … that appeared to be impersonating my father, an impersonation for which I could think of no reason at all.

CHAPTER SEVEN

AT HOME IN THE NHAMACOA
May 1995

I arrived back in Zimbabwe in a subdued mood. My visit to South Africa hadn't exactly turned out as I had expected it to, what with Dad dying and then some ghastly spirit pretending to be him and terrorising my mother and me.

O'D was waiting for me in Mutare. He was wearing a frayed brown jacket over a frayed and faded cotton shirt. I noticed that some of the shirt buttons were cracked. To complete this ensemble, he had added frayed khaki trousers and a pair of scuffed brown boots. He did not look like the successful sawmiller he and David and everyone else had told me he would rapidly become.

He was pleased to see me and led me over to the vehicle he had bought to replace the ancient Tabex pickup. This turned out to be an even more ancient Land Rover that looked as if it had been the first Land Rover ever produced by the Land Rover company in England and then shipped over to Mozambique.

Short-wheel based and squat, most of the paintwork had been rubbed off the Land Rover's body, leaving it a patchy aluminium, and if the word "grunge" could be used to describe a vehicle, this was how people would have described the car we were now using to take us around.

"Eeek," I said, and looked around somewhat furtively. "I hope we don't see anyone who knows us!"

"It's the only vehicle I could find," O'D explained. "You know how scarce things are in Mozambique."

The Land Rover showed its true colours once we left the tarred road into Chimoio and drove the 46 kilometres down to the sawmill. The corrugations were especially jarring in a vehicle without suspension and as we banged and jolted our way down the dirt road, we didn't talk much. This lack of conversation wasn't because we didn't have anything to say to each other, but because a thousand rattles drowned out our voices and anyway, we were too busy putting back bits and pieces which kept falling off the inside of the vehicle and sliding the windows shut. Red dust rose up in choking clouds through the floor and coated our hair, our faces, clothes and bodies. By the time we arrived in the Nhamacoa, I felt as if I had spent several hours in a concrete mixer.

The sun was already going down when O'D pulled up in front of the house. He took my suitcase out of the back of the Land Rover and we went inside, without opening the front door. This was because the house didn't have a front door, merely a large gaping hole where a door had once been.

Chuck and Eileen were in the sitting room. They were also wearing frayed clothes and were relaxing in two old Morris chairs with brown moth-eaten cushions near the west-facing window.

Like the door, the three metre long window was also a large gaping hole. Some attempt, however, had been made to protect the room and its occupants from the elements. In place of the missing glass, rolled up black plastic was attached to a piece of wood at the top of the windows and was obviously used as a blind. I noticed several large stones on the wide windowsill and deduced that these were used to weight down the plastic to prevent it from blowing in the wind.

The view from the window was stunning. Above an ocean of trees that went on and on seemingly forever, the darkening sky was awash with streaks of crimson and gold and mauve. A solitary evening star sparkled like a diamond.

Chuck and Eileen greeted me with a smile. "Had a good trip?"

Mitzi, comfortably ensconced on Eileen's lap, ignored me.

"It was all right," I said, smiling back weakly and trying not to sound grim.

Three paraffin lamps lit up the room but their golden glow couldn't hide the plain fact that since I had last been to the sawmill, Eileen had done absolutely nothing to have the walls scrubbed down and cleaned. They were still black with decades of smoke and mould and grime. What on earth had she been doing in the last six months with all the workers O'D was employing? The house resembled a … hovel!

I was a stickler for cleanliness and my mood darkened. We looked just like a bunch of American hillbillies now, I thought glumly, and Chuck and Eileen looked just like MAW and PAW!

We ate a supper of chicken curry and after Chuck had talked to O'D about the activities of the day, I was initiated into life in a broken-down house in a forest in Mozambique.

At seven o'clock, Chuck gave a huge yawn, forgetting to put a hand over his mouth and giving us a glimpse of his tonsils. "Time for bath and bed," he told us. "It's early to bed and early to rise in this place!" He heaved himself out of his chair and walked over to the west-facing window. Leaning over the windowsill, he shouted in the direction of the cook hut, a small construction made out of poles and untidy grass thrown up for a roof. "Avelino! Agua para banho! Chop chop!"

Avelino, a lugubrious looking fellow of mixed Mozambican and Portuguese parentage who had a shock of frizzy hair and who was a sort of Man Friday, staggered out of the cook hut and up the back stairs, carrying a large smoke-blackened tin filled with steaming water. Chuck met him at the top of the steps and the back door - another hole in the wall - and took it from him. Grasping the tin's two handles, he carried it down the corridor into the bathroom and I heard the sound of water being poured into a small tin bath.

Eileen picked up one of the three paraffin lamps lighting up the room. "Goodnight," she said, and followed by Mitzi, made her way down to the bathroom with the light, "see you in the morning."

"We have a water-saving system here," O'D told me. "Eileen always baths first and then Chuck baths in her water. They use half the hot water in the tin. When he's finished, he empties their bathwater into the cistern of the lavatory."

The primitive long-drop lavatory, I'd been glad to see, had disappeared during my absence and had been replaced by a proper, modern lavatory in the bathroom right inside the house. Without a water supply, however, the cistern had to be filled up with water by hand, a very common practice almost all over Mozambique.

In the dim light of a paraffin lamp, I bathed that night in a small tin tub in a bathroom where only a curtain strung up in the hole in the wall where the door had once been, gave us some privacy. However, as there were no ceilings in the house, only a grass roof, even the slightest sound anyone made could be heard very clearly.

I shot a glance at the white porcelain lavatory and its wooden seat just under the gaping windows. Sharing a house like this with strangers meant that you couldn't be inhibited when it came to normal – or abnormal - bodily functions ... especially in a country like Mozambique, where things often happened to us ... and we got diarrhoea ... or vomited ...

Still, being heard by everyone would always be highly embarrassing, even though we were all in the same boat.

While O'D bathed in my bathwater, I prepared myself for bed in the room opposite another curtained-off room where Chuck and Eileen and Mitzi, of course, were already all snoring their heads off.

My new bedroom was very spartan. Two green camp beds were set out side by side on the bare black concrete floor and neither of them had a mosquito net hanging over them to protect us from bites. A long built-in cupboard without doors was filled with some of O'D's tools and equipment. The window didn't even have black plastic for a blind and the door curtain was a capulana strung across the doorway on a wire.

"Chuck kicked one of the legs of your camp bed the other day and broke it," O'D told me when he climbed into a sleeping bag on his camp bed near the window. "We managed to fix it but now it tends to tip over if you're not careful."

"Why on earth did he do that?" I asked, annoyed. Chuck and Eileen were sleeping on a proper bed and mattress, their own from Matsinho.

"He was testing it to see how strong it was."

Although I was tired from my journey, it took time to fall asleep. Without doors and windows to restrain them, creatures of the night invaded the house. A bat flew in through the window and after fluttering around the room, hung on a beam not far from my camp bed, depositing disgusting bat droppings onto the floor. A shadowy shape with a long tail scuttled across the floor – a rat! – and disappeared into a pile of O'D's spare parts in the open cupboard. When another rat ran across the floor towards me, I sat up hurriedly and my camp bed tipped over and I rolled out onto the floor, still zipped up in my sleeping bag. Getting out of it, I righted my camp bed. Drat that Chuck!

The sound of drums floated over the forest, louder and louder ... boom boomboomboom ... boom boomboomboom ... BOOM BOMBOOMBOOM ...

As I lay carefully back down on my camp bed again, I knew I was in the real Africa now. That same Africa that my ancestors had known. But the problem with this was that I, along with about three quarters of the population of the African continent, had no desire whatsoever to live in the real Africa!

A gong woke me up the next morning at six o'clock. Not far from my window, I heard O'D's voice.

124

"Alfixa!" he called out.

"Pronto!" a voice replied.

"Daringua!"

"Pronto!" another voice replied.

"Fourpence ..."

Roll-call. Standing in front of a tree stump, O'D ticked off the names he'd written in The Time Book. We employed about forty workers now. They started early in the day, getting equipment ready to go out to work in the forest. We were cutting timber for a Portuguese company called Socinav, who were exporting the wood in the form of logs to Lisbon.

Leaning out of my window, I peered through the leaves of the big old mango tree next to my room and watched the workers loading equipment onto a trailer that was attached to the back of an ancient little blue Ford tractor. What a bunch they all were! Barefoot and dressed in an assortment of rags, most of them were illiterate and (with the exception of the two chainsaw operators, the tractor driver and foreman) this was the first job they had ever had in their lives.

Despite its size, the little tractor made quite a racket. Pulling the trailer loaded with men and equipment, it roared past the house and disappeared down the forest track in a cloud of dust. If all went well, it would be back at half past four, the time when our working day came to an end.

After breakfast, O'D drove off to Chimoio. We needed fuel for the vehicles. Living about fifty kilometres from the nearest petrol station, we had to transport big drums to town to fill up.

Left on my own, I was going to spend the morning sorting out our room and attempting to make it more liveable, if that was possible. But first, I wanted to see what Eileen was up to ...

As anyone who has ever lived in the bush will know, the small eccentricities which we all have and which we're usually able to overlook in normal circumstances often become magnified and completely take over our minds when people are forced to live together in difficult conditions and in a confined space.

Now, on my very first morning at the sawmill, it took me only about an hour or so to blot my copybook with Eileen and to upset her.

She was cutting up vegetables in the ruined shell of what had once been the kitchen when I walked in. Mitzi was lying next to the chopping board on the wide plank Chuck had placed on top of the broken worktop and giving a snuffle or two while she watched Eileen.

"Dogs shouldn't be anywhere near food," I told Eileen, picking Mitzi up and depositing her down on the floor. "They're dirty and it's so unhygienic."

Eileen bristled and her eyes grew beady at this slur concerning her beloved pet's cleanliness. She gave me a glare. "Mitzi's not dirty! She's perfectly clean! I shampooed her only last week in the bathroom!"

Her words made me pause for thought. Was I bathing in the same small tin tub also used by a grubby, snuffling little Pekinese dog? The bath probably wasn't even washed out afterwards.

"Gosh," I said, lost for words. It was rapidly becoming obvious that when it came to germs, Chuck and Eileen didn't have a clue!

I looked down at the chopping board and the mound of potatoes and carrots Eileen was busy cutting up. Where was her faithful cook, Sixpence, who had saved her and Chuck from being starved to death by Nelson at Matsinho?

"What happened to Sixpence?"

"Oh," Eileen heaved a sigh and chopped up a carrot in a particularly vicious way, "O'D fired him because he kept getting drunk. He came home one evening and found Sixpence lying on the kitchen floor, too drunk to cook supper and so he pulled him out of the kitchen and down the back stairs by his ankles. We could hear Sixpence's head clunking as it hit each step on the way down."

"O'D always gets very irritable when he's hungry," I informed Eileen.

"Well, since then I've had to do all the cooking."

"What a pity," I said, thinking that now I would, unfortunately, have to help her with the cooking. I didn't for one moment look forward to cooking in a stone-age style African bush kitchen but I really had no alternative. Even I couldn't be so selfish as to leave a 74 year old woman to slave over a mud brick stove in a hut every day!

"I've never cooked on a mud brick stove before," I told Eileen. "You'll have to show me what to do."

"Oh, it's very easy," Eileen said, sweeping the vegetables into some thick based cast iron pots, "as long as you can stand the heat and the smoke."

I helped her carry the pots down the back stairs and across to the cook hut. Although the hut was very primitive, it was surprisingly pleasant inside.

The stove was simple, with a waist-high back and two sides made with mud bricks that were cemented and plastered together with more mud. On the top, supported by the back and sides, was a thick metal plate and underneath the plate was a space with a grate, a little furnace, large enough for a wood fire.

Eileen put her pots down on top of a rickety wooden worktop and threw some more small pieces of wood from a pile on the ground into the fire under the metal plate. "You can adjust the heat of the metal plate by how much wood you put on the fire," she told me, placing the pots in the centre of the plate. "When the plate gets very hot, you boil things in the centre and then when you want them to simmer, you push the pots over onto the cooler sides."

Watching her, I saw that once you got the fire going at the right temperature in the stove, there was nothing to it really. The only disadvantage was that every now and then a big puff of smoke blew out through the cracks between the mud bricks and completely enveloped our faces.

While we were in the cook hut, a small procession of four or five youths, dripping with sweat and breathing heavily, walked out of the long grass and headed towards us. They were all balancing 20 litre plastic containers on their heads and when they arrived at the cook hut, they off-loaded their burdens down onto the ground with some relief.

"It's our water for bathing and for washing the dishes," Eileen told me. "The river's completely empty now, so they fill up with water from a hole we had to dig in the river bed. We heat the water up in those large black tin cans outside the cook hut."

"What about drinking water?" I asked.

"Oh, Chuck drives over to Macate with some containers and gets it from the village borehole. There's a hand pump and so we wait in line with the villagers until it's our turn."

I decided, without any opposition at all from Eileen, that she and I would take turns to do the cooking and that whoever did the cooking, would do all the washing up as well. This would give us each some completely free days when we didn't have to go anywhere near the cook hut at all.

While Eileen got on with the lunch, I walked around outside, getting my bearings. Under the shade of some mango trees not far from the back of the house, I noticed a long line of rabbit hutches, each hutch filled with one of these cuddly, fluffy little animals. No doubt Chuck was breeding them for food.

A lot of clucking from a large room underneath the house told me that Chuck was also breeding chickens and that one of them had just laid an egg. I looked into the room. It had a dirt floor and was filled with equipment and spares and tyres. There were chickens all over the place, laying eggs inside the tyres and sitting on them to hatch the eggs and scratching in the dirt and splattering everything with nasty-smelling black and white chicken droppings.

"Oh dear," I muttered to myself. "Oh dear oh dear oh dear!"

I walked away from the house, past the area where the large circular saw was in the process of being mounted. O'D had bought new discs and new stellite and tungsten insert teeth for the saw from England. Hopefully, it wouldn't be long before we started producing planks and making some real money to get us out of a fix we already appeared to have fallen into.

As we had feared, Carmen's bungling with the Deed of Loan had had some very bad consequences for us. In the short time left to us before the end of the cutting season, we hadn't been able to fell enough timber to see us through the first three months of the new year. We had managed to send John Phillips six thousand dollars, but this payment had meant we had later run low on funds. As a result, O'D and Caetano had taken out another loan with their Mozambican bank to tide us over.

My heart had given a flip of anxiety when I had heard this news. Two loans, one at 25% interest and now another at an incredible 44% interest!

"I knew it!" I had cried, beginning to hyperventilate. "We're going to lose Arrojela!"

"Don't worry," O'D had assured me. "We'll have the saw up and running soon and then we'll be able to pay back those loans in no time at all. You'll see."

On the other side of the saw, there was a makeshift workshop near the yellow container now housing the Kohler generator. In the shade of its grass roof, Chuck was lying on the ground, repairing something underneath the Gaz lorry. Avelino and a young worker called Pocas were helping him and as I strolled past them all, Chuck sat up with an annoyed roar and hit Avelino on top of his head with a spanner.

"Avelino," Chuck yelled, "how many times do I have to tell you ..."

Making my way through dry, yellow ankle-high grass, I decided to go and find out how the borehole drilling was getting on. The rig drilling the hole belonged to Vic Vorster, a wild-haired Zimbabwean with a somewhat maniacal look in his eye and because it was an old rig, it was working away very slowly.

"Good morning," I said to Vic's Zimbabwean workers. "Any luck with the water? How far down have you gone now?"

"We're down to 72 metres," they told me. "Mr. Pixley said that if we don't find water in the next metre or so, we may as well stop drilling."

My heart seemed to drop as deeply as the hole they had drilled. Vic was charging us U.S.$100 a metre whether we found water or not. If we stopped now, we would have to pay him U.S. $7,200 for nothing but a deep, dry hole!

Old Joaquim, who had originally shown the Magalhaes sawmill to Caetano, had told O'D there was water near a small incline not far from Chuck's rabbit hutches. Unfortunately, lack of telephonic communications had meant that the Water Engineer had come on a day when O'D had been away and he had chosen a spot that was proving waterless.

I was just about to turn around and go back to the house when the word 'EIGHTY' came into my mind, as if someone had whispered it to me. "No, don't stop yet," I said. "Drill down to eighty metres. I'm sure - really sure - we'll find water at eighty."

On the way back to the house again through the ankle-high grass, I got the first of the many frights I was to experience in the Nhamacoa. There was a loud hiss ... and I froze in mid stride. A snake! I turned my head in the direction of the sound and there it was, only a metre or so away from me. It had reared its green body up in the air in one of those stiff 'threatening to strike' poses and was eyeing me in a way I really, really didn't like.

I gave it the traditional greeting humans always give snakes. "Yeeow!" I cried and fled back to the house, too scared to look over my shoulder in case I saw the creature chasing after me.

At around about four o'clock in the afternoon, Fourpence, or Fo'pence as the Mozabicans called him, returned with the tractor and the workers. They'd had a good day's work in the forest and while they were busy offloading the equipment, Madeira, our Foreman, handed an exercise book over to Chuck. This was a record of the trees they had felled, with each individual tree's diameter and length worked out to give a total volume. Later on in the evening, all these measurements had to be checked and then transferred into a hardbound book called the Forestry Register.

During my absence, O'D had been the one to keep the Forestry Register up to date but now that I was back, this turned out to be my job as well, in between the cooking and the washing up.

It wasn't long before my passion for trees began to develop and although I didn't start growing them until I met someone called Allan Schwarz some years later, I began to read up on them and to wonder if I would be able to grow the more precious hardwoods from the seeds I found on the ground in the Nhamacoa. It had always been our intention, anyway, to replace the trees we felled by growing new ones from seed and reforesting.

At this time, the timber we were supplying to Socinav came from a lovely tree whose biological name is Pterocarpus Angolensis.

Apart from this name, the tree also has three other names in Southern Africa. In Mozambique it's called Umbila, in Zimbabwe they call it Mukwa and in South Africa, to complicate things even more, it's known as Kiaat.

The colour of this wood when it's turned into furniture and polished is a gorgeous deep golden brown and it has a lovely silky-smooth feel to it when you run your hand over it. It's a very popular wood with the local Mozambican carpenters because it's so easy to work with and even when it's still 'green' (full of moisture) and the planks have just come off the saw, there's very little shrinkage.

The sap of this tree is the colour of blood and in Zimbabwe they use it to make furniture oil. The sap also makes a very good dye, as we all found out when we inadvertently got it on our clothes and our clothes were ruined. No matter how often you wash your clothes, absolutely nothing removes an Umbila sap stain!

One fascinating fact I came across in our much-thumbed copy of Palgrave's famous book 'Trees of Southern Africa' was that before colonisation, the Africans used the root of this tree as a cure for malaria. Some old Southern African books I found later corroborated that this remedy worked.

Our customer, Socinav, wasn't at all interested in cures for malaria. They wanted the largest and most perfect of the Umbila logs we could cut down for them and they wanted them down at the port of Beira, in a hurry, to catch the ship to Portugal.

As there was little transport in the form of 20 ton trucks for hire at the time, this meant we had to transfer the logs to the railway station in Chimoio ourselves and load them into the wagons for their journey to Beira.

Without the help of a crane, the method we used consisted of muscle power in the form of our workers, or muscle power together with the aid of our tractor – the usual method we all used in Mozambique at that time to load timber.

First, O'D or Chuck supervised the loading of the Gaz and the trailer. Two long and sturdy poles were placed against one side of the lorry and then two ropes were tied to the top of these leggings. While the men pushed the log up the poles, other men (or the tractor) on the other side of the lorry, helped to pull the log up onto the vehicle with the ropes. It all looked pretty dangerous to me but thankfully we never had an accident.

To help the men work in unison with their pushing and pulling, a strong young man called Massoura sang and chanted out directions in his truly beautiful dark rich voice and they all sang and chanted back to him in wonderful harmony.

O'D and Chuck took turns to drive the loaded Gaz and trailer slowly out of the Nhamacoa and along the dusty corrugated road to the railway station and while one drove, the other supervised the loading at the station. When the logs were offloaded from the lorry, the whole performance was repeated all over again in order to load the logs into the wagons. It was heavy, heavy work.

One day while O'D was taking his turn at the railway station, a man approached him and asked him for a job. He was a tall man of about forty and his clothes hung in tatters on his strong frame. His name was Steven and although he admitted he was Zimbabwean and we weren't allowed to employ Zimbabweans, this didn't deter O'D.

"If you really want to work," O'D told Steven, "you can start right now."

Steven took a place among our team of workers and when the wagon was loaded with logs, he came back to the sawmill with them on the Gaz. He was grateful for a job. He hadn't eaten for a long time.

About ten days after my arrival at the sawmill, one of the young men who had been carrying containers of water up to the house from the hole in the riverbed told Eileen that he knew how to do housework. He was called Sabonette, which means Little Soap, and she decided to try him out.

The day Sabonette started working in the house was my cooking day, a day that consisted of a lot of walking up and down the back stairs.

He was busy sweeping the corridor when I left the cook hut and came upstairs to set the table for lunch. I put out plates and water glasses, knives and forks and once this was done, I went downstairs again for a final check on my simmering pots and pans.

There was no sign of him when I trudged back up the stairs again some minutes later and I thought he had finished cleaning and had left the house. How wrong I was! When I walked through into the main room, I saw a sight that rooted me to the floor with amazement. There was Sabonette, happily and carefully sweeping our plates and cutlery and everything else on the table with the dirty old broom he'd been using to sweep the corridor!

I let out a scream "AAAARGH!" and Sabonette's broom came to a stop on top of Chuck's plate.

"What do you think you're DOING?" I grabbed the broom out of his hands. "Out! Get back to the river!"

Alerted by my scream, Eileen came hurrying down the corridor. "What's going on?" she asked.

"I caught him in the act of sweeping the table - with THIS!" I cried, waving the dirty broom at her.

"Oh, my good grief!" Eileen exclaimed. "What a good thing you saw him doing it."

"Yes, isn't it?" I said. "And now I'm going to have to wash everything all over again!"

"I'll reset the table for you, while you're doing that," Eileen offered kindly. "I hope Avelino ironed the spare tablecloth!"

Down in the cook hut, I poured boiling water over the plates Sabonette had covered with germs. It was just as well I had caught him in the very act, I thought grimly to myself, because if I hadn't seen him, we would all have been eating off filthy, germ-ridden plates, totally unaware of their unhygienic state!

A few days later, another youth who had been carrying water up to the house told us that he, too, had once been a house worker and had been employed by no less a person than the Governor of Beira himself.

"Well, shall we try *him* out?" Eileen asked.

"Yes, why not," I replied.

Seven, as this young man was called, turned out to be a surprisingly good worker. A treasure, actually. He ironed our clothes beautifully, even though it was with the old-fashioned and cumbersome charcoal burning iron we had to use and he also turned out to be very useful when it came to watching our pots on the stove to see that they didn't run out of liquid. This left us free to do other more important things, such as reading or going for walks.

One morning, while Seven was keeping watch over her pots, Eileen went down the stairs to the cook hut and this time it was her turn to scream. I was working on the Forestry Register at the time and the sound made my pen jerk, leaving a squiggle on the page. What now? I wondered. Had she fallen down the stairs? Been bitten by a snake?

Before I could get up and put my head out of the window for a look, she came panting up the stairs and burst into the room. "You'll never guess what I've just found Seven doing!"

All sorts of hideous ideas came into my mind and I braced myself. "What, tell me."

"Well, I went down to the cook hut to check on things and I noticed a strange pot not belonging to us, bubbling away amongst all of ours. I looked inside it ..." here Eileen's voice quivered with pent up emotion "... and do you know what I saw?"

I shook my head. "No. What? What?"

"I saw ... MY ONLY GOOD PAIR OF CANVAS SHOES BOILING AWAY IN THIS POT!" Breathing heavily, Eileen sank down onto a chair. "I'd told him to clean them this morning but I hadn't realised that he thought they had to be boiled in a pot of water to be cleaned. Oh, I hope he hasn't ruined them! I don't have the money to buy new ones!"

Although I'd never been poor, I was beginning to get a pretty good idea of what it was like to be down and out and my heart went out to Eileen who, as usual, was dressed in one of her washed out and shapeless old shift dresses and wearing a pair of old scuffed black canvas shoes on her feet.

"Perhaps you caught him in time," I said hopefully, knowing that buying Eileen a new pair of canvas shoes would be last on the list of O'D's priorities.

"Oh, I hope so!" Eileen cried, still trembling from the shock of her discovery.

Luckily, Eileen's shoes survived their boiling and turned out to be undamaged. "You must never, NEVER, clean shoes by boiling them in a pot of water on the stove, Seven," she admonished him. "Do you understand?"

Downcast by the deep emotions he had aroused in the ample bosom of one of the women he worked for and by her loud and alarming reaction, a subdued Seven hung his head and replied "Yes, Meddem."

Although O'D and Chuck tried very hard to keep all the equipment under lock and key, things started disappearing. Losing our diesel and petrol to thieves was infuriating but it was the theft of their tools that caused the most anguish in O'D's and Chuck's hearts. Not only were all these screwdrivers and O'D's American Snap-on spanners expensive and impossible to replace in a country like Mozambique but they were also vital for the maintenance of our vehicles.

Larger items vanished into thin air too. Not long after my arrival, we discovered the brazen theft of one of the batteries for the brand new 180 kva Kohler generator that we hadn't even begun to use yet! Where were we going to find another of these batteries?

It didn't take much brainpower to work out who was responsible for all this criminal activity. We employed forty workers, most of whom appeared to be people without consciences and who thought that the only bad thing about stealing was … getting caught.

"You know what I think?" I asked O'D one afternoon after he had ranted over the disappearance of an expensive screwdriver David had given him for a present one Christmas.

"I have no idea what you think," O'D told me irritably.

"I think you should change your name. You should call yourself Ali Baba Pixley because you have Forty Thieves working for you."

O'D hadn't been at all amused by my suggestion. Apart from the fact that he and Chuck often had to resort to making their own home-made tools now, we were also losing quite a lot of money because of these thefts.

Questioning and threatening our workers with dire consequences if they didn't own up produced no results. They all looked at us with completely blank, expressionless faces, revealing no evidence of guilt or even a glimmer of remorse that they were stealing from the hand that was employing and feeding them.

134

Then one evening, even Mitzi disappeared!

Eileen was sitting in one of the old Morris chairs near the window, reading a book, when the gong struck half past four and work came to an end for the day. When Chuck came in from the workshop to wash his hands and to drink a refreshing cup of tea, he looked around the room and asked, "Where's Mitzi?"

"She was lying outside the front door, the last time I looked," Eileen replied.

"Well, she's not there now," Chuck told her.

Throwing down her book, Eileen hurriedly left her chair and rushed outside, Chuck following closely at her heels.

Although they looked all around the house, and then inside the house, Mitzi was nowhere to be seen. Becoming more and more distraught, they extended their search and with the help of Avelino, Pocas and Seven, they went further out, scouring the bushes and the long grass.

Dusk fell and when O'D returned from a fuel-buying trip to Chimoio, he joined in the hunt.

Stopping only for a bite to eat, the search went on but there was no familiar snuffling sound or even a stray paw print in the dusty ground to give us a clue as to what had caused the disappearance of a small Pekinese dog.

The hours ticked on until finally, towards ten o'clock, Chuck stopped shining his torch in the bushes and Eileen stopped calling her name. Like so many of our other things, Mitzi had vanished into thin air!

Eventually, Chuck and Eileen had their baths and went to bed and although they turned off their light, I'm sure that neither of them slept a wink that night ... because I never heard even the slightest snore coming from out of their room.

We woke up the next day to a lovely morning. High above us, two eagles rode on air currents in the pure blue sky of an African winter's day and somewhere to the east of us and not far from the house, baboons barked in the trees.

At roll call, O'D and Chuck questioned our workers about Mitzi, asking if they had seen or heard anything but they all shook their heads. Seven examined the long grass and bush around the house again and Alberto, the gardener, explored the area down by the dry Nhamacoa River, two hundred metres from the back of the house.

"Looking for Mitzi in this bush," O'D told me, "is like looking for a needle in a haystack."

As the day wore on, Eileen grew quieter and quieter and began to give in to her darker thoughts. At half past four when a worker struck the gong and Chuck came into the house for a wash and a cup of tea, she said, "Something terrible's happened to Mitzi. I can sense it, Chuck!"

"She'll turn up, old girl," Chuck said, trying to reassure her, "I'm sure she will," he repeated softly, trying to reassure himself as well. He gulped down some tea. "I'll go and have another look for her in a minute."

"The baboons ..." Eileen's face crumpled as she gave voice to the unthinkable and her worst fear of all "... the baboons may have torn her to pieces, Chuck." Tears welled up in her eyes and began to pour down her face like a rainstorm. She pulled a handkerchief out of a pocket in her dress and bowing her head, sobbed into it. "Torn her to pieces ... and eaten her ... oh, Mitzi ... Mitzi ... oh, my poor little Mitzi."

Supper, during Mitzi's second night of disappearance, was a gloomy affair. Chuck and Eileen barely ate anything, which for two people who loved their food so much, showed the extent of the anguish they were feeling at the loss of their beloved little dog.

We were drinking coffee when Chuck suddenly sat bolt upright in his chair.

"What is it, Chuck?" Eileen asked.

"Listen," he told her.

In the stillness of the night, we all listened and all we heard was the hooting of the owls and the high-pitched noise the cicadas were making in the long grass.

The next moment, Chuck leapt up from his chair and rushed out of the room.

Eileen looked after him, an expression of desperate hope in her red and swollen eyes. "Perhaps ..."

Within seconds, Chuck was back in the room, holding a small furry, orangey creature in his arms.

"Mitzi!" Eileen cried.

Mitzi snuffled happily at us.

Hardly able to believe the safe return of her little dog, Eileen jumped out of her chair and took Mitzi from Chuck, hugging her tightly to her chest and mingling tears and kisses onto the top of her head. "How did you know, Chuck?"

"I heard a faint noise which I thought sounded just like Mitzi and then when I went outside, there she was! Just sitting calmly only a few yards away from the front door."

Bending his head, he gave Mitzi's fur a couple of sniffs. "Someone kidnapped her alright," he told us. "She didn't just wander off by herself. There's a tell-tale smell about her. She smells all smoky as if she's been kept in a hut. Whoever took her must have had second thoughts about keeping her and sneaked up to the house while we were eating and left her near the door."

The thought of unknown people sneaking around a house such as ours, a house without windows or doors - and in the dark of night - wasn't a pleasant one.

"Who?" I wondered. "Who do you think snatched her, and why?"

"Oh, it was probably one of our workers," Chuck replied, "Probably someone working close to the house."

We never found out who had kidnapped Mitzi or why they had taken her. It was a mystery that remained a mystery.

After this experience, Eileen watched Mitzi like a hawk and when she went off to do something and didn't take Mitzi with her, she told Seven or Avelino (if he wasn't busy) to dog-sit and keep an eye on her.

One afternoon, when I was in the bathroom washing my hands in the enamel basin, I happened to look out of the window and caught sight of Avelino. He was standing in front of the ironing table in the shade of some mango trees and wielding the heavy old charcoal iron over a shirt … and there, as bold as brass, I saw a snuffling little Pekinese dog, sitting as unhygienically as ever - in the laundry basket, of all things - and on top of our newly washed clean clothes!

CHAPTER EIGHT

THE BEGINNING OF THE INVASION OF THE NHAMACOA

Although the blue Gaz performed well in the forest, working with only one vehicle was very limiting. Then, one day, Caetano heard that the Army needed some money and were going to raise funds by selling off some of their old vehicles. As one of these vehicles happened to be a Gaz – a green one, this time – and as O'D had become an ardent fan of these chunky little Russian lorries, he decided to buy it. It would help to push up our production.

Leaving Eileen, Mitzi and me behind in the Nhamacoa, O'D drove off early on a Saturday morning in the Land Rover, together with Chuck, Caetano, Avelino and Pocas to collect the other lorry. As it was in the port of Beira, a three and a half hour drive from the Nhamacoa, they would be away for the day.

In the forest, without workers to bother us, the time passed peacefully. Seven kept the fire going in the cook hut to heat the water and Eileen and I ate bread and cheese for lunch and spent the rest of the afternoon reading books.

When dusk fell, Eileen struck a match and carefully lit our three paraffin lamps, placing them strategically around the sitting room.

I pulled the black plastic blinds down over the glassless sitting room windows and anchored them onto the wide windowsills with several large stones. The blinds were useless at keeping people out but at least they stopped the bats from flying in.

"A little music?" Eileen asked.

"Why not," I said, and turned the radio on to Zimbabwe Radio One.

It was Eileen's sugar bean soup for supper, delicious with a couple of large dollops of Soya Sauce and a slice or two of bread and butter.

Sitting down at the table, we ate in the glow of lamplight. Two women and a Pekinese dog. In a forest in Mozambique.

"They're late," I said.

"It's a slow trip in that old Land Rover," Eileen reminded me.

The sound of drums floated through the trees, competing with Nat King Cole's lovely dark velvety voice on the radio. Boom boomboomboom... boom boomboomboom ...

"I hate those drums," Eileen muttered.

"Oh, why?" I asked.

"Because they're evil. They're calling up the spirits."

The rhythm of the drums reminded me of the old Western films I had seen years ago where Red Indians hopped around in a circle, gearing themselves up to attack wagon trains ... or remote homesteads ... moccasined feet sneaking around in the dark ...

A picture came into my mind, this time of a darker people, a barefoot people, sneaking around OUR house in the dark and looking for things to steal while O'D and Chuck were out of the way. A house with curtains for doors and black plastic for glass in the windows, not to mention the guard dog - a Pekinese who was so useless she had even allowed *herself* to be kidnapped!

"Aren't you afraid to be alone like this, especially at night, Eileen?"

Eileen looked up from her soup with surprise. "'Of course not," she said with a laugh. "It's only been a day and they'll probably be back any time now." She scooped up another spoonful of beans. "Once, while you were in South Africa, Chuck and O'D went off to get something and although they were only supposed to be away for a day and a night, they didn't come back for THREE days."

"Oh, how awful!" I said, imagining how I would have felt in her situation, left completely alone in the bush without money, without a phone or a car and not knowing what had happened to them. I would have disintegrated with fear, panicking and imagining all sorts of terrible things. "That must have been really worrying!"

"Oh, not at all," Eileen told me. "I knew they'd be back."

They didn't come back that night, so Eileen and I blew the flames out of the paraffin lamps and went to sleep with the black plastic blinds crackling and the curtain doors flapping in the breeze that always blows in the Nhamacoa.

They didn't come back in the morning either. Then, at about three o'clock in the afternoon, we heard the sound of a vehicle and leaned expectantly out of the east-facing sitting room window for a look down the forest track.

A dirty white 4 x 4 hurtled past us in a cloud of red dust and we caught a glimpse of several men crammed inside it. These were not men we knew and my heart gave a lurch. Bandits! I knew it ... I just KNEW it!

Seven ran behind the vehicle, to question and to interrogate its occupants. Oh, what could one young boy do to bandits?

Still leaning over the windowsill, we watched as Seven returned, bringing one of the men with him. The man was incredibly handsome and very light-skinned for a Mozambican. The reason for this, I knew, was because his grandfather had been a Belgian.

"Oh, hello Milton!" I greeted the Head of the dreaded Secret Police, and smiled the false smile we always give to those in Africa who hold the power of life and death over us.

I had met Milton during our Tabex farm days. Once, he had invited O'D and me to his house in Chimoio. Although the invitation had supposedly been for supper, it hadn't taken long for the real purpose of his hospitality to be revealed.

The evening had turned out to be rather bizarre, to say the least. After handing each of us a beer in his extremely over-furnished sitting room, Milton had waved a hand towards a table set only for two. "Eat! Eat!" he had commanded us. Obeying, we had sat down and helped ourselves to spaghetti and some kind of meat mixture and while we had eaten, Milton's heavily pregnant wife had joined us, and sitting down on a sofa, had retched agonizingly into a bucket.

During the meal, Milton had talked to O'D about a terrific money-spinning idea he had thought up - a partnership in a brothel in Chimoio!

Naturally enough, O'D had turned down Milton's offer but Milton had still managed to inveigle a 'loan' out of him.

Now, smiling a smile to match my own, Milton came towards us. Forgetting my name but a quick thinker on his feet as befitted a Secret Policeman he made up a title for me on the spur of the moment. "Aah, the Lady of the Forest!" he greeted me in return.

We all shook hands. "And where is your husband, O'D?" he asked me.

"He went to Beira," I told him.

"And they'll be coming back any minute now," Eileen informed him. "Any minute!"

"You shouldn't be here on your own," Milton told us sternly, "two women, with only one young boy to guard you."

"Oh, we're not afraid," Eileen said with a laugh and speaking for herself. "Nothing will happen to us!"

Milton's eyes took her in, wondering at her foolishness. He knew better than anyone what lay in mankind's heart and what it was capable of doing. After all, he was the head of a police department at the Cabeca Velha jail, a jail that had underground rooms for interrogating people.

"This is a very dangerous place," he told us and without giving us any explanation of his unexpected visit, turned to walk back to his 4 x 4. "You must get yourselves a proper guard - an armed guard."

From our position at the window, we watched the white 4 x 4 drive away, more slowly this time.

"That was funny," I said.

"Mmm," Eileen agreed, "the Head of the Secret Police ... now I wonder what they wanted."

"Well, whatever it is, at least we have nothing to fear from *them*," I informed her. "O'D loaned Milton some money about a year ago."

"Really? And how on earth did he manage to get O'D to do that?"

"Oh, he used a form of torture," I said, remembering Milton's wife throwing up while we ate.

"Hmm ..." Eileen said thoughtfully, "perhaps he came today because he wanted to pay the money back."

This time it was my turn to laugh. "Eileen, does it snow in the Kalahari?"

O'D and Chuck returned late that evening. There'd been a problem with the green Gaz. All the way back from Beira, it had stopped and started and as a result progress had been very slow.

"I don't think it's anything serious," Chuck told us. "The engine probably just needs a good clean and a bit of maintenance."

Chuck managed to get the green Gaz running well and with two lorries on the go, things began to look up.

Things began to look up in another direction too. Although cooking in the little cook hut had been fun for a while and a bit like being on a camping holiday, the effort of running up and down the kitchen stairs loaded down with pots and pans soon began to pall.

Then one evening, O'D came back from Chimoio with some news which sent both my spirits and Eileen's spiraling upwards with hope.

"I heard today that Biasse isn't working at Tabex anymore," he told us.

141

"Oh, has he been fired for breaking all their cups and saucers and plates?" I wanted to know.

"No," O'D said, "leaving Tabex was his own idea, apparently."

"Go and get him, O'D," I said, "before somebody else does!"

Biasse arrived a week later. He settled down well in the Nhamacoa and soon he and Seven were great friends, if you took into account all the talking and laughing that floated out from between the cook hut poles. The meals he produced were as tasty as ever and his culinary abilities seemed completely unaffected by the change from modern electric cooker to primitive mud-brick stove.

He hadn't been back with us for very long when I began to notice the unwelcome trickle of people into the Nhamacoa and to see for myself the start of the conflict between man and nature - and the devastating effect this was to have on both of them. Naturally enough, I was completely unaware that Biasse, my very own cook, was also playing a part in the deforestation of the Nhamacoa until the day I had a conversation with him about his family.

"This is very nice place, Madam," he told me enthusiastically one morning while he was preparing lunch. "Good for machamba!" He held up one of Alberto the gardener's large white cauliflowers, grown with water from the hole we had dug in the Nhamacoa River. "Maningui vegetables in your garden down by the river! Eeeeee! Good for mealies, too!"

"I'm glad you like it here, Biasse," I said, "but aren't you missing your family?"

"Ah, no, Madam," he told me cheerfully.

"Oh," I said, surprised to hear this from a man who was such a family man.

I soon found out why Biasse wasn't missing his family. The reason, it turned out, was because they were now all with him in the Nhamacoa!

Like so many other Mozambicans who were to come after him, he had met a man called Kashangamu and this man had sold him a piece of the forest.

"What!" I cried, aghast. "This is illegal, Biasse! This Kashangamu had no right to sell you land. The land belongs to the government. It's a forest. People aren't allowed to open machambas in forests!"

Biasse was unfazed. "It is land of Kashangamu, Madam," he explained. "Father of Kashangamu worked for Magalhaes.

142

Magalhaes give to Kashangamu when he leave this place before the guerra."

"Nonsense, Biasse! This forest never belonged to Magalhaes, so he couldn't have given land to Kashangamu's father. This man Kashangamu is just tricking you!"

Although money had changed hands, there had been no Deed of Sale or even a receipt from Kashangamu to record the purchase of the land by Biasse. However, this didn't worry Biasse in the least. As far as he was concerned, the land he had bought in the Nhamacoa from Kashangamu belonged to him.

While Biasse worked for us, his family worked on their newly acquired land. They built rudimentary huts out of poles and grass for themselves and chopped down trees, clearing the land to make it ready for the growing of maize when the rains came ... if the rains came ...

Almost three years had gone by since the start of the drought and there was still no hint of a break. Sometimes, a violent wind blew up and whipped across the forest. It ripped off parts of our grass roof and dislodged the rocks holding the black plastic down over our windows. With the wind came a rainstorm. A furious downpour of a rainstorm, bursting in through the holes in the roof and the walls and flooding all the rooms in our broken down house, while we rushed around, moving soaked bedding and wet furniture and books to safer and drier places. As quickly as it came, the wind and storm would disappear, leaving clear blue skies and the baking sunshine that turned the earth into cracks and dust.

Without rain or water in the rivers and dams, food was very, very scarce and so, during his fuel buying trips, O'D regularly scoured the Chimoio shops for sacks of maize meal for our workers and their families.

The maize he managed to buy from the shops in town was always stamped on the outside of the sacks with large black letters that read 'U.S. AID – NOT FOR SALE'. From this we deduced that somewhere along the line, someone was diverting American food aid to Mozambique – or to Zimbabwe – off the ships at the Ports and making a healthy profit by selling it to the shops. Shop owners took their cut too and, as usual, those who needed Western charity most of all were made to pay for it by their own venal and profiteering countrymen. So much for brotherly love in times of trouble!

Despite the lack of rain, the trickle of people coming into the Nhamacoa to open machambas continued. In the evenings and at night when I looked out of the windows and dazzled my eyes with the beauty of the starry skies of Africa, I often saw another more alarming sight as well. Fire! The red glow of fires mushrooming in the distant leafy hills and valleys of the Nhamacoa. Fires started by the people invading the forest.

Lying on my camp bed, I worried about these fires. I had seen how quickly grass burnt and we were surrounded by the stuff. And even worse, our roof was made out of grass! If a spark blew onto our roof and set it alight, would we wake up in time to save ourselves from the flaming, falling thatch?

While I lay awake, waiting for an ominous warning crackle or two, I marvelled at the sounds that filled the night. How busy the forest was after the sun had gone down!

Night apes screeched against the high-pitched background of a vast orchestra of cicadas. Owls hooted. Something made a grunting noise like a giant prehistoric pig. Something else, which I later discovered was a buck, gave a breathy warning BWAH! BWAH! A night bird joined in with its lovely bubbling call. And then there were the drums … always the drums.

Living like this in the forest and under such primitive conditions, I sometimes had the weird sensation that I had somehow flipped back in time and was living in the 1890's instead of the 1990's! It was as if I was reliving the life my ancestors had lived all those centuries ago when they had first sailed to Africa and settled in a continent that was alien to them in every way.

One morning, at about half past eleven, the grass just below the hill where we were living started to crackle.

A strong wind was blowing that day and the vegetation, of course, was tinder-dry from years of drought.

Fanned by the wind, the fire spread quickly and in no time at all we were enveloped in smoke so thick we could hardly breathe.

Tears streaming from their smarting eyes, O'D and Chuck ran from place to place, shouting orders to our workers, "Back burn! Back burn!" and they started fires of our own and burnt the land in front of the approaching fire in an attempt to stop it in its tracks.

I was standing not far from the house, mopping my own streaming eyes and watching the fire coming towards us, when I noticed a commotion going on above a tree directly in the path of the oncoming inferno. The tree was a thorn tree and its branches were weighed down with nests filled with newly hatched little weavers.

A small tragedy was about to occur, the first of the many little tragedies I would be witnessing during my years in the Nhamacoa.

Knowing what was going to happen and helpless to prevent it, a great cloud of the parent weavers circled frantically around and around over the top of the thorn tree, crying out their alarm. Too young to fly, the young hatchlings were going to be incinerated!

"No! Oh no!" I shouted, adding my own cries to those of the weavers as the fire roared towards the tree.

Only at the last minute, did the parent weavers stop their frantic circling over the thorn tree. When the fire reached the tree and its leaves began to catch alight, they knew it was all over. Flying off to another nearby tree, they settled down on its branches to watch.

They watched as the fire engulfed the tree and they watched as it consumed their nests and they watched as the little birds inside the nests were burnt to death.

And then, when it was over, they all rose up in a great cloud again and flew away, to the west. And to this day, fourteen years later, I have never again seen this particular type of weaver build a nest here in the Nhamacoa.

Despite our efforts to contain the fire, it spread. No sooner did we manage to stop it in one place, than it broke out in another. Soon, it encircled us on all sides. Caught in the middle of this hellish inferno, everyone tore small branches off the nearby trees and desperately beat at the flames.

"The rabbits!" Chuck shouted. "The fire's coming up towards the back of the house now! The hutches are going to go up!"

While they were beating out the flames around the rabbit hutches, one of the workers also suddenly remembered something. "A crianca!" he shouted, "The child!" A little boy of about three or four years old, left by himself in a hut not far from the river!

"That's it!" White in the face with fury, O'D threw down his branch and ran over to the Land Rover and jumped inside.

"What are you doing?" I shouted.

"I'm going to Macate to fetch the police!"

"It's not safe! You'll get burned!"

Without answering, O'D put his foot down and drove off down the track, disappearing into the smoke.

By the time he returned with two Macate policemen and the Chefe do Posto, a short and stocky man called Sainete, the fire had moved on, roaring over other hills and through other valleys, leaving us surrounded by charred and smoking blackness.

While the rabbits and the young boy had been saved, the roof of one of the houses we'd been in the process of repairing had been completely destroyed. Some off our workers' huts had also gone up in flames, causing them to lose the few possessions they owned. In a country that had nothing, even the loss of an old blanket, a tattered shirt, a pair of trousers was hard to bear.

"Kashangamu," one of our workers told the policemen. "The wives of Kashangamu are opening a machamba and they started the fire."

I pricked up my ears. Kashangamu … I knew that name. Biasse's estate agent!

"Ask him to come here," one of the policemen told the worker.

Kashangamu, it turned out, was not only the local Renamo representative in the area but also an important tribal chief and this probably explained why he appeared unperturbed by the presence of the Macate police. On good terms with them, he chatted away amiably, unrepentant about the damage his two careless wives had caused. After all, no one had died, had they? As for compensation … he gave a shrug …what did he have to give?

While O'D stood by, glowering and furious at the lack of concern the Mozambicans were showing about the damage the fire had wrought, Sainete also chatted away amiably with Chuck. Conversing in Shona, they talked about a subject close to both their hearts; chickens, ducks and goats.

"A goat …" Chuck's pale blue eyes lit up at Sainete's offer of the gift of one of his male goats. Unaware of the impact the animal was going to have on his future, he clapped Sainete on the shoulder. "I'll come and collect it from you the next time we fill up with water in Macate," he said and they both laughed happily.

The goat, when it came, had a dark, silky brown coat. He lived in the room under the house with the chickens, of course, and during the day left a trail of goat pellets all around the house. I noticed this when I sat down outside on the old paving to read a book and saw all the goat droppings under my feet … hundreds and hundreds of them … gosh, how much more unhygienic could Chuck get!

I was soon to discover just how much more unhygienic he could get.

One morning while we were eating breakfast, Chuck rubbed his stubbly chin thoughtfully and said "You know, I've been thinking. There's not much point in having just one goat. The next time I'm in Macate, I'm going to ask Sainete to sell me another one of his goats … a female, this time."

O'D looked up from his paw paw with a frown. "In that case, you'd better organise a pen for all your animals, Chuck. And don't forget to do something about those chickens of yours as well. I'm fed up with being woken up at three o'clock in the morning with cocks crowing on top of the roof."

And so Chuck added another animal to his growing menagerie and as he never got around to building a pen for the goats or a coop for his chickens, the manure around our house grew and grew.

CHAPTER NINE

CAETANO AND MR. GONCALVES, THE WITCH DOCTOR

"Aaah ... beautiful," Chuck said, with a sigh of contentment. Without taking his eyes off the sky, he drained the tea in his cup and set it down on the small Umbila coffee table he had made at Matsinho. The top of the table was the off-cut of a plank and the base was part of a log. "This is just like watching television, only a million times better."

"Yes," Eileen agreed and picked up the teapot to give Chuck's cup a refill. "And unlike television, there are no repeats. You can look at the sky every evening and never see the same sunset." She glanced down at her wristwatch. "Shall we turn the radio on? It's almost time."

We only listened to the radio now for one hour every evening, when Zimbabwe Radio One broadcast its music programme and the news. This was to conserve batteries. Our fortunes had suddenly taken a nose-dive and money had become extremely tight.

Sometime during the summer, Socinav, our one and only customer had unexpectedly disappeared! There were rumours that they had gone to the Cameroon or the Congo but wherever it was, their departure had left a large financial void in our lives. Timber buyers, as we had found to our dismay, were thin on the ground in Mozambique.

While O'D and Caetano searched for another customer, our money dwindled away and our debts piled up. We denied ourselves so we could pay the workers their wages every month and buy fuel for the tractor and lorries to keep things going.

Faruk, O'D's Indian friend, gave us limitless credit to buy the things we needed from his shop in Chimoio – more debt! – and we bought dried beans, rice, a chicken or two, salt, cooking oil, bath soap, toothpaste and shampoo.

We scraped along for what seemed like an eternity, deprivation begining to take its toll on all of us.

Still keeping his eyes glued on the sky, Chuck leaned back in his chair. "It would be a pity to break up this panoramic view with windows and glass again," he said thoughtfully. "I think we should leave it as it is."

While Eric Clapton sang a song on the radio telling us how he had shot the Sheriff, I gloomily surveyed the long wide hole in the sitting room's west wall. "The way things are going, we'll probably never have the money to buy glass for the windows."

"Oh, things could change," Chuck said, and remembering the terrible time when he and Eileen had lived on a handful of sadza a day, added reassuringly "anyway, whatever happens, I'll stick by O'D. I'll never forget how he helped us out when we were starving at Matsinho."

"Yes," Eileen agreed again, "we won't let O'D down now that things are going wrong for him, and at least we're not starving here, what with Alberto's vegetables and all the bananas, guavas and paw paws from the trees around the house."

"If only we had the money to buy a borehole pump," Chuck said, "then we could use the saw to turn the logs into planks. Planks are a much more saleable item. But planking's out of the question, because without a continuous supply of water to cool the saw blade, it will overheat."

"I know," I sighed. "Oh, why are there all these stumbling blocks and hindrances always stopping us from going ahead?"

A mysterious smile lit up Eileen's face. "Well," she said, "why don't we find out?" She heaved herself out of her chair and stood up. "I know just the right person to ask. Penny!"

Eileen went off to her bedroom to collect Penny and returned, carrying a white, pink-tinged crystal attached to a silver chain.

"Let's sit down at the table," she told me. "It'll be easier."

Eileen's relationship with Penny the Pendulum was a curious one. To her, the pendant was not just a little lump of rock and a length of metal chain, but it had a persona of its own, a feminine one, as well as being imbued with a kind of supernatural intelligence.

Leaning her right elbow on the table, she held the end of the chain up in the air between her thumb and forefinger so that the crystal was suspended over the table. "She answers questions with a 'yes' and a 'no'," Eileen explained to me. "When she swings around in a circle, it means 'yes' and when she swings backwards and forwards, it means 'no'. Now, are you ready?"

Not sure to whom Eileen was speaking, me or the pendant, I said "Mm."

"Right," Eileen said, "lets begin." She cleared her throat, "Hm, hm," and greeted the pendant politely, "Good evening, Penny. We'd like to ask you some questions and we'd be very glad if you'll give us some answers."

Penny appeared to quiver slightly on her chain in response.

"Good," Eileen said, and then, in a trembly voice, asked a question that surprised me. "Is O'D a good man?"

Penny thought about this for a while and then began to move around in a slow circle.

"She says yes," Eileen told me unnecessarily and gently stopped Penny's progress with her left hand, in preparation for her next question.

"Is Caetano a good man?"

The ridiculous nature of these questions had an unfortunate effect on me. A laugh threatened to burst out of my chest and before I could curb it, transformed itself into a smile that bloomed all over my face. Eileen noticed and gave me a look from narrowed, witchy looking eyes.

In answer, Penny began to swing around in another circle

"Alright," Eileen said, "now that we've got that out of the way," she gave me another look, "we can get on to the important things."

Penny told us several things in the next few minutes and when it came to the most important question of all as to whether or not we were going to make a success of the business, she was more than enthusiastic. Flying around in wide and exuberant circles, she assured us that by the end of October we would be on our way to riches!

Towards the end of October, things were no better and we were still held fast in the grip of our financial doldrums. Penny the Pendulum's ability to predict the future, it was obvious, was a dubious one.

"I can't understand it," Eileen said, "she's never been wrong before!"

Why we couldn't get on our feet was a mystery to all of us … with one exception, of course …

One morning, while we were eating a breakfast of toast and margarine and drinking coffee of an extremely fluffy and inferior type, we heard the sound of a familiar voice. It was a very distinctive voice and it was a voice that made you want to laugh when you heard it. It was speaking Portuguese very, very fast and the faster it spoke, the higher it rose until it sounded just like the voice of Speedy Gonzales, the Mexican cartoon mouse I used to watch on television decades ago when I was young.

"Caetano's here," I said, "and he's upset or excited about something."

We always looked forward to Caetano's visits and to seeing his happy, cheerful face. Nothing ever seemed to get him down and his optimism always raised our dented spirits. Now, however, even he seemed worried.

As he always did before coming inside the house, Caetano removed his dusty and broken size twelve shoes and left them outside before joining us in the sitting room. Sweating from his trip to the sawmill in the open back of a battered chappacem (taxi pickup) and then the six kilometre walk down the forest track, he sat down on a chair at the table and gratefully accepted a large glass filled with Mazoe Orange Juice.

"We must bring a witch doctor to the sawmill as soon as possible," he told us. "We need to find out why we're having all this terrible luck."

Eileen looked up from her toast. "Well, I hope you can find a real one this time, Caetano. I'm sure the one who held that ceremony here last year was a fake, tricking us into giving him a goat and all that alcohol."

Caetano nodded his head slowly. "Perhaps that's why we're having problems," he said. "Perhaps it's something to do with that ceremony …" an expression of fear flitted across his face "… perhaps, instead of placating the Spirit of this place, we offended it!"

Although he'd been baptised into the Roman Catholic faith, like many of his countrymen Caetano was still held captive by his culture and the things Mozambicans believed in. Things like witch doctors and evil spirits and the magical powers that animals could pass on to humans.

Once, when he and O'D had been driving around Guro (they travelled around a lot together and were soon to become as inseparable as twins), Caetano had become terribly excited when he had noticed a certain substance which had been deposited on the ground by one of Africa's largest animals.

"Stop! Stop! Stop the car!" he had shouted urgently at O'D. Thinking Caetano had spotted trouble, O'D had braked hurriedly. He'd been a bit puzzled when Caetano had jumped out of the vehicle, grabbed a hessian sack out of the open back and then loped off to the side of the road towards an enormous mound of what looked like dung. There, he'd bent down and had started shovelling it into the bag.

Returning to the car, Caetano had thrown the sack into the open back again. "Elephant dung!" he had explained to O'D with a great big grin all over his face. "I'm going to mix this with Denis' bathwater (Denis was his five year old son) and then he'll grow up as strong and as powerful as an elephant!"

Another time, in the Nhamacoa, when O'D had obliviously driven over a puff-adder not far from our front door and squashed it as flat as a pancake under his tyres, Caetano had been overcome by this stroke of good luck. Like his fellow Mozambicans, he firmly believed that if you find a snake in your house or your garden, someone who wished to harm you had sent it there.

"I wonder which of your enemies sent this snake to you?" Caetano, the Mozambican, had pondered. "Could it be Ataide in Machaze … or is it someone we don't even know about?"

"No one sent this snake, Caetano," O'D, the Englishman, had replied. "We're bound to get snakes around us. After all, we are living in a forest."

"That's the difference between Africans and Europeans," Caetano had mused. "To you, a snake is just a snake. To us, it's a deadly weapon sent to harm us by an enemy."

Caetano believed that witch doctors could make lightning crackle in a clear, cloudless blue sky and send lightning bolts straight into the houses of your enemies, frizzling them to death.

Caetano believed that witch doctors could put curses on people you hated and make them die and that they could call up spirits to visit you in your sleep to give you horrible dreams.

Caetano believed that a certain witch doctor at Dombe could even make you immune to bullets … by boiling you in a drum of water into which a magical potion had been mixed.

I'm sorry to say that when we had heard this last fantastical claim, O'D and I just hadn't been able to keep a straight face and had both burst out laughing uproariously at the pictures his words had conjured up in our minds.

"I wouldn't like to try this out for myself, Caetano," O'D, who liked to try out almost anything, had laughed.

"It's true!" Caetano had insisted, quite put out by our reaction.

152

It had been the Mozambican belief that spirits live in rivers, in mountains, in valleys and forests, that had made Caetano tell us we had to hold a ceremony at the old Magalhaes sawmill before Chuck could even begin to do any work there.

"If we do anything … ANYTHING AT ALL … without asking permission from the Spirit of the place … the Spirit of the Nhamacoa …" Caetano had warned O'D ominously, "we will have nothing but bad luck!"

Respectful of Caetano's culture and knowing that he wouldn't rest easy without a ceremony, O'D had agreed. "Alright, Caetano. Arrange it."

However, as the ceremony hadn't exactly turned out as Caetano had anticipated, it seemed we were now going to have to arrange another.

The witch doctor Caetano found this time to bring down to the sawmill was an extremely powerful witch doctor. His name was Mr. Goncalves and he had agreed to come down to the Nhamacoa on Sunday at twelve o'clock. O'D would have to collect him from Chimoio, of course, as he had no transport.

Biasse was not at all pleased when I told him to prepare a larger than usual Sunday meal of fried chicken, chips and salad for visitors that included a witch doctor.

His wrinkled face turned grim. "Witch doctor no good, Madam."

"He might be able to fix your back, Biasse." Biasse had been suffering a lot from backache.

Biasse's little figure stiffened at the thought of being touched by such a person. "Ah! No, Madam!"

"But this is your culture, Biasse. Don't you all go to witch doctors when you're sick?"

"Is not my culture, Madam," he told me proudly. "I Christian! Witch doctors are very bad men, very very bad! Kill people! My Church tell me never to go to witch doctor!"

Shortly before midday on Sunday, O'D arrived back at the sawmill in the Land Rover with Caetano and our visitors. Accompanying the witch doctor was a woman who turned out to be Mr. Goncalves' wife. Everyone came inside the house and we all settled down around the table in the sitting room.

While our visitors relaxed after their jolting, bone-rattling drive down to the Nhamacoa, I examined Mr. Goncalves. I had never met a witch doctor before and had expected him to look out of the ordinary and different from the rest of us. However, there was no aura of evil surrounding him that I could make out and he seemed a nice enough person, softly spoken and neatly dressed in a white open necked shirt and brown trousers. No, there was nothing at all in his small, lean physique or in his manner that gave even a hint that he was a witch doctor.

"Would you like to eat lunch now, Mr. Goncalves?" O'D asked.

Mr. Goncalves shook his head. "No, but I would like a little wine to drink."

As Caetano had told us Mr. Goncalves had requested red wine for the event, we had used some of our dwindling funds to buy a bottle. O'D opened the bottle but before he could pour more than three small mouthfuls into Mr. Goncalves' glass, the witch doctor held up a hand and stopped him. "It is enough," he said.

Closing his eyes, Mr. Goncalves drank down the wine in his glass.

He sat still in his chair for a few minutes, while we all watched him in silence and then he stood up. He picked up a small bag he had brought with him and walked over to a corner of the sitting room, near the east facing windows. Then he began to take off his clothes.

He slipped off his shoes and shrugged off his shirt. He unbuttoned his belt and stepped out of his trousers.

Clad only in a pair of black shorts, Mr. Goncalves opened his bag and pulled out a large square of black cloth. Spreading this out on the floor, he knelt down on it and began to prepare himself. He tied a thin white bandana around his forehead and wound a python skin around his waist. He opened a small pouch and, as if he was playing a game of dice, threw small stones across the cloth.

Then he closed his eyes and while he knelt there on the cloth, his wife leaned over him.

Mr. Goncalves had disappeared and in his place was the very powerful witch doctor Caetano had found.

As I examined his light brown and fine featured face closely for any trace of fakery, the witch doctor gave a convulsive jerk, and then another, as he went into a deep trance ... deeper ... and deeper ... and then he began to speak, calling up the spirit of the Nhamacoa.

It was a hot, still October afternoon, with not even a hint of a breeze but suddenly there was a small, strong gust of wind and out of nowhere a dust devil rose up out of the ground not far from the house and danced and whirled towards the window. Grains of sand blew into the room and sprinkled down on us all, onto our hair, onto our faces and onto our bare arms, almost as if we were being baptised.

Was this the spirit of the Nhamacoa, coming in the form of a dust devil? Feeling a little uneasy that a spirit might perhaps have touched me, I looked around at the others and raised my eyebrows. They ignored me.

The witch doctor's conversation with the spirit was a complicated one. For some reason, the spirit of the Nhamacoa only spoke Zulu and it was this language that came out of Mr. Goncalves' mouth in his entranced state. As none of us, naturally, understood Zulu, this was where Mrs. Goncalves came in, translating the Zulu into Shona for Caetano. Caetano then had to translate the Shona into Portuguese for O'D.

The spirit of the Nhamacoa was more than ready to tell us what was wrong. When words began to tumble out of the witch doctor's mouth in an aggrieved torrent, I leaned over towards O'D and whispered "What's he saying," Caetano's Portuguese was much too fast for me to understand.

"He's complaining about the ceremony we held here last year," O'D told me in a low voice, confirming Caetano's fears.

Suddenly, the tone of the witch doctor's voice changed. The volume increased alarmingly and the spirit now began to speak angrily … and accusingly …

Caetano gave a great start at its words. His eyes bulged out of his head with fear and tiny droplets of sweat popped out on his forehead.

"What's he saying?" I asked O'D in another whisper.

"The spirit's castigating Caetano," O'D muttered back at me "and blaming HIM for neglecting to see that the ceremony had been properly conducted ... no respect ... no one had shown him any respect ...offering him nothing at the ceremony … everyone eating everything ... drunk ... without giving a thought to him".

Leaving Caetano sitting limp and crushed in his chair, the spirit began to talk about something else that was on his mind. This time, it was Chuck's turn to give a violent start, his turn for his eyes to bulge out of his head with fear and little beads of sweat to pop out on his forehead!

I leaned over towards O'D. "What's he say …"

"SShh!" O'D told me. "Apparently Chuck's got a curse on him."

I leaned back in my chair and glared at Chuck. A curse! It was just like Chuck to come to us, bringing a curse with himself and not telling anybody about it. It was no wonder we were in such a fix!

Chuck raised a hand and nervously fingered a thin strip of leather around his neck. I had never noticed this before but now I saw that there was something attached to the leather, like a kind of amulet.

"He says Chuck brought this curse on himself," O'D told me, "by cheating and lying to Nelson who retaliated by going to a witch doctor at Matsinho. That thing he's wearing around his neck isn't strong enough to ward off the evil. He needs something much more powerful."

The spirit of the Nhamacoa talked to Mr. Goncalves for a very long time. Trapped in my chair, my eyes glazed over and I stopped listening and asking questions. Instead, little pictures began to form in my mind ... little pictures of golden, crispy chicken legs ... scrumptious chips as only Biasse could make them ... tomatoes sweetly ripened in the sun ...

Activated by my thoughts, my stomach gave a loud growl. I glanced at the clock on the wall. Four o'clock! No wonder my stomach was grumbling. It had had nothing but a slice of toast and margarine all day!

I wondered what the spirit would think if I disappeared downstairs into the cook hut? Would there be more bad luck?

When my hollow stomach gave another protesting growl, I stood up slowly and slipped out of the room.

Downstairs in the cook hut, Biasse was nowhere to be seen, but there, on the worktop was a large platter, piled high with golden pieces of fried chicken just waiting to be devoured.

I was ravenously eating my second chicken leg when a dumpy shadow fell across the doorway of the cook hut.

"I thought this was where you were going when you slipped out," Eileen said, grabbing a plate, "so I thought I'd join you. I'm so hungry, I feel quite faint!"

By the time Eileen and I had finished eating, the scene inside the house had changed. When we guiltily crept up the back stairs, we found Mr. Goncalves now busy cleaning our house. Still on his knees and using an imaginary little broom, he was making his way around the sitting room, sweeping 'bad spirits' out of the room before him.

156

Not knowing what to do, we all trailed behind him in a line, stopping every now and then when he found a particularly recalcitrant 'bad spirit' and had to attack it more vigorously with his invisible little broom.

Although it would have been a painful thing for most of us to travel across cement floors on our bare knees, Mr. Goncalves didn't seem to feel a thing. He made his way down the corridor … sweeping, sweeping … all around Chuck and Eileen's bedroom … sweeping, sweeping … and then into ours. The bathroom was next and then after a quick trip around the broken kitchen, he made his way out of the front door, still brushing away and now going down the old cement paving next to the house, until with a final flourish of his imaginery broom, he swept everything away into the air.

When Mr. Goncalves finally stood up, I gave an inward sigh of relief. It was over at last and we had come to the end of a very long day. But … oh, no! … it was not the end after all!

Going back into the house, Mr. Goncalves gathered together some little white pouches. These had the power to stop evil people from coming into your property, and walking normally on his feet again, he went from entrance to entrance around the sawmill and buried them.

In a hurry to get home to Chimoio now, Mr. Goncalves declined O'D's offer of food. This was just as well. After our visit to the cook hut, Eileen and I had left barely enough chicken for anyone!

It was only later that I realised that none of us had given a thought to holding a second ceremony to placate the spirit and we had also done exactly what the fake witch doctor and his people had done, eating almost everything and finishing off the wine.

In Africa, Africans take spirits and witch doctors seriously. O'D and I did not take them seriously. And that may … or may not … have had something to do with what was to happen to us some years later.

CHAPTER TEN

ANIMAL FARM

Soon after Mr. Goncalves' visit, our fortunes changed again when Empacol, another customer, arrived on the scene. Of course, this had nothing to do with the witch doctor and was probably the reason why none of us gave even a passing thought to arranging a second Mozambican 'good luck' ceremony.

Empacol was a Mozambican sawmill in the port of Beira and although they didn't pay as much as Socinave had paid us, we were spared the expense and extra work of transporting our logs to the Chimoio railway station and loading the timber onto trains. This was because Empacol sent their own transport in the form of ancient Mercedes Benz 20 ton lorries to collect our logs from the Nhamacoa and to laboriously drive them back down to Beira.

The relief we felt at the slight easing of our financial problems didn't last long. About a month after the witch doctor's visit, trouble reared its head in a new, but not unexpected, direction. While all of Chuck's animals were living free range lives, the four of us were kept cooped up in one small, broken down Portuguese house and our personalities began to clash in earnest.

One morning, Chuck returned from a water-collecting trip in Macate with two ducks.

"Ducks ..." I gave an inward groan. As well as the chickens and the goats and all their droppings, we were now going to have duck droppings as well!

"Where are you going to keep these ducks, Chuck?" I wanted to know.

"Oh, they'll have to sleep downstairs until I have time to build a pen," Chuck said.

"That room's already full to over-flowing with animals," I said, feeling myself beginning to fume and hearing my voice beginning to rise.

"I've just TOLD you, " Chuck said, his voice also beginning to rise "that I'll build a pen WHEN I HAVE THE TIME!"

Before you could even say 'Hey Presto!" the female duck had produced eggs and, fluffing out her feathers, sat down on them to keep them warm. Not long after this, the eggs hatched and several cute and fluffy little yellow ducklings emerged from their shells.

When the ducklings were about two weeks old, Chuck went downstairs one evening to check on them and to his horror, discovered that they were covered in ants. He cleaned off all the ants and putting the ducklings into a cardboard box with their mother, carried them up into the house.

"No!" I shouted furiously, outraged beyond measure by Chuck's continued and complete disregard of O'D's instructions concerning his animals. Not only had he made no effort to build a goat pen or coops for the chickens, he was now bringing animals into the house itself! "NO, I will NOT have ducks in the HOUSE, Chuck!"

Outraged in his turn at my hard heartedness, Chuck shouted furiously back at me. "They're being EATEN by ANTS downstairs! What do you expect me to DO?"

The ducks spent the night in Chuck and Eileen's bedroom and the next morning, Chuck poured old diesel down the ant holes.

Out of their cardboard box and downstairs again, the ducklings kept close to their mother as she moved around, pecking at insects on the ground.

Eileen bent down and picked up one of the fluffy little creatures. "Oh, Chuck," she exclaimed, cuddling the duckling under her chin, "aren't they lovely? Aren't they sweet? They're going to need water, you know. We must build a little duck pond for them, right here in front of their room."

The female goat Chuck had bought from Sainete had not only thrilled Chuck and Eileen but had thrilled the male goat as well and soon the consequences of Sainete's gift to Chuck became apparent.

The female goat became pregnant and produced two small goats and Chuck and Eileen were as excited as new parents. They brought the mother and her children to live under our house with the chickens and the ducks, a 'temporary' measure Chuck told me, while the male stayed in the pen O'D had finally ordered the workers to build for Chuck's goats.

The male goat didn't take to being separated from his family. Lonely on his own, he often found ways to escape out of his enclosure and galloping after the female goat, chased her around and around the house.

And like a thick carpet, millions of round brown goat pellets joined the chicken and duck droppings in the room under our house and around our house. We were more like a guano manufacturing factory now than a sawmill.

"This is disgusting," I complained to O'D. "We can't even walk around the house without being ankle-deep in animal manure!"

"I've had enough of this, Chuck," O'D told him. "Get some workers to make a coop for the chickens and ducks at the other end of the sawmill and make a separate pen for the female and the small goats."

Towards the end of the year, the strain of living together with our conflicting ideas about hygiene and animals became too much. Chuck and Eileen's sloppiness really, really irritated me and my preoccupation with germs and cleanliness upset them and tired them out. When the end came, it came quickly.

One Friday morning, after O'D had driven off to Chimoio in the Land Rover, Chuck, Eileen and I lingered on at the breakfast table. We talked about growing indigenous trees and how we'd been unable to get any of the Umbila seeds we had collected to germinate. Then the conversation moved on to the Jacaranda, that gorgeous purple-blossomed tree found in so many towns all over Southern Africa.

"Is that an indigenous tree, Chuck?" Eileen asked.

"Yes, it is," he told her through the mouthful of margarined toast he had crammed into his mouth.

"No, Chuck," I interrupted, "I'm sure it's not indigenous. Isn't the Jacaranda a South American tree, brought to Africa by the Portuguese from Brazil?"

Eileen gave me a cold look, annoyed that I was disputing Chuck's knowledge of Africa and the bush. "Oh, I'm sure Chuck knows what he's talking about, Val."

I pushed back my chair and stood up. "Oh well," I said, "I'm off to wash my hair, so if you want to use the bathroom, you'd better tell me now."

"No, you go ahead," Eileen replied, "we're still eating."

In the bathroom, I pulled the curtains shut. I removed the top from my bottle of shampoo and poured cold water from a large bathroom container into an enamel washbowl. When I put the container down, I stared at the water in the bowl. It had always been quite clear but today the colour was different. Today it was a strange pale biscuit colour. I remembered that the night before Chuck had mentioned that the water from the hole in the riverbed had been a bit dirty and for a moment I hesitated. Did I really want to wash my hair in water like this? Oh, it's only river water, I told myself and making up my mind, plunged my head into the bowl.

Immediately, a foul stench rose up out of the bowl and into my nostrils … the kind of stench you'd smell if a rat had fallen into the water and died and decayed in it.

"Aaaargh!" I gave a scream of horror and disgust and pulled my head out of the revolting liquid. Grabbing a towel, I wrapped it turban-style over my now vile, stinking, tresses and rushed down the corridor.

At the breakfast table, Chuck and Eileen were still placidly munching on toast when I burst into the room.

"This river water is absolutely stinking, Chuck!" I cried. "We can't use it. It must be thrown away at once. I can't wash my hair with anything like this!"

Chuck looked thoughtful. "Did you use the water from the white container or the yellow one?" he asked.

"The white one," I told him. "And the water's revolting! Fetid!"

"That's not river water," he told me. He took another bite out of his toast.

"Not …"

"It's the water the washermen used to wash our dirty clothes. To save water, I told them to pour it into the white container so that we can use it in the lavatory."

A foul dribble of water escaped out of my towel and ran down my face and neck. I mopped it up with one end of the towel. "Why didn't you tell me?"

Like most men who are confronted by an angry woman and know they're in the wrong, Chuck's eyes turned shifty. He chewed on, trying to get his brain to come up with a suitable excuse to exonerate himself from being the cause of making a woman's crowning glory smell like a garbage dump … and failed.

"I TOLD you I was going to wash my hair," I went on, my voice rising with outrage, "and you didn't say anything. And I went and saturated my hair with filthy, stinking water that was used to wash people's DIRTY SWEATY SOCKS … AND UNDERPANTS … AND …OOUUUGH!"

I stomped out of the room and went into the kitchen. Grabbing hold of a container of the clean and precious Macate water we only used for cooking and tea and coffee, I dragged it noisily along the floor, down the corridor and into the bathroom.

I rinsed and rinsed my hair and then I shampooed it. I scrubbed my scalp, washed my face and neck and rinsed my hair over and over again. By the time I was finished, I had used up a whole 20 litres of valuable clean water. But I didn't care.

Then, a few days later on Sunday, something else happened which caused even more friction between us all.

While Caetano and O'D were busy loading some equipment onto the blue Gaz with the help of a few workers, Chuck's male goat escaped from his enclosure and came chasing after the female goat. Like mad things, they galloped frenziedly around and around the lorry, blaring and crashing into equipment and getting in everyone's way.

Suddenly, O'D cracked.

Aptly describing the animal's character in a fierce, taut voice, he said "I've had enough of this fucking goat!"

He turned to the workers. "Go and catch that goat and tie it up on top of the lorry. I'm giving it to Caetano."

Eileen and I had been standing nearby and now she began to cry. Tears streaming down her face, she rushed over to the workshop in a stumbling run and shouted "Chuck! Chuck! Come quickly! O'D's giving our goat to Caetano! He's got no right! It's OUR goat!"

Chuck came out of the workshop, wiping his oily black hands on an oily black rag. "What the bloody hell do you think you're doing, upsetting Eileen like this?" he shouted at O'D.

O'D went white with fury.

"This is MY sawmill," he shouted, "and you work for ME, not the other way round! I've asked you over and over again to keep that goat penned up and out of my way but you won't listen. You NEVER listen! If you can't understand this and won't do what I ask, you and Eileen can pack your bags and get out of here right now!"

When O'D stopped shouting, there was a dead silence that was broken only by loud blaring bleats from the male goat, now protesting about being tied up on the lorry and struggling to free itself.

Eileen was the first to make a move. She turned away from us and ran back to the house, sobbing as if her heart was breaking.

After a while, I walked back to the house too. Inside, in the sitting room, Eileen sat hunched in the Morris chair, now sobbing into a white handkerchief.

"All this isn't good for me," she sniffed pitifully, in between sobs. "It's making me ill."

"Well," I said, sick at heart myself with the way things were going, "well, you and Chuck should have listened to O'D, you know, and kept that goat penned up as he asked you to."

"O'D has no right to give our goat to Caetano, no right at all!" Eileen cried, ignoring my words and proving how true O'D's claim had been that she and Chuck never listened. "It's OUR goat!"

No one ate lunch that day. The food sat untouched on the table. When O'D and Caetano drove off to Chimoio in the blue Gaz with the equipment they had loaded and the goat, Chuck and Eileen disappeared behind the curtains in their room. No one ate supper that evening either after O'D returned from Chimoio and so I gave it all away to the workers who were still awake. That night, Avelino and Pocas had an unexpected feast. Without a fridge, it was impossible to keep food in the torrid heat of the Mozambican summer.

The next morning, Chuck told O'D that he'd been thinking things over and had realised he'd been in the wrong. O'D accepted his apology and they decided that it would be best for all of us if Chuck began to renovate one of the other houses for himself and Eileen, so that we wouldn't be on each other's backs all the time.

While Chuck was organising eucalypt beams and thatching for another grass roof, Eileen gave me a clue as to what she and Chuck were planning.

We were in the sitting room at the time. I was busy filling in the Forestry Register Book and Eileen was reading another more exciting book of her own, when she put her book down and said "Chuck's brother-in-law is a very rich and important man, you know. He's got kapenta rigs on Cahora Bassa. (Kapenta is the name for the tiny sun-dried and salted fish Africans like to eat so much) "He's a very successful businessman," - here her voice lowered almost to a murmur - "not like some I could mention."

A few weeks later, Chuck drove the blue Gaz up to Chimoio and while he was there, made a phone call from the post office to his rich and successful brother-in-law. On his return, he told us that he and Eileen needed a rest and that they were going away for the weekend.

Then, on a Friday afternoon, a rusty old blue VW Golf with yellow Zimbabwean number plates jolted slowly down the forest track and stopped outside our house.

"Who's that?" I asked.

"Oh, that's our car and chauffeur," Eileen told me and headed for their bedroom. "Chuck! Chuck!" she called out, "Are you ready, Chuck? He's here!"

"See you on Monday," Chuck told us and together with Mitzi, of course and their two small weekend suitcases, they climbed into the car and drove away.

While they were away, I took the first opportunity I'd had since my arrival in the Nhamacoa to start cleaning all the black mould and old smoke stains off the sitting room walls. Although I'd managed to scrub the blackened and grimy tiles still attached to the bathroom and kitchen walls until they'd come up sparkling and white, Eileen had strenuously resisted my attempts to clean the rest of the house. "It's a waste of time," she had told me. "You'll never be able to get thirty years of dirt off these walls."

Now that she was safely out of the way, I rounded up Seven and a couple of other workers and handed out scrubbing brushes and buckets of soapy water. We pushed Chuck and Eileen's old furniture into the middle of the room and set to work.

Chuck and Eileen's weekend lengthened to more than the original weekend and the work O'D had organised with Chuck went undone. Already fed up with Chuck, O'D's temper began to fray around the edges.

Then, late one evening, a little, rusty VW Golf came jolting down the forest track and stopped outside our house. There was no "chauffeur" this time as Chuck was driving. When they walked into the house, I immediately noticed that something was missing. Where was Mitzi? Still in the car?

"You're late, Chuck," O'D greeted him.

Chuck mumbled something evasively and disappeared into his bedroom.

While Eileen took in the changed appearance of the sitting room - clean pale grey walls, a telltale bucket of soapy water and a scrubbing brush, some of her furniture still pushed against a wall - I took in her new and amazingly changed appearance.

Gone were the shapeless, frumpy, washed-out shift dresses she always wore and in their place was a strange new dress I had never seen on her before. White with large pink flowers scattered all over it, the dress was short and figure-hugging with a neckline so plunging it

164

made me gape. Was this a relic from her youthful days in the Swinging Sixties?

"Hello, Eileen," I said, and indicating the bucket and brush, added, "I didn't expect you back this evening."

"So I see," she replied, in a tone of voice that could only mean trouble. "Well, this is a nice welcome, I must say. No ' how was your week-end, Chuck?' or, 'did you enjoy yourselves, Eileen? Obviously nothing's changed around here." She turned on her heel and flounced her ample pink flowered bottom at me as she clumped her way down the corridor and disappeared into their room. "That's it! I've had enough! Chuck! Chuck! Come on, let's go!" she cried and, with the fate of their goat obviously still rankling, added "They're still as nasty as ever!"

Left standing in the sitting room, O'D and I listened to the sound of suitcases being pulled out and things being thrown into them. It didn't take Chuck and Eileen long to pack and within a few minutes they emerged from their room and climbed back into their borrowed car.

Following them outside, I said, "Goodbye," while Eileen glowered at me through the dusty windscreen and Chuck's eyes went all red and teary and he choked "I can't ... just can't go on ... sorry things had to end like this ..."

I turned away from them and went back into the house. Although O'D hadn't said a thing, his face was very white. Was he angry? Was he upset? Or, was he worried now that we were on our own?

The little car started up and O'D and I listened to the sound of Chuck and Eileen, our too-close companions of more than a year, driving away down the forest track and out of our lives.

"They left all their things behind," I said to O'D, "their furniture, their kitchen stuff, their books ... ALL their animals!"

"Oh, I expect Chuck will come and collect them when he's ready," O'D said.

A mix of feelings enveloped me. Relief that they had gone, mixed with a strange sense of regret and of loss. What a pity we hadn't been able to get along together. Although Chuck and Eileen hadn't exactly been our friends, they had been company in this wild and isolated forest. You needed support in the African bush, you needed people to turn to for help if you got sick or were injured, people to talk to and discuss things that were happening.

Now we were on our own. A sudden jolt of fear stabbed through me as the realisation dawned of what exactly this was going to mean. Now, except for O'D, I was going to be on MY own! Remembering what a fright Milton, the Secret Policeman, had given me when Eileen and I had been alone in the Nhamacoa, I wondered how on earth I was going to cope when O'D went into Chimoio on his fuel buying trips or into the forest with the blue Gaz. I'd been surrounded by people all my life and now, here I was, alone in a forest filled with trees and smothering grass ... living in a broken down house with no doors and windows and barefoot people tiptoeing around at night ...

When Caetano came down to the sawmill and heard that Chuck had left, little lines of worry appeared on his forehead. Mechanics who actually knew what they were doing were like gold dust in Mozambique. "We've got to find another mechanic in a hurry," he said, "but where?"

"There's one standing right in front of you, Caetano," I told him. "O'D used to work for the Americans in the Middle East, you know, fixing all the machinery on one of their oil rigs."

Soon we had fallen into a routine. While O'D worked in the forest, bringing in timber and repairing the lorries and tractor when they needed repairing, Caetano worked in Chimoio, dealing with the mountain of paperwork the Mozambican government departments always foisted onto us.

We were now almost at the end of the year and although we were making some money, it was all going on paying the worker's wages every month and repaying the expensive loan to the BPD Bank. We desperately needed a pump for the borehole so that we could have water of our own and could start planking, but buying the pump was always beyond us.

Eventually, in December, I made a hard decision – and a dangerous one. I would have to borrow money for the pump from a member of my family in Harare (more debt!) and on top of this, I would have to engage in the criminal activity called a 'KANDONGA' (smuggling) to get the money out of Zimbabwe and into Mozambique.

Currency restrictions were extremely tight in Zimbabwe. If I got caught smuggling a large amount of Zimbabwean dollars out of that country, I would end up in the most terrible trouble. All the money would be confiscated and I would be thrown into a Zimbabwean jail – a prospect too ghastly to even contemplate!

CHAPTER ELEVEN

KANDONGAS ACROSS THE BORDER

In Harare, I stayed with my cousin, Leslie, pondering for about a week on how I was going to smuggle fifty thousand Zimbabwean dollars (the equivalent of about four thousand U.S. dollars) across the border without being caught. The quantity of the notes made a bulky pile, difficult to hide.

As Leslie had just become a devout Christian, she made no suggestions to help me out and so I had to turn to my brother, David. David and his friend, John, who would be driving me back to Mozambique.

Two days before we were due to leave, David told me he had finally thought up a plan. "We'll buy twenty chickens," he said, "and stuff them with the money."

A vision came into my mind, of plump Zimbabwean Customs officials poking around a cold box overflowing with chickens. They would be sure to find the quantity suspicious.

"We'll just tell them we're having a big barbecue in Mozambique," David went on optimistically.

The vision grew worse as I saw a Customs official examine one of the chickens and, exclaiming "What is THIS?" pull an incriminating wad of Zimbabwean dollar notes out of its cavity.

"No," I said, "that's not a good idea. Not a good idea at all, David!"

While I wracked my brain for a foolproof plan, my mind roved over several other successful Kandongas that had been perpetrated in the past by various people I had known or seen at it.

There had been the time when the Tabex farm had needed a new water pump and Tim, one of the Zimbabwean farmers, had driven across the border into Zimbabwe to get one. In Mutare, he had cut off the bottom of a 210 litre drum and had put the pump inside it. It had been a tight fit but no one had remarked on the drum of 'fuel' in the back of his pick-up as he had driven through both Forbes and Machipanda border posts.

Another time, sitting in the pick-up at Machipanda border post, I had watched a band of about eleven barefoot and tattered

Mozambican women gear themselves up to blatantly smuggle eleven large sacks filled with bottles of Coca-Cola and Fanta out of Zimbabwe and into Mozambique.

Their Kandonga had been a simple but a daring one. Balancing the clinking sacks on top of their heads, the women had drawn together in a tight group. Then, at a whispered signal, they had stormed towards the wooden barrier blocking the road into Mozambique.

Taking everyone by surprise, especially the guard at the barrier, they had stampeded onwards, crashing so mightily against the wooden pole that it had cracked in half and fallen onto the ground A loud roar had risen up in the air from the spectators as everyone had exploded with laughter and the women had dumped their sacks down on the ground and had flung their arms around each other, laughing and dancing with triumph.

The women's extraordinary enterprise had put the Mozambican officials into such a good humour that day that they had decided not only to overlook the breaking of the law, not to mention the wooden barrier, but they had also waved everyone else through into Mozambique without bothering at all to check on their goods.

And then there had been the time when O'D had driven off to Mutare with Faruk, his Indian friend, to buy a mattress. They had gone in Faruk's pick-up and when Faruk had brought O'D back to our house on the Tabex farm, I had asked them if they would like some tea. "Yes, that would be nice," they had told me, and sitting down on the dralon-covered armchairs, they had immediately begun to take off their shoes and their socks.

At first I had thought that this was some sort of Islamic tea-drinking custom and that O'D was also removing his footwear in deference to Faruk's culture but then, when Zimbabwean dollars began to emerge from their socks, I had realised that the Customs officials had once again been foiled.

Eventually, on the day before I returned to Mozambique, I decided how I was going to carry out my own Kandonga. Like O'D and Faruk, I decided to wear the money. As far as I knew, searching the underclothes of white women was unheard of and quite unthinkable.

Choosing a fairly loose top and a gathered skirt, I hid the money around myself, under my clothes. In Leslie's bedroom, I carefully examined myself for telltale signs in her long mirror. A woman who looked a trifle too bulky to be true looked back at me and so I began to subtract the packets until I looked normal. This left me with four large wads of dollars and I had no idea whatsoever where to hide them.

John, David's friend, came to my rescue.

"Give the money to me," he said, "I've got a place I always use when I smuggle money out of the country," and unscrewing the plastic covers of the back lights of his 4 x 4, he stuffed the money inside, at the far end of the light compartments and screwed the back light covers on again.

During the journey, I became more and more nervous, worrying that something about my appearance would betray me at the border. The thought of jail terrified me. Another dread was that some of the money would fall out of my clothes, leaving an incriminating trail behind me as I walked across the floor of the Immigration and Customs building at Forbes. That would be just my luck!

Forbes Border Post was busy when we arrived. The path over the mountain separating Zimbabwe and Mozambique was busy too, with a very visible trail of people all Kandonga-ing away with large sacks and bundles on their heads. Inside the small building, pockets of potatoes and boxes of eggs, confiscated from unsuccessful Kandongas were piled up against the Immigration and Customs Officers' desks. No wonder they were all so plump!

At the crowded counter, I stayed close to David and John. Africa was macho country and as a woman and therefore a second-class person, I knew I would be ignored while they got all the attention.

"How many Zimbabwean dollars are you carrying?" a Customs Official asked us.

My heart gave a nervous thump at the question and a sudden explosion of perspiration misted my face like a veil. I turned my head towards the windows, pretending interest in the Vervets rummaging around the piles of empty crisp packets under the trees.

"About forty dollars between us," John lied, without blinking an eyelid.

Outside the building again, we walked past a dilapidated grey Peugeot Stationwagon where a large female Customs Official was examining the contents of the driver's suitcase. She had unearthed a hundred and thirty eight T-shirts which he was claiming were his personal clothes.

Grilling him, she asked "How is it - if these are your personal clothes as you are claiming - that these one hundred and thirty eight T-shirts are all still in their original pristine plastic packets?"

We climbed into the 4 x 4 and drove towards the barrier. The border guard examined our gate pass and then raised the pole and waved us through. It was only when Machipanda border post was completely out of sight that I closed my eyes and fell weakly back in my seat, blowing out a long breath of relief. I felt no guilt at what I had done. It had been the only way. Foreign currency was hard to get and life was short. Trying to find a legal way through the tangle of red tape African governments love so much just wasn't worth the effort.

One morning, a week later, O'D carefully lowered our new borehole pump down the 80 metre hole Vic Vorster's old rig had drilled. Then, checking that everything was in order, he turned on the generator.

As Vic's workers had told us they had found very little water, we waited tensely. Our whole future depended on the borehole. Was water going to come cascading out of the short hosepipe O'D had attached to the pump, or were we going to end up with an extremely expensive deep, dry, hole?

Nothing happened ... and then there was a gurgling sound. With a gush, precious sparkling clean water spouted out of the pipe and soaked into the hard, drought-stricken earth. Gathering all our plastic containers together, Seven hurriedly inserted the pipe into one of them and began to fill it up.

The hole pumped dry within 15 minutes and our spirits drooped with despair. "I'll try again this afternoon," O'D said "and see what happens."

In the afternoon, the borehole gave us another fifteen minutes of water before running dry and as it did this, day in and day out, we were grateful and learned to live with it. The water was just enough for our own personal needs and to operate the saw.

Our workers were grateful, too. No more sweating trips up and down to the hole in the riverbed with heavy containers on their heads. That was women's work! Now, using the new - and uncontaminated by Chuck - containers I had made O'D buy, Seven collected water from the borehole, a much, much shorter distance.

As we hadn't been able to find an experienced saw operator, O'D operated the saw himself at first. He'd never done this sort of thing before, of course, but he'd pored over books on saw milling and it hadn't appeared to be difficult. You just had to get a feel for the wood and know when you had hit a knot or a series of knots. The wood was extremely hard and the best way of cutting through a knot was by slowing down and easing the blade through it.

As he was now doing the work of three men - lorry driver, mechanic and saw operator - O'D soon turned his mind to finding a replacement to relieve him of at least one of these duties, preferably that of saw operator.

"Where on earth are we going to find someone who knows how to do this?" I wondered.

"I'm going to train one of our workers," O'D told me. "Someone who has enough common sense for this type of work."

There were not many of these, I can tell you! However, O'D's eye had fallen on Pocas, the bright and intelligent young Mozambican who used to help Chuck in the workshop.

Once he'd been shown what to do, Pocas sawed well and planks and beams began to pile up around the sawmill. Now all we had to do was to find customers to buy them. Something easier said than done!

One day, not long after Chuck and Eileen had left, Mario, the Chief of the Macate police, rode down the forest track on his ancient Honda government motorbike with a warning for us.

There was bandit activity in the area!

The warning made O'D realise I needed more protection than the mere presence of Biasse, Avelino and Pocas in the room underneath the house. "We need a night guard," he told me, "but for the life of me I can't think of anyone who would be trustworthy enough. Or brave enough."

While O'D and I were wondering where to find a suitable night guard, our Foreman, Madeira, and our workers came to us with the answer.

One evening, when they arrived back from working in the forest, they complained to O'D about Steven, the big, ragged, Zimbabwean he had employed at the Railway Station. Steven, they claimed, was always starting fights and threatening to kill them with his knife.

When O'D asked Steven to explain his behaviour, the man shrugged off the accusations and told O'D that as he had once been a soldier, he would prefer to guard our house and sawmill than work in the forest. He had, it seemed, been a member of the Zimbabwean fighter Tekere's group during the Rhodesian bush war.

O'D thought about Steven's suggestion for a while. He rather liked the Zimbabwean. He was strong and worked hard.

"I think we should try him out," he told me.

"Alright," I said.

The next day, O'D explained Steven's new duties to him. They were quite simple. His first priority was to protect me when O'D was away and then to make sure that no one stole any of our equipment or planks during the night.

Armed only with a paraffin lantern, Steven took up his duties and soon little scraps of paper, which looked as if they had been torn out of a school exercise book, began to appear all over the place. They were propped up on our equipment, they were stuck onto the windscreens or fuel tanks of our lorries and tractor, they were attached to various mango trees around the sawmill. All these notes had a message on them, a threatening message and were written in pencil in a large and uneven print.

'TSOTSIES WATCH OUT!" the notes read. "I AM WATCHING YOU!"

As these warnings were printed in English and our Tsotsies were Mozambicans who not only had no knowledge whatsoever of English but were mostly unable to read as well, it was difficult to gauge their effect.

Some evenings Steven brought a battered Bible to work with him. He had learnt a lot of it off by heart and often recited great reams of it to O'D with an enormous amount of fervour and passion. Whenever I saw him doing this, I would get a feeling that something was wrong with Steven, that something was wrong with his mind and that it had been broken in some way by the war and by the things he had seen … and the things he had done.

One late afternoon, while Steven was talking to O'D outside the house, he heard the baboons barking in the forest and the sound triggered off some of his wartime memories.

"I will never hunt and kill the baboons," he told O'D. "I will never kill and eat them like the Mozambican people do, because the baboons are my friends. Once, during the war in Rhodesia, they saved my life. This I will never forget."

He went on to tell O'D that he'd been trained to fight by the Chinese, in the training camps they had set up in Tanzania. It was the time of the Cold War and the Chinese had long term plans for Africa.

"The Chinese helped us a lot against the Rhodesians," he said. "There were many of us in their camps and when they thought we were ready to go back to Zimbabwe, they gave us guns and ammunition, uniforms and boots. When my unit and I got to the Zambezi, we paddled across the river in canoes at night and slipped into Zimbabwe. Then we began to make our way through the bush."

It was here that his unit had had their first and last encounter with the Rhodesian Army.

"One day," he told O'D, "we were moving through the bush when we had a contact with some Rhodesian soldiers. During the gunfight, they called up one of their helicopters to come and attack us and they killed all the men in my group. Only I was left alive and they would have killed me too, if it hadn't been for the baboons."

A troop of baboons had been close by when the fighting had begun and the sound of gunfire and the swooping helicopter had panicked them, sending them scrambling for safety.

"I grabbed at the opportunity," Steven said, "I bent down and with my hands on the ground, I imitated their movements, running among the baboons for cover. To the Rhodesians in the helicopter overhead, I looked just like another monkey … and so I escaped death, thanks to my friends, the baboons."

Only a few weeks after Steven had become our night guard, trouble reared its head. Someone, whom we strongly suspected was one of our workers, had reported him to the Department of Immigration and the Department was threatening to deport him. They'd been told he was a Zimbabwean and Zimbabweans didn't have official permission to work in Mozambique.

Distressed, he came to O'D and appealed for help. He didn't want to return to Zimbabwe, he told O'D, as there was now nothing there for him. He wanted to stay in Mozambique and make a new life here.

Wondering how to help Steven, O'D talked to Caetano. As a Mozambican, Caetano knew the ropes and with the help of a government official, quickly arranged some false papers for Steven, who now became … Stefano.

Thrilled with his new Mozambican papers and identity, Steven thanked O'D and told him that he was the only white man who had ever treated him decently in his entire life.

By the end of December, Pocas had sawn our logs into large piles of beautiful planks. He had a natural bent for mechanics and had quickly turned into something of an expert saw operator. As he was walking off on Saturday at 12 o'clock for his last weekend of the year, I smiled at him and said, "You're doing really great on the saw, Pocas!"

Strangely, Pocas didn't return my smile. He merely gave me a nod. "Thank you," he replied.

Alone in the forest, O'D and I hadn't had much of a Christmas and we didn't have much of a New Year, either. On the last day of the year, while the Vervet monkeys foraged in the mango trees outside our windows, we ate a simple lunch of Biasse's famous tuna fish cakes, crispy potato chips and a salad. We had no wine or even a glass of beer. But perhaps next year everything would be better - especially now that Chuck and the curse he had brought with him had gone!

CHAPTER TWELVE

BABES IN THE WOODS
1996

The new year began with another betrayal.

When Pocas didn't turn up for work on the 2nd of January, we thought at first that he had fallen ill, perhaps with malaria. However, when Caetano paid a visit to Pocas' family in Chimoio to find out what was going on, he soon discovered that we'd been the victims of some skullduggery by someone of a decidedly low-down, underhand, sneaky, sly disposition!

Yes, Chuck had done it again! Stabbed us in the back when we had least expected it.

Now working for his 'rich and successful' kapenta-fishing brother-in-law on Lake Cahora Bassa, Chuck had connived with Pocas behind our backs and had stolen him away from us by telling him that he was going to make him rich. This promise was to lure another of our workers away from us. A few weeks after Pocas' departure, Avelino also ran off to join Chuck.

As Chuck and Eileen had given us no indication as to when they would be returning for their belongings, I spent about a week packing up all their things into cardboard boxes to clear the house of their possessions … and their presence. The fact that they had left me to do this filled me with resentment and I was looking forward to Chuck's return to collect their stuff so that I could tell him exactly what I thought of him.

When time passed and Chuck didn't return for his possessions, O'D gave all the animals away to Caetano. Seven cleaned their smelly presence out from the room underneath the house and I used this room to store all their old furniture, their books, their bedding and kitchen equipment.

This left us with only the bare minimum in the house until Raimundo, a doddery and ancient carpenter O'D had found, could manufacture some furniture of our own out of some of our newly sawn planks.

There were no furniture shops in the country and so, like everyone else, we had to have all our furniture handmade by local carpenters. This, as you may imagine, took time and wouldn't have gone down at all well with Western people and their demands for instant gratification of their needs.

I had long since given up our little camp beds and for almost a year O'D and I had been sleeping on a mattress on the floor of our room. This had not only proved more comfortable for us, it had also been a popular move with the various insects sharing our abode. Stray scorpions, with hideous little scorpion babies piled up on top of their backs, clambered up off the floor and onto the blanket, while revolting fork-tailed and shiny blue-black centipedes slithered under a pillow or two. They all met with the same fate - squashed beyond recognition, either by a woman wielding a shoe or a Mozambican cook wielding a broom!

Now that we had the planks, Raimundo could make us a bed and we could sleep in safety, high up off the floor. And as well as our own table on which to eat our meals, he could make us chairs, window frames and much needed front and back doors.

Using his well-worn old hand tools from Portuguese Colonial days and aided by Luis Raoul, a much younger carpenter from the village of Macate, plus some war veterans who claimed they wanted to be trained as carpenters, Raimundo set to work.

Sawing and planing, nailing and glueing, the carpenters' shed was a hive of activity.

At last, several weeks later, a small procession of people trooped over to the house, proudly carrying a table, six chairs and two small bedside cupboards all made out of Umbila.

Raimundo's furniture was a little on the clumsy side, chunky with a ripple effect from the hand planing. It looked a lot like the sort of furniture Fred and Wilma Flintstone would have used in their home in Bedrock but I didn't complain. When you lived in a country that had nothing, you weren't fussy.

Now that Pocas had run off with Chuck, O'D cast his eyes once again over our workers. This time he decided to train no less than three of the most sensible ones to operate the saw, just in case Chuck made another sneaky hit and run raid on our resources.

Once he was sure the saw operators knew what they were doing, he went back to driving the blue Gaz early in the mornings into the forest, loading the little lorry with felled timber and bringing the logs back late in the evening to the sawmill.

Left on my own all day long, with only Biasse or Seven to talk to now and then, I turned to our shortwave radio for companionship. Knowing how I would need it now that Chuck and Eileen were gone, O'D always made sure I had a plentiful supply of batteries.

Without a telephone to speak to family or friends and in a country where an airmail letter took more than a month to reach its destination, the radio became my lifeline, connecting me in my isolation in the Nhamacoa to the rest of the world. It filled the empty silent house with music and voices, the voices of people who would never know that I existed but who became my friends and companions in the awful, awful loneliness I was now to experience.

Without my shortwave radio, I would have fallen apart.

The other thing I began to do, was to talk to God. When you're all alone in an African forest, you soon get to know who is important in the world.

Once, with the exception of my father who claimed to be an atheist, my family had belonged to the Anglican Church but had been chased away from it by The Very Reverend French Beytagh, the portly priest who had presided over it. Shocked by the revelation that my grandparents had forgotten to baptise my father, The Very Reverend had curtly told my mother not to bother bringing my father to him for burial if Dad should die.

The Very Reverend's threat hadn't worried my father. "I wouldn't want someone like *him* to bury me anyway," Dad had said.

Then, when my sister Jennifer was born, The Very Reverend had done it again, telling my mother to stay away from Church for the next two weeks as she was 'unclean.'

Deeply offended, my mother had taken The Very Reverend's advice to heart, and had stayed away not for two weeks but for good.

Although my mother had never set foot in Church again, she had forced me to endure two years of Confirmation classes and many, many long Sundays sitting in a pew in the Anglican Cathedral and listening to The Very Reverend's sermons. Sermons that were so unutterably boring and dreary, I never remembered anything he said. Immediately after my confirmation and the taking of Holy Communion, I had stopped going to Church. I had not found God in the Anglican Cathedral. It wasn't the kind of place you ran to. It was the kind of place you ran away from. And now, here I was, not in a cathedral but in a forest in Africa and trying to find Him again after all these years.

I had never spoken much to God before – The Very Reverend had never suggested that this was something we could do - but now I had long conversations with Him about everything. Quite often, when Biasse came into the sitting room, he caught me talking aloud to God and gave me peculiar looks, no doubt wondering if I was becoming 'bush happy' – an old White Southern African expression for 'nuts'.

"Just talking to myself, Biasse," I would explain with a reassuring smile. "Just talking to myself."

Clouds blew up and rain lashed the Nhamacoa. In the forest, O'D and his workers struggled in the deepening mud with the lorries and the tractor.

He had managed to find a driver for the green Gaz to replace Chuck. This was a rather fearsome looking man called Nunes who had once worked for Maciel at the Tabex farm until Maciel had fired him for something or other. Nunes was of Portuguese and Mozambican descent and had long black shaggy dreadlocks dangling wildly around his moustachioed yellow face that gave him an extremely villainous appearance. With Chuck and Eileen's exit and Nunes' entrance into our lives, we no longer looked like a bunch of hillbillies. We now looked like a bunch of South American desperados.

Our workers were afraid of Nunes and obeyed his orders without question. He had once worked for the Secret Police and this terrified them. With Nunes working for us, our production rose quite dramatically.

The rains brought more stress into my life. While O'D spent longer and longer in the forest, digging the lorries and tractor out of the mud, I sat alone in the dimly lit, broken down house in the evenings and as the hours dragged by, I worried.

I worried about O'D having an accident. I worried about how I would go about getting help without a telephone, without money, without friends. I worried about O'D never coming back from the forest ... disappearing ...

I worried about bandits paying me a visit. I worried about getting sick, about coming down with malaria, tick bite fever, cholera, blood poisoning from a scratch that turned bad, and dying alone while O'D was stuck in the mud in the forest ...

I had never worried much about anything before but now, living in the Nhamacoa forest, I became a lone worrier.

One black moonless night while I sat in a chair in the sitting room and waited for O'D to return from the forest, a wild and terrifying electrical storm blew up right overhead. Gale force winds from the east roared through the trees and bolts of lightning flashed all around the house, exploding with earsplitting cracking sounds.

As I sat on tensely, wondering whether the house was going to be hit, the rocks and stones holding down the black plastic blinds went flying. Driving rain poured through the windows in a horizontal flood and the paraffin lamps went out.

Groping around in pitch-blackness, I stumbled for safety down the corridor just as another mighty blast of wind ripped off part of the grass roof and more rain poured in on me.

In the bedroom, I threw myself face down onto the mattress. I was feeling a bit mad and wild myself. I was afraid the whole roof was going to be ripped off, that the raging storm was going to come right inside my house, leaving me defenceless and with nowhere to shelter.

An intense and awful feeling of absolute depair, of being completely forgotten by everyone, overwhelmed me and I burst into tears. "So lonely, oh, so lonely," I shouted into the storm, punctuating my words by beating at my pillow with my fists, "why ... WHY am I so alone, alone, ALONE ... "

"But you're not alone," a calm voice cut into my cries.

I stopped beating up my pillow and sat up slowly. Although I had never heard this voice before, I knew to whom it belonged.

The sound of the storm receded, along with the terrible feeling of isolation, and another feeling flooded through me. This was a feeling of such peace and security that it made me feel I could deal with anything that was going to be thrown at me. "Thank you," I said to the One I had been spending so much time talking to.

Of course I wasn't alone.

One evening, O'D arrived back at the sawmill from a fuel-buying trip to Chimoio looking rather upset and preoccupied.

"What's wrong?" I asked.

"It's Caetano," he told me. "He's got something on his mind and it isn't our business. In fact, he seems to have lost all interest in the business. Maybe it's because we're not doing well and making any money. Maybe he's thinking of going off on a venture of his own or with someone else."

The thought of losing Caetano made my heart sink. He had become more than a partner by now. He had become a friend. How would we cope without his cheerful and optimistic presence?

"It's always better to get the bad news over and done with quickly," I said. "Ask him what's wrong the next time you see him."

A few days later, O'D met Caetano at the Sports Clube, a place they now used as an informal office. They sat down at a table near the window and ordered a coffee for O'D and a Coke for Caetano. While they drank, O'D braced himself to ask the question that might bring all his dreams crashing down.

"Is something wrong, Caetano?"

Caetano looked down at the table and there was a long silence while he struggled to control the emotions that were tearing at his heart.

Then, unable to contain himself any longer, he burst into anguished tears and covering his face with his hands, cried for a long time.

Aghast, and not knowing what to do, O'D stared at him. Not only a man but an English one at that, he wasn't good at handling emotions.

At last, when the storm of Caetano's tears subsided, O'D dug a hand into a trouser pocket and pulled out a crumpled handkerchief.

"Here, Caetano," he said, knowing Caetano didn't possess such a thing as a handkerchief, "you'll need this."

Caetano took the handkerchief and after mopping his wet face with it, blew his nose noisily. "Marcelina … it's my wife …" Caetano managed to choke out eventually. "She's been sick for months now, with terrible pains in her stomach. I think … I think she's dying. I can't find anyone to help her. Whenever I take her to Chimoio hospital for an examination, the only thing they do is to give her a handful of aspirin. None of the doctors or nurses will even tell me what's wrong with her! I don't know where to go for help … or what to DO!

Now that he was out of dangerous emotional waters and back in his element of practicalities and action, things he did best, O'D took charge immediately.

Pushing his chair back, he stood up. "Come on, Caetano. Let's go and look for a doctor for your wife, right now. A good doctor."

The search was not an easy one and when they eventually found the 'good' doctor, he would do nothing until he received an upfront payment of five million meticais - about three hundred U.S. dollars!

Managing to scrape this extortionate sum up from somewhere, O'D paid the doctor and although he put Marcelina on an intravenous drip in Chimoio hospital and it seemed to help, her recovery was shortlived and her agonizing pains returned.

"I don't know what more I can do!" Caetano told O'D in despair.

"We'll have to take her back to that 5 million meticais doctor," O'D said.

"No," Caetano shook his head. "That doctor is no good. He didn't help her at all."

Beside himself with fear and misery, Caetano ran wildly around Chimoio, looking for someone else to help his wife and this time came across a nurse. Once again O'D handed over an extortionate amount of money, only to see Caetano's greatest fear come true. Marcelina died.

After the funeral, Caetano's face took on a haunted look. To his days of mourning for his wife, were added fears for his own life.

"He's having a lot of trouble from Marcelina's parents," O'D told me. "Not only are they blaming him for their daughter's death but they've also told him that they're arranging to get someone to kill HIM now, in revenge."

"What kind of people are these?" I wondered.

"They're from the Chitewa tribe, " he said, "and according to Caetano, the Chitewas are the most terrible people in the whole of Mozambique."

With what little money we'd had now reposing in the pockets of an unscrupulous doctor and nurse, O'D decided to sell the Mbaua logs we had cut down and had been going to turn into planks. It was easier, unfortunately, to find a buyer for logs than to find customers for our planks.

Umbaua, as mahogany is called in Mozambique, goes under the botanical name of Khaya Nyasica. The trees are huge, wide and tall and grow on the steep slopes leading down to rivers and streams. We had felled them while Chuck had still been working for us and he had told me that we would never be able to pull them up the hills and bring them back to the sawmill.

His words had filled me with irritation. "Then why the hell did we go to all the expense and time of cutting them down, if we're just going to leave them lying in the forest?"

Fortunately, O'D was not a Chuck. Enterprising and optimistic as ever, he had said, "Of course we'll get them up the hills. We'll winch them up." And that's just what he had done.

The buyer Caetano found for us came from Beira. He was Portuguese, middle aged and plump and arrived in a large and expensive white Landcruiser.

As his dark Mediterranean eyes took in our broken down house and our piles of unsold planks, he understood our circumstances immediately and naturally enough, decided to take advantage of them.

Standing amongst our Umbaua, he examined them with a deliberately jaundiced eye and shook his head. "Not good, not good," he pronounced and sent our hearts sinking. "You have cracks! Bad cracks!"

It was true. Some of the logs did have several visible cracks as well as some small holes.

Plucking a long blade of dry yellow grass out of the ground, the Portuguese pushed it into the holes and cracks as far as it would go. In some cases, the blade of grass disappeared up to a length of 6 or 9 inches.

Sighing dolefully with the disappointment of a man who had driven two hundred and forty kilometres for sub-standard logs, he explained to us that the price we wanted for the logs was far too high. That they were hardly worth buying. That he would have great difficulty working out how to saw logs with such bad cracks and still get enough planks out of them to make it worth his while. However, he *had* driven a long way to come and see us …

O'D and I exchanged a look. We had hoped that what had looked to us like magnificent mahogany was going to pull us out of the financial desert we were in but now it seemed we'd been fooling ourselves.

The Portuguese offered us a low price and despite being unsure of himself, O'D haggled with the Portuguese. This went on for some time in the hot sunshine until finally, the Portuguese couldn't be pressed any further and O'D gave in.

Our need for money was too desperate to turn the Portuguese down and he knew it.

Some days later, after the Portuguese buyer's lorries had taken away the Umbaua logs he had chosen, we rolled a few of the logs he had rejected onto the saw for planking.

Would they be as bad as the Portuguese had claimed ... or had we, in our ignorance, been taken for a ride?

Augusto, our young and capable saw operator, started up the saw and as the log moved slowly forward, began slicing it into planks - wide, beautiful, pale pink planks that would turn a dark red-brown when they dried out.

"There's nothing wrong with this wood," O'D said as we examined each plank when it came off the saw for stacking. The cracks and holes the Portuguese had made such a song and dance about were hardly worth worrying about. They didn't run the full length of the log and were only at the ends. " I had a feeling that Portuguese knew something I didn't know - and I was right! All we have to do is cut off the ends which have defects and we'll have perfect planks."

"He saw we were babes in the wood where the timber business is concerned and he lied to us, to trick us," I said.

O'D gave a resigned shrug. "That's business for you. We'll know better next time."

By now, things were hotting up in the forest and there was a lot of activity going on. Activity that wasn't coming from us, but from the Mozambican people.

It was becoming increasingly obvious to us that there was a war going on in the Nhamacoa. A war that had begun when the civil war between the ruling Frelimo party and the opposition Renamo party had come to an end in 1992. It was a war between the people and the forest, a war between the people and the animals, a war between the people and O'D, Caetano and me. And, alarmingly, it appeared that it was a war the people were going to win!

The trickle of people coming into the Nhamacoa had now turned into a stream. Day and night, we heard the chop chop chop of axes, the crashing sounds of trees falling over and the crackling of flames as the people set fire to the large areas of forest they were clearing in order to open new machambas to grow maize.

These new forest dwellers introduced themselves to O'D and his workers one day by starting a fire not far from where they were working. When O'D asked them quite politely to control their burning, they in turn behaved in a decidedly rude and un-neighbourly manner. Waving their pangas up in the air at him in a threatening way, they shouted belligerently "WE ARE MOZAMBICAN! THIS IS OUR LAND! WE CAN DO WHAT WE LIKE! IF YOU DON'T SHUT YOUR MOUTH, WE WILL CUT YOU AND YOUR WORKERS UP INTO LITTLE PIECES WITH OUR PANGAS - AND KILL YOU!"

As there is nothing less likely to promote goodwill and trust than the threat of being hacked to death, this meeting was to set the tone for the future relationship between the people and us, especially when the stream of invaders turned into an unstoppable torrent.

Aghast at what was taking place, we wrote letters of complaint to the Director of Agriculture and to the Department of Forestry. They didn't acknowledge our letters but responded by sending the Head of the District Department of Agriculture in Gondola to the Nhamacoa. His name was Mr. Manhoca, a rather unfortunate name meaning 'diarrhoea' in the local Chitewa dialect, and he came not to put a halt to the destruction of the forest but to aid it. Loaded down with large supplies of maize seed, Mr. Diarrhoea gave free handouts of seed to the people to plant in their new machambas!

The fact that the very Mozambican government officials who were supposed to protect the forest were themselves helping the population to destroy it filled me with panic. Frightening visions of financial loss and a lifetime of poverty flashed before my eyes. We had invested our hard-earned money in a forest that was now rapidly being turned into a desert!

"I think the Mozambican government has sold us a bum steer, as the Americans call it, " I said to O'D and Caetano. "At the rate these people are cutting down the forest, we'll be out of business before we've even started! What are we going to do?"

Ever optimistic and unfazed by the destructive behaviour of his countrymen, Caetano replied, "We'll just have to cut down the trees we need faster than the people are cutting them down."

O'D was as optimistic as Caetano. "That won't be a problem," he said with a grin. "We've got chainsaws and all they've got are axes."

When larger and larger areas of the forest began to disappear as if a gigantic swarm of locusts had been through it, even O'D and Caetano's optimism began to wilt. It was quite obvious that modern technology in the form of three heavy-duty Stihl chainsaws was no match at all for thousands of primitive Mozambican manual axes!

Unlike us, who only felled trees of a certain species and of a certain size, the people were cutting down everything in sight, leaving not one tree standing in the now bare brown and empty earth. And even worse, unlike us who *paid* the Department of Forestry for licences to cut timber, the people were cutting with impunity; breaking the law by cutting illegally without licences, as well as turning valuable indigenous hardwood trees into ash and smoke.

Sensing defeat in the face of the massive devastation going on around us, Caetano began to look for other ways to stave off what was beginning to look like certain financial ruin. "What we have to do," he told us, "is to get hold of another felling area. I'll start looking for one, right away."

From the way things were going, I could see that there was little likelihood that we were going to be able to pay John Phillips' loan back to him on time. To salvage something, I sent Willy a fax from the post office in Chimoio asking him not to renew our rental contract with our German tenant, Uwe Heitkamp, but to give him notice to leave our house and then to put Arrojela on the market. With the sale of Arrojela, we could pay back the loan and have plenty of money left over.

A few days later, Willy faxed back. Arrojela was up for sale.

We were not the only ones whose plans were going awry. About a month after they had run away from us, Pocas and Avelino returned from Cahora Bassa. The dreams Chuck had woven for them had fallen far short of reality. While Avelino came back to work for us, Pocas remained at home with an illness that no one could diagnose. Sadly, by the end of the year, young Pocas would be dead.

CHAPTER THIRTEEN

NORA SWETE AND THE NIPPA DEMON

I come now to a very strange part of my story. If you remember, at the beginning of our renovation of the old mud-brick house at Arrojela, O'D had been hit by a plank that flew off the roof in a seemingly 'freak' gust of wind. Then, after my father's funeral, my mother and I had been pretty shaken up by some eerie and ghostly sounds we had both heard during the night in the house in Kleinbrak. Now, in the Nhamacoa, O'D and I, along with about a dozen of our workers, were about to be given the fright of our lives when we watched a large Mozambican woman being transformed into a demon … in broad daylight … and in front of our very own eyes!

It all began with Daringua, and the awful mistake he made.

Daringua Dzadza and Alfixa Gatia were two of our most experienced chainsaw operators. We had stolen them from our longhaired, old Italian enemy, Giancarlo Bertuzzi and felt absolutely no remorse at our action. This was because we had discovered, much to our amazement and ire, that Bertuzzi had been cutting illegally in our part of the forest using a Department of Agriculture map that he had FORGED in order to enlarge his area with parts of ours. Only he knew how much of our timber he had purloined and so, as far as we were concerned, the gloves were off!

Pleased with our ability to hit back in the rough and tumble of the timber industry, we had no idea, however, what a fearful thing lay in the background of one of the two men we had 'head hunted'.

Both Daringua and Alfixa were in their forties and like the majority of Mozambicans, they followed the practice of polygamy. While Alfixa appeared to live a life of contentment with his two wives, the same couldn't be said for Daringua.

Short and plump, with a little pot-belly that hung over the belt of his trousers, Daringua had added a new woman to his family rather late in his life and what a woman she had turned out to be! A few months after tying the knot, poor old Daringua had discovered all sorts of things about his new wife. Things that were enough to chill the blood of a strong man …

Out of all the women he could have chosen to marry, it soon became dreadfully clear to him that he had tied himself to a woman who was possessed ... possessed by a demon!

Yes, a woman who was none other than the terrible Nora Swete!

Unaware of what was lurking under the seemingly placid surface of Daringua's second wife, Eileen used to buy tomatoes from Nora Swete. I had been present during some of these transactions so I had seen her a couple of times. Hardly a beauty, Nora Swete was a large, heavy-boned woman and as she worked extremely hard in her machamba, she was also immensely strong.

It was when Nora Swete decided to put the profits from her tomatoes into a more lucrative business, that she let the genie right out of the bottle!

Noticing a gap in the market, she began to turn sugar cane or very, very ripe bananas into Nippa, that heady brew rural folk like to drink so much. Unfortunately, Nippa is a potent drink and Nora, like all of us who like to cook and brew, was irresistibly tempted to have a taste of her concoction, and then another taste and another and another, until all her tastings led to a dreadful change in her character ... a change that could only be described as similar to the one that overtook Dr. Jekyll and turned him into Mr. Hyde.

O'D and I first became aware of Daringua's sinister matrimonial problems on a fine and sunny day in March.

One morning, while Biasse was busy currying a chicken in the cook hut for lunch and I was in the upstairs kitchen of the house preparing a lettuce, cucumber and tomato salad, garnished with cubed feta cheese and a sprinkling of oregano, I suddenly noticed that a strange quiet had descended over the normally noisy sawmill. Silence had replaced the whining sound of the saw slicing through logs and even the low hum of the generator had been stilled. Wondering if something had gone wrong, I placed a large net cover over my salad to protect it from flies and walked down to the saw to find out what was going on.

I was on my way across to the planking area, when I saw a sight that brought me up short. There, standing on the saw operator's small platform was a large woman. Nora Swete, Daringua's second wife. Waving her arms around, she appeared to be giving a speech to an audience of empty air while our saw workers, having abandoned the

187

saw to her, were tip-toeing among the planks and moving them from one place to another in uncharacteristic silence.

O'D was working on a piece of equipment near the workshop while Madeira, our foreman, and two or three other workers stood silently in a huddle next to him. I walked over to him.

"What's going on?" I asked O'D.

It was Madeira who answered me. "Too much Nippa. It has caused a confusion in her brain," he told me in a whisper, and added the warning, "Stay away from her. She could get violent."

"Are you mad, Madeira?" I whispered back tartly. Why on earth would I want to go near a large, immensely strong, drunk Mozambican woman?

Nora Swete's dark eyes caught mine and she stopped speaking in mid flow. The sight of me seemed to fill her with a strange excitement – and an anticipation – almost as if she was thinking "Ah, SHE's here!" Keeping her eyes fixed on me, she stepped off the platform and began to stride eagerly towards us. Alarmed by her purposeful approach and mindful of Madeira's warning, I shrank towards O'D for protection.

Halfway towards me, her eyes alighted on the blue Gaz, which was parked near us. The sight of the vehicle stopped her in her tracks and, distracted from her original purpose, she veered away from me and headed instead towards the lorry. Heaving herself up, she clambered awkwardly onto the open back of the Gaz and sat down on the spare tyre.

Unfolding a small cloth bundle she'd been carrying, she took out a large, grey-blue hardcover book that I saw was a Bible and opening it up in the middle, she balanced it carefully on top of her head.

For a while and with her hands folded on her lap, Nora Swete sat still and quiet on the tyre. On top of her head, the pages of the large Bible flipped over in the slight breeze.

And then, before our horrified gaze, Nora Swete underwent a hideous transformation!

Suddenly, her eyes rolled up in her head until her brown irises and black pupils disappeared completely, leaving only the whites glaring blankly out at us from her dark brown face.

Then, her mouth opened and the deep brassy tones of a man's voice boomed out from between her lips.

188

The hairs on my arms stood up as if I'd been electrified and an icy chill ran down my spine. This did not look like a drunk woman to me. I'd seen a lot of drunk people in the past and even I, in my younger days, had had a glass or two too much of wine, but none of us had ever reacted in *this* way! No, Madeira had not been telling me the truth.

This looked more like a woman who had been taken over by something supernatural ... something just like ... a demonic spirit!

Nora Swete, or whatever it was, spoke for some time in Chitewa, an indigenous language I naturally couldn't understand. Her ghastly eyes never left mine and I had the distinct impression that there was a mocking expression in those eyes, blank and white as they were. Incredibly, they seemed to be laughing at me ... and gloating ... as if she knew something I didn't know ...

"What's she saying?" I whispered to Madeira.

"Many things," he whispered back, "and all of it is rubbish."

"Oh come on, Madeira," I insisted, unconvinced by his reply. There was a definite whiff of ancient evil in the atmosphere and apart from that, what was the meaning of the open Bible balancing on top of her head? "Even if she *is* talking rubbish, I want to know what it is."

"It is nothing," Madeira shook his head, refusing to give me even an inkling of what everyone, except O'D and I, were hearing.

The booming voice went on and on until eventually I'd had enough. I decided to walk back to the house but not wanting to make any move to encourage whatever it was that had taken possession of Nora Swete to see this as an opportunity to rush at me and grapple with me, I slid imperceptibly over to the other side of O'D. Once I thought I was hidden from her view, I crept quickly behind a bush and then made my way back to the house in a roundabout way, screened by the long yellow grass.

Some time later, while I was sitting in a chair in the sitting room and trying to make sense of what I had just seen, out of the corner of my eye I noticed a movement at the east-facing window. I turned my head to have a look and gave a gasp of fright. Aah! Nora Swete! Horrified, I wondered if she had come looking for me. As her large form loomed into view, I sank down in the chair, trying to make myself as small as possible in an attempt to hide from her. Would she see me and if she did, what would she do? Forgetting to breathe with the suspense of it all, I watched her walk past the window. Fortunately, she didn't look in but stared straight ahead as she clumped on past. After she had gone, I sat up slowly and let out a long breath of relief. Wow! There was nothing like living in a house with glassless windows while a demon with blank white eyes and a booming voice walked on by.

At twelve o'clock, the gong rang out and O'D came in for lunch.

"Well," I said, "what did you think about THAT? It was a bit like that film "The Exorcist", wasn't it? Do you think she's possessed?"

"It certainly looked like it," O'D replied thoughtfully. "It's just as well her head didn't start revolving and whizzing around her neck."

I pictured the scene. "Imagine if it had! Our workers would have made a mad dash for it!"

"They wouldn't have been the only ones," he said. "We would probably have been in the lead."

"You bet!" I agreed, and we both laughed. Not because we thought it was funny but to ease the tension we felt. The devil had just paid us a visit and we knew it.

A few days later, Madeira and the workers had a meeting with O'D. They told him that Nora Swete was becoming more and more impossible to control and that during the night she had attacked and beaten up poor old Daringua - her own husband! - and then had left him tied up in his hut.

Managing to loosen his bonds and free himself in the morning when Nora Swete had gone off to her machamba, Daringua had discussed his marital problems with his fellow workers and they had come up with a solution. Nora had to be taken to Chissui where there was a clinic for the mentally disturbed and left there for treatment.

There had been one stumbling block, though, and that had been Nora Swete's abnormal and supernatural strength. How were they going to catch her and take her, against her will, to the clinic? After more discussion, they had finally come up with a plan, a plan that would, of course, necessitate O'D's help.

"We have decided, Patrao," Madeira told O'D, "to capture Nora Swete early on Sunday morning. Because she is so strong, we will have to take her by surprise and so we are going to visit Daringua, one by one, until there are about ten or twelve of us at his hut. When Nora Swete comes out, we will surround her and rush at her all at the same time, overwhelming her with our superior numbers. Then we will tie her up and bring her to you."

190

"Bring her to me ..." O'D repeated slowly, hoping that there was more to our workers' plan than this!

"Yes," Madeira went on. "If you agree, Patrao, we'll put her in the blue Gaz and you can drive us all to Chissui."

O'D gave his approval to the capture and intended incarceration of Nora Swete and early on Sunday morning a large group of people arrived at the sawmill. Nora Swete was amongst them, standing docile and quiet with her hands neatly and securely bound up with rope behind her broad back.

This morning there was nothing about her at all to indicate that from time to time she underwent a ghastly transformation. She looked just like an ordinary, if rather unattractive, Mozambican peasant woman wearing a faded cotton capulana and standing patiently with her big toes and bare feet in the dust. Yes, just an ordinary woman until, that is, you looked closely at her dark brown eyes ... and there it was ... a flicker of something red ... a kind of red glow ... just waiting ...

"Be careful," I warned O'D.

"Don't worry," he assured me. "I'm going to be inside the cab while they're all going to be outside, in the back with ... HER."

Nora Swete's delivery to the Chissui clinic went off uneventfully and naturally enough, I forgot all about her. Then, one afternoon, several weeks later, she came back into our lives in a decidedly unexpected way.

I was relaxing in a chair in the sitting room and reading a book to the soothing background music of Zimbabwe's Radio One, when suddenly and without any warning at all, I was blasted out of my seat by the magnified and stereophonic booming of indigenous African electric guitar music! Indigenous African electric guitar music battered at my eardrums, filled every corner of my house and drowned out the sound of my own music. I turned my radio off.

Shouting for Biasse over the incredible noise, I asked him what was happening.

"It is Nora Swete, Madam," he shouted back at me. "She is back from Chissui and giving a Nippa party!"

"Well," I shouted, "you go and tell her to turn the volume of her music down!"

For a moment Biasse stared at me in amazement. "Me, Madam?"

"Yes, you, Biasse! You're the only one here at the moment!"

A mutinous expression bloomed all over his face at the thought of having to give orders to a large demon-possessed woman with glaring blank white eyes.

"Go ON, Biasse!"

Biasse was away for a very long time and when he returned the music was, if anything, louder than ever.

"She says she will NOT turn down the music, Madam! And she says she wants to see *you*!"

"Me, Biasse?" Now it was my turn to stare at Biasse in amazement. No way was I going to pay a visit to the dreadful Nora Swete in her Nippa reeking hut!

In the evening, when O'D returned from Chimoio, he sent for Daringua and ordered him to tell his wife to turn down her music. Without a word and with an unreadable expression on his face, Daringua went off to his hut and didn't come back to work. The terrible music went on without a break for the rest of that night … and all of the next day … on and on … for three whole days and three whole nights, without even a minute's break. It disturbed my sleep, it jangled my nerves and it made my voice grow hoarse from shouting. At night I wrapped a pillow over my head and during the day, I walked around with wads of cotton wool stuffed into my ears. The music was a form of mental torture and I took it personally. The demon inside Nora Swete had it in for me!

"I'm going to crack if you don't do something," I threatened O'D.

At last, he drove off to Macate and reported Nora Swete for noise pollution. Sainete's young assistant didn't go for that but instead fined her for not having a licence to hold a Nippa party in the forest.

The music stopped at last and a few days later, Daringua wandered back to work as if nothing had happened. He had divorced Nora Swete, we were told, and she had packed up all her possessions and moved to a spot six kilometres away, near the turnoff where the forest track joins the road to Chimoio.

One day, the American missionary Kirby Jennings paid us a visit. He was showing the 'Jesus' film to the villagers in Macate. White haired and an old Africa hand soon to return to his own country, he had seen it all. Taking the opportunity of his wide experience, I asked him for his opinion concerning Nora Swete's terrifying metamorphis.

Visibly shaken by what I told him, Kirby Jenning's face paled a shade and grew very grave. "I've seen this before in Africa," he told me softly. "It's demon possession."

And staring intently into my eyes with a warning that chilled me, he added "You must be careful. Very, very careful."

CHAPTER FOURTEEN

THE DROUGHT BREAKS

Visitors started coming to the Nhamacoa. Other foresters, like Will Scholler and Andre Swanepoel. They came to see what we were up to and whether there were any opportunities to be had by getting to know us.

Scholler, who was white haired and tough, was originally from Namibia but now lived in Pietersburg, a city in South Africa that had once been a bastion of apartheid. Despite this, his partner and close friend for many decades was an Indian called Sabir and together they had set up a company with a high-ranking Mozambican government official to cut timber in the region of Quelimane.

Although I thought we were living rough, Scholler soon disabused me of this notion when he, Sabir and Izzy their mechanic, whose left eye disconcertingly stared off to the side instead of straight ahead, tramped into our house for coffee.

"Nice set-up you've got here, O'D," Scholler said, his steely eyes roving over the grass roof and the Fred Flintstone furniture in our sitting room.

"Oh, do you think so?" I asked, disbelievingly.

"You're living in luxury compared to us," he assured me. "We're sleeping in tents ... cooking over the coals ... and wallowing around in mud now that the drought's broken."

We weren't long into the conversation when Scholler said,"I see you've got the same problem we've got, O'D." He nodded his head at the west-facing window and the plume of smoke we could see rising up in the hills. "People moving into your area, chopping down trees and burning everything in sight. It's worse around us, though. Real devastation. We're inundated with people. The other day I asked them what they'd do when we moved camp and they laughed and told me that they'd move with us."

Andre Swanepoel arrived soon after Scholler. A short, slim man who chainsmoked and hid his eyes behind dark glasses, Andre lived in Zimbabwe. Felling timber to supply wood to his father's door-manufacturing factory in Pretoria, Andre had it in for the BBC. The population had also invaded his area and while they were chop chopping away at the forest around him, he had heard the BBC telling the world over his shortwave radio that it was people like Andre who were to blame for deforestation.

"I don't like the way they lump us all together," he grumped, "telling the world that we're the ones destroying the environment and cutting down all the trees. They should get their facts right instead of spreading misinformation. We're LEGAL foresters, paying for our licences and keeping to the rules. If they really knew what was going on – which they obviously don't! - they'd know that it's the people who are doing all the destruction to the forests, not us."

Wet and stormy weather now set in with a vengeance and work in the forest became hard and uncomfortable. Time and time again, rain drenched O'D and our workers and made them shiver. The country didn't have rain gear. The forest tracks ran with water and became slippery and dangerous and if you weren't a good driver, a loaded lorry and trailer could easily overturn.

O'D was still in the depths of the forest late one evening when I heard the commotion.

It came from the direction of two huts hidden in the bush not far from the back of the house, huts that housed our fearsome foreman Nunes and Mauricio, a pleasant old man who was our new mechanic.

The loud shouts and screams I now heard coming from Nunes' and Mauricio's huts were quite frightening and although I really didn't feel like going to investigate, I picked up my torch and went down the back stairs.

It had rained on and off all day long but now at last the heavy downpours had turned into a misty drizzle and through this drizzle, the beam of my torch picked out the figure of Mauricio. He was stumbling up the path towards me, crying and moaning and holding his hands over his mouth. Walking up to him, I shone the torchlight on his face and got something of a shock. His hands and his mouth were red and shiny with blood!

"Mauricio," I said, my heart beginning to thud fearfully in my chest, "what happened to you, Mauricio?"

"Nunes," he told me, through great, gulping sobs. "Putas. Three in his hut."

"Putas!" I exclaimed, angry that Nunes was harbouring prostitutes in his hut. And so close to my house! How dare he?

"They hit me," Mauricio cried pitifully. "They hit me … and broke one of my teeth!"

195

"Why?" I asked. "Why did they hit you, Mauricio?"

"They wanted to get into my hut … and I wouldn't let them ... and so they hit me!" he wailed.

Another figure appeared out of the night. Steven, with his lantern.

Thankfully I turned the problem over to him. "Go and tell those prostitutes that they have no right to be here on sawmill property, Steven. Tell them to get out of here, NOW!"

Steven's eyes lit up in the lamplight at the thought of some action.

"Can I hit them?" he asked me eagerly.

"No!" I exclaimed. Steven was a strong man and the last thing I needed was for him to injure the women and then tell everyone I had told him to do it. I could just see the headlines in the Mozambican newspapers. 'ZIMBABWEAN WAR VET MASQUERADING AS MOZAMBICAN NIGHTGUARD BEATS UP MOZAMBICAN WOMEN ON THE ORDERS OF WHITE FOREIGNER'. "No, just tell them to get out of here, right now. Okay?"

Steven disappeared down the path and I was left with the still blubbering Mauricio. He made a pathetic picture and so I gave him a sympathetic, consoling pat on his shoulder. "Wait here, Mauricio," I told him. "I'm going to get you some painkillers. You'll feel better in no time after you've taken them."

A few minutes later, while Mauricio was putting two Paracetamol pills into his bleeding mouth, we heard the sound of blows and some bloodcurdling screaming. My heart stood still. Now what? Steven emerged out of the long grass and strode towards us. His lantern had gone out.

"I had to hit them," he told me with some satisfaction. "They refused to leave. Then they kicked my lantern and broke it and so I gave them all something to remember."

On the way back to the house, I stopped off at the cook hut to pick up the pot Biasse had left simmering on the mud brick stove. How fortunate the trouble had been something I'd been able to handle on my own. Why did things always have to happen when O'D wasn't around?

In the sitting room, I sat down at the table and filled a soup bowl with Biasse's vegetable soup. It had pasta in it and made a substantial, warming meal on this wet and windy night.

The room was brighter and warmer too because we had replaced our black plastic blinds with some sleeping mat blinds. These were not only better at keeping the wind and rain out but improved the look of the house, giving it a nice cozy bush look on the inside and a nice casual bush look on the outside.

The day's wind, though, had blown some grass off the roof and it had sprung several leaks. Over the drip drip drip of water dripping into buckets, I listened to my static-filled radio. Sleep would be impossible, I knew, while O'D was in trouble somewhere in the forest.

It was about half past eleven when I heard the distant sound of a vehicle driving slowly along the forest track towards the house. I walked over to the east-facing window and, peering out through a gap in the sleeping mat blind, I saw a strange glowing light wavering down the track towards me. Something huge and lumbering seemed to be following behind it. Puzzled, I shone my torch in the direction of the peculiar light.

A running man wearing soaked and filthy clothes came into view. Holding a smouldering branch up in the air, he ran slowly down the track in front of the green Gaz. A Gaz loaded with logs and workers and that had no lights ... No lights on a black, moonless and starless night like this!

No one bothered to unload the logs. The moment O'D hit the brakes, everyone abandoned the Gaz and vanished into the night. They were wet and freezing. They were hungry. And they were tired.

In the sitting room, O'D rubbed his wet hair dry with a towel and drank a steaming cup of coffee.

It had rained so much in the forest during the day, he told me, that it had turned the ground into a sea of mud. On the way out, both lorries had sunk down to their axels and they had spent hours trying to dig them out.

In the end, they had succeeded in freeing the green Gaz, but they had had to leave the blue Gaz behind. Then, on the way home, the lights of the green Gaz had failed and as they had used up the torch batteries earlier on, O'D had had to think of other alternatives to light his way home.

Determined not to spend an uncomfortably soggy night in the forest without food and warmth, O'D's ever inventive brain had come up with an idea. He had turned to Nunes, who was sitting in the passenger seat next to him.

"Give me your cigarette lighter, Nunes," O'D had ordered.

197

By now, the rain had stopped and so O'D had comandeered one of the workers to run down the slippery, slidey forest roads and to hold Nunes' cheap plastic throwaway cigarette lighter and its tiny flame up in the air so that he could follow it. It hadn't exactly been easy driving behind the lighter, O'D told me. For some reason, the worker holding the lighter had irritatingly been unable to run in a straight line down the middle of the road. Running from left to right and then from right to left again, the tiny flame had weaved all over the place.

"He really confused me," O'D said, " and if I hadn't been careful, we would have been off the road and into the bush!"

When the lighter had run out of fuel, they had stopped near some huts and had asked for a burning branch or a glowing stick of wood to help them on their way but the villagers had refused to give them anything. According to local superstition, they believed that giving strangers a glowing coal or a burning branch after dark might result in their spirits being stolen from them.

Eventually, they had found a man who knew one of our workers. Reassured by a familiar face, he had parted with a small smouldering stick and this had been the strange wavering light I had seen coming towards me.

The rains stopped for a while and the sun came out. In the forest, O'D dug out the blue Gaz and brought it home.

Then, two days before the end of the month, O'D gave me some very bad news.

"We won't be able to pay the wages on Saturday," he told me. "We're broke. Flat, stony, broke."

We were in the sitting room at the time and I sank back in my chair, feeling panicky. No money! Just what I had always dreaded.

"How much do we actually have?"

O'D put his hand into one of his trouser pockets and pulled out a couple of coins. Five meticais! The only money we had in the world. Not even enough to buy a shoelace!

How ironic it was to be penniless while we were sitting on an enormous pile of valuable hardwood planks and beams!

"But there must be someone out there who wants to buy planks, surely!" I cried. "What are we going to do?"

"I don't know," O'D said. "Caetano and I have tried everything."

After hearing the dreadful news about the state of our finances, I went into the bedroom and closed the door. There was only one thing left to do now, I knew, and that was to speak to God and ask Him for help. This was not something the Anglican Church had ever told me we could do, but O'D and I were desperate and He was our last hope.

I sat down on the chair next to the window. "God," I begged, "God, we need money to pay our workers their wages. Help us, please! You're the only One who can do it."

The next morning, at around about ten o'clock, I heard the sound of a car driving slowly down the forest track towards us. My heart gave a little leap. Could this be a customer? The answer to my prayer? I peered out of the sitting room window but when I recognised the plump driver sitting behind the steering wheel of the white pickup as it drove slowly past the house, my spirits fell again. Oh, it was only Mendonca …

Teofilo Mendonca was from the Department of Labour in Chimoio and something of a special friend of O'D's, although I couldn't understand why. Smooth, plump and softly spoken, like most Mozambicans he was always wanting things from us. Things like whisky … or money … and once, O'D had even given him my old computer notebook and printer.

Disappointed, I turned away from the window. A 'wanting' person was the last person we needed in our situation. I didn't even bother going out to greet Mendonca, but picked up a book and began to read.

An hour went by before I heard the sound of Mendonca's vehicle starting up again and driving down the track. "Goodbye, goodbye," I muttered, as the sound of the pickup grew fainter and fainter.

O'D came into the sitting room, rather jauntily, I thought. I looked up from my book.

"I suppose Mendonca wanted some free wood from us and you gave it to him … for nothing," I said accusingly.

"Yes, he did want some wood," O'D told me. "Quite a lot of wood, in fact. He's building a house for himself."

Beginning to fume at the thought of such an expensive freebie while our workers went without their wages, I opened my mouth. But before I could say another word, O'D got in first.

"And he gave me this," he said.

He pulled some large bundles of meticais notes out of his trouser pockets and put them down on the table.

Amazed, I stared at the bundles. "Don't tell me he actually PAID for the wood!"

"Yes," O'D said and a great big grin lit up his face. "He got some money from somewhere ... and ... it's the exact amount we need to pay the workers!"

Awestruck and thrilled by this evidence that God had actually heard my prayer - and had answered it so speedily - I began to laugh. "A miracle! It's a miracle!" Imagine God answering my prayer! Imagine God using someone like Teofilo Mendonca to rescue us from the crisis we were in! If ever there was an unlikely tool ... but then God didn't have much to choose from in a country like Mozambique, did He?

In the bedroom, I sat down on the chair next to the window. Relieved that another crisis was over and overwhelmed by God's quick response, all I could say was "Oh God, thank you, thank you, thank you!"

In some strange way, Mendonca's visit and purchase of wood from us acted as a catalyst and released us from the terrible financial limbo that had held us in a stranglehold for so long.

A few days later, we had another visitor. This was a small man called Mr. Pasos who came on foot from Chimoio to buy planks from us. Then, when O'D went to Chimoio to buy fuel, he bumped into Clive who ordered some planks to make new decks for the Tabex trailers. Not long after this, Maciel, who was building a new house for himself, saw the timber Clive had bought and ordered wood for his kitchen cupboards.

Things were looking up a little - at last!

Mozambique was beginning to stir out of the ashes of war and reconstruction was finally in the air.

Word spread quickly that there was a small sawmill producing much needed timber and soon Government departments began to order our wood, along with Aid Agencies and Missionaries. They needed to repair existing schools, hospitals and clinics and to build new ones. The schools needed wooden beams for their roofs, doors and window frames, as well as desks and chairs for all the new pupils starting to get an education. Hospitals and clinics needed cupboards in which to keep their medical equipment. Churches needed benches.

Lorries began to arrive at the sawmill from Manica, from Inchope and even as far afield as Maputo!

And then there were the needs of the ordinary people ...

Jethro and Manuella who owned the little shop called Daisy Commercial in Macate bought planks for shelving and a widow called Argentina, who had little money, bartered for wood in a novel and most unusual way. Astutely deciding that O'D's weak spot was a sweet tooth, she offered a product of her own which she knew he just wouldn't be able to resist. Cakes! Every time Argentina needed some planks, she baked a delicious cake for O'D and after placing it on a tray, covered by a clean embroidered cloth to protect it from flies, she sent it off through the forest to us on the head of a young barefoot boy.

In no time at all, dozens of carpenters from Chimoio also began to make their way down to the sawmill. They came every day, on foot and clamouring for wood. To reach us, they caught chappas (beat-up old pickup taxis) at the market and travelled down in the open backs of these vehicles as far as the turnoff at Lica where they were dropped off. From the turnoff they walked the six kilometres down the forest track to us and then, after choosing their planks or beams with the help of Frank, our Cubicador, they walked the six kilometres back to the main road and sat and waited for another chappa to come along and take them back to Chimoio. A round trip of 76 kilometres. How about that for a shopping trip!

As we always cut our planks according to the size of the log unless a customer asked us for a special size, we had looked around for someone who could measure the volume of our planks and calculate the price of each individual piece of timber.

Hearing on the grapevine that we had started sawing, a small, bearded and often drunken man called Frank had approached O'D in town one day and had begged for a job. Frank had once worked at Tabex until O'D had fired him for being constantly drunk at work.

"I don't employ drunkards, Frank," O'D had told him sternly.

"I will mend my ways," Frank had promised. "I will only drink at weekends."

As Frank had been the only candidate for the job, it hadn't taken much begging from Frank for O'D to relent. "Alright, Frank," he had said. "See that you keep your promise."

Frank had turned out to be a pretty good Cubicador and as he spoke English very well, he soon became indispensable to me. He helped me out when I had trouble understanding a customer or they

201

had trouble understanding me. As I've said before, unlike O'D who has a natural talent for languages, my Portuguese wasn't (and still isn't) exactly wonderful.

Although every now and then we caught a whiff of Nippa on Frank's breath, he always insisted that this was only the residue of a couple of tots over the weekends and that he was keeping to his promise.

He did have one habit, though, which while it amused me, drove O'D to distraction. For some reason Frank always called me "Sir" and O'D "Madam".

"You've been drinking again, haven't you, Frank?" O'D would accuse him, irritated at being called Madam. "*I* am Sir and this", O'D would say, pointing at me, " is Madam!"

"Yes, Madam ... er ... Sir," Frank would stutter.

No matter how O'D went on at him, Frank continued to reverse our roles and as the years went by, O'D finally became reconciled to being called "Madam ...er ...Sir" and in my case "Sir ... er ... Madam".

As our sales increased daily and more and more people came down to us on foot, in pickups, in lorries and tractors with trailers, we realised we needed a day guard to supervise the activities of our customers. Customers who just might get carried away and walk off with some of our equipment instead of buying our timber.

The Mozambican we employed as our day guard was called Uonatomale Tepo but he insisted that we call him 'Cinco Metro'. He was very proud of this nickname as it means five metres and had been given to him because he was unusually tall for a Mozambican.

Raimundo built a wooden guard hut for Cinco Metro a short distance away from our house and together with a wooden pole as a barrier and an exercise book and a Chinese ballpoint pen, he set about controlling our customers.

Selling timber to a mass of customers who had no transport meant that we had to provide the transport. So, twice a week, O'D loaded our customers' wood onto the back of the blue Gaz and drove it into Chimoio where, at the estaleiro Caetano had rented from his friend Joao de Conceicao, he was besieged by a crowd of waiting carpenters, all waving their facturas (receipts) at him. When their wood was off-loaded, the carpenters hired chovas (a large type of wheelbarrow) and pushed their planks to their houses or primitive little workshops.

Now that we finally had customers, the money we were earning not only went into paying off the awful BPD bank loan a little faster but we even had some left over to buy a much needed item or two, as well as some bags of whitewash.

And so Seven, a young man of many talents, tied a plastic bag suicidally over his head to protect himself from paint splotches and set about turning our old ramshackle Portuguese house into a vision of sparkling white.

With the coming of the rains, it seemed our long financial drought was also over.

O'D Pixley

Caetano, O'D's Mozambican partner at Nhamacoa sawmill (1992 – 2002)

As we were, in the beginning - 1994

Me

Biasse, our cook, who made my life in the forest easier.

Above: The cook hut – my first kitchen in the Nhamacoa. Alberto, the gardener standing in front of it. Below: Our workers, with Frank in the front holding the hat.

Above: Loading logs the hard way – by hand. Below: Fernandinho bringing logs back to the sawmill with the MTZ Russian tractor.

Above: Azelia, Frank's wife who worked for us for 8 years in the Nhamacoa.
Below: The blue Gaz 66 Russian lorry driving over a makeshift plank bridge.

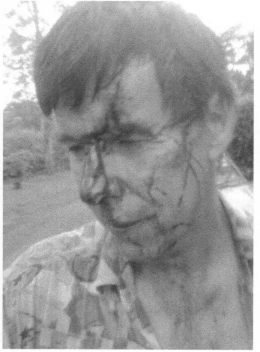

Above: Sawing planks for the reconstruction of schools, hospitals, clinics and churches, which had been ruined during the civil war.

On the left: O'D wounded by the bandits who attacked our house in the forest with an AK47, a pistol and machetes on 5 December 2010

Our house in the Nhamacoa foerest, before and after.

CHAPTER FIFTEEN

A SITTING TENANT CALLED UWE

One morning, O'D woke up feeling terribly ill. The whites of his eyes had turned a dull yellow and he told me that he thought he had malaria. Even worse, that he thought his malaria was cerebral!

"You'll have to tie me down if I go off my head and start thrashing around and raving," he warned me.

His words horrified me. Tie him down! A doctor, O'D had to get to a doctor! But how?

"I can't drive the blue Gaz!" I cried. I didn't have the strength to drive this lorry and besides that, my feet couldn't even reach the pedals.

O'D climbed groggily out of bed. He pulled on some clothes. "Doesn't matter," he said. "I can drive myself to the hospital. I'll take Avelino with me."

While I stayed at home, worrying and on tenterhooks, O'D somehow got himself to the hospital. There, Pepe, a nurse O'D knew well, confirmed that he had malaria, bad malaria, and injected him with Halfan.

Managing to drive himself back home again, O'D collapsed weakly into bed. Sweating and freezing and complaining of an agonising headache, he vomited a thin stream of yellow into the plastic bowl I held under his chin.

This time, I knew, he was surely going to die. I had never seen him look so ill, not even when he had been brought down with that hepatitis he had caught from Mr. Mabaleza, the witch doctor.

In the bathroom, I poured water into the plastic bowl, rinsing it out and flushing its contents down the lavatory.

A terrible dread filled me and I tried to stamp it down. Oh, what were we doing in this wild and isolated place, all alone and miles away from medical help? Without even a telephone?

I sat down on the edge of the bed and stared at O'D helplessly. "God," I begged silently, "please don't let O'D die. Oh, please, don't let him die…"

O'D opened his eyes and caught me staring at him. Understanding my fear, he gave me a ghastly smile of reassurance. "Don't worry," he muttered, "I'm not going to die."

"Promise," I said, wanting to cry.

"Promise," he said, and closed his eyes again.

That night I dreamed a strange dream about O'D and my father. In the dream, I saw O'D climbing high mountains until he finally arrived at a small village in Tibet.

A little white road led up past a row of wooden houses on the mountainside and O'D walked up this road until he came to a house with its shutters thrown wide open.

Standing under the window, he looked up and called out, "I'm here!" and although he didn't put in an appearance, a voice that I knew was my father's called back to him, "It's not time yet!"

When I woke up in the morning, I knew O'D was going to be alright. The meaning of the dream had been clear.

While O'D lay sick in bed, customers continued to pour into the sawmill and as we had no way now of transporting their purchases to Chimoio, the piles of planks and beams waiting delivery rose higher and higher. What we needed was a reliable driver who could stand in for O'D and wouldn't smash up our one and only good vehicle. But where to find one?

About five days after O'D had fallen ill, Frank appeared at the east-facing sitting room window, accompanied by a tall and well-built Mozambican with a pleasant face and a wispy beard that ended in a straggly point.

"This is Mr. Fernand, Sir ... er ... Madam," Frank introduced us. "He is a driver and needs a job. He wonders if you would like to employ him now that the boss is ill."

"Are you a real driver with a real driving licence?" I asked Fernand.

He pulled a small card out of his shirt pocket. It claimed to be a Mozambican driving licence and came with a photograph. Carefully, I checked the photograph, comparing it with Fernand's face in front of me. Everything looked alright, but I knew that papers meant nothing in Mozambique. As for his driving ability, we would only find out about this when he had driven off into the distance with our precious Gaz.

In the bedroom, I showed Fernand's driving licence to O'D. "Well, what do you think?" I asked. "Shall we let him drive the blue Gaz?"

"We haven't got any choice," he replied weakly.

For once, luck was with us. Fernand turned out to be a capable and reliable driver and it seemed we had found a treasure. While O'D languished in bed, work continued. Logs were brought in, sawn into planks and beams, bought and paid for by our customers and transported to Chimoio every day by Fernand who never put a dent into the blue Gaz.

Fernand also kept us in contact with Caetano and the outside world and began to bring faxes back to us from the post office. These faxes were from Willy in the Algarve and they were not good news.

He had put Arrojela on the market, Willy told us, and although there had been a lot of interest, there was a problem. A big Germanic problem. Despite being given several weeks' notice to move out, our German tenant, Uwe Heitkamp, was still in the house! And not only that, but he was also behaving in such an obnoxious manner that he was driving away dozens of potential buyers.

When Willy arrived with people who were interested in buying Arrojela, Uwe turned nasty. Rudely refusing access to our house, he sometimes even slammed the door shut right in Willy's face.

So much for Uwe's promise to O'D that he wouldn't cause any problems if we should put Arrojela up for sale! The pony-tailed German had turned himself into a 'sitting tenant', another bullying Hitler, illegally occupying territory that didn't belong to him.

"Send a fax to Willy," O'D instructed me from his sick bed, "and tell him to remove our generator and the two water pumps from Arrojela. Cutting off his electricity and water will be sure to get Uwe off our land!"

The fax we received back from Willy astonished us. He had been in contact with a lawyer, he told us, and it appeared that Uwe could take *US* to court if we took away his right to electricity and water.

"But Uwe's in *our* house, *illegally!*" I exclaimed. "Don't *we* have any rights?"

"Send a fax to Willy," O'D instructed me weakly from his pillows. "Tell him to get a Court Order to remove Uwe from Arrojela!"

212

The fax Fernand brought back from the post office in Chimoio filled O'D and me with incredulity. "Can only get a Court Order if you take Uwe to court," Willy told us, "and that might take months - even a year."

So much for the Algarvean system of justice!

Faxes flew between Mozambique and Portugal but Uwe remained obdurate and now even began to threaten *us*! He had been to see his lawyer in Lagos and she ... She? Could this be Carmen again? ... had told him that we had been in the wrong to rent Arrojela out to him in the first place; that we had neglected to obtain a certain paper from the Council certifying that Arrojela was in a habitable state and as a result, Uwe could take us to court for renting Arrojela out to him under false pretences!

Uwe's arrogance enraged me. How dared this German carry on like this in MY house!

No one had forced him to rent our house and he had lived in it quite happily for almost six years, paying only a nominal rent of one hundred and ninety eight pounds a month.

And how, I wanted to know, did someone like Uwe get to have more rights to MY house than I did?

We were fast approaching the two year deadline of John Phillip's loan to us and with Uwe messing around like this, there was the danger of Arrojela falling into John Phillips' hands for a quarter of her value, leaving us with absolutely nothing. Trapped in the Nhamacoa by malaria as well as a lack of money for an airfare to Portugal to sort things out, O'D and I wracked our brains on how to deal with the German. How were we going to get the wretched man out of Arrojela before time ran out for us?

We were still in a deadlock with Uwe when O'D finally felt well enough to get out of bed. Driving up to Chimoio in the blue Gaz, he met Caetano and Caetano had a suggestion. Mr. Goncalves had disappeared but there was another witch doctor in Chimoio and he was sure the man would know how to get Uwe out of our house, out of Arrojela and out of our lives.

In his little brick house in a crowded suburb of town, the witch doctor listened intently to what O'D had to tell him.

"You must write a letter to the German" he told O'D, "bring it to me and I will put a curse on it. The letter must be put into his hand personally and it will make him leave your house and your property immediately."

213

The fact that the cursed letter to Uwe would have to be sent in the form of a fax didn't faze the witch doctor. Letter or fax, a curse was a curse. The only thing that O'D had to ensure, however, was that the cursed fax had to be put into Uwe's hand personally by the person who received it at the other end.

Once again enlisting Willy's aid, O'D sent the fax off to the Algarve. Now Uwe would have to watch out! Now Uwe would get his comeuppance!

Convinced that our German squatter would shortly be fleeing Arrojela for unspecified reasons, O'D turned his mind to more pleasant things and went back to work.

Unbeknown to O'D, however, when the cursed fax came out of the fax machine in Willy's house in the Algarve, his plan began to unravel.

Loathe to endure another unpleasant encounter with the belligerent German on his own, Willy persuaded Tom Waterer, a visiting cousin of the Pixley brothers, to accompany him to Arrojela. When they arrived at the house, they found no one there - much to Willy's relief! - and so he decided to ignore the witch doctor's instructions to personally hand O'D's message to Uwe. Getting out of the car, he slipped the cursed fax through the crack under the front door and then, duty done, he got back into the car and he and Tom drove away.

In the meantime, O'D and Caetano were making preparations to begin felling in Machaze, the new felling area Caetano had found. They had sent equipment and a group of our workers to set up a base camp there but already it was becoming obvious that this was going to be a difficult place in which to operate. It was far from us, the roads were in a terrible condition and the local Administrator, his assistants and the police were unfriendly, unhelpful and extremely corrupt.

Within a few weeks, our small band of workers was in trouble with the locals. Enticing women away from their husbands, they were embroiled in fights and wrote letters, written on scrappy pieces of paper torn out of exercise books, telling us they had been thrown into jail and begging us to get them out.

And then trouble of another sort reared its head when we sent Fernand off to Machaze in the blue Gaz loaded down with equipment and pulling a tractor on a trailer.

While waiting several hours at the market for Caetano to give him a paper from the bureaucratically slow Department of Forestry,

Fernand, flamboyantly dressed for the journey in cowboy boots and a white cowboy hat glittering with sequins, got bored and decided to overcome this boredom in the usual Mozambican way. By the time Caetano arrived, our driver was too drunk to stand and was lolling around on the ground against one of the Gaz's front tyres.

"What are we going to do with him?" Caetano asked O'D.

"Fire him and look for another driver," O'D replied.

Caetano found another driver called Tacarinduwya and warning the man about drinking while driving, O'D entrusted the blue Gaz to him. Travelling up to Machaze without a problem, Tacariunduwya deposited our equipment and more workers at base camp and returned safely back to the Nhamacoa. Thinking that all was now going well in our new area, O'D and Caetano put Machaze out of their minds for a while.

In October, we received a marvellous order from John Fortescue of Msasa timbers for his door manufacturing company in Zimbabwe. The order was for twelve cubic metres of first class Umbila and would go a long way towards paying off our debts.

Luck, it seemed, was at last on our side and our fortunes had finally turned around.

When the Msasa timber order was completed, Fortescue and his partner Clive Walsh drove down to visit us and to check on the quality of the planks. Pleased with what they saw, they told us they would be sending their driver and lorry to transport the wood to Zimbabwe. Fortescue would deal with the paperwork on his side of the border and we would, of course, deal with the paperwork on the Mozambican side.

Caetano dealt with our export paperwork and was surprised when the official at the Chamber of Commerce in Beira handed one particular paper back to him, telling him it wasn't needed. For a moment, Caetano thought about questioning this but then, deciding that the bureaucrats knew what they were doing, he gave a shrug and travelled back to Chimoio.

With all the documents approved and stamped, O'D phoned Fortescue and he sent his driver Mescheck to pick up the timber.

In the blue Gaz, O'D followed the lorry to the border, seeing it through Machipanda without any complications and waving Mescheck goodbye when he drove across the Munene River towards Forbes Border Post.

An hour or so later, O'D was back in Chimoio and sitting with Caetano at the Sports Clube when the hammer blows began to rain down on them. Bad news came thick and fast, just like the messengers who had come to tell Job of his losses.

The first messenger to arrive was Momahd. Returning from Machaze on a chappa, he had terrible, heart-stopping news about Alfixa, our chainsaw operator.

Alfixa had cut down a tree, Momahd told O'D and Caetano, and when he had leapt out of its way while it was falling, he had caught his foot in some undergrowth and had, himself, fallen ... right in its path! The tree had crashed down on top of one of his legs, crushing and smashing it.

"We carried him to the only clinic in the area," Momahd went on, "but the people there couldn't do anything to help. So we hired a driver and his pickup and we took Alfixa across the Zimbabwean border to Chipinge, the nearest place to Machaze where there is a hospital."

The journey to Chipinge had taken two long and agonising days in the dilapidated old car and by the time the doctor at the hospital had examined Alfixa's leg, it was rotten and full of maggots.

"The doctor cut off Alfixas' leg," Momahd said. "He cut it off above the knee."

While they were listening, appalled, to the awful accident that had happened to Alfixa, another messenger arrived at the Sports Clube with bad news from Faruk, O'D's Indian shopkeeper friend.

There had been several phone calls for O'D on Faruk's shop phone, Faruk's messenger told O'D and Caetano, as well as some faxes on Faruk's shop fax machine. The calls and the faxes had all been from someone called Fortescue who had had a very loud shouting voice over the phone and although Faruk couldn't understand a word of English, it hadn't been difficult to get the idea that this Fortescue had been very angry about something.

Still benumbed by the news about Alfixa, O'D and Caetano hurried off to Faruk's shop. What had gone wrong now? Inside, Faruk handed over some long white pieces of paper.

Scrawled in extremely large and menacing black handwriting, the faxes read:

MESCHECK IS STUCK WITH THE LORRY AT THE BORDER!

ERRORS IN EXPORT PAPERS!

MY LORRY IS NEEDED IN SOUTH AFRICA URGENTLY!
YOU BETTER DO SOMETHING TO UNSTICK THE
LORRY - OR ELSE!!!!

It seemed we had been sabotaged! The paper Caetano had handed to the Customs official in Beira and which the man had handed back to him, telling him it was no longer needed, was apparently vital to the export. Without it, Fortescue would have to pay extremely high import duties on the wood he had bought from us!

Dazed by these events and trying to gather his wits together, O'D phoned Fortescue.

"I'm going to send another driver to the border with a car," Fortescue told O'D, knowing our situation with regard to vehicles. "Mescheck can meet you in Chimoio with this car and take you to Beira to get the missing paper stamped."

By the time the Beira Chamber of Commerce had dealt with the missing paper, Fortescue's lorry had been stuck at the border for three days and our popularity rating with Fortescue had sunk to an all-time low. In fact, he never again gave us another order and his was the first and last export of timber we ever did.

Alfixa received excellent treatment at Chipinge hospital. Taking the loss of his leg philosophically, he told us that it had happened because 'it was his time'. At first, he learned to walk with crutches and then later, when he was ready for it, we took him to a clinic in Beira where he was measured and fitted with a brown plastic leg. It was a very cheap leg, but it was all that was available, and every now and then he complained that the screws were coming lose and O'D would make him take it off and fix it for him.

By now our stress levels had risen to a new high and the news that Uwe was still at Arrojela and in our house didn't help. The power of Mozambican witch doctors, it appeared, could not extend across continents and had no effect on big belligerent Germans. It was time we started issuing threats of our own.

Writing one last fax to our unwelcome tenant, we told him how much money we were going to lose because of his actions and that if he didn't get out of our house right away, we were going to take him to court no matter how long it would take and sue him for damages for the loss of our house and the losses he had caused to our company.

This fax brought a reaction from Uwe. Contacting Willy, he told him that he would agree to leave our house but only on one condition. That he could continue to live there for another two months … RENT FREE!

"I wish we could afford to hire a hit man," I told O'D.

There was nothing for it but to agree to Uwe's outrageous demands.

Later on, we discovered why Uwe had been so reluctant to move out of Arrojela. He had bought a plot of land and had been busy building a house. As his house wasn't quite ready for habitation, he had decided to remain nicely ensconced in ours.

Although the success of his blackmail sweetened Uwe's mood and he graciously allowed Willy to bring people to look Arrojela over, the damage his recalcitrance had done couldn't be repaired. We had run out of time and the best buyers had been driven away. In a hurry now, we were forced to accept the only offer Willy received, an offer that was thirty thousand pounds well below Arrojela's value.

The day I lost Arrojela I put on a black T-shirt and black jeans to match my black mood. Sitting in a chair in the sitting room, I brooded on the terrible loss of my lovely house and of my security. Everyone had assured me that Arrojela would be safe, would never slip out of my hands … and now it belonged to someone else! I would never again cook in the pretty kitchen with the hand-painted tiles of purple grapes and ochre pears from Lisbon, never again amble through the hills, along paths so heavily scented with the fragrance of wild herbs, never again escape from the sun by sitting on the shady banks of the stream and cooling my feet in the running water …

This was all Chuck's fault! And Carmen's!

If Chuck hadn't interfered and messed up our plans for Matsinho, we would never have come to the Nhamacoa, never have had to take a loan out on Arrojela. And as for Carmen's contribution to my loss, if she hadn't been so incompetent and taken so long to get the paperwork in order, we wouldn't have had this trouble in paying John Phillips back.

O'D came into the sitting room for a drink of water. "Why are you looking like a Hell's Angel?" he asked me.

"Because I feel like one," I said. "This is how losing my house makes me feel. It makes me wish I had a motorcycle and could drive it backwards and forwards over Chuck and Carmen."

"It was my house, too," O'D said, and turned to hurry outside to avoid what he knew was coming.

218

"It's not the same for a man," I said, talking to his rapidly retreating back and beginning to lose it. "A woman's house is A WOMAN'S HOUSE! And look at what I've got IN ITS PLACE! A broken-down, window-less, grass-roofed shack in the middle of nowhere that ISN'T EVEN MIIIIIINE!"

Frustratedly left to myself, I mulled over my loss, wondering in amazement and some disbelief at how people we barely knew could have had such a damaging effect on our lives. And how none of them had even cared about what they had done, even getting angry with us! Chuck rushing off like that, making out that we were too difficult, Carmen angrily demanding an apology from O'D ... and as for Uwe ... UWE! causing us to lose thirty thousand pounds on Arrojela ...

How untrustworthy and dishonest everyone was!

A tear trickled down my cheek and plopped onto my black T-shirt. I had planned to grow old at Arrojela but now I knew I would never see it again.

At the end of the year, Steven, our night guard, fell ill with malaria and although O'D took him to Chimoio Hospital where they dosed him with a course of chloroquine he never seemed able to shake off the illness. He lost weight and his once powerful physique shrank until his clothes hung on him and he was just a shadow of the man he'd been when he'd first come to work for us.

O'D and I wondered if Steven's loss of weight meant that he had AIDS but our workers told us that he was smoking a lot of mbanje and even sprinkling large quantities of the drug onto his sadza at mealtimes as if it was a condiment!

Then one Sunday morning at about 10 o'clock, Steven stumbled down the track towards our house and collapsed down onto the dry brittle yellow grass just outside our front door. He lay on his back on the ground with his eyes closed and in a weak voice told us he was dying.

He certainly looked in a bad way. His chest was heaving up and down erratically and his whole body was trembling.

Alarmed, I looked up from Steven and at O'D. "You'd better take him to hospital right away!"

Steven's eyes flickered open. "No," he gasped, "I don't want to go to Chimoio. I want to go home to Masvingo. I want to die in my own country, Zimbabwe."

"Well," O'D said doubtfully, "I can give you the wages we owe you, Steven, but you don't look as if you're in any condition to travel."

Steven closed his eyes again. Sweat streamed down his face and trickled off his neck, onto the ground. "I want to go back home to Masvingo," he insisted, "I want to go back to Zimbabwe."

"Alright," O'D gave in. He went into the house and came back with Steven's wages, as well as a bonus of some Zimbabwe dollars we still had from the days when we used to cross the border to buy things and to visit friends. He put the money into Steven's right hand and Steven clutched the notes to his chest.

"I will rest here for a while," he told us.

We stood over Steven while he lay on the ground. I shook my head at O'D. We were looking down on a man who was not going to get his wish to die at home in Masvingo. Steven probably wouldn't even make it back to his hut in the Nhamacoa. How sad, how terribly terribly sad.

Steven's lips moved and he mumbled something from the battered Bible he had always carried around with him until it had fallen to pieces and the pages had blown away in the wind. This gave me an idea. I went into the house and came out with my own Bible. Compared to Steven's Bible, mine looked almost new although I'd had it for years. I took it with me wherever I went, like some talisman or good luck charm but shamefully, unlike Steven, I never read or opened it unless I wanted to find the answer to a Biblical clue in a crossword puzzle.

"Here, Steven." I bent down and carefully placed my Bible onto his chest. "Here's a new Bible for you."

Books were expensive, precious luxuries for Africans and he would, I knew, never be able to buy another Bible for himself. If he lived, of course.

Steven's left hand eagerly clutched the Bible to his chest. Unlike the money in his right hand, the Bible seemed to calm him ... even to strengthen him a little. After lying on the ground for another half an hour or so, he managed to raise himself up and swaying a little, walked weakly off down the forest track, beginning his journey back to Masvingo.

"I wonder if he'll get there," I murmured.

"Who knows," O'D replied.

Just before Christmas, I decided to have a springclean. Chuck had never come back for the stuff he and Eileen had left behind and as a whole year had gone by with no sign of him, I decided to give everything to our workers.

In the room underneath the house, I opened the cardboard boxes into which I had packed all their things, and got something of a surprise. Where were all Chuck and Eileen's blankets and pillows, their pots and pans, their plates, their soup bowls, their cups, their glasses, their knives and forks? Box after box was empty!

Kneeling in front of the last box, I opened it up and peered inside. Oh, this one actually still seemed to have something in it … there, in the corner … Putting my hand down inside the box, I pulled the object out. It was an old pink knitted teacosy with a moth hole in it.

Holding the old teacosy in my hands, I sat back on my heels. Well, well, well. It seemed that the workers had already known what my thoughts were going to be long before *I* had even known them and that throughout the year, they had helped themselves to all the contents of the boxes during the long, dark nights.

I was beginning to get the idea that the human race was a stuff up. Was there anyone out there who could still be trusted?

I dropped Eileen's old teacosy back into the cardboard box and stood up. "Happy Christmas, everyone," I said, "and goodwill to all men."

CHAPTER SIXTEEN

THE RETURN OF NORA SWETE
1997

After Steven left, we turned some of our workers into night guards and they armed themselves with pangas and large sticks and reluctantly and nervously patrolled around the house and the woodsheds. They weren't at all happy about this because there was a ghost roaming around the sawmill after dark and several local people had seen it, down by the river and at other times near the house and the saw.

This was the first time O'D and I had heard about the sawmill ghost but our new guards assured us that it did exist and that it terrified all who saw it by moving towards them threateningly with flashing red and green lights.

"Red and green flashing lights ..." O'D said, musingly. "Sounds like traffic lights ..."

"You know what I think?" I asked O'D, as I often did.

He gave me a look. "No, I have no idea what you're thinking," he replied, as he often did.

"I think this 'ghost' they're talking about was Steven's lantern." After Nunes' prostitutes had kicked Steven's lantern, it had developed a fault and had irritatingly flashed on and off all the time. "The locals were probably frightened when he wandered around at night and all they could see was this flashing light."

"Mmm," O'D said thoughtfully. "You could be right ... and there could be some benefits in this for us."

Hopefully, these stories of the flashing phantom would spread all over the area and prove to be a better deterrent than our reluctant guards at keeping the thieves away.

Early one morning, about two weeks after Steven had left for Masvingo, I wandered into the sitting room. Biasse and Seven were standing in the room and I noticed that both of them wore worried expressions on their faces. I opened my mouth to say good morning but before I could utter a word, Biasse got in first.

"I dunno about your radio, Madam," he said.

I looked at him blankly for a moment. 'I dunno about your radio' was a decidedly strange way to greet me at the start of a new day.

"What about my radio, Biasse?"

"It is gone, Madam."

Gone? I turned towards the bookcase and was shocked to see that Biasse was right. The spot where my radio had stood for the last two years was ... empty! Despair gripped my heart. The chance of finding another shortwave radio was practically zero, especially in Mozambique. Oh, what a disaster!

I ran out of the sitting room, out of the front door. Outside, I gave a loud scream of anguish.

My scream was so loud that everyone heard it, even over the sound of the generator and the whine of the saw. Everything ground to a sudden halt. Startled, our workers turned to stare in my direction. O'D come running up to me, alarm all over his face.

"My radio's gone!" I screamed, close to tears at the loss of the only companion, the only friend, I had in this solitary life I was leading. "GONE! Someone stole it in the night! I can't live here without my radio! I can't! I just CAN'T!"

O'D put a comforting arm around me. "We'll get it back," he assured me. "We did the last time it was stolen. Remember? That time when we went off to Harare for a long weekend and the Tabex guard stole it from under Biasse's nose?"

I shook my head, hopelessly. Finding a radio thief in the forest wouldn't be as easy as finding the thief on the Tabex farm. "No, we won't get it back this time. I know we won't."

Biasse thoughtfully brought up the kettle from the cook hut for coffee and I calmed down a little. Desperate for the return of my radio, I came up with an idea.

"What about offering a reward for it?" I suggested. "If it hasn't gone too far, someone will know who has it."

The word went out through our workers. A reward was offered and a promise that secrecy would shroud the identity of any informer.

Three days went by, days that were incredibly long and incredibly silent.

Then one morning, Cinco Metro sidled up to the open sitting room window and, dramatically looking around to make sure that no one was watching, put a hand over his mouth and, from behind his palm, whispered "There is a man here with a secret".

223

"Oh, and what is this secret, Cinco Metro?" I asked.

"Sshh!" He hissed and looked around dramatically again, thoroughly enjoying himself. "He has come about the reward. He wants to speak to the boss about it."

My heart gave a thump of hope. This had to be news about my radio!

"Well then," I whispered back at Cinco Metro, "go and call the boss ... but do it secretly, for Heavens sakes!"

Delighted with my instructions, Cinco Metro rushed off to get O'D.

When O'D walked up from the sawmill, a young man with twisted legs and a pole for a crutch moved laboriously over to speak to him. After a few minutes of more whispered conversation with O'D, he left.

"What's up?" I asked O'D. "Is this anything to do with my radio?"

O'D nodded his head. "Might be. Apparently, his uncle recently bought a radio with two aerials like ours ... from Steven ..."

My mouth fell open. "Steven!"

"... and paid him for it with thirty two chickens."

"Steven ..." I said again. "I thought he'd gone back to Zimbabwe ... to die."

A grim smile flitted across O'D's face. "No," he told me. "It seems that Steven's very much alive and kicking and living not far from us."

Later that afternoon, when Caetano arrived at the sawmill, he and O'D drove off into the forest in the blue Gaz. They returned an hour later, with huge grins ... and my radio!

"We gave the young fellow his reward," O'D told me while I examined the radio. To my dismay, it had deteriorated in the short time it had been away and looked a bit battered. One aerial was bent and the other had been broken off at the base. "We also had to pay his uncle some money, to reimburse him for the thirty two chickens," he went on. "It *was* Steven. He never did go back to Zimbabwe. We drove over to his machamba to speak to him and the moment he saw us, he ran away and disappeared into the bush."

"They broke it," I said. "They broke my radio and now it will never work again."

"Oh, I'm sure I can fix it," O'D said. "It's only the aerials." And while I looked on anxiously, he sat down and repaired the radio and by that afternoon, I had my unseen friends back again, to keep me company in the Nhamacoa.

The ease with which Steven had been able to climb through our unprotected sitting room windows and to escape again, undetected, with my radio made us renew our efforts to find a reliable and relatively honest night guard.

For a month or so, we tried out two guards sent to us from the Chimoio police. However, when Frank discovered they were helping the locals at the Lica turnoff to steal our planks in the dark of night, we fired them and the search for guards went on.

Finally, we found someone. This was a tall, thin man called Lovad who seemed a fairly sensible and responsible person.

One evening, some months after we had employed Lovad, he came to work and told us he was feeling ill with malaria. As we always had a supply of choroquine and paracetamol at hand in the house (chloroquine worked well at this time), O'D gave Lovad a course of these pills, taking great care to explain the dosage to him and even writing this down on the outside of the little brown packets he put them into:

Day one   4 chloroquine pills + 2 Paracetamol pills
Day two   4 chloroquine pills + 2 Paracetamol pills
Day three   2 chloroquine pills + 2 Paracetamol pills

Assuring O'D that he understood his instructions completely, Lovad went home to take his pills and to lie sweating and freezing on his sleeping mat in his hut. He would not be back for work, we knew, for several days.

Lovad surprised us, however, by appearing for duty the very next evening and by looking quite fit and strong.

"Lovad," O'D asked, "are you sure you're ready to start work again?"

"Yes, Patrao," Lovad replied cheerfully, "I'm completely cured."

"Well, even though you may feel better after one day, Lovad," O'D warned, "you must still finish all the pills I gave you."

Lovad's reply startled and alarmed both of us.

"I *have* finished all the pills, Patrao," he told O'D, and pulling three little crumpled brown envelopes out of the top pocket of his green guard's uniform, showed us that they were completely empty.

Our mouths fell open. Lovad had swallowed down all sixteen pills in one go!

For the next few days we watched Lovad closely, wondering if he was going to drop dead. The large dosage of chloroquine he had taken had certainly been effective in killing off all the malaria bubbling away in his bloodstream - would it do the same to him?

Time passed and as Lovad remained hale and hearty, we turned our attention to another problem, that of finding a suitable driver to replace Tacarinduwya, who, we had discovered, was also a drinking driver like Fernand.

As driving licences meant nothing in Mozambique and the only way we could test a driver's abilities was to put them into one of our lorries, O'D used the green Gaz for testing purposes. When driver after driver failed to reach O'D's standard, our assistant tractor driver Zerouso piped up.

"I know how to drive a lorry, Patrao."

"Why didn't you tell me before, then?" O'D asked, and prepared both himself and Zerouso for a test drive in the green Gaz.

Inside the cab, he went through the various gears and pedals with Zerouso to refresh his memory and then, when Zerouso assured O'D that he understood everything, he climbed out and clambered up into the open back of the lorry, not wanting to be trapped in the cab if Zerouso did anything stupid.

Zerouso turned on the ignition, pulled away with a succession of fearsome jerks and then, ignoring the track, drove flat out through the bush, lurching and bouncing straight over rocks and bushes and even flattening small trees!

Certain that the drive was going to end in disaster, I realised O'D had come to the same conclusion when I saw him fling himself off the back of the lorry to save himself just like a stuntman in a film. When he landed on the ground and rolled in the dirt, I cried "WOW!" and clapped my hands over my eyes. Was he hurt? Had he broken some bones?

Through the spaces in between my fingers, I saw O'D rise to his feet, red with dust. "ZEROUSO!" he screamed. "BRAKE! PUT YOUR FOOT ON THE BRAKE, YOU BLOODY FOOL!"

Almost invisible in the cloud of dust Zerouso had stirred up, the green Gaz came to a screeching, shuddering halt and stalled. O'D ran up to it. Remarkably, it was undamaged despite all the large and unusual obstacles Zerouso had driven it over.

"Get out, Zerouso," O'D said grimly, wrenching the driver's door open. "Why did you pretend you could drive when you obviously know NOTHING ABOUT DRIVING AT ALL!"

Zerouso was unrepentant. "It wasn't my fault, Patrao!" His voice rose up in an accusing whine. "This lorry's dangerous. Very dangerous! It's got something wrong with it. It almost killed me!"

Our next would-be driver arrived early one morning from Chimoio. He was a small fat man and although he looked as if his feet would barely reach the pedals of a lorry, he possessed a driver's licence stating that he was, indeed, a bona fide lorry driver.

This time, O'D sent him off in the green Gaz with Naison, our workforce supervisor in the forest.

While the man started up the green Gaz, O'D and I stood in front of the house and watched. We watched, wincing, as the Gaz laboured down the track, gears grating horribly as the driver forced them into position. We were still watching when our green lorry rounded the bend in the track and disappeared from sight. A disappearance that coincided with a sound - an almighty BANGING sound - that reverberated all over the forest causing the Vervet monkeys to chuck chuck chuck! in alarm and O'D and I to exchange a look.

We said nothing until we saw Naison walking back down the track towards us, alone.

"Well," I said, "at least HE isn't dead."

O'D looked grim. "If the driver isn't dead, he soon *will* be if he's smashed up my lorry."

Naison stopped in front of us. His face was expressionless. "Patrao," he said, "the driver lost control of the Gaz when we went around the bend ... and drove it straight into a tree."

"Is he hurt?" I asked.

"No," Naison told us. "He's gone."

Anticipating O'D's reaction to the destruction of the green Gaz, the man had fled.

We walked down the track with Naison and rounded the bend towards the scene of the crime. The green Gaz was a sorry sight, its front embedded into the trunk of a large eucalyptus tree. Water was still spurting out of the mangled radiator and the cab was crumpled beyond repair. On the ground, shards of glass glittered in the sunlight from the smashed windscreen.

"Well, that's the end of the green Gaz," I said.

"Perhaps not," O'D, who could repair almost anything, muttered.

Towing his wrecked lorry back to the workshop with the blue Gaz, he examined it. Luckily, the engine had come through the accident unscathed and as he just happened to have a spare cab among all the spare parts he was always buying, it wasn't long before he had the green Gaz on the road again. The only part that was missing was the windscreen.

"I'm not going to bother buying another windscreen," O'D told me grimly. "The quality of Mozambican drivers is so low, it'll probably only be a matter of days before they shatter it. Whoever drives the green Gaz will just have to put up with it as it is."

Now Naison stepped into the breach. "I know how to drive, Patrao," he said. "I don't have a driving licence but I learned to drive in Zimbabwe."

O'D examined him thoughtfully. Naison could only see clearly with his left eye, the right eye being covered with cloudy white cataracts.

"Alright," O'D came to a decision. "Let's give you a test and see how you get on."

The test drive satisfied O'D and the next morning, he set off into the forest in the blue Gaz with the workers, while Naison and Madeira followed in the green Gaz. Using a one-eyed driver who didn't have a driving licence meant nothing to us anymore. We had tried out so many Mozambican drivers who did have driving licences and who had damaged our lorry and been a danger to our workers that Naison was a relief to us all. Reliable, slow and careful, the only thing he wouldn't be able to do would be to drive anywhere out of the forest.

Naison had been driving for some weeks without any problems whatsoever when something quite worrying happened.

Our workers usually returned from the forest just before sundown but one night they didn't return at all. O'D and I waited and waited for them until the moon rose high in the starry night sky and it grew very late. What on earth could have happened? Had there been a breakdown? If so, why had no one run back through the forest as they normally did, to tell us about it? Or had there been an accident ... with Naison, our one-eyed, unlicenced driver at the steering wheel?

Early the next morning, just as O'D was about to go and look for our missing workers, we heard a familiar rumbling sound. And there, around the bend in the track, came Naison in the green Gaz loaded down with logs, followed closely by Fo'pence on the tractor with the trailer full of workers. Looking even more dishevelled than usual, they all slumped with exhaustion.

As Fo'pence drove slowly past the house, Madeira jumped off the trailer and came over to us.

"Bom dia, Patrao," he greeted O'D tiredly.

"Bom dia, Madeira," O'D said. "Well? Why are you so late?"

Madeira gave a shudder. "Something terrible happened to us last night, Patrao. Something very terrible. And it was all the fault of the scouts! They forgot to tell us there were graves near the panga pangas they had found ... and we cut the panga pangas down without making an offering to the Spirits!"

This oversight had angered the spirits and there had been breakdowns, tyres puncturing and a big black mamba slithering in and out of the Gaz cab! Forced to spend the night in the forest, our workers had huddled supperless around a small fire, hearing eerie sounds and seeing strange and frightening things. These things had included all the tractor tyres deflating and inflating themselves - all at the same time - and all night long!

In the morning, our forest crew had hastily made amends to the spirits. Kneeling down near the graves and with a few words of apology, they had placed a small offering of tobacco down on the ground.

Not long after our workers' scary experience in the panga panga grove, we found a driver for the blue Gaz. This was a man called Sabao who had worked for a Zimbabwean Construction Company until they had fired him for driving down a road he shouldn't have been driving down.

Sabao turned out to be a surprisingly good driver. With a penchant for the colour pink, he turned up for work every day in his driver's outfit which consisted of a pale rose-pink track suit, pale pink flip flops and a pale pink floppy cloth hat.

Nora Swete made her re-appearance in our lives early one morning when Sabao was driving down the forest track in the blue Gaz with a load of wood for our customers in Chimoio. Afonso, our chainsaw operator was with him that day, together with the little son of another of our workers.

Sabao and Afonso were chatting away happily without a care in the world when they turned a corner and saw a sight so terrible that it froze their blood and cut their words off in mid-stream. There, in the middle of the track and blocking their way stood a woman, a large, heavy-boned woman with a sack by her side and an enxada (hoe) in her hands. Nora Swete!

Unerringly sensing trouble, Sabao screeched to a halt and as Nora advanced menacingly towards them, Afonso pushed the little boy down to the floor of the cab to hide him and then, to save himself, jumped out of the Gaz and fled into the long grass, leaving Sabao to fend for himself.

Nora Swete stopped in front of the Gaz and raising her enxada high up in the air, smashed the big metal blade right through the middle of the windscreen! Shaking with terror, Sabao somehow managed to put the Gaz into reverse and roared backwards down the track to get away from her.

Mr. Alberto, the local Frelimo Party secretary, was all dressed up and on his way to town when he heard the tinkling sound of glass being smashed and the roaring sound of an engine being strained. Allowing his curiosity to get the better of him, he went to investigate and instantly regretted it.

Catching sight of Mr. Alberto in his bright yellow-gold shirt and smart maroon trousers, Nora Swete's eyes lit up with a pleasure that was enough to make any man's heart quake. He turned to flee … too late! … and found himself captive when a big strong hand shot out and grabbed his arm, jerking him up short.

"Kneel down!" Nora Swete ordered and pointed a large finger at a spot on the ground in front of her bare feet.

Trembling with fear and not knowing how to get himself out of the bad situation he had so suddenly found himself in, Mr. Alberto obediently knelt down on the dusty ground.

Nora Swete opened her sack and dug inside it with her hands. "Purification!" she boomed brassily at Mr. Alberto, "you need to be purified!" and to his consternation, she began to pour handfuls of salt all over him, rubbing it into his shaven head, all over his face, his neck, his arms, his yellow-gold shirt, his maroon trousers and his shoes. She went on and on … until the salt stuck to his sweating brown skin in a thick coating and turned it white from head to toe and he looked just like Lot's wife, who had turned into a pillar of salt when she had been unable to resist looking back at Sodom.

Escape came for Mr. Alberto when another unsuspecting traveller stepped out of the long grass and onto the forest track.

"Kneel!" Nora Swete's voice boomed out and in that second when she turned away from him and grabbed hold of her new victim, Mr. Alberto took the opportunity to dart off into the grass and vanish from sight.

Mr. Alberto didn't go to town that day. Apart from having to do something about his changed appearance, he had had quite a shock and needed to get over it. He walked back the way he had come, up the steep path through the trees and past his gaping wife. Inside his hut, he took off his salty clothes and then, wrapping a capulana around himself, he walked down a gentle slope towards a spot where his banana trees grew and where there was a little stream.

Throwing off his capulana, Mr. Alberto stepped into the stream. He lay down in it and let the water run over him, washing and washing away the salt that covered his body.

Nora Swete would have to do another stint in Chissui. She was obviously quite out of control … again!

And as for the blue Gaz and the large hole Nora Swete had smashed into its windscreen …

Well, O'D's reaction was predictable. "Another windscreen gone," he grumped. "Well, that's too bad. Sabao will just have to put up with driving it around as it is."

CHAPTER SEVENTEEN

BLACK KITTY

It was about ten o'clock in the morning when Black Kitty came across the puff-adder or the mvumbi, as the Mozambicans call it.

The snake, so ugly and so poisonous, was lying half hidden amongst the piles of dry, coppery brown leaves under the mango trees not far from the back stairs.

The fight was short and vicious.

Attacking from behind, Black Kitty lunged at the snake's neck and the snake reared up, opening its mouth wide and making a hideous roaring hissing sound.

Again Black Kitty struck, so fast the action was just a blur and again the puff-adder reared up and hissed.

Nearby, O'D, Seven and I stood tensely watching, not daring to make a sound in case we distracted Black Kitty and the snake's fangs found its mark in our young cat.

And then it was all over. Black Kitty struck one last time and the puff- adder lay dead. Disdainfully turning his back on the reptile, Black Kitty padded off through the leaves. Another one bites the dust. He hated snakes.

Seven bent down to scoop up the lifeless body of the puff-adder with a stick. According to African tradition, the snake must be thrown into the fire to prevent its mate from coming to look for it.

"E um bom cacador!" Seven grinned admiringly. "He's a good hunter!" Like most of our workers, he was proud of Black Kitty's hunting prowess.

I had met Black Kitty for the first time when I had gone down to the cook hut to speak to Biasse one morning and had seen a tiny kitten sitting just inside the cook hut door. What a little beauty it was! Pure black and velvety as a moonless African night, with eyes the deep green of emeralds.

"Is this your kitten, Biasse?" I had asked, bending down to stroke the kitten on its head. It had purred loudly, obviously used to humans.

"No, Madam. It's a kits from the bush."

"Then I'll have him," I had said, and picking up Black Kitty, had taken him upstairs to his new home.

For a bush cat, it hadn't taken Black Kitty long to feel at ease with us and to luxuriate in his new surroundings. In no time at all, he was sporting with the mosquito net over our bed, trying to force his face and body through the fine transparent material and then, when he failed, climbing its high folds right up to the top and then joyfully swinging and sliding and bouncing around on it. Although Black Kitty's claws ripped holes in the mosquito net, his antics were so hilarious we made no effort to stop his games. In any case, we had several other nets.

We had been plagued with rats and had battled with them ever since we had arrived in the Nhamacoa and although we bought traps at the market, the rat population had been too overwhelming to exterminate until, that is, Black Kitty had come onto the scene.

A formidable little hunter, he had cleared the house of rats and the entire area around it and then had gone on to bigger things, such as rabbits, which were often much larger than Black Kitty himself. Using the house as his den, he stored the dead rabbits either in O'D's tool cupboard in the spare bedroom or in the gap underneath the bookcase and made us feel quite queasy when we came across him munching on them with a lot of cracking and crunching of bones. A voracious eater, he left nothing behind, even eating up all the fur.

Fearless as he was, there was one animal that terrified him.

One afternoon, the baboons arrived and began to forage in the mango trees outside the sitting room window. Black Kitty had been sitting on the wide windowsill at the time and the sight of the creatures made him tremble violently from head to foot.

"Are these the ones who bit off your tail?" I asked Black Kitty.

Someone or something had either cut or bitten his tail and although it had healed completely, it was only half the length it should have been.

Black Kitty and I spent a lot of our time together. He became my companion and whenever I went for a walk down to the saw or along the forest track, he would come with me for the walk just like a dog. He liked being carried and when we turned to go back to the house, I would pick him up and he would purr with happiness.

One afternoon, when I was carrying him back from the saw, I felt his small body suddenly stiffen and heard his purrs turn into a menacing and rather frightening growl. Wondering what was wrong, I

233

stopped walking and looked in the same direction he was looking. And there, on the branch of a small tree right next to me, I saw it. A long green snake! Attuned to the natural world as I was not, Black Kitty made me realise how I blundered around in the forest, completely oblivious of all the creatures living so close around me. Unaware that they were watching me, I rarely saw them or heard them until they, themselves, gave me a warning hiss or a fright when they slithered or darted away.

I noticed Black Kitty's appreciation of music one afternoon when he was lying sprawled out on the carpet in the sitting room. Zimbabwe's Radio One was playing a particularly toe-tapping tune at the time and Black Kitty's short tail was keeping perfect time to its rhythm. Twirling his tail joyously from side to side, Black Kitty swung it to the left and then to the right, following the beat of the music as it went faster and faster and then slowing down as the tune slowed down. When the music came to an end, Black Kitty's tail gave a final flourish in the air before it stopped moving and lay still.

One day, Black Kitty disappeared. He vanished as Mitzi had vanished, without leaving any clues behind. At first we thought that his hunting expeditions had taken him further than normal but when the days passed and there was still no sign of him, we began to think that something terrible had happened.

"The baboons," I said, tearfully echoing Eileen's words of so long ago, "perhaps the baboons have killed him."

"Don't even think about it," O'D who loved Black Kitty as much as I did, told me. "He'll be back. I'm sure of it."

We were standing outside the house one late afternoon when we heard the faint weak miaow. "What's that? Listen," O'D said, just as Black Kitty came out of the long tall grass, dragging himself towards us, along with the snare that he had walked into.

He was a pitiful sight. For three days and three nights he had fought a desperate battle for survival while the wire of the snare had tightened and tightened so much around his neck that it had cut a bloody groove deep into the skin and had twisted between his legs, leaving wounds there as well. Exhausted and wounded and weak, he had fought on until, miraculously, the wire had snapped and he was free.

"The pliers! Get the pliers!" O'D ordered and when I came back with them, he carefully and gently cut the wire around Black Kitty's bloodied neck and removed the snare.

"Is he going to be alright?" I asked.

"I don't know," O'D replied.

Without a Vet, there was nothing we could do to help Black Kitty except to bring him into the safety of the house and give him water to drink and a little food. Tired out by his ordeal, he fell into a deep sleep and when he woke up, he began licking and licking at the wounds he could reach.

After about ten days, Black Kitty's injuries had healed and he was almost back to his old self again - almost, because later on when his fur grew over the scars, he was no longer a pure black cat. A fine white line of fur, like a necklace, now encircled his neck where the wire had bitten into it and another white strip ran down the inside of one of his legs.

Now that it was too late to save Arrojela, we were, ironically, earning a lot of money. As Chimoio's banks were notorious for their inefficiency, we hid this money in O'D's clothes cupboard, on the shelf where he kept his socks and underwear and T- shirts; a shelf that was always so untidy we were sure it would be too off-putting for any thief to contemplate searching.

Sometimes there was more than ninety million meticais hidden under O'D's clothes and after we had paid off all our debts, we decided to spend our profits on a much-needed article. A brand new Toyota pickup!

It's quite true to say that you only really appreciate something when you've been through a long period of deprivation.

The shiny white Toyota delighted us. It spelled freedom. Now we could drive across the border into Zimbabwe to see family and friends and buy the things we needed. When O'D parked the pickup under the shelter next to the east-facing sitting room windows, I ran my hands over its smooth shiny surface, touching a headlight, a windscreen wiper, as if I had never seen a car before.

In the house, one evening, O'D tried out the car alarm. "I wonder if I can lock and alarm the pickup from inside the sitting room," he said.

Lovad just happened to be ambling past the pickup when O'D squeezed the little plastic disc and the pickup made a high-pitched beeping sound and flashed its lights at him. "Aargh!" Lovad gave a startled shout and backed away from the empty pickup, examining it warily from a distance. Ah! The new car had a spirit in it!

Despite the dusty roads, the white Toyota always left the Nhamacoa in a spotless and gleaming state. Seven saw to that. He liked to keep things clean, although there were times when his enthusiasm for cleaning things carried him away and made him forgetful of past mistakes.

One Saturday afternoon when O'D and I were relaxing in the sitting room and reading books, Seven appeared in the doorway and hovered there, timidly.

O'D looked up from his book with irritation. He never liked being bothered by workers over the weekend. "Well, what is it, Seven?" he asked.

A picture of misery, Seven crept further into the room and shoved a tray at O'D.

We stared at the tray. There was a tiny shoe on top of it, a shoe that would have fitted a child of about five years old.

Suddenly, O'D let out what could only be described as a loud whooping howl.

Seven started back in fright at the sound.

"It's mine!" O'D spluttered, with another howl of suppressed laughter. "It's one of those animal skin shoes I bought at that safari shop in Zimbabwe. Seven's gone and miniaturised it by boiling it in a pot of water!"

Soon after the debacle of O'D's shoe, Seven decided to get married and like Daringua, he made an unwise choice. Although the girl he chose as his bride was beautiful and sparkling, she was also the deaf mute daughter of a Prophetess.

One day, Biasse came to me with a worried look on his face.

"It is Seven, Madam," he told me, "he has found an evil object in a corner of his hut. He thinks the Prophetess, his mother-in-law, has sent it there. She hates him and is wanting to kill him."

"To kill him? Oh, surely not, Biasse. He's probably just imagining all of this. You know how superstitious he is."

Biasse's face turned grim. "I think not, Madam."

We burned the evil object in a small clearing Seven made among the trees not far from the house. It was a thin cord on which seeds had been strung and I thought it could have been a clumsy attempt by someone to make a necklace but Biasse and Seven wouldn't have it. This was a fetish and they knew all about these things. The object was definitely evil and had been deliberately put into Seven's hut in order to harm him.

236

After Seven had thrown the evil object into the fire, he knelt down on the ground and repeated a prayer of protection I had found in the new Bible I had bought to replace the one I had given to Steven. Biblically ignorant as I was, I had spent hours rifling through its pages until at last I had come across something, coupled with a threat from God about what he did to wicked people, which I thought might suit Seven's situation. Standing behind the kneeling Seven, I read the passage out and he repeated it aloud in Shona.

A few days later, Seven did not appear for work. Although it had been burned, it seemed the evil object had done what it had been sent to do. His young wife had run back to her Prophetess mother and Seven now lay as stiff as a plank in his hut, completely paralysed from head to foot!

"I'm sure it's got absolutely nothing to do with that thing he found in his hut," I told O'D. "It's just in his mind."

Seven, like all Mozambicans, firmly believed in the power of witchcraft. Once, he had come to me to ask for money because he was suffering from bad pains in his legs. Thinking that he intended going to the Macate clinic for medical treatment, I had given him the money. Instead, he had gone to a curandeiro (a traditional healer) living in the forest not far from us and had returned, completely cured.

"Look, Meddem," he had told me, holding out a hand, "look what the curandeiro found in my legs!"

For a moment I had stared blankly at his outstretched hand. In the palm lay four rusty and bent nails and two razor blades. How was this possible?

"An enemy sent these things into my legs," Seven had explained excitedly, seeing my lack of understanding, "to hurt them and give them pain! And the curandeiro took them out!"

I had pictured the crafty curandeiro's slight of hand. Well, no matter. His rusty nails and razor blades had probably had a better effect on someone as gullible as Seven than a couple of Western pills would have had.

Now Seven lay as stiff as a board, convinced that the Prophetess's fetish was at work.

"You'd better take him to the hospital," I told O'D.

Two workers carried Seven over to the Toyota pickup. One held him under his arms while the other held him by his ankles. Stretched out straight and stiff between them, his body resisted gravity and didn't droop in the middle as a body would normally have done. They lay him down in the pickup's open back.

At Chimoio hospital, doctors and nurses examined Seven. They could find nothing physically wrong with him, they told O'D. However, they had seen this condition before. It was something to do with a fetish.

Seven's lips, the only part of him that wasn't paralysed, moved. "A witch doctor," he begged. "There is a witch doctor who can help me. Take me to him."

The witch doctor Seven insisted on seeing lived deep in the bush and apparently was the only one who had the knowledge to cure him.

Once again, our workers put Seven into the back of the pickup and O'D drove off with them all. When the dusty bush road petered out and the Toyota could go no further, he stopped the car and the two workers climbed out. For several kilometres, they staggered through the bush carrying Seven's rigid form between them until finally, they arrived at the witch doctor's hut.

It was to be about four or five months before we saw Seven again. The fetish, it seemed, had been a powerful one and took time to remove.

Fortunately, Seven's absence did little to disrupt work in the house. By this time, I had employed Azelia to wash our clothes and she now took on Seven's duties as well.

Azelia was Frank's pretty wife and she was as tall and slender as a model. She often sang while she ironed our clothes with the old fashioned, heavy charcoal iron. She was happy because she was earning money to spend on herself and didn't have to rely on Frank who often drank up his wages. After Seven had turned into a human plank and had disappeared into a faraway witch doctor's hut, she was happier than ever. She and Seven hadn't been too fond of each other, often bickering while they worked, and now, to her delight, he was gone.

In June, a rather ugly little incident occurred which showed me quite clearly to what extent I could rely on day guard Cinco Metro (and Frank!) for protection.

About a month earlier, three men in a white twenty tonner with Maputo number plates had appeared at the sawmill and had chosen seven first class panga panga planks. As they hadn't had enough money to pay for the planks, they had asked me to accept a small deposit in order to keep the planks for them until their return with the balance of the money two days later. I had agreed, and had told Frank to put the wood aside for them.

The weeks had flown by without a return visit from the Maputo men and then, during a run on timber when carpenters from Chimoio had even been standing in a bunchy queue by the saw itself, waiting to buy planks from logs in the process of being sawn up, Frank and I had decided to sell Maputo men's panga panga planks to a desperate customer.

"After all, Sir ... er ... Madam," Frank had told me, "we agreed to put the planks aside for two days only and it is now more than a month."

"Yes, Frank," I said, "and when ...or if ... they do come back, we'll just return their deposit."

As luck would have it, the Maputo men put in an appearance the very next day and on one of the three days a week when O'D was always away from the sawmill.

"You sold OUR planks?" they asked incredulously, standing in a group with Frank and Cinco Metro outside the east-facing window of the sitting room.

Inside the sitting room and on the other side of the open window, I handed back their small deposit. "Sorry," I told them, "but you told us you were coming back in two days' time and that was over a month ago. We don't normally hold timber for people, anyway."

One of the men moved closer to the windowsill and glared at me. "You must pay us compensation," he demanded menacingly. "Compensation for our fuel. We drove all the way from Maputo to collect our planks and now you tell us you have sold them. You have wasted our fuel!"

Growling in agreement, his two companions also pressed closer to the windowsill.

"Don't be ridiculous!" I retorted, knowing full well that they hadn't driven a distance of over one thousand kilometres just for seven planks. They had had other reasons for coming to Chimoio, other business. "I'm not going to pay you anything!"

The man's right hand shot out and shoved hard at my left shoulder, "We want compensation!"

The force of the shove jerked me backwards and I felt a flash of fury.

"Don't touch me!" I told him.

239

In answer, he gave my left shoulder another hard shove with his right hand. "GIVE US COMPENSATION!"

"Alright," I said tightly, "you asked for it," and turning away from the window, I walked quickly over to the corner of the sitting room where we kept Lovad's rifle. It had no bullets in it as O'D always took the magazine out in the morning but that didn't matter. With the element of surprise in mind, I walked back to the window making sure to keep the rifle out of Maputo men's sight.

Standing in front of them again, I hissed "Get out of here," with a menace of my own and slowly slid the barrel of the rifle threateningly over the windowsill, pointing it straight into the eyeballs of the man who had shoved me. "Get out of here, right now!"

The reaction I got was satisfying.

Ten panic-stricken eyes bulged with terror and Frank and Cinco Metro shouted, "No, Sir! No, Madam! No, Senhora! Don't shoot!" and pushed Maputo men down to the ground to protect them from me before dropping down themselves.

I looked over the windowsill at all the men, including Frank and Cinco Metro, now cowering down on the ground with their hands covering their heads. "I told you to go," I said coldly. "Now, GO!"

Slowly, they all stood up. The man who had shoved me looked at me with pure hatred. "You'd better never leave this place," he spat out. "You'd better never come to Maputo … because if we ever see you there …" he made a slitting movement at his throat with his hand "… we will KILL you!"

I raised the rifle and, making sure he would notice, slowly squeezed at the trigger with my finger.

"Go!" Frank pushed at the man, "Go on!" and at last they walked off towards their lorry. The twenty tonner started up with an angry roar, gears clashed and as they drove away, the man who had shoved me shouted something I didn't hear over the engine noise and made another slitting motion at his throat. And then they were gone.

"Cowards," I muttered. They would not have behaved like this, I knew, if O'D had been around. African men always thought they could browbeat a woman on her own.

And as for Frank and Cinco Metro …

I stared at them with disgust. They had completely failed to protect me. "Well, what are you lolling about for? Get back to work."

My safety in the Nhamacoa, it seemed, lay in my own hands.

When O'D and Caetano went to Machaze, my belief that Seven's paralysis was 'all in his mind' and nothing to do with witchcraft took a bit of a battering.

Ataide, a Mozambican forester, was felling trees in our area and they had driven off to sort him out, leaving me alone in the Nhamacoa for two days and two nights.

During the night before O'D's return, my sleep was continually disrupted by bursts of incredibly bright light that dazzled my eyes and came from dozens of little creatures, dancing and twittering around me.

Held almost in a trance-like grip, I didn't know whether I was asleep or awake.

In the morning, I dragged myself out of bed, totally exhausted.

When O'D and Caetano arrived back from Machaze at about midday, I mentioned my tiring night.

"Funny you should say that," O'D said, "Caetano and I had quite an argument with Ataide and the Machaze Administrator. The last thing we heard was that Ataide had gone off to see a witch doctor. The witch doctor must have decided to do something to you."

"To me? Why me?" I asked, outraged.

"Witch doctors often call on the spirits to attack the people who are the closest to the person they want to harm," Caetano explained, "The closest and the weakest. People like the wives and the children."

O'D and Caetano didn't succeed in sorting out Ataide. He sorted them out, instead. While he carried on felling with impunity, Geronimo, the Director of Agriculture at this time, sent them a letter, telling them they had committed misdemeanours under Article something or other and that he was, therefore, expelling them from Machaze.

Enraged, O'D and Caetano decided to contest this expulsion and made an appointment with Geronimo.

Their visit appeared to put him on the spot. Unable to explain the obscure Article that had been used to expel them from their area, Geronimo resolved the problem by tearing the letter in half and throwing the pieces into his wastepaper basket. Then he brought the visit to an end, leaving O'D and Caetano in limbo.

The reason for our expulsion from Machaze soon became clear when we discovered who was taking over our felling area in Machaze.

A Portuguese forester called Souza, who had teamed up with none other than the Machaze Administrator!

Deciding to take their complaint higher, O'D and Caetano made an appointment with Felicio Zacharias, the Governor of Manica Province. As well as talking about their unfair expulsion from Machaze, this would also be an ideal opportunity to talk about the terrible destruction going on in the Nhamacoa.

The visit with the Governor didn't go as well as they had hoped.

Glaring at them with dislike across his empty desk, Felicio Zacharias had given O'D and his complaints short shrift.

"Foresters are nothing but trouble," he told them coldly. "If it was up to me, I would ban all timber companies and foresters from operating in Mozambique."

And when it came to the wholesale deforestation that was going on all over the country, it was the foresters, he told them, who were the cause of this. *THEY* were the people who were to blame for the loss of this valuable natural resource; *THEY* were to blame for the fact that future generations of Mozambicans would not be able to enjoy their indigenous forests in the years to come!

For a few seconds, O'D and Caetano sat in amazed silence, digesting the Governor's tirade. The way he was deliberately turning a blind eye to the activities of the population and blaming us for the appalling desertification of the Nhamacoa was particularly infuriating, not to mention downright insulting.

O'D opened his mouth, preparing to give the Governor an angry blast but before he could even utter a word, Caetano's big size twelve shoe pressed down hard on top of O'D's size eight shoe, crushing O'D's foot with this by now well-known signal of Caetano's to cool it, to reign in his temper and to watch his words. A confrontation with such a man as Felicio Zacharias would do us more harm than good.

Heeding Caetano's warning, O'D closed his mouth again.

With nothing left to say, O'D and Caetano stood up, glad to leave the hostile atmosphere of the Governor's office.

Being kicked out of Machaze by a crooked forester and a corrupt government official put both O'D and Caetano into a black mood for a while.

Then Caetano rallied and put the loss behind him. "Never mind," he told us. "We'll just have to look for something else."

The new area on which Caetano's eyes fell was situated in Guro and although he had gone through the usual bureaucratic route and had been granted the area, it soon became clear that here, too, something peculiar was afoot and blocking our way.

The stumbling block, Caetano discovered, turned out to be a charming Italian with long floaty grey hair, twinkling little eyes and a character that could only be described as unutterably roguish. Our old enemy, Bertuzzi, who had stolen a large amount of timber out of our area in the Nhamacoa by fraudulently enlarging the forestry map of his area to include part of ours!

"He's also got an area in Guro," Caetano told us. "It's near the one we've been allocated and now he's laying claim to ours as well, even stating that our area has been registered at the Land Office as his!"

While O'D and Caetano were trying to sort out this complication at the Forestry Department, Bertuzzi came up with what he thought was a foolproof plan to get his hands on our area.

Furtively meeting up with Caetano in Chimoio, Bertuzzi made him an offer he was sure Caetano wouldn't be able to resist. A partnership, a car and the sum of a hundred million meticais - if Caetano signed our area in Guro over to him!

"Do notta tella O'D aboutta dis," Bertuzzi advised Caetano.

When Caetano told O'D about Bertuzzi's offer, O'D flew into a tremendous rage. Alone, he drove furiously over to Bertuzzi's house in Chimoio and burst inside without even knocking on the front door.

Confronting the long-haired Italian in his sitting room, he shouted "What the hell do you think you're up to, Bertuzzi? What the hell do you think you're doing, trying to bribe my partner away from me!"

"I am an old man," Bertuzzi defended himself. "I have to look after myself, before it is too late!"

"Well you're bloody well not going to do it at our expense!" O'D shouted and stormed out of the house again, slamming the front door shut with such force that it almost fell off its hinges.

Sitting at the Sports Clube with Caetano, O'D still simmered with rage while he nursed the hand he had hurt by slamming Bertuzzi's front door.

"I'd like to make *his* life difficult for a change," he said. "What can we do to the little mafiosi?"

A thoughtful glint came into Caetano's eyes. "Romana, my sister, works at the Finance Department," he said. "Perhaps I can drop a word or two that Bertuzzi is evading his financial obligations to the country."

For the next three days, Bertuzzi's Landcruiser was parked outside the Department of Finance while he explained himself.

Then, Caetano heard that Bertuzzi was about to lose his area adjoining ours in the Nhamacoa. Busy with his other areas, he had neglected to work it for some time and the Forestry Department now considered that he had abandoned it.

"Get hold of it, quick!" O'D told Caetano.

Bertuzzi objected to our application for his area in the Nhamacoa but this time luck was with us - for a change! - and it was given to us.

Towards the end of the year, Seven unexpectedly returned to work, cheerful and supple, and now it was Biasse's turn to undergo tragedy.

"My daughter is sick, Master," he told O'D one day, standing next to the barefoot twelve year old girl dressed in a pink cotton dress. "She has pain in the stomach and is not able to eat."

Chimoio hospital diagnosed stomach cancer and when Biasse saw that the doctors there were unable to do anything to save his daughter, he ignored their objections and brought her home to die amongst the familiar faces of her family who loved her.

One afternoon, soon after his daughter's death, Biasse came into the sitting room and began dusting.

"You know, Madam," he said without looking at me and flicking his yellow duster erratically over the bookcase, "I think someone in Nhamacoa put a curse on my daughter, to make her sick, to make her die."

Sighing inwardly, I put down the pen I was using to fill in the Forestry Registry book. Always the witchcraft. "No Biasse," I said, "this hasn't happened because of a curse. People in Europe also get this sickness and no one in Europe puts curses on people."

Unconvinced, Biasse stopped his distracted dusting.

"I would like to take my thirty days' holiday, Madam, and go away for a while."

"Of course, Biasse. I'll give you your holiday money and you can go right away if you like."

"It is because my head is not right, Madam," Biasse told me, still not looking at me. "Something in my head is not right."

Thirty days passed and each day after that I waited for Biasse to come back.

There was no word from him and then I heard from one of the workers that he had moved his whole family away from the Nhamacoa and had gone back to his home in Antennas. There was another new Administrator at the Tabex farm, a bachelor from Portugal, and Biasse was working for him now.

I was upset that Biasse had disappeared back to the Tabex farm without saying a word to me, especially as we had been together for so many years. I missed his cheerful presence. I also missed his cooking. Now I would have to go back to the wretched cook hut! The very thought of slaving away in its smoky, fiery furnace of an interior filled me with rebellion.

"Cook in it yourself, if you want hot meals," I told O'D. "I'm only going to do salads from now on."

The threat of salads galvanized O'D.

He drove down to Beira and returned with large cardboard crates in the open back of the Toyota pickup. A gas cooker, all the way from Brazil! A large gas/electric deep freeze from South Africa! A Defy Automaid washing machine, also all the way from South Africa and … a white enamel bath!

The cooker from Brazil was a little scary. When I gently ran a soft, damp sponge over it to clean it, all the oven temperatures displayed on its white enamelled front and numbered one to five, disappeared! After that, it was all down to guesswork.

The washing machine was a thing of wonder to Azelia. Completely fascinated by it, she often knelt down in front of its window to watch the washing going around and around in a sea of bubbles as if she was watching a particularly engrossing soap opera on television.

Azelia still used the charcoal iron when the generator wasn't running and although she was a good ironer, there were times when she was a trifle careless when it came to errant little pieces of red hot charcoal falling out of an overloaded charcoal iron.

One morning, after she had carried a pile of newly ironed clothes into the sitting room and had carefully placed the pile onto a chair, I noticed a burn hole in my newest pair of jeans. And there, in the identical spot, another burn hole in O'D's jeans!

Marching down the back stairs to the laundry room, I placed the jeans on top of the ironing table and turned to confront Azelia and Seven.

"What is this?" I asked sternly, pointing a finger at the two burn holes.

Seven and Azelia bent their heads over the jeans and examined the holes in interested silence.

At last Seven looked up. "It is a hole!" he told me, triumphantly.

"Yes!" Azelia looked up, sharing his triumph,"it is a hole!"

"I KNOW it is a hole!" I said annoyed, and rephrased my question. "What I would like to know is HOW DID THESE HOLES GET THERE?"

Once again, Seven and Azelia bent their heads and made an examination of the holes. "The iron!" Seven finally told me.

"Yes!" Azelia agreed excitedly. "The iron! It is the iron that made the holes!"

Although O'D found the time to install and plumb in our new modern appliances, the white bath lay next to a wall on the verandah, neglected and unused. And although I reminded O'D over and over again that the little tin bath in the bathroom needed replacing, my words fell on deaf ears.

CHAPTER EIGHTEEN

MR. YING, MR. CHANG AND MR. DELIGONG
1998

At the beginning of the new year, O'D and Caetano decided to expand their horizons. They had always wanted to start up a small factory to make quality furniture for export and so they put together a project to apply for finance from the International Finance Corporation.

"I think I'll deliver the project myself," Caetano decided. "Then we'll know for certain that the IFC got it."

The thought of Caetano travelling to Maputo on his own worried me. Although South African tourists were beginning to rave about the city, a three-day stay in the 5-star Polana Hotel, eating prawns and enjoying the nightlife hardly gave anyone indepth knowledge of the real Maputo. The real Maputo had a very murky side away from the tourist haunts and was well known for its crime, its drug and human trafficking, it's violence and murders. And then there was the memory, still fresh in my mind, of my own very nasty encounter with those woodbuyers from Maputo ...

There were bad guys out there!

Although Caetano was adept at karate, thanks to the Koreans, I thought he could still do with some extra protection.

"How about taking my Habanero Pepper Spray along with you, Caetano?" I suggested, holding up the personal defence weapon I had recently bought in Harare. In large white letters printed on its black wrapper, the can boasted a 'NEW IMPROVED KNOCKDOWN FORMULA!'

Caetano didn't say no.

A few days later, with my Habanero Pepper Spray safely tucked away in his jacket pocket, he boarded a bus for Maputo and set off on the 1,200 kilometre trip.

When he arrived back in Chimoio all in one piece and came down to the sawmill, I asked for the return of my spraycan.

To my surprise, this request brought a strange reaction from O'D and Caetano. They exchanged looks and then promptly burst out into loud roars of laughter.

"What?" I asked. "What's so funny?"

"He used it," O'D grinned.

"On the bus," Caetano laughed.

"On the bus!" I exclaimed.

Caetano's use of the Habanero spray, it turned out, had been an unplanned action, with consequences that could well have provoked dangerous 'bus rage' among his fellow passengers.

During the long and hot journey inside the crowded, stuffy bus, the passengers had grown drowsy and had fallen asleep. Caetano had also dozed off, quite unaware that he had dislodged the cap of the spraycan in his jacket pocket by sitting on it and that his weight had been pressing down on the nozzle, releasing its contents.

The first indication he'd had about the peppery gas escaping from his jacket pocket was when a peculiar buzzing sound like the sound of angry bees had penetrated his drowsy torpor and he had felt a painful burning, stinging sensation in his eyes. Waking up, he had looked around the bus through a blur of tears and had found a scene of agitation and indignation. His fellow passengers heaved and surged around in their seats. Tears of pain rolled down their faces. They exclaimed, they began to shout, to get angry.

It hadn't taken long for Caetano's quick mind to put two and two together. A furtive feel of his fingers in his jacket pocket confirmed his suspicions that the NEW IMPROVED KNOCKDOWN FORMULA! had been to blame for the pandemonium and immediately, his strong survival and self-preservation instincts had kicked in. Knowing the character of his fellow passengers and fearing they would beat him up, throw him off the bus and dump him in the middle of nowhere, he had joined in with the noisy upheaval in order to divert the finger of suspicion from being pointed at him.

"What's going on?" he had shouted, mopping at his burning, streaming eyes. "What's happening? Open the windows! Let the air circulate!"

The air had finally cleared and to Caetano's relief, the mystery of the strange and peppery attack on the travellers' eyeballs had remained just that. A mystery.

"Well," I said. "At least we now know that this Habanero pepper spray does actually work. I'll get another one, the next time we go to Harare."

The new year also brought us some new and rather eccentric customers. They were the advance party of what was later to become something of an invasion from a far off country. A country that already had strong ties with Africa, not only by supporting its liberation movement with military training and guns but also by selling the many products that we all so reluctantly had no alternative but to buy. Yes, China!

One late evening in the Nhamacoa, when the sun was just on the point of vanishing down behind the trees and turning everything the mauve of dusk, Ying Investments paid us a visit. They jolted along the rutted forest track towards our house in their white Toyota 4 x 4 and parked under the eucalypt tree near our bedroom windows.

I was in the bedroom at the time and although I peered out of the window, I couldn't make out who our visitors were because their faces were completely obscured by the thick red dust that coated their windscreen.

"Who on earth are these people?" I asked O'D who was standing outside, not far away. "Do you know them?"

"Yes ..." he told me, somewhat thoughtfully, "it's ... the Chinese."

The Toyota's doors flew open and Mr. Ying, Mr. Chang and Mr. Deligong clambered out, accompanied by Fernando, their Mozambican interpreter. Smiling broadly, they rushed over to O'D and surrounded him, greeting him by vigorously pumping his hand up and down. There was a lot of loud chattering and a lot of what sounded like "Ha! Augh!" and "Hai!"

Turning away from O'D, they went back to the Toyota and began to pull something out of it. I leaned out of the window.

"O'D," I asked ominously, sensing that everyone knew something I didn't know, "what are the Chinese doing, coming to see us NOW?"

A peculiar look spread itself all over O'D's face. A sort of ... uneasy look. "They say they've come for supper ..." he said slowly "... and that they're going to spend the night in our house."

"WHAT!" I cried, horrified.

Under normal circumstances, I might just have been able to put up with four unexpected guests for the night, but these weren't normal circumstances. And to make things even worse, we had just eaten the last of our food this very evening! I now had nothing in the house to give anybody, not even a can of beans or a slice of bread. The cupboard was completely, absolutely bare - except for an unopened one-litre bottle of virgin olive oil all the way from Portugal.

Our empty larder hadn't worried me, as we had intended to replenish our food stocks in the morning, by driving across the border to Mutare and to TM Supermarket. But now ...

"They can't spend the *night*!" I hissed. "There's nothing to eat and there's nowhere for them to sleep! Tell them to go away!"

"I can't tell them to go away," O'D said, the peculiar look on his face intensifying and confirming my suspicions that he had invited the Chinese to supper and then had forgotten all about it.

With a sinking heart, I went outside. For a moment, I had the faint hope that the Chinese had brought some food with them, as one usually does in Africa, when visiting in the bush, but this hope faded when I saw that the only nourishment they had in the 4 x 4 was a crate of beer - which they had already started drinking.

"Ah!" Mr. Ying said, dark brown eyes beaming at me through his spectacles as he pumped my hand up and down vigorously.

"Mr. Ying," I began, giving him a weak smile in return. "I'm afraid that there's been some kind of mistake. We have no food in the house to give to you. And I'm sorry, but there aren't any beds for you to sleep on, either."

My bad news did not seem to deflect the Chinese from their determination to spend the night in our house and it also seemed that they did not understand what 'no food' meant either.

Mr. Deligong, who was quite muscley and could have passed for a Triad if he had worn a red bandana tied around his shaggy midnight black hair, gave me their order for supper, as if I were a restaurant owner. "We like chicken very much," he beamed, "FRIED chicken."

"Ah! FRIED chicken!" Mr. Ying repeated happily, rubbing his hands with anticipation. "I like very much FRIED chicken!"

I turned to O'D who, so far, had been of no help in getting us out of this dilemma into which he had put us. From the expression on his face, I could see that his brain had seized up for the moment and that it would be up to me. I wracked my own brains for a solution and the names "Jethro" and "Daisy Commercial" popped into my head.

I turned to O'D. "I think the best thing to do," I said, "is to go to Macate and buy some cans of tuna and sardines from Jethro's shop."

My culinary suggestions wiped the smiles off the Chinese' faces.

Mr. Chang's pleasant schoolteacher face lost its smooth inscrutability. "Fish ... Cans!" he cried, aghast at the prospect. "We buy ... CHICKENS!"

Having once bought a Macate chicken, which had resembled a rubber imitation of a chicken rather than the real thing, I thought this was a bad idea. However, in the face of such strong opposition when it came to eating anything else, I knew that any warnings from me would be brushed aside.

Mr. Chang opened more bottles of beer and they all piled into the dusty Toyota, with O'D in the front to show them the way to Macate.

"Soon! Back soon!" Mr. Ying shouted cheerfully, with a wave of his beer bottle at me through his open window.

And then they jolted off down the forest track, drinking and driving and talking and laughing.

After they left, I went into the house and gloomily sat down on the sofa to wait for them to come back from their trip. I remembered the last time Mr. Chang and Mr. Deligong had visited us to talk about buying our timber. On that occasion, they had irritated me immensely by running around excitedly with their cameras and taking photographs of our dilapidated grass-roofed house and glassless windows with their reed sleeping mat blinds ... behaving as if O'D and I were a primitive, prehistoric caveman couple whom the world had thought was extinct, but whom they, Mr. Chang and Mr. Deligong, had discovered was alive and well ... and living in the Nhamacoa forest in Mozambique.

They were all in a merry mood and emanating strong beery fumes when they came back. This was a consequence, O'D told me, of sitting in Jethro's bar for over two and a half hours while they waited for an old villager to catch two chickens, to kill them, pluck them, clean them and then charge 200 per cent more for them than the shops in Chimoio would have charged for them.

"Chickens!" Mr. Deligong triumphantly brandished the two large chickens at me. "Oil! We need oil!"

As the only oil I had left was my precious unopened bottle of olive oil, I balked for a second, wondering why they hadn't bought oil in Macate.

"Forgot," O'D told me and added knowledgeably, "They won't need much,"

"Oh, alright," I said, knowing I had no option.

When I grudgingly handed the precious bottle over, I forced myself to ask another question. "Do you need some help with the chickens?"

Mr. Deligong's teeth flashed a sparkle of white in the paraffin lamplight. "No. I expert chicken frier!" he told me.

I was relieved to hear this. It took away any guilt I might have felt when I watched him walk down the back stairs and into the fiery furnace of the cook hut, followed by Mr. Chang and Fernando.

Left with the company of the non-English speaking Mr. Ying, O'D and I were at a bit of a loss for a few seconds. However, Mr. Ying soon put us at ease. Drinking down two thirds of his bottle of beer all in one go, he beamed expansively at us and asked "Opera? You like opera? Ah! Western opera good! Very good!

Flinging his arms out wide, he threw back his head and drew in a long, deep breath that expanded his blue-shirted chest. Then, he opened his mouth and in a loud, emotional and dramatic operatic voice, sang a snatch of song in Chinese. "Aida," he informed us, pausing for breath. "You like?"

O"D and I nodded our heads, smiling. "Yes," we told him. "Good. Very good!"

Flinging his arms out wide again, Mr. Ying treated us to another snatch of song, which sounded exactly like the first. "La Traviata," he informed us, stopping for another breath. "You like?"

"Yes, very nice! Very good!" O'D and I nodded and smiled politely again.

Although I was beginning to feel like some kind of head-nodding doll, our appreciation encouraged Mr. Ying and for the next ten minutes he treated us to more songs which all sounded identical to us but which he told us were excerpts from Bizet's Carmen, Puccini's Madam Butterfly and La Boheme.

When at last his singing came to an end, I said "Aaah…" and clapped my hands in applause. This pleased Mr. Ying and he bowed several times, as if he had been performing on a stage instead of in a ramshackle house in a Mozambican forest.

Opening another bottle of beer, he took a long swig to moisten his dry throat and then turned his attention to his surroundings. His bespectacled and inquisitive eyes flitted up towards the ceiling, taking in the dry yellow grass; they moved down to the windows and examined the sleeping mats hanging from our glassless windows; they rested on the two paraffin lamps strategically placed on the bookcase and the table to light up the dim room; they drifted interestedly over the enormous spider web woven from window to ceiling and occupied by our fat resident golden orb spider.

He gave a loud laugh. "Ha haaa! You! English bushman!" he exclaimed exuberantly and clapped O'D so hard on a shoulder O'D staggered. "English bushman!" he repeated and gave O'D another powerful clap on the shoulder. "I make you rich," he promised, beaming at us, " RICH! I invite you to house in Beijing. Beijing good! House good!"

Although it was nice to hear that Mr. Ying intended to make us rich and was inviting us to visit his house in Beijing, I was beginning to feel a little drained. There is nothing so exhausting as trying to carry on a conversation with someone who only speaks a few words of your language while you don't speak their language at all.

Fortunately, rescue was at hand. Black Kitty padded panther-like into the sitting room and Mr. Ying gave another loud exclamation, this time not of amusement but of delight. "Aaaah, cat!" he cried. "CAT! I like cat very much! Very much!"

He knelt down on the carpet in front of Black Kitty and, pinning him down onto the ground, began to stroke him with long, hard strokes. Irate at being squashed almost flat down onto his stomach on the floor by a stranger, Black Kitty reacted with a loud, fierce hiss and struggled free, giving Mr. Ying a long scratch in the process. Mr. Ying started back from him and without another look at our Chinese guest, Black Kitty jumped up onto the windowsill and began to lick himself clean of Mr. Ying's fingerprints.

Mr. Ying stood up, rubbing his arm. He seemed a little hurt by Black Kitty's unfriendly behaviour towards him. "I go see chicken," he told us and promptly left the room to cover his loss of face.

Taken by surprise at his quick exit and as a result forgetting to give him a torch to light his way in the dark, O'D and I listened to Mr. Ying walk down the back stairs and onto the crumbling, uneven brick path. When we heard a shout ... AAARRGH! ... and the sound of a body falling over, we looked at each other speechlessly, fearing the worst. What NOW?

Mr. Ying came hobbling back into the sitting room a few seconds later. With agony etched all over his face, he sank down onto the carpet with a moan of pain and began to massage an ankle.

My heart also sank. This unwelcome and unexpected visit by the Chinese was fast lurching towards disaster! First, no food and now, perhaps a broken ankle!

O'D knelt down beside Mr. Ying and together they carefully examined his sock and trainer-encased ankle. "Probably just a sprain," O'D muttered. "Pity we haven't got any ice. A cold compress would probably help."

Mr. Ying tightened his lips bravely and allowed O'D to gently massage his ankle. After a while, he rose slowly and unsteadily to his feet with O'D's help and limped over to a chair. A sprain, only a slight sprain. Despite this, Mr. Ying's cheerful mood dissipated and a glittery look replaced the pleasant, friendly look in his brown eyes. We were no longer amusing and had changed from being English bushmen into English barbarians.

Mr. Deligong's arrival into the sitting room instantly lightened our dark moods. He came in triumphantly, holding aloft a large plate piled high with beautifully golden, crispy-fried chicken and with a flourish, placed this onto the table.

His sore ankle forgotten, Mr. Ying's eyes shone with anticipation behind his spectacles. He was starving! Mr. Deligong filled each plate with a portion of his exquisitely cooked birds and, sitting down at the table, we picked up our knives and forks.

As I had feared, the Macate chicken lived up to its reputation. Despite all the care and attention lavished on it from Mr. Deligong sweating away in the cook hut, it resisted all our efforts to penetrate its tough meat with our eating utensils. Within seconds, chicken portions were skidding around our plates ...   bouncing rubberly onto the tablecloth and ... oops, sorry, Mr. Ying! ... into each other's plates ... as if we were playing a game of tiddlywinks!

As I stretched out my fingers to retrieve my chicken from Mr. Ying's plate, Mr. Chang's chicken leapt across the table and knocked over the salt cellar and then Mr. Deligong's chicken bounced out of his plate, off the table and onto the floor. He bent down and scooped it up and then, ignoring the dust and Black Kitty hairs now coating it unhygienically, sank his teeth into it.

Mr. Ying's eyes grew annoyed and when Mr. Chang also discarded his knife and fork and grabbed hold of his chicken with his hands, tearing at it with his teeth, he decided to follow their example. Unfortunately, his old teeth weren't up to it and after a few fruitless bites which left no impression on its tough skin, he threw his chicken disgustedly back down onto his plate and glared at it. Supper with English bushmen - hah!

"Beer!" he demanded. Then, while Mr. Deligong, Mr. Chang and Fernando determinedly gnawed their way like wild animals through their chicken, my chicken, Mr. Ying's chicken and O'D's chicken, Mr. Ying sat in his chair, drinking beer after beer and sulking.

There were no more songs or laughs and as soon as the chicken was gone, the Chinese went to sleep, without washing or even brushing their teeth.

Mr. Deligong, Mr. Chang and Fernando curled up on the carpet without pillows or blankets and a hungry Mr. Ying threw himself grumpily down onto the narrow camp bed O'D put together for him. Unlike the others, Mr. Ying slept under a mosquito net O'D had suspended from a beam of the sitting room's grass roof. After what Mr. Ying had been through, we knew it would be just his luck - and ours - for him to get bitten by a mosquito and laid low with malaria of the worst sort if we didn't do something to protect him.

The Chinese left early the next morning and we never saw Mr. Ying, Mr. Chang and Mr. Deligong again. A few weeks later, Caetano told us that a Mr. Luke Chen was taking charge of Ying Investments and that Ying Investments was now called Chen Investments.

And although we never saw Fernando again either, we did hear news of him.

It seemed that Fernando had gone on to work as Mr. Chen's interpreter and one day, when he'd been left alone in Mr. Chen's office in Beira, he had noticed that Mr. Chen had carelessly left some keys lying around. Deciding to use the keys to explore the contents of the drawers of Mr. Chen's locked desk, his searching fingers had alighted upon Mr. Chen's chequebook, a chequebook even more carelessly containing a blank cheque ... and signed by Mr. Chen himself!

By the time Mr. Chen had returned to his office, Fernando had been long gone ... after cashing the cheque at the bank for the sum of U.S.$4,000.

Mr. Chen had put a reward out for the capture of the renegade Fernando, adding the private threat that when caught, he was going to rip Fernando's head off. The Chinese obviously took a very dim view of anyone cheating them out of their money.

Then, when we started selling logs to Mr. Chen at the port of Beira, we made the interesting discovery that this dim view only applied when the Chinese were being cheated and that they were quite happy to cheat *us* if they could get away with it. Far from making us rich, they were enriching themselves at our expense!

It was Caetano and his sharp eyes who picked up the Chinese scam. When our logs were being measured in Beira, the real volume of each log was deliberately and sneakily being decreased so that we ended up losing two cubic metres of logs and the Chinese gaining two cubic metres every time we sold a twenty cubic metre lorry load of timber to them!

Back at the sawmill and aghast at the way we were being cheated, Caetano's voice rose higher and higher with indignation as he described this Chinese double-dealing to us.

We wondered what we should do. Should we tell Mr. Chen the game was up and remonstrate with him? Or would it have more effect if we told Mr. Chen that we were going to rip HIS head off?

Caetano was silent for a while. Then, suddenly cheerful, he said, "We won't say anything to Chen because I've got a much better idea. We won't get angry, we'll get even ... the Mozambican way."

The next time our wood went down to Beira to Mr. Chen, Caetano had a quiet word with Mr. Chen's Mozambican cubicador. Some money changed hands. And the volume of the wood we sold to Mr. Chen increased dramatically, to much more than we had transported down to him!

Even the wily Chinese, it seemed, were no match for the Mozambicans when it came to trickery!

In the middle of the year, Caetano contacted the IFC and made an appointment with them to find out if our project for the financing of a furniture-making factory had been accepted. Then, leaving me at home in the Nhamacoa, O'D and Caetano drove off together in the pickup to Maputo.

Their visit to the IFC didn't take long. No sooner had they stepped inside an office and sat down in some chairs, than they found themselves outside the IFC office again and in the street ... in the pickup ... and driving back home.

The IFC, it seemed, had made them drive a round trip of 2,200 kilometres - all for nothing!

They were tired and angry when they arrived back in the Nhamacoa with their expensive and rejected project. The IFC man hadn't really explained anything properly to them, except to say that the IFC didn't lend funds to a company whose partners had a 50-50 share in their company!

We weren't the only ones to find our bright ideas rejected by the various International Development Funds organized by Donor countries and the World Bank.

In Harare, Caroline had begun to make beautiful duvet covers out of unbleached calico, hand-painted with brilliantly coloured ethnic designs. Needing funds to develop her idea further, she approached her bank. They in turn pointed her in the direction of another International Development Fund, set up to help entrepreneurs in Zimbabwe. The Fund, according to Caroline's bank manager, was bulging with money, just waiting to be given away to people like her.

Although her samples were stunningly beautiful, she also came across a brick wall with her small project. This time, no reason at all was given for the refusal to help provide finance for twelve sewing machines, an interlocker and start up money to buy bolts of cloth from David Whitehead Textiles.

We were in Harare when a despondent Caroline told us the news of her fiscal rejection. Unlike the International Development Fund who didn't appear to know a good idea when they saw it, I was sure Caroline was on to a good thing and offered our help. We didn't have enough money to set up a furniture-making factory, but we did have enough to set up her duvet business.

Within no time at all, Caroline's little factory took off and soon she was supplying thirty shops all over England.

Spring came to the Nhamacoa. Trees, which had lost their foliage and had grown bare and skeletal over the dry winter months, now began to sprout tender, tiny green leaves … and Black Kitty got restless.

We had never taken Black Kitty across the Zimbabwean border to be neutered by a Mutare Vet and so we weren't surprised by his reaction to all the budding and blooming that was going on around us. In the evenings, he would stand quite still outside the house, his tail stiff and quivering and his emerald eyes fixed on the forest track leading off to the south of us. Then he would pad off down the track and we wouldn't see him again for two or three days.

As Black Kitty always returned home to us, I harboured the hope that despite his wanderings he would continue to live with us permanently. But one evening, this hope was dashed.

Lovad and I were standing outside on the grass near the verandah at about six o'clock when the call of the wild exerted its final and powerful pull on Black Kitty. For the last time and without even a backward glance at me, he started off down the forest track and disappeared around the bend.

I never saw Black Kitty again, and I missed him. I missed him a lot.

CHAPTER NINETEEN

ENCOUNTERS WITH THE MATACENA
AND OTHER WILD ANIMALS
1999

It was Conceicao, Maciel's wife, who had first warned me about that hideous little Mozambican creature, the Matacena. "You must be careful, Vaal," she had told me all those years ago on the Tabex farm, "you must never walk around barefoot or wear open sandals. The Matacena is very, very dangerous!"

In the Nhamacoa, our workers often fell victim to this dreadful little worm that lived in the soil and burrowed into your toes, laying its eggs right near the nails. They dug the worms out with a needle and then poured petrol or diesel into the holes to sterilise them.

The thought of one of these Matacenas wreaking havoc in my toes terrified me and so I *was* very, very careful.

One afternoon, when I walked over to the garden to check on the tomatoes and the lettuce, my right foot sank into a patch of soft ground and soil filled the grey leather moccasins I was wearing. "Uh oh," I thought to myself and immediately turned for the house. Rushing into the bathroom, I took off my shoes and washed my feet in the bath. I gave my shoes a clean as well, shaking them out and wiping them inside with a wet, soapy cloth. Hopefully, these precautions would keep me safe.

I was standing in front of my easel a week or so later, finishing off a watercolour of some ragged children playing in the road of a small Mozambican town, when I felt the twinge. It was sharp and painful and was followed by a second and a third twinge a few seconds later. What was this? I wondered. Sitting down on the sofa, I examined the little toe on my right foot. Nothing. Everything looked quite normal. I stood up again. Perhaps the twinges had only been a sort of cramp, or pins and needles from standing so long at the easel.

We were spending a weekend in Harare when the twinge turned vicious. It woke me up at two o'clock in the morning, stabbing at my foot like red-hot knives and leaving me gasping and clutching at my foot with agony. A doctor! I needed a doctor!

By the time the sun had come up and we were on our way to see Dr. Featherstone, the mysterious pain had subsided - but not for long, I knew.

"Lucky this happened to me now, while we're in Zimbabwe," I said to O'D during the drive. "At least I can be sure of getting good medical attention here."

When he stopped the car under the Jacaranda trees next to Dr. Featherstone's surgery, I got out and limped over to his door. It was closed and there was a notice on it. Dr. Featherstone, the doctor who had looked after us since our arrival in Southern Africa had left ... and gone off to England!

Panic began to rise up in me. "He's gone!" I cried, getting back into the car. "What am I going to do now?"

"We'll just have to find another doctor," O'D told me.

"But where? WHERE?" I asked, my voice rising. There had been a steady drain of professionals like Dr. Featherstone from Zimbabwe over the last couple of years. President Mugabe's murky diamond-mining ventures with the Zimbabwean Army in the Democratic Republic of the Congo had seen to this. They were costing the country a fortune. There was a problem with foreign currency, another problem with fuel and as a result businesses were beginning to suffer. Our small ethnic duvet business with David and Caroline, so successful a year ago, was beginning to struggle now, what with the ever-increasing cost of electricity, fuel and fabric from David Whitehead Textiles. This unaccustomed hardship was making Zimbabweans restless. Some were leaving for greener pastures and others were complaining, complaining about Mugabe quite openly and aggressively on radio phone-in programmes!

The Medical Centre wasn't far from Dr. Featherstone's deserted surgery and there, much to my relief, we found a Dr. Watermeyer who was prepared to see me if I was prepared to wait. Naturally, I waited, and while I sat there, the plump and elderly receptionist made her feelings known about doctors who ran off to England and left their patients in the lurch.

"Dereliction of duty!" she sniffed huffily. "Just out for the money and couldn't care less about the sick!"

"Well, he does have a large family to support," I defended Dr. Featherstone. "He's got a wife and five children."

"That's no excuse," she snapped. "Times are tough for all of us. How are ordinary Zimbabweans going to cope if all our doctors run away to Europe and America because they want more money?"

How, indeed? I had no argument with that. Living in Mozambique, I had long ago come to realise how frightening life was when you were ill and you more or less had to doctor yourself.

Dr. Watermeyer was young and tall, with a long blonde ponytail that bounced around her head when she moved. She glanced down at the card her elderly receptionist had handed to her. "Mmm ... one of Dr. Featherstone's patients," she said disapprovingly. "What's the problem?"

"I keep getting a terrible pain in one of my toes," I told her. "There seems to be a tiny yellow mark there, and" I held up my left hand "I've also been getting the same pain in my left index finger."

Without touching my finger, Dr. Watermeyer examined the tiny yellow mark on it. "I don't know what this is," she told me, "it looks like an infection."

"Perhaps if you opened it up, we'd find out," I suggested.

In her examination room, she reluctantly pulled on some surgical gloves and picked up a needle. I held out my finger and she made a small incision where the yellow mark was.

A little white worm with a black head popped out of the incision and Dr. Watermeyer stepped back from me, a look of revulsion on her face. Ugh!

Without speaking, she removed the worm from my finger and after placing the needle and the worm on a white saucer, gingerly dabbed my finger with cotton wool soaked in Eusol. Then she peeled off her surgical gloves and placing a foot on the pedal of a white rubbish bin, raised the lid and carefully threw the gloves inside.

"What about my toe?" I reminded her.

Dr. Watermeyer turned a blank face towards me. It was obvious she had no intention of subjecting herself to the sight of yet another disgusting worm. "It looks like an infection caused by wearing tight shoes," she told me dismissively.

"But I never wear tight shoes," I objected.

Ignoring my denial, she sat down at her desk and began to write out a prescription. "You can deal with the infection yourself, when you get home," she told me. "Soak your foot in a bowl of hot water with green soap and then squeeze out the pus." She held the prescription out to me "and this is for a course of penicillin."

Back home in the Nhamacoa that night, I followed Dr. Watermeyer's instructions, soaking my right foot in a plastic bowl of hot water with a lump of green Sunlight soap wrapped around the little toe to draw out the 'infection'. Then, when O'D and I thought my toe had been soaked for long enough, O'D carefully cut into the tiny yellow mark with a sterlised razor blade. Half a worm emerged ...

"Where's the other half?" I asked.

"Doesn't seem to be here," O'D said thoughtfully, examining the tiny cut he had made.

"Must have disintegrated during that soaking with the green soap," I said.

"Well, it's gone now," O'D said, giving the little cut a dab with disinfectant. "Your finger doesn't bother you anymore, does it?"

"No," I said, "my finger's fine."

Although I took the penicillin Dr. Watermeyer prescribed, the painful twinges in my toe didn't go away. They were especially bad at night and by the middle of the week, I had made another worrying discovery. Dr. Watermeyer's antibiotics were proving as useless as her diagnosis.

"What's happening?" I asked O'D one night while I lay on the bed with my foot on top of the blanket. "Why isn't the penicillin working?"

"Give it time," O'D told me.

"But my foot seems to be swelling up," I said, an icy feeling of terror beginning to form in my heart "and there's a black mark - a **black mark, O'D,** that's getting bigger too!" I sat up and bending my head, fearfully sniffed at the toe. "I'm sure I'm getting ... gangrene!"

"Of course you're not getting gangrene," O'D told me, reassuringly. "That's just a little bruise on your toe."

By Friday, I had to sleep with my foot hanging down over the side of the bed. The pain was ratcheting up and paracetamol was useless. On Saturday night I couldn't sleep at all. Waves of agonising, excruciating pain knifed and rampaged through my foot without a break and in the end I left the bed and hobbled into the sitting room where I lit a paraffin lamp.

The pain was unbearable ... **unbearable** ... as if a shoal of piranhas was eating away at my foot, tearing and shredding at it with sharp teeth ... oh, what a nightmare this was turning into! I was going to die, I knew ... I'd been to a doctor, a doctor in Harare ... and now, here I was, going through this hell ... how was it possible ...

Another terrible pain ripped through my foot and I felt myself beginning to break, to lose control, to disintegrate under its power. "God! Oh God!" I cried as tears of agony poured down my face. "Help me! Oh, help me, God! God! Oh, God!"

Oh, what a pity Dr. Featherstone had gone to England ... oh, this would never have happened if I'd been able to see him ...

The thought of Dr. Featherstone triggered off a memory. The pills! Oh, of course ... the pills!

I hobbled over to our First Aid box, opened its lid and frantically began to rummage around in it, looking for the very powerful painkillers I had managed to talk Dr. Featherstone into prescribing for us. I didn't know what they were but he had prescribed them - reluctantly - when I had told him we would be in the bush, miles away from hospitals and doctors and might need them if we had a terrible accident, like the loss of a leg or something ...

When my trembling fingers at last found the little plastic packet of pills, I filled a glass with water and drank down the painkillers. Aaah ... magic, just like magic, their effect was almost instant. Within a few minutes, the terrible pain started melting away.

In the morning, we set off for Mutare and help. Although I'd been able to conquer the pain with the runaway Dr. Featherstone's help, daylight had revealed a shocking sight. During the night my foot had swelled up enormously and was now the size of a small melon. My toes resembled fat sausages about to burst out of their skins and the black mark had grown frighteningly larger. Even my ankle rippled ominously with swollen, stretched skin.

During the drive to the border, my thoughts were as black as the mark on my toe. I had put my faith in modern medicine and a presumably well-trained doctor and this was the result. Possible gangrene ... and amputation! I would have been better off if I'd gone to Mario, the nurse at Macate, or even a Mozambican witch doctor or curandeiro! Now I might have to lose a toe or ... the thought made me shudder with horror ... even lose a foot!

My entry into the small clinic in Mutare caused something of a sensation. The waiting room was full of people who all appeared to be in the full bloom of enviable good health. As I hobbled towards an empty chair, clutching onto O'D's arm for support, everyone gaped at the awful sight of my foot.

Two African nurses dressed in pale green uniforms appeared in the doorway of an examination room and, trying unsuccessfully to hide the horror in their dark brown eyes, asked "Are you diabetic?"

"No," I told them, "I'm not diabetic. This is the work of a worm."

"A worm?" They gasped. "What kind of worm would do this to you?"

I felt like bursting into tears, breaking down into sobs. "A Mozambican worm," I said. "A Mozambican worm called ... The Matacena!"

Ten minutes later and accompanied by O'D and the two nurses, I lay back on an examination couch while a youngish African doctor in shirtsleeves inspected my foot and gave me some alarming news.

"I'm not qualified enough to deal with this sort of thing," he told me. "I've asked the nurses to try and find a Specialist. In the meantime," he picked up what looked like a long drinking straw, "we're going to try and draw out the infection." Without giving me time to flinch, he plunged the straw-like object straight into the top of my swollen foot and then stood back to watch the result.

While we all stared at the straw in silence and waited for something to happen, grisly images of myself began to unfold in front of my eyes, like a film. A horror film.

At first, I saw myself stomping around the sawmill with a cheap brown plastic foot. Then the pictures grew worse and I saw myself hopping around without a leg. Deteriorating even further, my imagination travelled a ghastly path until it brought me to the final scene where I lay in a coffin, having died in dreadful agony, while African doctors and nurses stood looking on, helplessly wringing their hands and not having a clue what to do!

At last, the doctor bent over my foot and pulled out the empty straw. "Nothing," he said.

There was a sudden commotion at the door and a whirlwind of a man blew into the room and filled it with his energy. "Ah, Dr. Umbawa, the Specialist!" the young Doctor told me, with relief evident in his voice.

Short and stocky, Dr. Umbawa spoke with an American accent, having trained in Chicago and there was something infinitely reassuring about his presence. This was a man who knew exactly what he was doing. Overcome with the same relief the young Doctor had felt, I had to restrain myself from throwing my arms around Dr. Umbawa. I was safe now, I knew. I wasn't going to die after all.

Dr. Umbawa gave me different antibiotics to take and two days' later when the swelling in my foot had subsided we drove across the border again to see him. He hadn't liked the look of the black mark on my little toe. It seemed my fears about gangrene hadn't been so fanciful after all. The Matacena had stopped the blood circulating in my toe.

"The skin on your toe has gone rotten," he told me, "and the only way I can save your toe is to shave off all the skin."

At the little Mutare clinic, I lay down in the examination room, accompanied again by O'D and the two nurses.

"This is going to hurt like hell," Dr. Umbawa encouraged me and raised the giant needle he was about to inject into my foot. "You'd better hold on to one of the nurse's hands."

A nurse standing next to me held out her left hand and I grasped it. The needle plunged into my foot. I gave a shout and crunched her hand. "Sorry!" I gasped. "It's okay," she smiled.

For a while I watched Dr. Umbawa skillfully at work on my toe with his scalpel. "I'm gonna get the worm that did this!" he muttered fiercely, as he cut away at the enemy. "I'm gonna get that worm!" And then, when my toe had turned into a bloody little red stub, I looked away, out of the window where small fluffy white clouds floated serenely across the blue sky. I was lucky, I knew, oh so lucky that Dr. Umbawa had been on the scene. That he hadn't joined those other doctors who had gone to other countries and left us to suffer and perhaps die because there was no one to help us. Lucky too, that he'd trained in Chicago, America ... unlike Dr. Watermeyer who had made a wrong diagnosis, prescribed the wrong antibiotic and suggested the wrong treatment and who had probably trained herself ... probably from one of those teach yourself books ... A 'Teach yourself to be a Doctor' book ...

My recovery was slow and lasted for more than a month. Warned by the nurses not to put a foot outside the house until the bandages were ready to come off, I spent my time sitting on the sofa, reading books and hobbling around the kitchen on the heel of my bandaged foot to cook meals. Bathing was a bit awkward too, as I had to put my foot in a plastic bag to keep it dry and bath with my right leg on the outside of our small tin bath.

To lessen the trauma of my experience, people started giving me gifts.

One day, after a trip to the clinic to see the nurses for a check up, we arrived back home to discover that Alfixa had paid us a visit. He had come down to the sawmill with an old maize sack slung over a shoulder and had handed its contents over to Seven for safekeeping. "For the Senhora," he had told Seven.

When we walked into the sitting room, Seven pointed at a large plastic bowl he had turned upside down on the floor. "A gata," he told me, and raising one side of the bowl off the floor, he showed me the tiny kitten he had imprisoned inside it.

Skin and bone, but with a distended stomach as round and hard as a golf ball, the little kitten was a pale grey tabby with black feet and huge green eyes.

Like Black Kitty, it didn't take long for Miss Sydney, as I called the kitten, to make herself at home. In the night hours and feeling lonely, she made her way out of the sitting room and into our bedroom, where she jumped onto our bed and using a fold in the mosquito net as a hammock, went blissfully to sleep on top of O'D's obliviously snoring head. This caused a bit of disturbance, as you can imagine.

Feeling a hot, furry little weight on top of his head O'D woke up and, mistaking it for one of those huge hairy spiders that run around the Nhamacoa, lurched out of bed with a strangled shout of alarm "Whazzat?"

During the day, Miss Sydney sat on my lap and kept me company while I read and I would have had no idea at all what a vindictive, jealous, little bully she was until Achim, a German missionary who held the strong belief that love always conquers evil, also decided to give us a gift.

On the drive back from another check up at the clinic in Mutare, O'D turned in at Moyo Mukuru, Achim's Mission. "Just stopping off to collect the puppy," he told me. "She's a sort of Rhodesian Ridgeback."

Miss Sydney's reaction when the puppy ran into the house was alarming. Taking one look at the interloper, she raised her tiny body up into a hoop shape, puffed out her fur as if she'd been electrified and let out a frightening banshee shriek. Then, launching her tiny body forward, she stuck a painful claw into the pup's nose as a declaration of war.

We called the puppy Bandit, a very appropriate name for a dog that ran off with everything she could get her paws on. When Luis Raoul made her a splendid doghouse out of mahogany, Bandit set about furnishing its interior with all sorts of things she purloined - one of the worker's hats which she chewed up, shoes, some of O'D's spanners, pieces of wood, a couple of my capulanas, and the odd sweater or two.

Miss Sydney bullied Bandit unmercifully, craftily taking advantage of my presence to protect her from any retaliation. While I sat on the sofa reading, with Miss Sydney on my lap and Bandit lying on the floor next to my bandaged foot, she would often lean over my knees and give Bandit a gratuitous slap on her head. Then, when the dog looked up in surprise, one of Miss Sydney's tiny black paws would shoot out and hit Bandit viciously on the nose five times with a right and a left so fast that the action was just a blur, Whap! Whap! Whap! Whap! Whap!

When my bandages came off for the last time, they revealed a toe that looked perfectly normal except for its bright lobster pink colour. Although this faded over time, the same couldn't be said for my fear of the tiny worm that had almost cost me my foot.

The ending of my captivity brought freedom to Miss Sydney and Bandit as well. No longer voluntarily tied to the sofa with me, they now followed me outside and while I walked around under the trees and down the forest track, they chased butterflies and investigated holes. With the expansion of their world and so many new things to explore and examine, their attention was diverted from each other and an uneasy truce developed between them. Knowing no fear, Bandit often followed strange scents with her pointy nose and heedlessly plunged into tall grass, disappearing completely from view.

Miss Sydney, too, behaved recklessly. Despite her tiny size, her ego was enormous. Nothing seemed to scare her, as we were soon to find out when O'D began to have his encounters with snakes.

It all began early one morning when he went to switch on the saw.

Standing in front of the switchbox, he opened its small door and was about to stick his hand inside the box when his eyes caught sight of something black coiled up amongst the electrical wires. A small snake! This gave him a bit of a shock, of course, but it was only the prelude to more and even bigger shocks that were to come later on that evening and the following afternoon.

We were having sugar bean soup and bread rolls for supper and as it was already dark that evening, O'D was the one who (thankfully) went down the stairs to get the butter from the deep freeze in the room under the house.

He'd only been gone for a few seconds when I heard him shouting urgently for me.

"Val! Val! Bring the torch! Quickly!"

I grabbed the torch and ran down the back stairs.

"What is it?"

"Shine the torch over there," he ordered, with what sounded like a quiver in his voice as he pointed a finger at a spot on the ground, "but be careful and don't come any closer. I think I've just been walking next to a giant snake!"

A giant snake! With a hand that trembled, I shone the torch on the ground. What I saw made me catch my breath with awe. "Wow!" Unknowingly, O'D had been ambling along the side of the house in the company of a five metre long python!

According to my snake book, pythons are non-venomous and kill their prey (small buck, rabbits, cane rats and so on) by constricting them until all their bones were crushed.

Although the book also mentioned that pythons rarely attacked humans, it had admitted that there had been cases of young herd boys being crushed and swallowed. Mindful of this, I kept a safe distance between myself and the snake, just in case this one happened to be the rare exception!

As wary as I was, O'D armed himself with a long pole. "I'm going to re-direct the python away from the house," he told me, "and send it down towards the river."

He was just giving the python a gentle prod with the pole when Sydney and Bandit appeared on the scene and caused a little bit of chaos. Filled with the curiosity of the young, they foolishly ran right up to the snake for an investigative sniff. They were both just the right size for a python's dinner and for a heart-stopping moment I thought the tiny Miss Sydney had had it!

She danced around the python's head and its large dark eyes, gleaming in the torchlight, turned to look sideways at her.

Alarmed, I gave a shout. "Get away from there, you crazy cat!"

My shout did the trick. More frightened by my shout than by an enormous snake, dog and cat both leapt out of the way.

With O'D's help in the form of several more prods, the python wended its slow and majestic way across the ground towards the mango trees and then, when it reached the mass of tall yellow grass growing down to the Nhamacoa River, it slid inside and disappeared.

"Phew!" I breathed a long sigh of relief. "For a moment there, I thought that python was going to have Miss Sydney for an entrée."

"For a moment there, I thought *I* was going to be the python's entrée," O'D said. "I almost walked on top of it!"

Back in the sitting room, a rather unwelcome thought occurred to me. "That's the second time today that a snake has given you a fright, O'D," I said. "You'd better be careful. Things actually do seem to go in threes."

The next day, at four o'clock in the afternoon, I carried Bandit's food bowl out to her and put it down as usual next to her doghouse. The bowl was filled with Zimbabwe's nourishing 'Rambo' dog food, on top of which I had placed a large banana. Bandit loved bananas almost as much as she loved bones.

She ran up to the bowl, eager as always to eat, but then surprised me by suddenly leaping back from it as if she'd been stung. Legs flying around wildly with panic, she charged back into the house where she sat shivering violently in the corridor just inside the open front door.

I stared at her in amazement. What on earth was going on? "Don't you like your food today, Bandit?"

Bandit paid no attention to me but kept her soft brown eyes riveted on the white bath which O'D had still not installed in the bathroom and was leaning against the verandah wall near her doghouse.

"O … kay," I said slowly, as I nervously followed Bandit's example and began to edge towards the front door, keeping my eyes fixed on the bath. "So it's not your food that's bad, Bandit … it's something else."

I'd only taken a few steps away when something began to slide out from behind the bath towards me. It was black and menacing and seemed to go on and on and on. It chilled my blood and gave me as big a fright as it had given my dog.

A Mozambican Spitting Cobra!

The snake saw me standing a short distance away from it and rose up in the air, threateningly spreading out its hood.

For a split second I stared into its two black eyes, staring so intently back at me. These snakes, I had read, could shoot their venom straight into your eyes over a distance of three metres.

I flung myself at the door, scrambling for safety very much like Bandit had done, and then peered cautiously around the doorframe to see if certain death was following me.

It wasn't. My rapid disappearance, it seemed, had reassured the cobra. Deflating its hood, it turned away from the house and began to glide off in the opposite direction.

On its way to the bush, it slid underneath our red Toyota pickup and then, vanished up into the engine compartment of our car!

Thunderstruck, I stared at our pickup, now home to a deadly serpent. How on earth were we going to get rid of our new sitting tenant? There was only one thing to do. Filling my lungs to capacity with air and hoping that O'D and some of our workers would hear me, I shouted "O'D! O'D! Cobra! COBRA!" at the top of my voice.

Fortunately, they were working near the avocado trees not far away and came running to the rescue, armed with sticks.

"There's a cobra in the engine of the car," I told O'D, pointing a finger at the pickup, "I've just seen it going in there!"

O'D turned to look at the pickup and irritated me with his answer. "Oh, I doubt if it actually went inside," he said, "you just thought it did. And if it *did* go in there, it probably got out again. It's probably gone by now."

"It's not gone!" I cried. "Believe me! I was watching it all the time. It went up into the engine and it didn't come out again!"

Heaving a sigh of resignation, O'D walked over to the pickup to humour me. Certain that he was right and the cobra had gone, he opened the bonnet ... lifted it up ... gave a loud and peculiar high-pitched scream ... and then slammed the bonnet shut again.

"I told you it was in there," I said.

Shaken by the sight of a large Mozambican Spitting Cobra coiled up on top of the engine of his car and looking at him with its black eyes, O'D said, "It will probably leave by itself."

"But how will we know that it's left unless we actually see it leaving? It might not leave ..." I shuddered at the thought of driving around with a dangerous snake "... it might end up under the seat!"

"It can't get from the engine into the cab," O'D assured me. "It's completely closed off."

For a while, he stared at the pickup in silence and despite himself, I could see my words working on his mind. He would have to do something. If he didn't, he might well find himself driving around with a dangerous snake in the car.

Walking over to the pickup, he gingerly opened the driver's door and put the car into neutral gear. "Push," he ordered our workers and from outside the car, grasped the steering wheel with one hand.

Slowly, they pushed the Toyota a little distance away from the house and then O'D walked reluctantly around to the bonnet.

"Wait!" I cried. "You'll all need safety goggles to protect your eyes. I'll go and get some for you."

"I don't need goggles," O'D said grumpily. He glanced around at his small band of workers. "Do any of you want to wear goggles?"

Taking their cue from their boss, they all shook their heads.

"Alright," he told them. "Let's get this snake out of the car."

O'D carefully opened the bonnet of the car again and while he and our workers tried to extricate the cobra with their sticks, I went back inside the house.

Not only did I close the door, just in case an angry snake decided to use the house as a refuge but I also secured it with the wooden Fred Flintstone-type locks Raimundo had made. I shut all the windows as well and then I went back into the sitting room and picked up a book. It was far too nerve-wracking to watch O'D and our workers dealing with such a deadly snake.

With my nose in my book, I didn't see O'D try out his usual method of persuading a snake to leave by prodding at it with a long stick. This time, however, the snake refused to take the hint. It retreated deeper into the bits and pieces of the motor and then it disappeared completely down a hole - a hole which led directly into the front of the cab!

Dumbfounded, O'D let down his guard. He looked in through the open door and the cobra, on the floor by the driver's seat, grasped at its opportunity. As quick as a flash and only a short distance away from O'D, it squirted its venom straight into his left eye.

Clutching at his face, he staggered back in shock and pain

The first I knew of this was when I heard O'D hammering and battering at the locked front door and shouting at me at the top of his voice.

"Let me in! Open the bloody door! Open the bloody door and let me in!"

Heart thudding in my chest, I threw down my book and ran to the door, fearing the worst. We were miles away from proper medical attention and something awful had obviously happened. Had he been given a lethal bite ? Who would be able to help us? And how long did he have to live ...

I wrenched the door open and O'D rushed inside.

"My eye," he shouted, "poison in my left eye!"

This information immediately filled me with panic. I remembered reading that the venom from a Spitting Cobra could destroy your eyesight. Scar your eyes and blind you for the rest of your life! Was O'D going to go blind? Oh, what were we going to do? What were we going to DO? Then, another memory flashed into my mind. The memory of an old black and white wildlife film I had once watched years ago, showing a cobra shooting its venom onto the protective glasses of the producer of the film. They had mentioned an antidote ...

I ran to the table and grabbed a carton of Ultra Mel.

"Milk! We've got to wash out your eye with milk, O'D!"

While O'D forced his eye open, I poured milk into it, over and over again. Milk ran down his face, onto his clothes, splashed onto the floor and lay in white pools and puddles around his feet.

"Maybe we need more," he gasped.

I ripped open another carton.

After we'd gone through about two litres of milk in our fear and panic, O'D said, "Alright. I think that's enough."

I examined his eye. It was a frightening scarlet colour. "How does it feel?" I asked, fearfully. "Can you see out of it?"

"No," he answered. "It's very blurry and it hurts like hell. I think I'd better get over to Macate and talk to Mario about this."

Mario gave O'D a bottle of saline solution and told him to bathe his eye with it as well to soothe the pain. The milk, it seemed, had been the right thing to use and within a few days, O'D's eye was back to normal ... thanks to an ancient film I had seen when I was young.

Later on in the week, O'D and Caetano drove off to Gondola and during the drive, O'D began to tell Caetano about his encounter with the Spitting Cobra. When he got to the part where the cobra had disappeared down the hole in the bodywork and had exited into the Toyota's cab, Caetano, who like most of us was dead scared of snakes,

thought the snake was still lurking menacingly around in the car …
perhaps even under the very seat that he, Caetano, was sitting on …

"Cobra?" Caetano's dark eyes widened with terror. "A cobra
in the car?"

Before O'D could say another word, Caetano reacted in a way
he hadn't for one moment anticipated. With a wild, jerky movement,
he unbuckled his seat belt and threw it off. Then he flung open the
door, preparing to leap out of the speeding car and into a road full of
traffic, to safety.

"No!" O'D took a hand off the steering wheel and grabbed
Caetano's arm, at the same time slowing the pickup. "Caetano, no!"
he shouted. "The cobra's dead! Dead! Don't jump!"

"Dead …" The glazed look of panic in Caetano's eyes cleared
and he closed the door, falling back limply against the seat. A little
embarrassed, he gave a shaky laugh. "I thought it was still here," he
said. "A cobra! A cobra in the car with us!"

"Caetano," O'D said, "do you think I'd be driving around in
my car knowing that there's a snake in it? Even I'm not that mad!"

It's true to say that quite often something good comes out of
something bad. The fact that the bath had been used as a hiding place
by a venomous snake which had attacked him, galvanized O'D into
action as I had never been able to do. In no time at all, the white bath
was installed in the bathroom. Now at last I was able to lie down in
the bath, to luxuriate in it by covering myself up to the neck with
water. And all because of a Mozambican Spitting Cobra!

Some weeks later, something else was to happen to brighten up
my life. I was sitting at my desk in the spare bedroom and typing some
letters on my thirty year old Facit manual typewriter, when I heard a
little knock at the door. I looked up and there, standing in the
doorway, was a familiar and very welcome little figure.

"Biasse!" I cried, with delight.

"Hello, Madam," he said. "I'm sorry I left the way I did. Can I
come back and work for you again?"

There had been quite a few changes during Biasse's absence
and so when he started work again and stood in front of the gleaming
white Brazilian cooker, I spent some time carefully explaining the
dangers of gas to him. Unfortunately, I didn't take into account the
equally dangerous Mozambican matches we used to light the gas
cooker. These matchboxes were filled with matches whose heads
irritatingly fell off - or flew off - when you struck them. So, it was

273

only a matter of time before the combination of gas and faulty Mozambican matches led to an alarming incident.

One morning, while I was typing in the spare bedroom again, a peculiar and rather unpleasant odour began to drift down the corridor and then into the room. I stopped typing and raised my nose to sniff at the air, to identify the smell. It was not the aroma of food being cooked … or even of food being burnt, but … my fingers fell off the typewriter keys and I leapt up from my chair … it was the scent of … GAS!

I ran madly down the corridor and when I got to the kitchen doorway, I saw Biasse bending down in front of the open oven with a match and a matchbox in his hands. A little pile of matches without heads lay scattered on the floor by his feet and the room reeked with the gas escaping out of the turned on oven.

"No!" I shouted at the very same moment that Biasse struck another match, successfully this time.

WHUMPH! An enormous sheet of blue flame shot out from the bottom of the cooker, around Biasse's veldskoens and across the kitchen floor.

Biasse turned to me. "I dunno about these matches, Madam. They're no good."

I was doubly grateful for Biasse's return on the day when O'D worked hard on repairing the tractor engine and turned the soapy water in the new bath into an increasingly oily, dirty, black colour everytime he washed his hands and arms in it.

Saving and recycling water was all very well, I thought, as I stood over my no longer pristine white bath but this was too much! No way did I want to use this water again, not even in the loo!

Bending over the bath, I felt around in the opaque water for the chain that was attached to the plug. It was obviously a Chinese chain and plug, because it had come away from the bath on the very first day we had used it. My fingers brushed against something … aha! … and I grasped hold of it, pulled it out of the water and up in the air, expecting to see the white plug … but instead … saw that my fingers were clutching the long, water-slimy tail of a large and soggy brown rat with little black eyes and sticking out teeth that had been lying dead in the black bathwater for some time …

"AAAAAAARRRRRRGGGGGGGGHHHHHH"

The dead rat dropped out of my nerveless fingers, back into the oily black bathwater. Oughh, oughh, oughh! Shuddering with disgust,

I grabbed the bottle of Dettol, pouring disinfectant over my hands and washing them over and over and over again.

"BIASSE!"

He put his head around the doorway. "Madam?"

I pointed at the bath with a Dettol smelling finger. "There's a big dead rat in the bath, Biasse. Please get rid of it!"

One evening, towards the end of the year, the usual gentle soothing music on Zimbabwe Radio One was rudely interrupted. "People are rioting in the centre of Harare!" the announcer told us urgently. "They're overturning cars and setting fire to them! Smashing shop windows and looting! The Riot Police are out, with tear gas!"

It seemed that the simmering dissatisfaction with the rising price of fuel, food and other basics of life had suddenly erupted in the capital city. I took heed of the signs and made a decision.

"I think it would be a good idea to take all our money out of Stanbic bank," I told O'D."

As Zimbabwean banks were much more efficient than the banks in Mozambique and, believe it or not, our bank in Guernsey in the Channel Islands, we had transferred some of our Arrojela money to a sterling account in Stanbic Bank. It had made the money easier to get at when we needed it.

At the Mutare Branch of Stanbic, the Manager tried to persuade us to leave the money where it was. "Your money will be quite safe," she assured us.

"I'm sure it will be," I told her, " but I have this feeling ..."

As Stanbic Mutare didn't have the foreign currency available to pay us out in sterling, they turned our Arrojela money into Thomas Cook Sterling Travellers cheques instead. The wad was thick and there was a lot of signing to do.

"We'll open another account with you when the trouble's over," I told the Manager when we finally stood up to leave But as it turned out, we never did. And the trouble didn't go away. It only got worse. Much worse.

At the end of the year I began to dream strange and unsettling dreams. Dreams about demons with chalk white faces and evil eyes as black as soot, dreams about the devil. They stretched out long arms to catch hold of me and I had to fight and fight and fight them off.

The dreams were so terrifying that I always cried out in my sleep and woke O'D up and he wasted no time in shaking me awake.

My dreams frightened him, too, because the sounds I made when I struggled to call out for help were peculiarly eerie and quavering and gave him a pretty good idea of the unpleasantness of what was going on in my subconcious mind.

I put my dreams down to the unsettling situation and the awful things happening just across the border from us. I had no way of telling, of course, that some of the dreams I dreamed would actually come true, especially the most chilling one of them all …

CHAPTER TWENTY

A DREAM IN THE NIGHT

"Aaah ...!" I woke up with a gasp, my heart thumping frantically into the mattress and looked through the folds of the mosquito net at the bedroom door, still expecting to see him standing there. But there was no one and the door was closed, not open.

I hadn't been able to see his face, because he'd been silhouetted against the orange glow from the paraffin lamp in the bathroom. He hadn't been alone either. As I had stared at him, I'd seen another figure flit quickly past, behind his back, and then disappear. I had known why he was standing there in the open doorway. He was there because he had come to kill me.

"O'D," I shook his shoulder, not wanting to be alone with my fear. I needed to share it and to be reassured. "O'D, wake up!"

"Whaza matta?" O'D's voice asked sleepily in the darkness of the bedroom.

"A horrible nightmare, of a man standing in the doorway. It was so real ... so real, that for a moment I didn't know whether I was awake or asleep. He was going to kill me!"

O'D's response to my frightening explanation came in the form of a soft burbling snore, followed by some little popping sounds, like a baby blowing spit bubbles.

Ignored, I lay back on the bed, listening to the night sounds in the Nhamacoa forest and trying to blot out the dream. An owl hooted in the big mango tree next to the house and the sound of drums drifted through the trees ... louder and louder ... as it was wafted along on the wind. Eileen had hated the drums and I had grown to hate them too. There was something evil about the way they invaded and manipulated my dreams while I slept, giving them a whiff of the witchcraft that was practiced not only in the forest, but also all over Mozambique.

Witchcraft ...

At first, O'D and I had been sceptical when Caetano had told us of the powers of witch doctors ... but then we had seen Mr. Goncalves call up a twirling dust devil straight out of the ground ... and then we had seen the demonic Nora Swete ... seen with our very own eyes ...

It was no wonder I dreamed weird dreams, living with all this stuff around me in the forest. It was impossible to avoid, because it came TO you, uninvited – just like the drums. They were so loud now that they seemed to be right in the room with me, beating and beating at my ears. They never broke up O'D's sleep or disturbed him. Only me. Sometimes I had the uneasy feeling that this was deliberate and that they were meant to disturb me, because something in the forest didn't like me ...

I pulled a pillow over my head to muffle the drumming. "Oh, shut up," I whispered. "Shut up, shut up, SHUT UP!" A terrible blood-curdling scream cut right through the drumbeats and the feathers of my pillow. I felt O'D's body jump a little on the bed but he didn't wake up. I knew the horrible scream well. It came from the night apes living in the trees just below our house. Under cover of darkness, the forest was noisy with activity and the air was often filled with some pretty hair-raising sounds.

Still awake and unable to go back to sleep, I unmuffled my ears. While I lay on my back with my eyes closed, I listened to the bubbling sound of a nightbird I was never able to identify and tried to think of something pleasant. But my mind refused to obey me. Instead, it fearfully went over and over my dream, replaying it like a repeat on television. Every now and then, I forced myself to open my eyes to stare at the door, just in case it was ajar ... just in case someone *was* standing there, waiting to do something incredibly evil ...

But the door stayed closed and eventually, towards dawn, I drifted off to sleep.

The dream stayed with me for a long time, filling me with unease and making me edgy, jumpy. How real it had been! And how terrifying! As the months went by, however, and life went on without even the hint of any personal danger, the dream began to fade, as all dreams tend to do. I had no idea, of course, that it had been a prophetic dream - a truly prophetic dream - and that an unseen and sinister hand would soon begin to set the stage and to engineer my meeting with the man he was sending to kill me.

CHAPTER TWENTY ONE

THE WORLD'S BIGGEST PARTY
2000

Towards the end of 1999, the world began making plans to celebrate the new millennium. People in the developed countries of the world were splurging enormous amounts of money in preparation for the greatest party the earth had ever seen and champagne producers were rubbing their hands in anticipation of unheard of profits.

O'D, too, became caught up in the world's festive preparations. A few days before the New Year, he splurged out on a couple of bottles of red Portuguese wine, several cases of Manica beer and some Chinese firecrackers he bought from Riaz, Faruk's brother.

"I thought it would be nice to see the New Year in with a fireworks display," he told me, "but the only ones I could find in the whole of Chimoio are these three rockets."

"Hmm ..." I said, "Chinese ... I hope they don't blow your fingers off. And before you shoot them up over the forest, I think you'd better go over to Macate and ask Mario for permission. We don't want to get into trouble with people thinking we're starting a revolution."

When O'D returned from Macate some hours and several beers later with Mario, the Policeman and Mario, the Nurse, he only brought back two rockets. Mario, the Policeman, had taken one for himself as he and the villagers of Macate had also wanted to celebrate the New Year with us. The plan was for O'D to shoot off his two rockets at midnight and then, when Mario saw these flare up in the night sky, he would shoot off his rocket as well.

On the eve of 2000, while O'D and his workers and their wives sat outside and drank beer under the starry sky, I sat on the sofa in the sitting room with a glass of red wine and listened to the BBC World Service, waiting for the countdown to midnight and the sound of Big Ben striking the hour. Bandit, as usual, lay on the carpet close to my feet while a small, pure white cat called Grumpy curled up on my lap in the space usually occupied by Miss Sydney. Miss Sydney was sulking and nowhere to be seen. Beside herself with fury at the gift Caetano had given us, she alternated between bullying Grumpy unmercifully and disappearing out of the house for hours on end.

Listening to the world's hectic celebrations gave me a strange dark feeling of foreboding. They were throwing a massive birthday party but they hadn't invited the very person whose birthday they were celebrating. If they disregarded Jesus Christ, why were they having this party? Surely they realised that the earth was much older than 2000 years? What they were doing seemed completely illogical

An uneasy thought popped into my mind. The world was going to pay for this omission, I was sure of it …

Fifteen minutes to midnight, the BBC let me down. "Wouldn't you just know it," I complained to O'D through the sitting room window, "the BBC's gone off the air!"

"Keep your eye on the clock, then," O'D ordered, "and let me know when it's twelve o'clock."

At midnight, I called out "Happy New Year!" and O'D shot off his two Chinese rockets in swift succession into the starry sky above the forest.

The earsplitting, yowling, screeching sound was terrifying. It sounded just like war and was greeted with loud shrieks and screams of fright from the occupants of the various huts dotted around us. One more to go. Turning our eyes in the direction of the night sky above Macate, we waited and waited … in vain. Where was Mario's rocket?

"Must've downed one Nippa too many and shot it off in the wrong direction," O'D decided.

Back in the house, I had a premonition and shared it with O'D. "You know," I said, "It's been such a dry year, I think we're in for another drought."

On the 8th January, O'D and Caetano made a very uncomfortable bus ride down to Maputo to buy a new Toyota pickup. This was because Toyota in Beira hadn't had one pickup for sale! In Maputo, they bought a red one, not because they liked the colour but because here again, Toyota only had one red pickup for sale. They made the long drive back to the Nhamacoa just in time, because my prediction that we were in for another drought turned out to be totally wrong.

When the rains first came, the big warm drops spattered on the parched dry brown earth and left round spots in the dust and a deliciously fresh clean fragrance in the air. At first, the rain was soft with a silky, swishing whispering sound and then, when the swollen purple-black clouds burst, water hurtled down from the sky, pounding and roaring so loudly on our grass roof that we had to shout to be heard. Thunder rolled around overhead and while lightning bolts cracked violently all around us, two young cats and a dog cowered underneath the sofa, shivering with terror.

Day after day, the rain poured down.

Our workers' mud huts collapsed. Our house sprang a dozen leaks. In the forest where Naison and his crew were working, the Muanga River rose so fast that our lorries and tractors couldn't get across and were stranded. Leaving two unfortunate workers behind with some food to guard the vehicles, Naison and his men removed their clothes, tied them in bundles on top of their heads and swam across the swollen river. It took them two days to walk back to the sawmill.

When the rain considerately stopped for a week and the level of the river fell again, we took the opportunity of getting our vehicles back to the sawmill. Just as well, because this time, when it began to rain again, it didn't stop until parts of southern Mozambique looked just like an enormous lake.

In Manica Province, we wallowed around in a sea of mud. Swollen rivers cut us off from Maputo and the sawmills that bought our timber disappeared under water. In the forest, our logs were bogged down in places no lorry or tractor could get to and our own sawmill was silent. Everything ground to a standstill, including our income. Vegetables and maize turned black and rotted in the ground and food became scarce.

The weeks passed slowly while we waited for the rain to stop and the water to drain away. Money ran low, food even lower and life turned very tough for our workers and ourselves. We were back to living off Faruk's bounty and buying dried beans, tins of tuna, chickens and maize on credit from his shop.

We lost about three quarters of our local business at this time. Many of the small carpenters who had done so much to help our sawmill along stopped buying planks from the stock we still held in the Nhamacoa. No doubt this was because of the knock-on effect the floods had had on all businesses and there were no customers or work for them. Unfortunately, these carpenters were never able to get on their feet again and consequently vanished from our lives. Their loss was a big blow to us.

We'd been at a standstill for about five long months when Caetano found a way out of our financial dilemma. Or so we all thought. Little did we know at the time that his solution would bring a new person into our lives and that this would set the stage for the terrible and tragic events that were to take place two years later, in 2002.

Along with the floods, there had also been a cyclone called Eline and she had knocked down a vast quantity of trees along the Mozambican/Zimbabwean border, in the pine plantations at Tsetsserra.

"I heard the other day that the government's looking for private companies to pull the pine, saw it up and sell it before it's destroyed or burnt in the queimadas," Caetano told us. "So far, only a couple of people have taken up the offer. If we can scrape enough money together to buy the licence, I'm sure I can organise a contract with IAC (the government sawmill) to supply them with the pine."

Caetano talked to IAC, we scraped the money together and with Caetano now driving the white pickup and in charge of the venture, Fo'pence and our workers set up camp at Tsetsserra.

Unfortunately, there had been a change at the Department of Forestry. Ana Paula had left to work for an Aid Agency and had been replaced by a man called Ribeiro who had spent some time in Cuba and who abhorred private enterprise. Despite the fall of Communism, Ribeiro remained a loyal and rabid follower of this failed ideology and had wanted the work at Tsetsserra to be done by a co-operative of local people - with himself in charge.

When his ideas came to nothing, he worked off his disappointment on Caetano, harassing him with frequent visits to castigate and criticise. The work was being badly done! It was too slow! Too inefficient! Caetano should never have been given the job! He didn't know what he was doing!

One day, Nhaca, the new Governor of Manica Province, also paid Caetano a visit at Tsetsserra. He looked around at the work in progress and was full of praise for Caetano's organisation. How well the work was being done! So quickly! So efficiently! Used to Ribeiro's unflagging criticism, Caetano was completely taken aback by the Governor's compliments, so at variance with the Head of Forestry's unpleasantness. What were we to think?

Shortly after the Governor's visit, the local people began to stir up trouble. They got in the way, they hindered and prevented

Fo'pence and our workers from pulling the pine and complained to Ribeiro that the work should have been given to them to do.

Ribeiro promptly suspended our operations and told Caetano that he and the local population had had a meeting and had decided to buy a saw, form themselves into a co-operative and do the work themselves.

Incensed by it all, Caetano disputed Ribeiro's right to suspend our work. Ribeiro dug his heels in and rather than leave our workers idling away their time, we brought them back to the Nhamacoa. The pine which Fo'pence had pulled and which Ribeiro was refusing to allow us to supply to IAC lay in a safe estaleiro, awaiting its fate. We left our chainsaw operator, Caetano Jorge, to guard it. After all, it had cost us money to pull. Money for the licence, money for fuel, money for our worker's wages and their food. Were Ribeiro and his so-called 'Co-operative' going to compensate us for this?

While the dispute was raging, the local population carelessly started a forest fire that got out of control and also began to rage in Tsetsserra. It roared through the thousands of hectares of fallen pine, sending them up in smoke and leaving piles of ash.

When the fires died down, Caetano drove off to Tsetsserra to check on our own pine, although he knew the timber had been pulled into a well-cleared estaleiro and should have been quite safe.

On reaching his destination, he got a shock.

The estaleiro was untouched by fire ... Caetano Jorge was still there ... but the pine ... worth six hundred million meticais (U.S. $25,000) ... was gone! Caetano Jorge was guarding an empty estaleiro!

Caetano tottered out of the pickup. What had happened to our timber?

"The foreigner came and took it away," Caetano Jorge explained.

"The foreigner ... what foreigner?" Caetano's voice rose up in astonishment.

"The one the Company gave the wood to." Caetano Jorge went on.

"WHAT?" Caetano's voice rose higher.

Realising that something was wrong from the strong reaction his words were causing, Caetano Jorge's voice began to falter. "He told me the Company had given him permission ... given him permission ... to take the wood away."

283

How Caetano ever got safely back to Chimoio down the steep roads of Tsetsserra in his disturbed frame of mind, we never knew. First Ribeiro on his back, messing everything up and now this!

By the time he found Jan Westh, the Dane who owned the company Aloe Vera and who had stolen our pine, Westh had already sawn it all up into planks at his sawmill and transported it away for sale.

The confrontation between Caetano and Westh had been brief. Showing absolutely no sign of guilt or remorse, Westh was quite barefaced about his theft. Yes, he admitted, he had taken the pine. He would recompense Caetano for this, of course, by giving him what the pine was worth ... six million meticais (U.S. $250).

"Six million ..."

Caetano took Westh's offer as a personal insult, which indeed it was. Turning on his heel, he jumped into his pickup and drove off to the Police Station. He was going to have the Dane from squeaky-clean Denmark arrested!

O'D and I were in town on the day Jan Westh was taken in for questioning. We were driving down the main road towards the roundabout when we heard a 'toot' behind us and saw Caetano grinning broadly through his windscreen at us. We pulled off the road and stopped under the shade of a tree. Caetano pulled up behind us.

"The police arrested Westh this morning and when he was questioned by Mr. Shutar of the Commercial Fraud Section, he admitted everything. Everything!" Caetano laughed triumphantly. "They've got him in a cell at Primeira Esquadra now."

We were still gloating and wondering if Westh was occupying O'D's old maggot-infested cell, when Treciano arrived. Treciano was a tough Mozambican war veteran Caetano had employed to work at our estaleiro in town and to deal with our paperwork. He habitually wore a lugubrious expression on his craggy face and now looked more lugubrious than ever with the news he had for us. News that completely wiped the smiles off our faces.

"The criminal Westh is out of jail," he told us. "A Danish organisation got him out."

Furious that some interfering Europeans had perverted the course of justice, Caetano decided on a rash course of action.

"Westh's not going to get away with stealing our timber!" he fumed. "We'll take him to court!"

284

O'D shook his head. "You know the justice system in Mozambique is as corrupt as hell, Caetano. And anyway, after all that's happened this year, we just don't have the money to throw away on lawyers."

Caetano was silent for a while. He was as fed up as I was with all these people who were always stealing from us and getting away with it. Eventually he said, "We can do it through IPAJ, the legal service available to people who can't afford lawyers."

"Alright, Caetano," O'D said, "If you really want the Company to take Westh to court, take him to court. But you deal with it all. I don't want to have anything to do with it."

Caetano nodded his head. "I'll start on it right away," he said. "We can't afford to let him get away with what he's done. We've lost too much money already."

The news that we were going to take Westh to court brought a warning from Jinho, one of our Mozambican friends. "Let's hope you don't get Judge Magaia trying the case," he told us. "He's got a really bad reputation!"

Our financial position was now grimmer than ever. What with the floods, the Communist Ribeiro and the thieving Dane, we were almost at the end of our resources. There was nothing left for it but to start using the small nest egg that remained from the sale of Arrojela.

"What we have to do now," Caetano told us, "is to find another area, far away from Ribeiro's jurisdiction."

The area Caetano found for us was in Tete Province, about an eight hour drive from the Nhamacoa. It was a dry part of Mozambique, hideously hot and at the time more or less ignored by the rest of the country. With some of the money from Arrojela, we bought a licence to cut some Leadwood and sold it to Mr. Chen of Chen Investments. It helped, for a while.

While this was going on, there was chaos and disaster of another sort unfolding across the border from us, in Zimbabwe.

Ignoring the end-of-year riots in Harare and disregarding his people's feelings and their growing dissatisfaction with his rule, President Mugabe held a referendum to change the Constitution and to give himself the powers of a dictator. The Zimbabwean people responded with a resounding 'NO!' Used to adulation, this rejection shocked him and he reacted by throwing his toys out of the cot in a rage.

Through a haze of fury, he looked around for a scapegoat and a way to bolster his waning popularity and came up with some really bad ideas. Blaming the whites, a new opposition party called the MDC and the British for Zimbabwe's troubles, he organized the violent invasion of white-owned farms, supposedly to redistribute the land to landless indigenous people.

The 'War Vets' spearheaded these invasions. These were young men who were much too young to be the real War Veterans and whose leaders had given themselves ridiculous names like Hitler Hunzvi, Stalin Mau Mau and Black Jesus.

They began their campaign with a series of horrifying acts, the first of which took place on a farm east of Harare when they abducted a white farmer called David Stevens and dragged him off to the local police station. Hearing the news of the abduction, five other farmers rushed off to the police station to help him but on their arrival, they discovered that the War Vets had taken David Stevens off to their headquarters where they had beaten him, tortured him, forced him to drink diesel and then shot him in the head and back.

Where were the police while all this had been going on? we all asked.

With this murder, the violence escalated. Farmhouses were surrounded by the War Vets and their screaming mobs armed with machetes, axes and sticks who drummed their drums all day and all night long. When they got their hands on the farmers, they beat them up, smashing and breaking bones, sometimes killing them, sometimes simply evicting them and their families. Then the farmhouses were looted and trashed and the farm animals sometimes also killed; horses set on fire and cattle herded into dams and drowned. Having done their worst, the War Vets and their followers set about parcelling out the farmland amongst themselves.

White Zimbabwean farmers weren't the only ones targeted by the violence. Hundreds of thousands of farm labourers and their children lost their jobs and their homes when they were also evicted along with their former employers, the farmers. Forced to live from hand to mouth in the bush, they began to starve.

And in Harare, my young nephew Thomas woke up in the middle of the night, screaming from nightmares. The Wovets, as he called the War Vets, terrified him. One day he had seen Fatima, the family's maid, standing at the sink in the kitchen and washing the dishes while tears streamed silently down her face. She had just heard the news that her brother who had gone to the family home in one of the rural areas had been beaten to death by the Wovets on suspicion of being a supporter of the MDC opposition party.

Now, when O'D and I drove across the border to shop in Mutare or to visit David and Caroline in Harare, we took our own supplies of fuel in jerrycans tied up in the back of the pickup. There were long petrol queues in Zimbabwe and no guarantee of fuel.

Along with other industries in Zimbabwe, our small and once successful ethnic duvet business with David and Caroline took a nose-dive. Manufacturing costs were now just too high to carry on.

Sadly, my brother and his family decided to go back to London and like so many others, they would never return to Zimbabwe or Africa.

There were a lot of things to sort out, though, before their departure. Another job for Fatima, if possible. And then there were their animals, the three dogs and the three cats. The animals, unfortunately, would all have to be put down.

When Caroline walked into the Highlands Veterinary Surgery to make the arrangements, she walked into a scene of chaos. The rooms were bursting with traumatised people and their pets, grown men breaking down in tears and weeping at the thought of what they had to do. Growing pale and unable to join them, Caroline fled.

A South African organisation offered help, flying Zimbabwean dogs out of the country and into South Africa, to new homes on farms on that side of the border. With the reprieve of the family's dogs, that left their three cats: Stinky, a large and laid-back handsome ginger with a propensity to emit incredibly noxious fumes from his nether regions, hence the name! Sidney, a small and dapper cat in black and white, and a fat and cuddly grey tabby with a gammy leg, called Huffle. As there were no offers of help for the cats, I rashly forgot our own Miss Sydney's reaction to Grumpy and made an offer of my own. It would be a shame to put the family pets to death.

"We'll take them," I told Caroline. "Organise their papers for the border crossing into Mozambique."

On the day of their evacuation from Zimbabwe, Caroline gave each cat a pill with their breakfast. This was a sleeping pill the Vet had given to her, to keep the animals sleeping and calm during their six to seven hour journey to their new home. Unfortunately, Stinky, who was a voracious eater, greedily ate up all his food and then proceeded to gobble up some of Huffle's and Sidney's as well – ending up with a double dose of the drug!

During the journey to the border, Stinky slept the hours away in the enormous cardboard crate in the back of our pickup, completely oblivious that he was being transported away from his home. The same couldn't be said of his companions. Wide-awake thanks to Stinky, they began their attempt to escape from their prison.

Halfway home, I looked out of the pickup's back window at the crate to check all was well and saw eyes staring back at me through the airholes O'D had cut out for them. "They're awake!" I told O'D. "Don't worry," he replied. "They can't get out."

It was early evening by the time we arrived back in the Nhamacoa. Miss Sydney was nowhere to be seen but little Grumpy was home when O'D and Seven carried the crate of cats into the sitting room. They turned it on its side – slowly - and then O'D opened the lid. Three cats, one groggy and two clear-headed, cautiously tiptoed out and looked around the room, completely disorientated.

Just then, Miss Sydney padded into the house. In the sitting room doorway, she paused for one second, taking in the scene with her green eyes and then she reacted.

As if she'd received an electric shock, she leapt up into the air, fur and legs shooting out in all directions and let out a terrible screech. O'D, Seven and I fell back with shock, while Bandit scrambled over to the sofa in panic and squeezed herself under it for safety. Grumpy, Stinky, Huffle and Sidney scattered in all directions and cowered under chairs.

For several minutes Miss Sydney raged and rampaged around the room, pouring out all the pain her anguished little heart felt at the loss of her status. Just a few months ago she had been the only spoilt and pampered pet in the house and now she was just one of many. Eventually, she wore herself out and with a final angry hiss, ran out of the room and out of the house.

"Oh, what are we going to do now?" I asked, my heart sinking at the thought of all the tantrums that were going to shatter the peace of my house.

"She'll get over it," O'D said, turning his attention to the cardboard crate. He turned it upright again and examined its interior which showed clear evidence of Sidney and Huffle's escape attempt.

"Look at this," he told me, with a chuckle of admiration. "Sid and Huffle almost succeeded in chewing their way out of it. We got home just in time!"

Miss Sydney never did get over it. If anything, her fury increased. She especially hated Sidney, not only for his presence but for sharing her name. She tussled with Stinky. The one she really had it in for, though, was Huffle who appeared to be the dominant cat. Embarking on a bitter battle with Huffle, who had taken up residence on the grass roof of the house to get away from it all, she instigated yowling catfights that raged ceaselessly above our heads. They only came to a halt when Miss Sydney fell off the roof into a drum of water and had to be rescued by Seven.

Surprisingly, there was someone who benefitted from the chaos. Fighting on so many fronts left Miss Sydney little time to turn her attention to Grumpy. Before the arrival of the Zimbabweans, she had completely demoralised him with her constant bullying. Nerves shattered, he had been a candidate for a cat psychiatrist, timidly creeping around and jumping with terror at things that only he could see. The slightest sound frightened him, he was scared of his own shadow and even of his food bowl. Now, Stinky took him under his wing and acting as a role model, gave him some measure of protection. Glueing himself to his ginger hero, Grumpy began to blossom.

Mozambicans treated the turmoil in Zimbabwe with the same hard-hearted approach Miss Sydney had treated our refugees.

In the past, they had often cast envious eyes at the good life the Zimbabweans were enjoying on the other side of their border. Boasts from Zimbabweans that Zimbabwe was the best country in the world had irritated the Mozambicans. Now, they were gleefully appalled at the way Zimbabwe was rushing towards its ruin - learning nothing from its neighbour Mozambique which had gone to its ruin in almost the same way thirty years ago when it had kicked out the Portuguese.

Jethro, Manuella and Argentina paid us a visit from Macate, speeding past our house in their battered pickup and a cloud of red dust. "We've come to invade your sawmill!" they shouted, and screamed with laughter.

"You can have it," O'D told them.

Mario, the policeman, told us he was horrified to hear how the Zimbabwean police stood by and watched as two members of the opposition party MDC were torched by the War Vets and burnt to death in their car. "This is not the way the police should behave," he told us self-righteously. "It's the duty of the police to protect people and to ensure that law and order prevails."

Ironically, two years later, Mario's words and the very man himself would be put to the test. And he would fail. Fail miserably.

Not long after the arrival of the Zimbabwean refugees, we noticed a difference in Miss Sydney's figure - a definite bulging around the stomach - and began to suspect that her absences from the house had had more to do with increasing the feline population in the Nhamacoa than with her sulking. Although we had taken Bandit to be spayed by Dr. Hangartner, the Vet in Mutare, in the turmoil of our lives we hadn't managed to take Miss Sydney.

This forgetfulness on our part led Miss Sydney, one afternoon, to give birth to four little kittens in the most comfortable spot she could find - yes, on our bed. Surprisingly, there was absolutely no mess. O'D found a cardboard box and filled it with a soft blanket. He put the box in a quiet, dark corner of our bedroom and transferred Spike, Raji, Jasper and Missy into it. And Miss Sydney purred with a contentment we hadn't heard for a very long time.

Cats now took over our house. In a matter of a few months we had gone from owning one dog and one cat to owning one dog and nine cats! Hygiene flew out of the window as cat hairs flew around and floated thickly in the air. The cats slept all over the place; on the bed, on the chairs, in the paper trays on O'D's desk and in Sidney's case, in the vegetable rack, amongst the tomatoes, carrots and green peppers!

"I now like Jacques, who work for Master Maciel," Biasse grumbled, remembering his friend who cooked for Maciel's 27 cats. "Cook for the kits!"

CHAPTER TWENTY TWO

BRENDA, THE MONKEY LADY

As if the deluge of rain that had turned part of Mozambique into a vast lake in the year 2000 hadn't been enough, when the 2001 rains arrived, we were treated to a repeat performance of another flood.

Once again, everything ground to a halt for about six months and once again, we were brought to the financial brink. The only way we managed to keep our heads above the water this time was by resorting to the use of our Arrojela funds. 2001, we knew now, was going to be a make or break year but in the meantime, we would just have to tighten our belts and sit it out, waiting for the waters to subside and the mud to dry out.

It was around about this time, too, that Seven disappeared out of our lives. One morning, he came to me and told me that someone was once again tormenting him with nails and razor blades in his legs.

"I am suffering very much, Meddem. I need to go to a curandeiro."

Tired of Seven's preoccupation with witchcraft, I was impatient with him. "Oh for Heaven's sakes, Seven, if there's something wrong with your legs it would be much better if you went to Chimoio hospital instead of these curandeiros of yours!"

"Yes, Meddem," he said, softly. "Yes, Meddem."

I was to regret my impatience, because the next day Seven didn't come to work. He didn't come to work the day after that either and although I asked our workers if they knew what had happened to him, nobody could tell me anything. He simply vanished into thin air.

With my mind filled with all the problems we were having, I didn't notice that one of our cats also had a problem. There were now so many of them, it was difficult to give each cat individual attention.

One afternoon, Stinky came to talk to me and to ask for help. I was in the kitchen when he padded slowly into the room. He came right up to me and with a pitiful miaow, stared into my eyes for a long moment. Then, with a sigh, he collapsed weakly onto the floor and closed his eyes. Looking down at him, I noticed that the inside of his right ear was completely encrusted with some kind of brown stuff –

obviously an infection - and was horrified. His ear looked a complete mess! How could I have missed seeing this?

"Oh, Stinky, I'm so sorry," I said, and vowed to pay more attention to all the animals from then on.

The next day we put Stinky into a cat box and made a hurried trip across the border to see Dr. Hangartner. In an old house set in a pleasant leafy street near the centre of the town, we waited for his verdict.

"I've had a good look at … er … Stinky Pixley," Dr. Hangartner told us, trying unsuccessfully not to laugh at the name, "and he's going to need an operation. He's got a polyp growing in his ear canal that's causing the problem. It has to be removed." He paused for a moment and then admitted, "And to be quite honest, I've never done this operation before, so I can't guarantee its success."

O'D and I craned our necks upwards at the Vet. He was so tall that you almost fell over backwards when you looked up at him. "What's the alternative?" O'D asked.

"None," the Vet replied.

We left Stinky with Dr. Hangartner and drove back home.

A few days later, when O'D drove up to Chimoio to phone Dr. Hangartner from the post office about the results of Stinky's operation, the Vet gave him some alarming news. He had discovered that Stinky was also the owner of a defective heart! He was suffering from Feline Cardio Myopathy, an enlarged heart caused by the modern habit of feeding generations of cats from tinned cat food that lacked the vitamin, Taurine.

And not only that, while the polyp-removing operation had been successful, Stinky had caught cat flu from another cat in the cage next to his and was very sick indeed. Although Dr. Hangartner was doing everything he could to keep him alive, it was touch and go!

Amazingly, Stinky pulled through. This, of course, was largely due to Dr. Hangartner's medical skill, although Stinky also did his bit. Despite being the owner of a flabby enlarged heart, he had the spirit of a lion and a strong and tenacious will to live.

On our first visit to see Stinky while he recuperated in Dr. Hangartner's care, the Vet told us a little about the operation.

"The polyp was so deep in the ear canal that I decided to try using liquid nitrogen to remove it," he told us "Then, when that didn't work, I had to cut into the back of the ear to get at it." He looked

292

pleased with himself. "And I'm glad to say, it all went very successfully."

We were pleased with Dr. Hangartner as well. We were in the middle of thanking him for saving Stinky when a woman with short black hair came rushing breathlessly into the room.

"My fiancée," Dr. Hangartner introduced us. "She asked me to let her know when you'd be here. She wanted to see what kind of people would call their cat 'Stinky'."

"Actually," I said, glad to disappoint Dr. Hangartner's fiancée, "we were not the ones who called Stinky 'Stinky'."

Dr. Hangartner and his bride-to-be exchanged knowing looks. "We've heard that one before," Dr. Hangartner's fiancée said with a smirk.

"It was my brother David and his family," I told them, remembering how Caroline had been too embarrassed to tell their Vet in Highlands Stinky's real name and had pretended he was called 'Marmalade'. I had tried calling him 'Marmalade' when he'd first arrived in the Nhamacoa but it had been quite obvious that he hadn't had a clue that this was supposed to be him.

"Sometimes they fed him kapenta," I went on, "that dried fish. It made him very … er … windy."

Dr. Hangartner and his fiancée burst out laughing at my story.

"It's true," I insisted.

We brought Stinky home some weeks later. He was a lucky cat, because if he had become ill a year or two in the future, he would have died. Because by that time there wouldn't be any well-qualified Vets left in Mutare.

From time to time, O'D and Caetano drove to Maringue, a new felling area Caetano had found, to check on the state of the ground. Unfortunately, it was still too wet to work there and so our panga panga logs languished in the mud and we signed more of our Arrojela Travellers Cheques to keep us all going.

It was during one of these trips to Sofala Province that O'D saw Mogsie. He and Caetano had just driven out of Beira when O'D noticed a small cat struggling to pull itself along the side of the busy main road. The cat's thick grey and white fur was bedraggled and wet with sweat and its little pink tongue was hanging out with thirst. Unable to bear the pitiful sight, O'D brought the red Toyota to a screeching halt and jumped out.

"What's the matter?" Caetano asked, bewildered and wondering if their abrupt stop meant there was something wrong with the pickup.

O'D bent down and scooped the little cat up off the ground. "Here, you hold it," he told Caetano and put the animal onto a surprised Caetano's lap. "We have to go back into Beira to find a Vet, Caetano. This cat's hurt. We can't leave it here, it'll get run over."

In Beira they found something that passed for a Veterinary Surgery and left the cat there, together with some money for its medical treatment and food. Unfortunately, it turned out that the little cat had a dislocated hip and there wasn't anyone qualified enough at the Surgery to deal with this sort of thing. There was nothing for it but to drive down to Beira again and to bring the cat back to the Nhamacoa.

"I hope you don't mind," O'D told me, "but I just can't leave her to die."

"Of course you can't," I agreed.

We now had one dog and TEN cats!

The Mog or Mogsie, as I called her, was the sweetest little cat. Although she was greeted with a few hisses from the other nine cats, they didn't seem to mind her arrival too much and even Miss Sydney, who usually made the most fuss, only gave her a couple of bats on the head with her little black paw to show her who was the boss. They knew she was no threat to them.

By this time, Dr. Hangartner had sold his practice and together with his new wife had fled by way of a cargo boat to greener pastures in Australia. It was becoming more and more difficult for us to find medical help now, not only for ourselves but also for our animals.

However, there still remained one other well qualified Vet in Mutare and that was Dr. Mafara, who, like Dr. Umbawa, had also been trained in America.

Dr. Mafara gave Mogsie an x-ray and told us her hip appeared to have been dislocated for such a long time that he would have to operate on it to get it back into place. She also had a chest infection and would need antibiotics.

Leaving Mogsie in Dr. Mafara's competent hands, we drove back across the border to Mozambique.

We kept in touch with Mogsie's progress by using the post office phone to speak to Brenda, Dr. Mafara's receptionist. She had a real love for animals and was exactly the sort of person a Vet should have working for him. A couple of weeks later, when we told her we would be in Mutare for the day, she told us to bring our cat box. Just in case Mogsie was ready to come home.

Dr. Mafara's surgery was also in an old house in a shady garden. As O'D wanted to get some spares from Toyota, he dropped me off in the meantime.

Crunching noisily across the gravel drive towards reception, I stepped out of the sunlight and into the cool front room and was met by quite a comical sight.

There was Brenda, large, plump and motherly looking, sitting placidly behind the reception counter with a tiny Vervet monkey attached to the top of her short dark hair like a yarmulke. Another slightly larger Vervet was entwined around her neck like a scarf, munching on the green pea it was holding in one of its tiny hands.

"Hi, Brenda," I said.

"Oh, hello," she replied. "As I told O'D on the phone, Mogsie's had her operation. She's much better now ..."

Startled by my appearance and my unfamiliar voice, the monkey around Brenda's neck suddenly decided to panic. Dropping the pea, it scrambled to the top of her head for safety and immediately began to jostle and fight for space with the other Vervet already there.

" ... Ow! OW!" Brenda gave a scream of pain as the two struggling Vervets dug their fingers into her scalp to stop themselves from falling off her head.

Raising her hands, she wrenched at one of the Vervets and tried to detach its hands from her hair to pull it off her head while still continuing to talk to me "...but it would probably be better if you waited for Blessing ... he'll be back soon ... to talk about her ..."

Red in the face from the struggle, Brenda finally managed to prise the smallest monkey off her head "In the meantime," she gasped, holding the monkey in her arms and cuddling it like a baby, "I'll take you to see her."

I followed her down the corridor and into another room, laughing to myself at the sight she made. With a baby Vervet still firmly perched on top of her head, she looked hilarious from behind, as if she was wearing a monkey hat.

Mogsie did, indeed, seem better. When I put a finger into her cage to stroke her on her head, she squashed her head against the bars and purred at me as loudly as a contented lion. "O'D's coming to see you in a minute, little Mogsie," I told her. "And then maybe we'll be able to take you home."

Back in reception again, I leaned against the counter where Brenda and her Vervets were once again ensconced in her chair. Realising I wasn't a threat, the little animals were back to munching on their green peas.

"Where did you get the monkeys?" I asked.

Brenda heaved a sigh. "People keep bringing them in. These are the sixth and seventh baby Vervets I've been given to look after." She gave me a wry smile, "People are beginning to call me a rather unfortunate name - the Monkey Lady!" and bending her head over the tiny monkey she was cuddling, she kissed it right on the mouth.

"Gosh, Brenda!" I exclaimed, "I really don't think you should do that. You might get all sorts of germs ... even Ebola ... that terrible hemorrhagic disease with blood coming out of you everywhere!"

She ignored me and went on stroking the tiny creature gently. "They're so sweet," she said fondly. "They're just like little babies."

The Vervets certainly were sweet although I wouldn't have wanted them attached to the back of *my* head all day. "Who is bringing them to you and why?"

Brenda's plump face turned grim. "People are buying them off the side of the road and bringing them to me. The locals are killing their mothers for bushmeat and selling the babies. One of the little Vervets still had its umbilical cord ..."

"Oh ..." I turned away from the counter, feeling sick. "How can they do that ... how can anyone kill something that's just given birth ..."

"I know," Brenda said. "It's horrible, but that's what's been happening."

"Why don't you contact the World Wildlife people in London?" I asked. "Maybe they'd be able to help."

Brenda gave a contemptuous snort and like most people in Southern Africa, spoke her mind. "Oh, them," she said dismissively, "they're just a lot of useless old farts, full of hot air. A waste of time ... they never do anything ... they just talk. I've been sending the Vervets on to a private game park but the way things are going in this country, I don't know if even *their* animals are going to be safe."

Blessing, Dr. Mafara's assistant, pronounced Mogsie to be fully repaired and so we took her home. There was one thing that I

296

noticed about her, though. Mogsie couldn't look up. She could only look straight ahead. There must have been more damage to her than we had originally thought. However, she didn't seem to be in any pain and when she was back home again, I often picked her up and carried her around so that she could see a bit more of the world than what was just straight ahead of her and low down on the ground.

A happy little cat, she had a particularly raucous purr. Food made her happy and being picked up and cuddled made her happy. Her moments of greatest happiness, though, came when she saw O'D. She knew he had saved her and she adored him with all her little cat heart. She often showed off for him, with a little trick she thought would amaze him. Lying on her back on the sitting room carpet, she would roll over onto her left side and then turn her head to look at him, expecting praise. When O'D exclaimed "Mogsie!" in admiration, she waved all her paws delightedly in the air and then rolled over onto her right side and looked at him, waiting for another "Mogsie!". This performance could go on for quite some time.

In the evenings, when she heard the sound of the red Toyota pulling up in front of the house, she always clambered off the chair she was lying on and went to the door to greet him. He was the love of her life and her purrs when he picked her up were lionesque in their roaring quality.

On the 18th October, O'D fired Frank.

One morning at roll call, O'D noticed that Frank could barely manage to stand without supporting himself against one of our other workers.

"Frank!" O'D said. "You're drunk! What did I tell you would happen if you came to work drunk?"

"I'm ... nosh drunk, Madam ... er ... Shir ... er ..." Frank protested, staggering up to O'D and inflaming a temper already inflamed by enveloping him in foul and noxious clouds of Nippa fumes.

"Not drunk? You're stinking of Nippa!" O'D gave Frank a push in the direction of the forest track. "Go home. Go on! You've had your last warning. You're fired, Frank!"

From my bedroom window, I watched Frank weaving his drunken way along the forest track, back towards the hut he shared with Azelia. As he finally staggered around the bend and disappeared from sight, I shook my head and heaved a long sigh.

I was sorry to see Frank go, not only because I had a soft spot for him but because I doubted whether we were going to find another Mozambican who spoke and wrote English as well as he did. Frank had been my go-between when I needed help to understand a worker or a customer. My Portuguese would never be up to much and I often needed an interpreter. Even more importantly, he was also a known quantity and had been trustworthy to a certain extent when it had come to the large sums of money we had handled together.

"What are we going to do, now?" I asked O'D at breakfast. "You know how difficult it's going to be to find another cubicador. They all want to work in the towns."

"Oh, someone is sure to come along," O'D told me, "and if they don't, we'll just have to try and train one of our workers."

In the afternoon, three days later, O'D and I were standing and talking outside the house when we saw a figure striding purposefully down the forest track towards us.

He was a polite and pleasant young man and he told O'D that his name was Samsone Joao. He had come all the way from Beira and he was looking for a job.

"What kind of job?" O'D asked.

"A cubicador," Samsone Joao replied.

O'D and I exchanged a look.

"A cubicador ..." I repeated, amazed.

After a small test, to see whether Samsone Joao did, in fact, know how to measure timber and work out their volumes, O'D employed him.

"He's quick and he's bright," O'D told me.

"Well," I said, "what a coincidence! One cubicador walks off into the distance, just as another cubicador comes walking out of the blue to replace him! Isn't this just the most extraordinary piece of luck?"

O'D was thoughtful for a moment. "Hmm. It certainly is peculiar," he muttered, "but as for luck, only time will tell whether it's going to be good luck ... or bad luck."

At the end of the year, Azelia brought me news of Seven. We were in the kitchen at the time, measuring out some Sunlight dishwashing liquid and diluting it with water, when she casually mentioned she had spoken to him at the market in Macate on Saturday afternoon.

"He was selling tomatoes, Dona. Small, bad looking tomatoes and he was talking about his machamba and about being a farmer. He was laughing, laughing like a mad person."

"Mad …" I said.

"Yes, and he looked dreadful! All his hair has fallen out and he is thin, very very thin."

Suddenly, I felt a terrible sense of urgency. "Do you know where he's living, Azelia?"

She shrugged. "No, Dona."

"Well, we've got to find him and bring him back here."

She stared at me in amazement. "But why?" she asked. "He's mad!"

"He's not mad," I said. "He's sick. Will you try and find out where he is, Azelia? Ask people if they know?"

She was silent for a while and I remembered how she and Seven had often bickered. "Alright, Dona," she said eventually and with some reluctance. "I will ask."

I would find Seven, I thought, and then we would take him straight to hospital, get him well again and feed him up.

But before I could find Seven, something was to happen that would put all thoughts of him out of my head for a while. And then, when I finally did remember him again, it was only to discover that his fate had been taken out of my hands.

CHAPTER TWENTY THREE

MURDER IN THE NHAMACOA
2002

Whenever I think of what happened to us all in 2002, a passage from the Bible comes into my mind. It's that part of the book of Job where God asks Satan what he's been up to and the devil replies "From going to and fro on the earth, and from walking back and forth on it."

And during all his walking back and forth, Satan paid me and Caetano and O'D a visit in the Nhamacoa … and our lives were changed forever.

I didn't know, of course, that I had been 'set-up' until much later and oh, what a set-up it was. A neat little series of events, which started with Frank being fired and which then led, step by cunning step, towards its planned conclusion, when it exploded in the ultimate evil of all … murder!

In the beginning of the year, Murray Dawson paid us an unexpected visit.

Murray was - or used to be - a successful Zimbabwean commercial farmer and an old friend of Paul and my sister Jenny. It had been years since we had last seen Murray and then he'd been brown haired and clean-shaven. This long lapse in time was to cause a little confusion, especially when he pulled up at our house at exactly the same moment as Allan Schwarz who had come to pick up some Umbila he had bought from us.

"Hello, O'D!" Murray greeted Allan, as they both clambered out of their pickups.

When Allan denied being O'D, Murray walked over to O'D, who stared at him blankly, trying to pinpoint where he had met him before. Who was this bespectacled man whose face was almost entirely hidden beneath a great fuzz of white?

"Murray Dawson!" Murray told us, and held out his hand

Although we were pleased to see Murray again, the reason for his visit wasn't a good one.

He sat down in our sitting room and while he drank a cold can of Castle and smoked a harsh Madison cigarette, he told us what had brought him across the border, into Mozambique. "She came with her

War Vets to take my farm," Murray said, in his dry, rough voice. "Sabina, that old sister of Mugabe's. Naturally, I decided to **resist** her … with some **force**! I got all my farmworkers together and we attacked them …" he paused to swig down some more beer.

"And then?" I asked.

"They attacked us **back** … with some **force**!" Murray said, and with a dry laugh, added. "They gave us a real thrashing … and we had to run away."

"So Mugabe's sister took your farm," I said.

"She did, indeed," Murray drawled. "And then they trashed my house. Terry's living in town now."

The farm, just outside Harare, had been in Murray's family since the 1930's and after Murray had taken charge of it, he had made a tremendous success of growing vegetables for export to the U.K. A bachelor, he looked after his sister, who was divorced and his brother, Terry, who was wheelchair bound. Now, with his livelihood suddenly wrenched away from him, like many other Zimbabwean farmers he'd been forced to look across Zimbabwe's borders for a new start in life.

Although Murray had only been in Mozambique for a few days, some locals had already given him the traditional welcome Mozambicans give visitors to their country.

This event had taken place one afternoon when he had noticed he was driving his khaki-coloured Toyota Landcruiser on 'empty' and had innocently driven into a petrol station to fill up. When the petrol attendant had tried to charge him for more diesel than the Toyota's fuel tank was capable of taking, Murray had balked. An argument had broken out. Murray had called for buckets, and in the presence of a stray policeman, the Toyota's fuel tank had been emptied out into the buckets in order to measure the fuel.

When these measurements proved that some trickery had, indeed, been afoot, the owner of the petrol station had suddenly appeared and had tried to hit Murray with a baseball bat! Then, the man had run off, only to reappear some minutes later with a policeman of a higher rank than the one Murray had found.

This policeman had hauled Murray off to the local police station and there had told him that he had two choices. "You either pay the petrol station owner the money you owe him," he had told Murray grimly, "or you go to jail!"

Murray had paid up.

"I'm living at the Chibuku factory outside Chimoio until I get sorted out." Murray told us. "I'm looking for a suitable piece of land to farm, and perhaps somewhere to start up a butchery."

Murray's presence cheered us up a bit. By now, almost all of our friends and family had fled Zimbabwe and this had left us feeling a little lonely. There was no longer any reason to make the drive to Harare and even Mutare was beginning to look a little bare of people we knew.

A few days after Murray's visit, one of our workers in Maringue brought a message from Fernand, who was once again driving for us. The blue Gaz had a problem and had broken down.

The news put O'D in a bit of a quandary. He was going to have to rush off on a 200 kilometre trip to fix the lorry and he was going to have to leave me alone in the Nhamacoa - without a night guard. This lack of a night guard had occurred when Lovad had decided to give up work for a while and O'D hadn't been able to find anyone to replace him. As a result, he was forced to use some rather unlikely characters to keep me safe.

"I've told Samsone Joao to spend the night in the guardhouse to guard the timber," O'D told me, "and Biasse can sleep in the room under the house. You'll have Bandit, as well, so you should be alright."

"Yes, I'm sure I'll be alright," I agreed, although it was doubtful whether a small, skinny and elderly cook of sixty six would be of much help if I should find myself in a desperate situation. And as for Bandit … well, despite being a Rhodesian ridgeback and a breed famed for its courage and lion-hunting abilities, so far she hadn't lived up to this reputation. She was ludicrously scared of people who wore hats and when a car jolted down the forest track towards our house, she usually made a mad dash for the bedroom, scrambling wildly under the bed and hiding until she thought all danger was passed and it was safe to come out! With protectors like these, I knew I was on my own - not that I had any of my usual feelings of foreboding that 'something bad' was going to happen.

In fact, I'd become rather blasé where my safety was concerned. After all, I'd now spent seven years living in an African forest and in a house with flimsy sleeping mat blinds over the windows and nothing had happened to me. Except, of course, for the theft of my shortwave radio! Now, however, I was much more secure than I'd been in those days. Shortly before the floods of 2000, we had

302

discarded the sleeping mats and installed glass windows in all but one room in the house. The exception was the spare bedroom. The window in this room still had its blind but it was too high to get into, unless you used a ladder.

O'D set off early on Saturday, the 12th January. He and Caetano were meeting up with Murray in Chimoio because they were going to drive to Maringue with Murray in his Landcruiser. There was a lot of mud around and O'D didn't think our Toyota Hilux would be up to it.

"I might be able to make it back home tonight," O'D told me, starting up the red Toyota. "It depends on how quickly I can fix the Gaz."

"Okay," I said. "I'll see you when I see you."

O'D had only been gone for a couple of hours when something quite out of the ordinary occurred.

I was sitting at the table, breakfasting on toast and marmalade when Biasse came into the sitting room. "Customer, Madam!" he told me.

I looked up in surprise. Customers on a Saturday had always been rare, even during the years when our sawmill had been at its busiest. "Who is it, Biasse?"

"It is Mr. Bonjasse, Madam," he told me, and added proudly with a broad smile. "Family of mine!"

Mr. Bonjasse was a very pleasant and softly spoken man. He needed Umbila, he told me, and rather a lot of it.

Biasse called Samsone Joao and together Mr. Bonjasse and our new cubicador walked over to the timber and spent some time picking through the piles of planks, choosing some and discarding others.

When they were finally finished, they stood outside my sitting room window and Samsone Joao handed me his measurements. Mr. Bonjasse had certainly bought a good quantity of timber - eight million meticais worth - and a windfall to us at this time, broke as we were!

Mr. Bonjasse now began the laborious task of counting out the grubby, tattered meticais notes to pay me and while he was busy, I just happened to glance up and noticed a peculiar expression on Samsone Joao's face. He just couldn't tear his eyes away from the money. He was mesmerised by it …

A tiny warning light flashed briefly on in my mind - what did we really know about our new cubicador? - but I dismissed it. We *all* had our eyes glued on the notes, because it was easy to miscount and make a mistake.

When the transaction was over, I gathered up the money – oh, what a lucky day this was turning out to be! - and took it off to the bedroom. The best place to stash it, of course, was in O'D's cupboard.

I opened the door. His clothes were in a mess, so I rummaged around until I found four of his socks and stuffed the meticais inside them. It would take a thief a long time to find it in this shambles!

The rest of the day passed peacefully. With nothing to do except please myself, I spent my time reading "Hill Towns" by Anne Rivers Siddons. This was a wonderfully amusing read about five Americans who were travelling around Italy in the company of Sam, a famous American artist and his wife, Ada, who lived in Rome. The story was so engrossing that I lost myself completely in it and for a few delightful hours I was far, far away from the Nhamacoa.

In the evening, I lit some paraffin lamps and went early to bed. Just in case O'D was able to make it home in the night after all, I left one paraffin lamp alight in the sitting room and another in the bathroom. It would save him from stumbling around in the dark.

I was propped up against my pillows reading "Hill Towns" again when some rather weird and disturbing things began to happen.

I had just got to a very satisfactory part of the book where Cat's obnoxious husband American Joe had been clowning around and showing off in front of some English aristocrats and had fallen into the fetid and foul waters of a Venetian canal, when out of the corner of my eye, I caught a movement at the end of my bed.

I looked up from my book and what I saw set an icy chill tingling along my spine.

The corner of the mosquito net at the end of the bed … on my side of the bed … appeared to be raising itself up off the floor … into the air … and then dropping softly down onto the edge of the bed!

For a moment, time seemed to stand still. Hardly daring to breathe and hardly able to believe what I had seen, I froze. Was someone UNDER my BED!

Slowly, I put my book down next to me on the sheet. Slowly, I took off my glasses and put them down next to my book. I was going to have to get out of bed and have a look … my heart cringed at the thought … oh no, oh no, oh no … yes, I was going to HAVE to do it … couldn't just ignore it …

I steeled myself ... perhaps it was only one of the cats, with a rat ... and leapt out of bed ... threw myself onto my knees on the floor ... looked under the bed ...

Nothing! Just a couple of dust balls Biasse had missed with his broom.

I stood up slowly and looked around the room, wondering what had caused the mosquito net to move. It couldn't have been the wind. The bedroom door was closed and so were the windows. Puzzled, I pulled the net off the edge of the bed and back down to the floor.

"What could it have been? What?" I asked myself aloud. It had looked almost as if someone had raised the net up to get inside ...

An unwelcome explanation to my question suddenly popped into my head. Could it be that another of O'D and Caetano's enemies had gone to a witch doctor? Could it be that he had sent another evil spirit or two to torment me in my sleep?

I glared irritably around the room at the thought. "Why, oh why do things always happen to me when O'D's away?" I asked, still speaking out aloud to myself.

Getting no reply, I got back into bed, put my glasses on again and picked up 'Hill Towns.' I would read for a little longer.

When my eyes grew tired, I turned off the light. For a few minutes, I lay on my back and looked at the starry sky through the window and then, despite the suspicion that I was now sharing my room with some vile Mozambican evil spirit, I turned over onto my side and immediately fell asleep, until about three o'clock in the morning ...

I don't know what woke me up, then. Perhaps it was the creak of the door, or perhaps it was a ... touch. But one moment I was soundly, deeply asleep and the next moment, just as if someone had given me a hard push in the middle of my back, I found myself sitting straight up in bed in one swift, smooth, movement.

The bedroom door was open. A man stood in the doorway, silhouetted by the orange glow of the paraffin lamp I had left burning in the bathroom.

For an instant we stared at each other through the folds of the mosquito net   hanging around my bed.

I felt a sense of déjà vu and it confused me. This had happened before ... in a dream. Was this a recurrence of the frightening dream I had had two years ago?

No ...

305

Ice filled my veins and I felt a hideous downward spiraling of dread …

No … this wasn't a repeat of my dream. This was the dream come true … this was the man I had dreamed was going to kill me. My dream killer had finally turned into terrifying reality!

Before I could make a move to try and save myself, the man was at my bedside. One hand shot through the mosquito net and grabbed me violently around my neck. The other hand clamped itself over my mouth. I sat frozen, while jangled thoughts roiled through my mind all at the same time as fast as the speed of light and I shuddered inwardly with the horror, the terror of it all. No one to help me. There was no one to help me. I was alone … completely alone … and I was going to die. Die horribly, I knew. Die! MURDERED! Oh, my …

And then, something strange happened, something very strange. Every vestige of the fear that was enveloping me suddenly melted away and I was filled with a peace so deep that my rioting, panicking, terror-stricken mind was completely stilled. And into this peace, this calm, I heard a voice speak to me.

"Although there is no one here to hear you," the voice said, "you must scream."

I drew in a deep breath and because the man's hand was over my mouth, I screamed from the back of my throat. The sound was guttural, ugly, horrible. I screamed over and over again, without taking in any more breaths.

Something clattered down onto the concrete floor next to my bed. The choking grip on my neck disappeared. The man turned away from me and fled across the room towards the door.

Astonished by his flight and hardly able to believe my miraculous escape from certain death, I took full advantage of my now unfettered throat and abandoned myself to a series of bloodcurdling screams, in my mind's eye seeing the killer running down the corridor … out of the house … and down the forest track …

When I thought that the man was safely gone, I stopped screaming and got out of bed. I turned on the torch and shone its beam on the floor, looking for the thing he had dropped with a clattering sound.

Aah … a knife. The handle was wooden, old and weathered. The blade was rusty except for the end, which had been sharpened into a hook and glinted silver in the torchlight. It looked more like a ripping knife than a stabbing knife. It looked as if it had been especially sharpened … just for me.

I picked up the knife and walked out of the bedroom, into the corridor. The front door was half open and as I approached it, it flew wide open and banged against the wall as another man burst into the corridor. He was small and skinny and was dressed only in a pair of old navy blue shorts. In his right hand he held a panga, a machete.

Biasse … too late to take part in the action.

Through the now wide-open doorway, I caught sight of Bandit. Confused and a little groggy, she was standing staring down the forest track and barking little barks with question marks after them. Woof? Woof? Woof?

"Madam! Madam! What happened? Why were you screaming?" Biasse asked, echoing Bandit's thoughts.

"Someone's just tried to kill me, Biasse," I told him, with a sense of incredulity, disbelief, at what had almost happened to me. "Someone's just tried to KILL me … with this knife!"

Biassse looked at the knife and then looked wildly up and down the corridor. "But where is Samsone Joao?" he asked.

"I don't know, Biasse," I said. Who cared where Samsone Joao was.

"But he should be here! He should have come when you screamed!"

A fiery and agonizing pain bit into my face, under my left eye, on my right cheek and on my lips. My fingers flew up to my face. What was this, now?

"Biasse," I asked, growing cold with fear all over again, "is there some Mozambican poison that burns like … fire?"

"I dunno, Madam. But where is Samsone Joao?"

Panicking, I ran into the bathroom and examined my face in the mirror. My skin was covered with large blisters. Welts. My tongue felt strange and there was a peculiar metallic taste in my mouth. I opened my mouth and stuck my tongue out, and felt a jolt of shock. The left half of my tongue had turned completely black!

With trembling fingers, I soaped my face and rinsed it over and over again with cold water. What on earth was this stuff on my face? Eventually, when I thought I had done my best to wash off whatever it was, I patted myself dry with a towel and walked slowly back down the corridor and into the sitting room.

Wearily, I sank down onto a chair at the table. It seemed I hadn't escaped death after all. Not content with trying to kill me with a knife, the cowardly wretch who had come to attack me while I was asleep had poisoned me as well!

A blue and white carton of Ultra Mel on the table caught my eye. Milk … Some poisons were supposed to be neutralized by milk … weren't they? I stood up, walked over to a small cupboard and took out a glass. Our First Aid box lay on a nearby shelf and I opened the lid and pulled out a large wad of cotton wool. I sat down at the table again, filled the glass with milk and drank it all down in one go. I filled the glass a second time and drank some more. I poured milk onto the cotton wool and dabbed it all over the welts and blisters on my face.

"Is anything missing, Madam? Has anything been stolen?"

I glanced around the room, lit only by the paraffin lamp. Since our arrival in the Nhamacoa, O'D and I had become minimalists. We didn't have anything of value that would have caused someone to go to such lengths as murder in order to steal. The clock was still on the wall, its hands ticking towards ten past three. Our old battered shortwave radio was still in the place it had occupied on top of the bookcase for the last seven years. The large coffee tin, though, which was full of coins, had vanished.

"The tin of change is gone, Biasse."

"So," Biasse said grimly, satisfied that he had found the motive for the attack. "I go look for Samsone Joao, now."

The memory of my dream came back to me. Although only one man had tried to kill me tonight, in my dream there had been two men.

"No. No, Biasse. There might be others out there in the dark, and if you go outside, they might attack you, too."

Biasse laughed derisively. "There is no one outside now, Madam. You frightened them away with your screaming."

"We'll wait," I told him firmly. "We'll wait until it gets lighter and then we'll both go and look for Samsone Joao."

Reluctantly, Biassse hunched down on the floor in front of the open door, his panga across his knees. I sat on at the table, alternately drinking milk and dabbing more milk on my face. Wrapped up in our thoughts, we waited in silence for the stars to grow dim and the black sky to lighten.

"Eh!" Biasse's voice said suddenly from his position near the front door. 'EH! The mosquito saved you, Madam!"

"The mosquito?" Being saved by a mosquito would be a first!

"The mosquito! The mosquito!" he repeated impatiently, getting to his feet and walking into the sitting room. "The mosquito around the bed."

"Oh, the net."

"Yes," he said. "Without the mosquito, you would be dead now. Dead ..."

His voice trailed off and a look of pure horror spread over his wrinkled face "... and when the Master came back from Maringue and found you dead, I would have been in trouble. Eeeeee! Maningui trouble! Maningui! Maningui! MANINGUI! EEEEEEEEE!"

"Oh, don't be silly, Biasse. How could anyone blame you?"

"Because I was supposed to protect you, Madam! Eeeee! If the mosquito hadn't saved you ... eeeeeeeeeeee!"

I poured another glass of milk, not sharing Biasse's relief. My attacker might not have killed me with his knife but I was still dying ... poisoned ... in a Mozambican forest. Oh, how ironic, how weird that my life should end like this! I had never planned on coming back to Africa and it certainly hadn't been my idea to live like a recluse in a forest ...

"Madam," Biasse's voice interrupted my bleak thoughts, "I go look for Samsone Joao now."

I looked out of the window. Although it was still dark, the night sky had lightened a fraction and dawn wasn't very far away. "Alright, Biasse. I'll come with you."

Leaving the house open, we started walking towards the little wooden guardhouse where Samsone Joao had been told to spend the night. I went with some reluctance, dreading what we were going to find. As we picked our way over piles of bark and around logs, my imagination took flight and hideous pictures of Samsone Joao filled my mind. Pictures of the poor boy lying dead on the floor of the guardhouse and in a great pool of blood; bright red sticky blood, from the long gaping gash in his throat ...

"He is not here," Biasse muttered, as we walked up to the guardhouse. We looked inside. Except for the small fire that still flickered on the dirt floor, it was eerily empty.

"I wonder where he is?" Biasse asked himself thoughtfully.

"Perhaps he's dead, Biasse," I said fearfully. I looked around, wondering if there were eyes watching us. "Perhaps they killed him and dragged his body behind a bush."

Biasse gave a snort of laughter at my naivete. How was it possible for someone born in Africa and growing up in Africa to be so … stupid?

"I go to speak to Majuda, the tractor driver, now, Madam," he told me and turned away from the guardhouse. "He lives with Samsone Joao, not far away."

This time I didn't argue. "Oh, alright, Biasse."

Back in the house, I just had time to dab more milk onto my face and drink down another glassful when Biasse returned with Majuda. I went outside.

"Listen to this, Madam, to what Majuda has to say," Biasse told me grimly.

I turned to Majuda. He was a stocky, middle-aged man who was also supposed to be a witch doctor.

"I was asleep, Senhora, when the door of the hut banged open and woke me up," he told me. "Samsone Joao came running in. He grabbed his small bag and started throwing his clothes into it. When I asked him what he was doing, he told me he was taking his clothes down to the river to wash them."

This time *I* gave a snort of laughter. "What time was this? Do you know?"

"Sometime around three o'clock."

Biasse looked at me with a 'I told you so' gleam in his old eyes. "It WAS him," he said. "You should have let me go look for him, Madam."

I ignored him. "Majuda," I said, "go to the police in Macate and tell them that someone has just tried to kill me. Tell them to radio the police in Chimoio. Perhaps we can still catch him. After that, tell them to come and speak to me."

Majuda nodded his head. "Yes, Senhora."

"Perhaps you can find a chappa to take you there," I told him. "I'll give you some money."

The round trip fare to Macate was only twelve thousand meticais but as Samsone Joao had run off with the tin of change, I had to raid O'D's socks and give Majuda one of Mr. Bonjasse's notes, a one hundred thousand meticais note.

310

After Majuda had gone, Biasse and I walked around the house, wondering how Samsone Joao had managed to get in. It didn't take us long to figure it out.

"Oh look, Biasse," I exclaimed, "look at this!"

There, on the ground underneath the spare bedroom window, lay two rather grubby white trainers and a sweat-stained cap, neatly placed next to each other and waiting for the return of their owner.

"Ah!" Biasse said with a triumphant smile, pleased that his suspicions were confirmed with concrete evidence. "Samsone Joao's shoes and cap!"

"There's no way he could have got up there by himself," I said, thinking that my dream had been right. There *had* been two men. "It's much too high. He must have had help, Biasse."

I was surprised when Majuda arrived back from Macate by himself. Thinking, as we all do about our lives, that my life was of such supreme importance that the Macate police would pull out all the stops to catch my would be killer, I was taken aback by their lack of reaction.

"A policeman will be coming soon," Majuda told me.I

I held out my hand, palm upwards. "Where's my change, Majuda? Twelve from one hundred equals eighty eight."

"The police took the eighty eight thousand," he said. "The Sergeant's in Chimoio and the constable wouldn't come unless I gave him money to buy beer and wine."

"What!" I exclaimed, outraged. For crying out aloud, someone had just tried to KILL me and the police wouldn't come unless they were given money to buy BEER and WINE?

Biasse and I were standing outside the house when, quite some time later, we saw a policeman on an old black bicycle pedalling unsteadily down the forest track towards us. When he was almost abreast of us, he stopped pedalling and put on the brakes in the Mozambican way by taking a foot off a pedal and placing it down hard on top of the front tyre to stop it from going around. Dismounting, he leaned the bicycle against a tree and approached us.

"Boa tarde!" I said sarcastically.

"Bom dia," he replied, my sarcasm going over his head. "I hope you appreciate the trouble I've gone to, cycling all this way from Macate to see you."

I stepped back from the cloud of sour red wine fumes he was breathing into my face and glared at him. "Have you spoken to the

311

Chimoio police over your radio about the man who attacked me ..." I showed him the knife "... with this?"

He barely glanced at the knife. "No," he said laconically, "the radio's battery is flat."

"The Chefe do Posto's got a radio in his office," I reminded him crossly. "Why didn't you use his?"

"Locked," he said laconically. "The Chefe's in Chimoio for the weekend."

The constable fumbled around in his shirt pocket until he managed to pull out a ballpoint pen and a tiny notebook. He poised the pen over a blank page. "Name?" he asked, peering blearily up at me through a haze of alcohol.

"P. I. X. L. E. Y," I spelled out slowly in Portuguese.

B ... ?" the constable began.

Suddenly, I'd had enough. The reeking policeman was dreadful. Useless. I threw my hands up in the air. "Oh, nao faz mal! Never mind!"

There was the sound of a car and O'D drove up in the red Toyota. He stopped the pickup next to us and took in the scene. "You look awful," he greeted me.

Suddenly, I was mad. "You'd also look awful," I said grittily, "if someone had tried to murder YOU!"

O'D got out of the car. "Did he ... touch ... you?" he asked, voicing the fear that crouched like a leopard in the back of the minds of all of us who live in modern Africa.

"No," I said. "Apart from trying to strangle me, poison me and stab me to death with a knife, he didn't touch me."

The policeman staggered over to O'D. "Name?" he asked, enveloping O'D with his sour fumes while his pen trembled over his notebook.

O'D stepped back from him. "Name? You should bloody well know my name by now, after all these years! You're supposed to be the police!"

The policeman squinted down at his notebook. "B ...?" he asked, and poised his pen over the page.

With a brief and curt explanation of what had taken place, O'D sent the policeman back to Macate with a flea in his ear. No doubt, he would inform Mario as soon as possible and no doubt, Mario would take appropriate action.

I was standing, still with the knife in my hand, under the spare bedroom window and showing Samsone Joao's shoes and cap to O'D, when the white Toyota arrived. Caetano climbed out and walked over to us. His eyes took in the state of my face. "What has happened?" he asked.

I opened my mouth to tell him but before I could say anything, Biasse butted in. "Samsone Joao tried to kill the Madam," he told Caetano and although he hadn't been anywhere near me at the time, he gave Caetano and O'D a vivid and graphic re-enactment of what - according to his imagination - had taken place.

Playing two roles simultaneously – mine and Samsone Joao's – Biasse attacked himself. His two hands flew up to his neck and while they tried to strangle him, he put up a tremendous struggle. Now trying to strangle himself, now trying to fight off the choking grip, he staggered around the grass. Eyes bulging with terror, he put on a high falsetto voice to represent mine and cried "Help! Help!" So desperate was his struggle for survival, that at one stage he almost fell over and ended up by having to put his arms around the trunk of the big old mango tree for support, coughing with the exertion of it all.

Biasse's performance was so funny that I burst out laughing and had to lean against the spare bedroom wall, myself, for support.

O'D and Caetano stared at me.

"This isn't a laughing matter," O'D told me pompously.

I stopped laughing and felt myself start to fume. So far, not one person had asked me how I was feeling or had even offered any words of sympathy. No doubt, this was because they were men and were treating me exactly as they would have treated each other if someone had tried to kill them. A certain degree of resentment began to bubble up inside me at the ill treatment I was getting from everyone. "Don't tell me what to do, O'D Pixley!" I yelled. "It's MY murder and I'll laugh if I want to!"

In the short silence that followed my outburst, I felt a twinge in my lip and this reminded me of something. I turned to Caetano. "Samsone Joao put something … some kind of poison … on my face. It burnt like fire. Do you have any idea what it is, Caetano?"

Caetano didn't even have to think about it, he knew his fellow Mozambicans so well. "Battery acid," he told me without any hesitation. "Battery acid, to blind you."

Battery acid! I touched the welts and blisters, so close to my left eye and blanched. What a narrow escape I'd had! If Samsone

313

Joao's hand had been just a fraction higher up my face, the acid would have gone right into my eye … or eyes …

I shuddered. I was not a person, I knew, who would have been able to cope with a life of blindness.

Caetano bent down and picked up one of Samsone Joao's trainers. He took the knife from my hand. "I'm going to Dombe now," he said grimly. "To that powerful witch doctor there. I'm going to arrange for him to strike down Samsone Joao with a bolt of lightning and kill him." He climbed back into the white Toyota and started it up.

"But he's just come back from a four hundred kilometre trip," I protested. "Dombe and back is another three hundred!"

"He wants to do it," O'D said.

In the afternoon, Murray came to visit. I was sitting on the sofa when he walked into the sitting room. His step faltered as his eyes took in my battered and bruised face, one eye looking decidedly black. Warily he walked over to an armchair not far from me and sat uneasily down on it. Obviously O'D and I had had a humdinger of a fight and I had come off the worst!

"Someone tried to kill me at three o'clock this morning, Murray."

"Oh," he said, relieved to hear O'D wasn't the culprit. He lit up a Madison and puffed out some pungent smoke. "Well, I'm glad I didn't come to visit you only to see you being carried out through the front door in a box."

I spent the next two weeks cloistered in the house. Except for Caetano, Biasse and Azelia, I wanted nothing to do with the Mozambicans. They were treacherous people who smiled at your face while plotting to stick a knife in your back. "Frank can deal with all our workers and our customers," I told O'D. "I don't want to see any of them."

O'D had re-employed our bearded and often drunken little cubicador. After all, Frank's misdemeanours paled when compared to Samsone Joao's.

Left alone, I washed the mosquito net over and over again in the washing machine to remove the unwelcome reminder of Samsone Joao's presence in the room. The battery acid he had put on his hand had left a remarkably clear yellow-brown imprint of his palm and five fingers splayed across the net. When the imprint had faded until it was

314

no longer unsettling, I sewed up the holes his knife had ripped in the net.

I often thought about the voice that had saved my life, as well as my eyesight. It was the voice, I was sure, of the One I had spent so much time talking to since I had come to live in the Nhamacoa Forest.

In the bedroom, I closed the door and sat down on the chair near the window, the chair I used when I had something special to ask God.

"It was You, I know, who spoke to me and saved my life and my eyes," I said, and burst into tears. "And I thank you. Thank you, thank you, thank you. You left it jolly late, though ... "

God had let Samsone Joao take me right to the brink - had let me look over the edge right into the dark and terrifying face of death - before he had rescued me, just in the nick of time. How amazing, and how ... nerve shattering!

There were quite a few other things to wonder about and to puzzle over. One was the warning dream I'd had two years before. What had been the point of it? It hadn't shown me Samsone Joao's face or that of his accomplice and there hadn't even been any indication as to when it was going to come true.

And as for that weird little incident where the mosquito net had risen up in the air and then had fallen down onto the edge of my bed ... Well, I never was able to work out what that was all about. It was a mystery then and it remains a mystery to me to this day.

I put an end to my self-imposed seclusion one afternoon, at about two o'clock, by walking out of the front door and across the drive to some long wooden tables under a large and leafy shade tree. I had planted hundreds of panga panga seeds in little clay pots on top of these tables and now I was pleased to see they had all germinated.

While I was examining the tender little pale-green leaves, I noticed someone walking down the forest track towards me. "Oh, it's Seven!" I said to myself. "And how well he looks. I wonder why Azelia told me he looked sick?" But when the figure came nearer, I saw I was wrong and that the man was Maqui, not Seven.

This mistake jogged my memory. I'd been on the point of trying to find Seven when Samsone Joao had attacked me and diverted my thoughts away from him. After that, I'd been so wrapped up in myself that I'd forgotten all about him. I had to find him, had to help him. I would definitely do something about him tomorrow, I promised myself, first thing tomorrow.

The next morning just after roll call, when I was sitting up in bed and drinking a cup of tea, the door opened and O'D came into the room. He sat down on the carved mahogany chest opposite the bed.

"Seven's dead," he told me baldly.

Shock jolted through me. Dead? Seven, dead! I'd been thinking about him only yesterday. "When did he die?" I asked.

"They found him lying dead on the forest track about two o'clock yesterday afternoon. Apparently he'd starved to death. He'd been living under a makeshift grass and pole shelter not far from here. He didn't have any possessions. Not a blanket or even a cooking pot."

I felt my eyes begin to prick with tears. "He must have sold them for food," I said, remembering the pots and pans I had given to him. "Oh, that poor, poor boy. Why didn't he come to us for help?"

When I was up and dressed, I called Azelia upstairs.

"Seven is dead, Azelia," I told her, although I was sure she already knew.

She put on a sad face. "Yes, Dona."

"You knew where he was living, didn't you? Not far from here. Why didn't you tell me? We might have been able to save him."

Her face went blank. "Dona?"

I gave up. "Alright. You can go back to your ironing."

The police never did make any attempt to catch Samsone Joao. Although everyone knew about the attack, Mario never came near us despite all the help O'D had given him over the years.

"Police no good," Biasse told me sourly. "Samsone Joao far away now. Maybe over the border in Zimbabwe, but ..." he hesitated "... but when he see police not even try to catch him, maybe he come back here."

"Come back ... here?"

"Maybe, Madam. He know the Master goes away often. One day, Maringue. One day, Tete. And you by yourself, here in the house."

"That's a great thought, Biasse," I said dryly. "Thanks!"

As it was doubtful whether Mario had informed the Chimoio police about the incident, O'D decided to write a letter of complaint to the Governor of Manica Province and to give it to him in person.

In the Governor's building in the centre of Chimoio, the receptionist told O'D that the Governor was away on holiday for a month. However, the Assistant to the Governor was available.

When the man appeared, O'D handed him the letter and told him about Samsone Joao.

The Assistant to the Governor had his own ideas about the attack. Dismissing the money Mr.Bonjasse had given to me as the motive, he added insult to injury by making an insinuating suggestion. "Perhaps," he told O'D thoughtfully, "the Senhora was attacked … because she ill-treated your worker…?"

I stared at him with disgust – how DARED he? – and restrained myself from ill-treating *him* by battering him over the head with my handbag. So that's the direction we were going to take, was it?

"Right!" I said. "I've had enough of this!" and without another word, I stormed out of the room and clattered noisily down the stairs.

We met Caetano for lunch, in a clean and pretty little restaurant in the fairgrounds. He and O'D ordered curried prawns on a bed of rice. I ordered a Heineken beer.

While they ate and I drank, Caetano told me the witch doctor at Dombe had refused to do anything about Samsone Joao unless I personally went to see him.

The thought filled me with repugnance. "No," I said. No way was I going to be lured by a witch doctor into sitting in his murky, smoky hut while evil swirled all around me and contaminated me.

Caetano let out a sigh of irritation. "But you *must* go," he said, "otherwise Samsone Joao will get away with what he did."

Not wanting to hurt Caetano's feelings - after all, he had made a three hundred kilometre trip to avenge me - I made an excuse I knew he would accept.

"I can't, Caetano," I told him. "It's against my religion. God will be terribly angry with me if I killed anyone."

With another sigh, this time of resignation, Caetano nodded his head. He understood. It was just that, living in a country without justice, who else could you go to for help if you didn't go to a witch doctor?

He began to talk to O'D about other things and while they talked, memories of Seven came drifting into my mind. Poor Seven, maybe he'd still be alive if I hadn't been so impatient with him and his fetishes; with those imaginary razor blades and nails he always thought an enemy had sent to lodge in his legs. I heard an echo of his voice, as it had been on that day I'd told him it was all nonsense. "Yes,

317

Meddem," he had said softly, "Yes, Meddem," and that had been the last I'd ever seen of him. Oh, what a waste of a life. He'd barely reached the age of thirty.

Tears I couldn't stop began to stream down my face. They plopped into my glass of beer and onto the pink tablecloth. Caetano and O'D stopped talking and shifted uneasily in their chairs.

"You're embarrassing Caetano," O'D told me.

"Why?" I sniffed. "*He* cried in front of *you* at the Sports Clube when his wife was dying, didn't he?"

When the Governor returned from his holiday, he read O'D's letter and sent Wilson, the Head of the Gondola police, to visit us. Wilson and his constables spent more time squabbling with Majuda about the missing eighty thousand meticais than worrying about a killer on the loose and so, in the end, we pinned Samsone Joao's photograph up on the Shoprite notice board with a warning to everyone buying their groceries to watch out for this man, because he was dangerous.

CHAPTER TWENTY FOUR

BETTER EYESIGHT WITHOUT GLASSES

A few weeks later, almost exactly one month after Samsone Joao had tried to blind me, another dream I'd had, this time in 1998, came true.

The dream had been a very simple one. In it, I had seen myself sitting in a chair and reading a book - reading WITHOUT the reading glasses I'd had to use ever since I'd left the Algarve.

In the morning when I'd woken up, I had told O'D about the dream, saying "Oh, if only it would come true!"

I was now on my second pair of reading glasses and my eyesight without them had deteriorated so much that I couldn't see anything close up. My face in the mirror was a blur and the print in a book or a magazine was a faint, grey, wavering line.

Then, two weeks after my dream, an uncanny thing had happened.

We had driven across the border to Mutare to do some shopping and while I'd been browsing around the magazine rack in Meikles Department Store, my bespectacled eyes had caught sight of a book incongruously placed amongst the "Fair Lady" and "News Week" magazines. It had been a white paperback and on the front, in large bold black print, were the words

W. H. BATES, M.D.
BETTER EYESIGHT WITHOUT GLASSES

Well, I had thought to myself, if this isn't an omen, what is? It was almost as if someone had deliberately placed the book in the magazine rack, especially for me!

Naturally, I had bought the book and on the drive back home had eagerly started to read it.

I had spent the next couple of days poring over Dr. Bates' book and had discovered that we held the same opinion about spectacles.

He was scathing about glasses, calling them ugly little optic crutches, and even went so far as to state that they made people's eyesight worse!

"Persons with presbyopia," Dr. Bates stated, "who put on glasses because they cannot read fine print, too often find that after they have worn them for a time, they cannot, without their aid, read the larger print that was perfectly plain to them before."

Yes! This was exactly what had had happened to me in the Algarve!

"I couldn't agree with you more, Dr. Bates," I had said, speaking out aloud.

The remedy for bad eyesight according to Dr. Bates came down to nothing more than relaxation and exercising the eye muscles.

As I had read on, it had begun to occur to me that there was something a little strange about Dr. Bates' book, a slightly old-fashioned air about his words, such as his paragraph about lying down while reading a book. This, he said, although generally considered by his fellow ophthalmologists to be bad for the eyes was, in his opinion, a most delightful position in which to read!

And as for Dr. Bates' eye exercises! I had read about covering my eyes with the palms of my hands and imagining the blackest of black, standing outdoors and moving my head from side to side to let hot sunshine fall on my eyelids, shifting and swinging, and the reading of the tiniest of print in a dim room. It had been hard to believe that anything so simple - and so weird – could actually have a positive effect.

I wonder ... I had said to myself, and turning to the front page of Dr. Bates' book to see where and when it had been published, had got something of a surprise ...

New York ... 1919 ...

Dr. Bates' ideas had first seen the light of day almost eighty years ago!

Slowly, I had put the book down, wondering if it was worthwhile reading to the end. After all, if Dr. Bates' theories and exercises *had* worked, why were millions and millions of people all over the world continuing to wear glasses right up to the end of the 20th Century?

Still, what did I have to lose by trying out the exercises? I had picked up his book again and had read on.

I had read on until I had come to the part where Dr. Bates told the reader that his exercises wouldn't have any effect unless they threw away their glasses and then, I had balked. I needed my glasses to fill in the forestry registers, to write out facturas and guias, to count our customers' money. Oh no, I couldn't do away with my glasses. I wouldn't be able to do any work without them.

And so, instead of putting away my glasses, I had put away Dr. Bates' book.

It was a long four years later, in the middle of February 2002, when Dr. Bates' book made a sudden and unexpected comeback into my life.

I was sitting in a chair near the bedroom window on a Sunday morning and reading another of Anne Rivers Siddons' books, this time an intriguing tale about a discarded Coca-Cola executive's wife, some swans, two old lesbians and a one-legged man, when I heard the loud chattering sound of a Vervet monkey. Looking up from my book, I saw the monkey sitting on a branch of the tall eucalypt tree just outside my window. This was a bit of luck, I thought. Up till now, I'd never been able to get near enough to a Vervet to photograph it because Bandit kept as close to me as a shadow and, thanks to Lovad, had the habit of chasing anything that moved. Now, however, Bandit had gone for a walk with O'D and was safely out of the way.

Throwing my book down, I rushed over to the cupboard and pulled out the camera. Back at the window, I looked down to take off the lens cap ... and it was then that disaster struck.

My reading glasses, which I had forgotten to take off in my hurry, slid down my nose and before I could put out a hand to save them, slipped off and fell onto the cement floor with a small smashing sound.

All thoughts of photographing monkeys forgotten, I put the camera carefully on top of the dressing table and with a sinking heart, bent down to pick up my glasses. Oh, no ... what a thing to happen ... this was awful ... awful! The left lens was completely shattered. What was I going to do now? They were the only pair I had. There weren't any opticians in Chimoio and no chemist or shop where I could buy one of those stand-by reading glasses over the counter. How was I going to read and write, paint or sew?

And even worse, what about all those prawns I had taken out of the deep freeze to defrost for lunch? It was Biasse's weekend off so *I* had to de-vein them. Would I even be able to see the veins with my naked eyes to remove them?

Holding my broken glasses in my hand, I sank back down onto the chair and burst into a flood of tears. Africa ... Mozambique ... was really, really, getting me down.

Some time later, after I had mopped my face and pulled myself together, I stood in front of the worktop in the kitchen. I picked up a limp, defrosted prawn and stared at it. I could barely make out its black vein but it was too late, now, to put the wretched things back in the deep freeze.

I picked up a sharp knife and, straining my eyes to see, began to cut. It all went very slowly because there were dozens of the damned things and my eyes began to hurt and then tears started running down my face with the incredible pain of trying to focus on pulling out all those little black lines.

Just as I was finishing off the last prawn, O'D and a panting, grinning Bandit came into the kitchen, back from their walk.

"What's the matter? Why are you crying?" O'D asked, taken aback by the sight of me, weeping over a pile of prawns. He picked up a prawn and sniffed at it. "Don't tell me they've gone bad overnight."

I turned away from the prawns and buried my face in his chest. "I've broken my glasses!" I howled, wetting his shirt as my tears of strain turned into tears of despair and self-pity. "I can't do ANYTHING without them!"

O'D gave me some comforting pats. "Maybe I can fix them, temporarily," he said "Go and get them."

Although O'D was very good at fixing things, even he couldn't do anything about the shattered lens. "Beyond repair," he told me, "it looks as if we'll have to go across the border. You'll just have to hold out for a few days."

On Monday, O'D drove off to Chimoio to buy fuel and food and when he came home in the evening, the news he brought was bad.

He had tried to phone J. Doaks, the opticians in Harare who had supplied me with my last pair of glasses, but there had been no reply.

Then, he had discovered that because it was the run-up to the Zimbabwean elections, Mugabe was now refusing to let anyone with EU and U.S. passports into Zimbabwe!

The bad timing of my glasses breaking just when Mugabe was putting his anti-foreigner action into practice overcame me. I felt I was being personally persecuted. Why, oh why, had my glasses broken NOW and not at another more convenient time? Why? WHY?

"I wonder how Mugabe would feel without *his* glasses!" I said bitterly.

I moped around for a week, not able to do anything at all. My books lay unopened. My typewriter rested idle and silent on my desk. My watercolour box remained closed. It was incredibly boring and I fumed with frustration. How long, oh how long was this going to go on for?

And then, at the end of the week, I noticed something peculiar. Was it my imagination or had my eyesight actually improved a little?

"Why don't you try out those eye exercises in that book you bought all those years ago?" O'D suggested.

"I think I will," I said, "if I can find it after all this time!"

It took me a while to search for Dr. Bates' book but at last I came across it, tucked away at the back of the big bookcase in the spare bedroom.

Back in the sitting room, I cleaned four years of dust off the cover and opened it at random. The lines of print on the pages were wavy, the faintest of grey and completely blurred. Just as I knew they would be. How was I going to read the book now, without help? I moved over to the window. Perhaps I would be able to make the words out with sunlight streaming onto the page and lighting them up.

"Some ... people ..." I read aloud, while tears of pain streamed from my eyes with the strain of it all "... who ... break ... their ... glasses ... find ... that ... their ... eyesight ... improves ...while ... they ... are ... waiting ... for ... their ... new ... ones..."

I looked up from the book. How remarkable that I should have opened it at this particular page and read something that seemed to apply directly to me. Yes, I had noticed this very thing. It was almost as if the dead Dr. Bates was speaking to me!

As the strain to read any more was too much for me, I had to ask O'D to help me out by reading the exercises to me. For some reason, this made him grumpy, especially as I asked him that evening while he was reading a book of his own in bed. "What's the first exercise you have to do?" he asked, impatiently flipping through the pages of Dr. Bates' book.

"I don't know," I told him. "You know I can't see a thing."

"Well, how am *I* supposed to know what you've got to do?" he grumped.

"Just read the Contents," I said grittily. "That's why books have them."

O'D irritably turned to the beginning of the book and read down the list of chapters. "What glasses do to us ... Strain ... Central Fixation ... Palming ..."

"That's it!" I told him. "Palming. Read it out to me."

323

With a sigh, O'D obeyed. "What next?" he asked and read down the list of chapters again.

"Shifting and Swinging," I told him.

After a few brief explanatory sentences, he put Dr. Bates' book down and picked up his own. It was a Louis L'Amour and although it had been written about fifty years ago, there were passages in it about how we were destroying our environment and the only home we humans had to live on. Obviously Louis L'Amour had been aware of what was happening long before our modern scientists woke up to what we were doing.

It wasn't easy to do Dr. Bates' exercises when O'D was away or busy and oh, how I struggled.

I palmed, trying to imagine the blackest of black but never succeeded. I planted my feet one foot apart and swung my arms and body in a semi-circle from side to side, my eyes following the swing. I pinned the Snellen Eye Chart that had come with the book on the sitting room wall and tried to read the letters.

Barely able to make out Dr.Bates' instructions, I strained to make out his words. This was excruciatingly painful, until one day I actually managed to read one of his sentences without O'D's help. "Staring at a word causes strain," Dr. Bates had written. "Don't stare. Shift!"

Suddenly, it all fell into place. Of course! That was it! As I moved my eyes along a line of words without really trying to read them, I discovered I could make them out - not perfectly, but at least without the pain.

My next instruction from Dr. Bates was to read the smallest print I could find for about five minutes every day … and in dim light!

I wondered where I was going to find tiny print. O'D and I didn't have anything that small in the house - or did we?

I found my tiny reading matter in the bathroom. First on the tube of Colgate toothpaste '… change your toothbrush every three months. Visit your dentist twice a year …' and then on the back of bottles '… one tablespoon of Dettol to a medium size bath of warm water will kill the Bilharzia cecariae …' and on the tubes of mosquito repellent '… harmful to some furniture, plastics, rubber and painted surfaces …'

As you may imagine, there is nothing more boring than reading the words on toothpaste tubes, deodorants and shampoos over and over again and I would probably have given up with this exercise if, one day, I hadn't come across the little Bible with the wooden cover when I was dusting the books off in the bookcase. The Bible had been given to my father when he had gone off to fight in the Sahara desert during the Second World War and had become mine after he had died.

I had never read it but now, finally, I opened it up. The words were tiny and the print had almost faded away with age in some of the paragraphs. To add to my difficulty, the English was the old English of 'thees' and 'thous' but I forced myself to read a chapter, anyway, of the New Testament every day.

"I WILL see without glasses," I told myself. "I WILL!

As I hopped around the Gospels, I came across some interesting verses, some of which appeared be speaking directly to me. One of these was John 10, Verse 27. 'My sheep hear my voice,' Jesus said, 'and I know them …'

His words made me sit up and think. Hear His voice …

'My Father, who is greater than all,' He went on, 'has given them to me and no one is able to snatch them out of my Father's hand …'

No one … no one … is able to snatch them out of my Father's hand …

It took me a mere three weeks to get my eyesight without glasses back. Now, when I looked at a book, a magazine or a newspaper, the words on the pages were no longer blurred or faint and grey, but almost black. Despite my progress though, there was still some faint double imaging around the letters. This made me feel impatient.

I picked up Dr. Bates' book and, as so often happened, it fell open at a page that gave me some good advice. 'You wouldn't expect a man who has been ill and spent months in bed recuperating, to suddenly get out of his bed and run a marathon, would you?' Dr. Bates admonished me. 'The same applies to people who have been wearing glasses for some time. Discretion must be used.'

"Of course," I said. "Of course."

While I practiced Dr. Bates' exercises and read the little Bible, a thought flitted into my head. If it hadn't been for that Vervet monkey, I wouldn't have broken my glasses. And if it hadn't been for President Mugabe closing the border to foreigners at that particular time, I would merely have bought new glasses from a Zimbabwean optician. Dr. Bates' book would have continued gathering dust in my bookcase ... and my father's little Bible would have remained unopened.

As so often happened in the Nhamacoa, I had the feeling that I was taking part in a play that someone was writing for me to live out in my life, a someone who was setting the scenes but not giving ME the script for MY part. The fact that I was now reading the Bible, pointed a finger in only one direction.

God ...

The novel way God engineered situations, even using quite drastic measures to get my attention, impressed me. Although I knew that it hadn't been God who had set up my intended murder, He had left it to the very last second to rescue me ... and then, even going to the lengths of breaking my glasses to get me to read His Word! He was showing me that He was serious about my getting to know Him and that I'd better not ignore Him.

At the end of February, we were in trouble again. Money had run out and we were forced to resort once again to our Arrojela travellers cheques. This time, however, when we went to the Bank of Mozambique that usually changed our cheques, we were in for another of those shocks Mozambique was throwing at us with such abandon.

At the counter, the teller pushed the cheque back at us and told us that new regulations had come through from Maputo. No more pound sterling traveller cheques were to be changed. Euro travellers cheques and U.S. dollar travellers cheques, yes - but not pounds!

Astonished by this news, O'D demanded to see the manager.

In his office, O'D, Caetano and I sat down and the manager repeated the story the teller had told us. Almost begging him to do what banks were damn well supposed to do, even Caetano, who was always optimistic no matter what happened, seemed beaten down by the never-ending battering we were being given on all fronts.

The bank manager was inflexible. "Take them to BIM at the airport in Beira," he told us. "They'll cash them there for you."

This advice to make a 400 kilometre round trip to cash a travellers cheque soured our mood even further. Apart from the terrible waste of money, we didn't even have enough fuel in the pickup to make the journey!

We left his office and trudged around to all the other banks in Chimoio. They all told us the same thing. Go to BIM in Beira.

Without even enough money to buy a Coke or a Lemon Twist at a café, we stood under the shade of a tree for a while, debating on what to do next. Then, the image of a bespectacled face almost hidden by a fuzz of white popped into my mind. "Perhaps Murray will be able to help," I suggested. "Zimbabweans always want foreign currency."

At the Chibuku factory, Murray's new and spartan home that was furnished with a desk, a telephone and a camp bed, Murray opened his safe and revealed an enormous pile of meticais. We handed over our cheques and Murray gave us some of his meticais. He knew a Zimbabwean pilot, he told us, who often flew to London. He would give our Travellers Cheques to him.

We now had a new Head of Forestry in Chimoio. The Communist Ribeiro had gone and had been replaced by Cremildo Rungo.

Caetano got on well with Rungo and soon he had secured another cutting area for us, this time in Gondola and much nearer to home. Here, Caetano organised our workers and they set to work, felling panga panga. And things started looking up for us again.

CHAPTER TWENTY FIVE

THE TRIAL OF JAN WESTH

When he heard the news that the Dane, Jan Westh, was finally going to be brought to trial for stealing our pine at Tsetsserra, Caetano was jubilant. He had, after all, waited two long years for this. Justice – at last!

The only fly in the ointment was that the Judge trying the case would be - yes, just our luck! - the corrupt Judge we'd been warned about. The dreaded Judge Magaia.

The trial was scheduled for the morning of the 23rd April and so, when we saw Caetano's white pickup jolting down the track towards us in the afternoon we thought it was all over.

One look at the expression on his face, however, when he swung his long legs out of the pickup, told us quite a different story.

"How did it go?" O'D asked, although he already knew something was wrong.

A torrent of indignation and outrage poured out of Caetano, so fast I couldn't understand a word. Faster and faster he spoke, all his words running into each other and the pitch of his voice rising to heights I'd never heard before.

Something must be very wrong!

"What's happened?" I asked. "What's happened?"

O'D's face was grim. "When Caetano arrived at the Court House this morning, he discovered the trial had been cancelled - because Westh left Mozambique for Denmark on the 19th April!"

"What!" I cried, my voice rising as high as Caetano's had done. "How could they have let him leave! He committed a crime! And why didn't Nelson, who is supposed to be Caetano's legal aid, tell him about this four days ago?"

"Mozambican justice … just as I thought!" O'D said, furious at this evidence of sneaky manoeuvreing behind our backs by Westh and the Chimoio Judiciary. "Don't worry, Caetano, even though Westh's managed to skip the country, we're not going to take this lying down!"

The next morning O'D met Caetano in town. When they spoke to Nelson about the Dane's disappearance, he merely shrugged his shoulders. Apparently Westh's father had suddenly fallen ill in

Denmark and Judge Magaio had compassionately allowed him to fly back home.

"And if Westh doesn't come back," O'D asked Nelson, "what then? How are we going to get our timber or our money back from him?"

"Oh, he'll come back," Nelson answered carelessly.

Deciding to complain to Judge Sambo, the Judge President, about the irregular way in which our case against Westh was being handled, O'D and Caetano made an appointment with his secretary to see him the following day.

Their meeting with Judge Sambo was very satisfactory. He flew into a rage when he heard how Judge Magaio had allowed Westh to leave Mozambique without doing anything to ensure his return. He assured them he would investigate and heads would roll.

In the middle of May, Caetano brought us more news about Westh. News that totally surprised us. The Dane was back in town!

"Westh's new trial date is set for June now," Caetano told us. "The 10th June ... that is, if he doesn't disappear again!"

June arrived. In the sitting room, I turned the page on the Zimbabwean wildlife calendar I had hung on the wall and exchanged May's photograph of an elephant for June's photograph of a buffalo.

At first, the buffalo looked innocuous enough - a bit worn and moth-eaten, with patchy white marks on its horns - but it wasn't long before I noticed something strange about it, something that gave me a distinctly uneasy feeling. During the day, the animal looked just like it was, a buffalo. At night, however, by the glow of paraffin light, it underwent a peculiar metamorphosis. It turned into a rather hideous and sinister horned man ... a sort of devil creature ...

One evening, even O'D who wasn't particularly observant about things like this, asked me if I had noticed the buffalo's strangely altered appearance at night. Even he, it seemed, found the image disturbing ...

We weren't the only ones who were feeling uneasy. In the weeks running up to the trial, Caetano became uncharacteristically more and more jittery. Although the evidence against Westh was solid and the Dane's confession was on record at the Commercial Fraud Squad's office, he was beginning to think that something fishy was afoot.

When Westh's lawyer came searching for him and even visited his house one evening, Caetano hid himself away, refusing to see or talk to the man.

Then, when Caetano came down with a cold that turned chesty and gave him a persistent cough that no cough syrup would cure, his thoughts turned to witchcraft. Westh's workers had caused his illness – he was sure of it!

"They'll lose their jobs if Westh has to pay us back our six hundred million meticais," Caetano told us. "They probably went to a feiticeiro to make me sick ... to stop the trial. They probably took something of mine to the feiticeiro."

"Like what, Caetano?" O'D asked, thinking how unlikely this was.

"It could be anything!" Caetano cried. "Maybe even the footprints I made in the sand outside Westh's sawmill!"

Although Caetano's fears seemed a bit far-fetched to us, especially the bit about Westh's workers scooping up his sandy footprints, he became more and more nervous and turned to witchcraft himself for protection, employing a series of witch doctors, each one supposedly more powerful than the one before - and each one charging a more exorbitant fee than the one before.

At first, he paid them large sums of money to perform ceremonies around his house to protect himself and his family. And then, on the eve of Westh's trial, he decided that O'D and I were also in danger and needed protection.

"I'm bringing an extremely powerful feiticeira this time," Caetano told O'D. "A woman. She's the sister of the one I went to see at Dombe. I'm going to bring her down to the sawmill this evening!"

Clouds blew up over the Nhamacoa in the afternoon and when Caetano arrived with the feiticeira, the normally blue winter sky had turned grey. A chilly wind blew and it began to drizzle.

The feiticeira was a disappointment. Caetano had described her as extremely powerful and so I had expected to see a woman who would look the part. But when she climbed out of the white pickup, she looked just like any other young African woman, with a baby tied onto her back with a sun-faded capulana. Several children of various ages jumped out of the open back of the pickup. These, Caetano told us, were also the feiticeira's children.

This time, unwilling to have a witch doctor inside our house again, O'D brought three chairs out onto the verandah for us to sit on. The woman untied her capulana and gave her baby to one of the older children to hold. Opening a bundle she had brought with her, she pulled out the obligatory black cloth and spread it on the floor in front of her. Then, she settled down on the cloth and began to transform herself. A magnificent headdress of long green-black feathers emerged from her bundle to adorn her head. Strange objects dangling from a thin strip of leather were tied around her neck and waist. In a matter of minutes, the ordinary young woman had completely vanished and in her place sat a feiticeira.

The feiticeira turned to O'D. "Beer!" she demanded.

He handed her a large bottle of the locally made 'Manica' beer and, tilting her feathered head backwards, she raised the bottle to her lips and drained its entire gassy contents all in one go.

Then, when she finally put the bottle down, her body gave a sudden jerk. Loud and horrible grunting growling noises erupted up from her chest and exploded out of her mouth.

An enormous feeling of tiredness swept over me and something else that resembled boredom. Oh, for Heaven's Sakes ... surely not again! Was the woman now in the process of turning herself into some kind of wild animal ... a jackal or perhaps a hyena ... treating us to another demonic possession, like Nora Swete when she had paid us that visit? The thought was unbearable. I'd really had more than enough of all this African preoccupation with witchcraft. I made a move to stand up, to leave.

"She's only belching," O'D told me.

The feiticeira growled again and opened her mouth wide ... and a great spray of Manica beer shot out of her and onto the verandah wall.

I leaned back again in my chair, annoyance replacing my boredom. Now Biasse would have to get busy with a bucket of soapy water and a scrubbing brush tomorrow morning. I really couldn't have the beery contents of a witch doctor's stomach all over my walls.

Having relieved herself of her heartburn, the feiticeira picked up a small pouch and scattered its contents onto the black cloth. Then, after spending some long minutes studying the small pebbles and bones that lay there, she gave us her verdict.

It seemed we were entering a time of danger ... great danger ... and needed protection from the dark forces swirling around us ... but although we had enemies, we would be successful … if we protected ourselves …

Sitting next to me, Caetano spoke at length with the feiticeira. Shivering slightly and huddled in his chair with his arms wrapped around himself for protection against the chill wet wind, he talked and while he talked, he coughed.

At last it was over. All that was left to do now was to walk around and place the usual little bags of magic potion at all the entrances into the house and into our land to protect us from evil.

As Caetano stood up, his face pinched with cold, a powerful, terrible and dark feeling of foreboding knifed through me. Alarmed, I turned to O'D.

"Maybe we should try to get him to Mutare, to see a doctor before the trial."

"Caetano's going to be just fine," O'D assured me with a smile. "He's a big, fit, strong man. He's only got a cold that's hard to shake off."

When the feiticeira, now looking like a young African woman with a baby on her back again, climbed into Caetano's pickup, I watched them all drive off down the forest track until they vanished in the gloomy twilight. O'D was right, I assured myself. Caetano *was* a big, fit, strong man. No need to worry. No need at all.

In the kitchen, I lit a match to heat up Biasse's vegetable soup on the gas cooker and while I waited for it to grow hot, I sat down on the sofa in the sitting room. As so often happened now in the evenings, my eyes were irresistibly drawn to the calendar on the wall opposite the sofa. Tonight, after the feiticeira's visit and the terrible sense of foreboding I had felt about Caetano, there seemed to be something especially evil … especially menacing … about the image of the horned man.

Aaah … creepy! With a shudder of revulsion, I jumped up from the sofa and went over to the radio to search the wavebands. What we needed this evening to dispel the rather unpleasant vibrations the feiticeira had left behind was some music! Sadly, I was out of luck. Zimbabwe Radio One, which had sustained us for so long in our isolation, was gone, and never to return. Inexplicably destroyed by Jonathan Moyo, Mugabe's Minister of Information.

There was nothing for it but to settle for the BBC.

Monday, the 10th June arrived and to our relief, Jan Westh's trial did take place.

O'D and I didn't go near the Court House but Caetano gleefully kept us up to date with the proceedings.

"I think Judge Sambo must have said something to Magaia," Caetano reported back, "because when Magaia came into the courtroom, he glared at me and asked 'Do you have a problem with me, Mr. Caetano?' Before I could even open my mouth to answer him, he ordered me to be quiet by barking 'Don't speak! Don't speak!' at me."

Over the next few days, as the trial progressed, Judge Magaia's irritation with Caetano continued to show itself.

When Caetano stood up to give evidence and waved his arms excitedly in the air during his description as to how Westh had tricked our guard into allowing the Dane to cart all our pine away, the Judge gave him another baleful glare.

"Don't gesticulate!" Magaia barked. "You are not allowed to gesticulate in my courtroom, Mr. Caetano, and if you gesticulate again, I will fine you!"

When it came to Jan Westh's turn to speak, he explained to Judge Magaia that his action had not been one of theft but of preservation. He had noticed a large forest fire approaching and as we hadn't bothered to protect our logs by pulling them into an estaleiro, he had taken them. If he hadn't done this, they would have been burnt to a cinder.

Unfortunately for Westh, when his own cubicador was questioned, the man forgot which side he was on. He admitted that not only had our logs been pulled into a well-cleared estaleiro but that they had not been in any danger at all of being consumed by fire.

At the end of everybody's testimonies, the Judge appeared satisfied. "The case is clear," he declared. "The Sentence of this Court will be read out on Friday, 14th June."

"Westh's lawyer tried to bribe me - right there in the courtroom!" Caetano told us with a grin of satisfaction. "He offered me two hundred million meticais if I agreed to have the case against Westh dismissed."

Scenting success, Caetano had turned down the bribe. His mood was upbeat and he was going in for the kill. He certainly wasn't going to let Westh wriggle out of paying the six hundred million meticais he owed us. As Judge Magaia had stated ... the Case was clear!

Friday the 14th dawned, warm and sunny.

At the Court House Caetano and Jan Westh sat waiting in the courtroom. They didn't speak to each other and the silence in the room was only broken by Caetano's persistent cough. Westh was clutching a bulging briefcase and the sight of it caused Caetano's heart to thunder in his chest with excitement. The briefcase, he was sure, contained the six hundred million meticais Westh owed us for our stolen pine. We had won - and Westh knew it!

Caetano and Jan Westh sat for a long time, waiting for Judge Magaia to put in an appearance. Eventually, after being kept on hold for some hours, a clerk appeared with a message. Judge Magaia had fallen ill and the reading of the Sentence was cancelled until further notice.

His high hopes dashed, Caetano slowly stood up. Now that everything was at a standstill again, he might as well take the opportunity of going to see a doctor about his chest and his cough.

The Fatima Clinic was only a short distance away. New, spotlessly clean and built with local Indian money, it promised to give better medical service than Chimoio hospital and had had a well-trained doctor all the way from India to deal with patients.

At the Fatima, a Mozambican doctor examined Caetano and arranged some blood tests. Unfortunately, the well-trained Indian doctor had gone back to India, it seemed, and the clinic now used the services of the same doctors who worked at Chimoio Hospital.

"You have bronchitis," the doctor told Caetano, "and you have malaria, as well. Malaria of the 'one cross' variety."

Although his malaria was not of the serious kind, being 'one cross' malaria', it was the type that was difficult to treat and cure. Feeling too tired and weak to go back home and treat himself with pills, Caetano decided to put his trust in the Fatima Clinic. He booked himself in.

We were all relieved when we heard Caetano was in the Fatima. He was in safe hands, we thought, safer than he would have been in Chimoio Hospital.

On Saturday, at lunchtime, O'D paid Caetano a visit at the Fatima. They didn't talk much because Caetano was busy throwing up. While he was there at his bedside, O'D saw the doctor giving Caetano three large Fansidar tablets to drink down and when Caetano lay back on the bed again and gave him a weak grin, O'D said, "I'll see you on Monday, Caetano." He could see Caetano was going to be alright.

Fansidar is a powerful anti-malarial drug and it seemed to do the trick, because by the afternoon, Caetano was standing on the Clinic's verandah, cheerfully talking to a daughter he had never known he'd had. The girl had appeared out of nowhere all these years later and Caetano had been delighted to meet her, exclaiming with surprise and laughter at her existence.

"He'll be out of the Clinic soon," O'D told me, "probably at the beginning of next week."

I was in the bathroom on Sunday morning when I heard the car. I was giving O'D's dirty clothes a pre-soak and a pre-scrub in the bath before putting them in the washing machine.

Wondering who was paying us a visit so early on a Sunday morning, I went to the bedroom for a look through the window. Caetano's white Toyota pickup drove past and I caught a glimpse of two men inside the cab. Oh, Caetano ... and wearing dark glasses ... he'd obviously made a quick recovery and was now well enough to leave the Fatima and to drive down to us in the Nhamacoa.

Glad to see how much better he was, I went back to the bathroom to finish off my washing. I would go outside to greet him in a minute or so.

I was holding one of O'D's shirts up in the air over the bath and examining it for resistant dirty stains when he came into the bathroom and stood in the doorway. There was a strange look on his face, an expression I had never seen before.

"Caetano's dead," he said.

The floor seemed to shift underneath my feet. The wet shirt fell out of my fingers, back into the bath with a small splash and I heard the loud, high-pitched wail of an African woman - "Nooooooooooooooooooo nooooooooooooooo not our Caetano! Oh, nooooooooooooooooooo not our Caetano!" - and realised that the wail was coming from me.

I turned and fell against O'D's chest. He put his arms around me. "But I've just seen him drive up!" I cried against his shirt. "Wearing dark glasses ... in the white pickup!"

"That's Mr. Leite, a friend of Caetano's family," O'D told me. "Treciano's with him."

Outside, Mr. Leite and Treciano stood next to Caetano's car. Their faces were stricken with grief and shock at the suddenness and unexpectedness of it all.

"He seemed so much better on Saturday afternoon, when he stood on the verandah talking to his daughter," Mr. Leite told us. "Nobody can believe he's dead. One moment alive and laughing, the next moment ... dead!"

"How?" I asked, forcing the word from between lips that felt numb.

"The doctor put him on a drip on Saturday night," Mr. Leite said. "He had convulsions at four o'clock this morning ... and died."

A drip? As well as the Fansidar? What kind of a drip?

While Mr. Leite and Treciano and O'D talked, I paced up and down the brown winter grass. Overhead, the sun seemed too harsh, too brassy, in a sky too blue. Everything looked wrong, felt wrong, was wrong.

Caetano dead. Caetano DEAD! How was this possible? No, it couldn't be true. He'd been getting treatment in the Fatima. The Fatima! This was just a dream ... another of those nightmares I sometimes had that seemed so real but were just dreams ... yes, this was just another of those nightmares ...

I straightened up, suddenly conscious of a terrible pain in my stomach. Without realising it, I'd been pacing backwards and forwards bent over, with my arms clutching my stomach. Caetano dead! Oh, no, noooooooooooooooooooooo!

"I have to go into Chimoio," O'D told me. "There are arrangements to make."

"Alright," I said.

After they had all driven away, I walked into the kitchen. "Mr. Caetano's dead, Biasse," I told him, although I was sure he already knew. His little face was as wooden as an African mask.

Outside again, I sat down on a tree stump, my mind full of Caetano. Through a blur of tears, I looked down the forest track, a track filled with so many memories and so many images of Caetano.

There was Caetano, walking towards me with broken, dusty shoes and red dust in his hair ... Caetano speeding down the track on the motorbike ... jolting down the track in the white Toyota pickup ... Caetano driving three hundred kilometres all the way to Dombe and back, just to get a witch doctor to frazzle Samsone Joao with a bolt of lightning for me ... Caetano pepper-spraying the passengers on a bus to Maputo ... Caetano, almost throwing himself out of the red Toyota and into the traffic when he thought O'D was driving around with a Mozambican Spitting Cobra under the seat ...

Caetano, laughing and optimistic despite all our disappointments ... still full of plans ... plans for a cashew nut farm in Tete, a small hotel on the beach under the coconut trees at Inhassora ... a holiday in Portugal to visit the Palace in Sintra ...

Holding us up ... we'd been like three sides of an arch ... and now that he was dead and his side was gone, the arch had fallen down ...

Caetano, dead ... cut off in mid-life ...

How could he be DEAD?

Tears poured down my face. Oh, Caetano ... oh, dear, dear Caetano ... how are we going to go on without you?

"Why, God?" I asked. "Why did you let him die? You saved me, why didn't you save him? Why? We loved him!"

From that moment on, I stopped talking to God. He had let us down and I couldn't understand it.

O'D returned from town in the late afternoon. He had spent some time with Caetano's family, giving them money to organise the funeral. They were all in a state of shock ... disbelief. Caetano had been in the Fatima, the FATIMA! He'd been getting better ... they'd seen it for themselves!

They hadn't been able to find a coffin large enough to fit Caetano and so Romana, his sister, had had to drive across the border into Zimbabwe to buy one in Mutare. The funeral was set for Tuesday, in two days' time.

When O'D sat down tiredly on the sofa, he told me some news that made my heart leap with wild hope. "Apparently Caetano's body was still warm at eight o'clock this morning."

"Perhaps he's not dead after all, then!" I cried. "Perhaps they've made a mistake and he's only in a coma!"

"No," O'D said heavily. "He's dead alright."

A terrible feeling of vulnerability and loneliness swept over me, adding to my feelings of grief and anguish and loss. "I don't want to live here anymore, not now that Caetano's gone."

"I don't either," O'D said, and bending his head down into his hands, he burst into tears and wept for a long time for his friend.

The adventure was over.

The next day, after O'D had driven off to Chimoio to make more arrangements for Caetano's funeral, Frank appeared at the sitting room window.

"Yes, Frank?" I asked.

"You know, Madam," Frank said, for once getting it right and not calling me 'Sir', "I was in Chimoio on Saturday afternoon and I came across the mother of Mr. Caetano. She said she had just been to see him at the Fatima. 'You don't have to worry about your boss, Frank,' she told me. 'He's so much better he'll probably be back at work next week.' It is very strange, Madam. Very strange that he is now dead."

I let out a sigh and shook my head. "Frank," I said, " You're not the only one who thinks it's strange. We *all* do."

CHAPTER TWENTY SIX

THE FUNERAL

I dreaded Caetano's funeral.

When the day came around, I dressed in the drabbest of my clothes. O'D put on his grey suit and his old Etonian tie, in honour of his friend.

At Caetano's house, the house he had shared with his mother and Denis, his young son, we joined the large crowd that had gathered there. They were waiting for the car to arrive from the morgue with Caetano's coffin.

While we were standing, waiting, Caetano's old uncle walked over to speak to O'D. "I have to tell you something," he said urgently. He was agitated and it was obvious that something was weighing on his mind. "I have to tell you about something strange that I noticed about Caetano at the morgue."

The old uncle had been with the family when they had gone to the hospital morgue to get Caetano. Except for the old uncle, they had all been too afraid to touch his dead body and so he had been the one to haul Caetano's corpse up into the coffin.

"As I put my hands under his armpits and pulled him upright," the old uncle told O'D, "a very peculiar thing happened. A large gout of yellow liquid gushed out of his mouth like a river. This liquid had the very strong smell of medication and ..."

The arrival of the Station Wagon containing the coffin cut short the old uncle's story. Some men took the coffin out of the car and carried it over to a table that had been placed under the trees next to the house. Once the coffin was safely on top of the table, they opened the lid. Women began to sing. The song was soft and sad and incredibly sweet, made sweeter by the perfect and beautiful silky harmony of their voices. "Why have you left us?" I heard them sing, although I knew I was imagining the words as they were singing in a language I couldn't understand. As everyone started to move forward in a slow line to look at Caetano's face for the last time, we forgot the old uncle and whatever it was that he had so urgently wanted to tell O'D.

When O'D walked over to the coffin and looked down at Caetano's face, tears ran down his face. A Mozambican standing nearby called out to him. "Be a man!"

I remembered the shortest sentence I had read in my father's little Bible. 'Jesus wept.' If Jesus himself had cried for his dead friend Lazarus, then it was perfectly alright for O'D to cry for his friend. I opened my mouth to tell this to the Mozambican but then I closed it again.

Caetano's Zimbabwean coffin was white and when it was my turn to say goodbye to him, I saw that it was still too small for him. They had had to bend his knees and turn him sideways at the waist to fit him in and to hide this, they had placed a lacey white cloth over him up to his shoulders.

The lace didn't hide the ugly brown suit his sister Romana had bought for him. In life, Caetano had hated suits and had never worn them. Now that he was dead, he was being buried in one.

I looked down at his face. "Goodbye, Caetano," I said softly, even though I knew he was somewhere else and that there was nothing but his empty shell in the coffin. "Goodbye." The coffin lid was closed and the men carried it back to the Station Wagon.

In the red pickup, its open back loaded down with mourners, we joined the long convoy of lorries, old pickups and cars driving slowly on the road out of Chimoio to the cemetery. On the lead car, someone held up the large cross that was always held up to show that this was a funeral procession.

The cemetery was a sea of sand. There were no headstones, just little mounds of earth and some handwritten signs made out of cardboard to indicate the site of a grave.

The gravediggers were still working on Caetano's grave. His size had taken them by surprise. The coffin wouldn't fit and while we waited, they dug away to enlarge the hole.

The women sang their beautiful, silky song again and when at last Caetano vanished into the sandy earth, I looked up. It was a sunshiny day and high overhead an eagle soared along on the wind currents in the clear blue winter sky.

A woman thrust a red Barberton daisy into my hand and as the crowd surged forward towards the grave, I was pushed along with them. We placed our flowers on the new mound of sand and then I walked back to O'D. An old man with sad eyes and long straggly grey hair was standing with him. Bertuzzi. He opened his arms wide and I

340

walked into the arms of our old Italian enemy and cried all over his khaki-clad shoulder.

"Oh, that beautiful boy," Bertuzzi mourned. "Oh, that beautiful, beautiful boy."

We drove back to Caetano's house, with the thought of saying a few words to Caetano's mother and his sister but when we stepped into his small house, we stepped into the deepest of black. All the windows had been covered, it was stifling and airless and as we fumbled our way towards a room, we heard a scream and then a voice crying out, "Romana! Romana has fainted!"

"We'll speak to them another time," O'D said.

On the drive out of town, I said "I don't want to go home. I want to be with my kind of people. Let's go and see Murray."

The Chibuku factory was a hive of activity. The car park was full of expensive 4 x 4s with their yellow Zimbabwean number plates and inside the large, barnlike main room, Murray sat behind a desk, smoking a Madison and drinking a beer. The room heaved with people. Mostly farmers like Murray who had been kicked off their farms, they were looking for a safehaven and a new start in life. The room vibrated with the stress and trauma of the shock and loss the Zimbabweans were experiencing.

Murray eyed our clothes.

"We've just been to a funeral," I explained. "Our partner died."

A Zimbabwen woman wearing a scruffy navy anorak looked up. "Oh, I'm sorry to hear that," she said. "Was it someone we knew?"

"No," I replied. "Our partner was Mozambican."

The sympathetic look vanished from her face. "Oh, only a black," she said dismissively.

I opened my mouth to tell her that what she had just said was the reason she was now in Mozambique instead of Zimbabwe but for the second time that day I closed my mouth and said nothing.

We stayed for a while, talking and drinking a beer and then we drove home.

They weren't my kind of people after all.

One night, about a week after Caetano's funeral, a rather disturbing thing occurred.

O'D was already in bed, reading a book to take his mind off events and I was brushing my hair in front of the mirror when everything seemed to change and to slip out of kilter, as if I was caught between two dimensions. All of a sudden, in front of my eyes, I saw a thick white outline like an aura surrounding my reflection in the mirror, my hand and the hairbrush I was holding, even the mirror itself ...

And then, in the left side of the mirror, Caetano appeared. He was wearing a mustard-coloured sweater with a hole in the elbow and the expression in his dark eyes was infinitely sad. "Don't worry, Senhora," he told me gently. "Don't worry."

Startled, I stepped back from the mirror and noticed that the white aura was outlining everything else in the room as well ... the mosquito net, the chair, the bed, O'D ... the sight was so disorientating, it made me lose my balance and I fell against the bed.

O'D looked up from his book. "What's wrong?" he asked.

I pushed myself upright and all of a sudden everything was back to normal again. "I thought I saw Caetano in the mirror," I told him. "He was wearing a very ugly sweater I'd never seen him wearing before."

O'D gave me a blank look, not understanding.

I got into bed. What had happened was just caused by stress, I told myself. My imagination playing tricks on me.

My head sank down onto the pillow and I closed my eyes. Yes, just stress. That's what it was. Wasn't it?

CHAPTER TWENTY SEVEN

THE PISTACHIO GREEN JUDGE

A few days after the funeral, Nelson Batista, the IPAJ clerk Caetano had employed to deal with the court case, contacted O'D. Judge Magaia had recovered from his illness and Westh's sentencing was now set for the 24th June.

We had dreaded Caetano's funeral and now we dreaded going to the Court House. With Caetano gone, we had the feeling that things weren't going to go well. Still numb from the shock of his unexpected death, we looked around for some support. Apart from the small pocket tape recorder I was taking with me to secretly record the proceedings, we also needed human witnesses and friends to give us advice.

At the Court House, a nondescript building that looked like a block of flats built in the 1960's, we met up with Treciano, Jinho and Joao de Conceciao who had let us use his land for our estaleiro in Chimoio.

We climbed the stairs to the first floor and were met by Nelson. We would have to wait, apparently, because Judge Magaia was still working on the Sentence - writing it all out by hand!

With nowhere to sit, we stood in the long corridor. Men and women holding papers and files bustled importantly past us, amongst them a particularly stocky man who strode towards us with arms pumping and footsteps cracking like gunshots on the cement floor. With his yellow face and strange dark eyes that looked as if they had been outlined with kohl, he looked as if he had come straight out of an Egyptian wall painting.

Jinho bent his head towards me and whispered, "That's the Judge President. Judge Sambo."

At last a clerk appeared and motioned for us to enter the courtroom. We went in and sat down. I had wanted to see the man who had been the cause of our troubles but I was disappointed. We were the only ones in the room.

I looked over at Nelson who had seated himself in a chair next to the wall, away from us. "Where's Jan Westh?" I asked.

He answered with a shrug.

There was a commotion at the door and a very plump, very dark and smooth-skinned man swept in. He was dressed in a well-cut and eye-catching pistachio green suit and looked just like a large pale green ice cream with a black currant decorating the top of it. A clerk handed him a black robe and he put it on over his suit.

"Stand up! Stand up!" Nelson hissed.

We all rose to our feet.

The Judge sat down and settled himself behind his desk.

"Sit down! Sit down!" Nelson hissed.

We all sat down again.

There was silence as Judge Magaia surveyed our small group with a baleful glare. Then he barked some angry words at O'D and me. Unable to understand what he was shouting, we stared dumbly back at him.

Jinho, who was sitting next to me, leaned over towards O'D on the other side of me. "Uncross your legs!" he whispered. "Quickly! He says you are not allowed to cross your legs in his court and he's going to fine you if you don't uncross them!"

O'D and I hastily uncrossed our legs and planted our feet side by side on the floor.

With a last warning glare at us, Judge Magaia began to speak.

Careful not to let the Judge see me, I turned on my little tape recorder.

A terrible clacking sound suddenly started up, filling the room and completely drowning out the Judge's voice. The clerk who had handed Judge Magaia his black robe, was now sitting on a chair in front of an ancient black manual typewriter and pounding away to take down the words the Judge was uttering.

Just our luck, I thought, and turned off the tape recorder.

Judge Magaia turned to Nelson and the typewriter fell silent.

The sentencing of Jan Westh was not going to take place today after all.

The Chimoio Judiciary, it seemed, had neglected to tell the Danish criminal to put in an appearance!

Judge Magaia stood up. The sentencing of Westh was now set for the 26th June, he told us, and swept out of the room.

Downstairs, we stood next to the pickup preparing to go our separate ways. "I have a bad feeling about all of this," I said to Jinho.

He made no effort to reassure me. Crippled in one leg from polio since the age of two, Jinho had had dealings of his own with the Chimoio Judiciary.

It had begun one day when he'd been innocently sitting under the umbrella of a small outdoor café and munching on a Mozambican type of hamburger. A waiter had approached him and had demanded payment.

"Wait until I have finished," Jinho had told the waiter, reluctant to dirty his hands with money while he was in the middle of eating his food.

Then the owner of the café had appeared. He had made the same demand and when Jinho had refused to pay until he had finished eating, he had roughly pushed Jinho off his chair, throwing him onto the ground!

Jinho had pulled himself to his feet, he had paid the café owner for his half-eaten hamburger now lying in the dirt and then he had gone off to take the café owner to court.

Although he had won the case and the café owner had been sentenced to pay Jinho the sum of seven million meticais in damages, the man had never done so.

Now Jinho merely said, "Let's wait and see what happens on the 26th."

On the 26th June, we were back in the courtroom again for the third attempt to sentence Jan Westh. Strangely, the man who was the cause of the court case was still not present to hear the Court's verdict. "Where's Jan Westh?" I asked Nelson. How was it POSSIBLE that the Chimoio Judiciary could let the Dane get away with not attending his own sentencing?

Nelson gave me a shrug and a rather mocking smile. "Perhaps he's gone to Denmark again, to see his father."

A green-garbed figure swept plumply through the door. We all stood up. Judge Magaia donned the black robe and sat down behind his desk. We all sat down on our chairs again, O'D and I taking care not to cross our legs.

The Judge eyed us with what appeared to be his habitual expression - the baleful glare - and, disappointed not to find anything to threaten us about, began to read out Jan Westh's sentence. At once, the dreadful clacking sound began from the ancient typewriter and completely drowned out his voice.

345

For what seemed like an eternity of excruciating boredom, we sat and watched the Judge mouthing five and half pages of words that we couldn't hear. Eventually, he stopped speaking, the clacking typewriter fell silent and he gathered his papers together. When he swept out of the room, we were no wiser than when he had come in.

Nelson walked over to O'D. "You won!" he told him. "Westh has to either return your pine or pay you the six hundred million by the 24th July. If he doesn't, he will go to jail for two years." He paused. "Now you have to take out another court case against Westh."

"What for?" O'D asked curtly. He'd had more than enough of Westh and the Chimoio Judiciary. "The Judge has sentenced Westh and that's that." He looked away from Nelson towards the door, eager to get out of the Court House.

Contempt flitted across Nelson's face as he looked at O'D and his lips curled up in a horrible sneer. Taken aback by the ugliness of Nelson's expression, I wondered why on earth Caetano had chosen someone like him to deal with the court case.

"But you must," Nelson insisted.

"No," O'D said, oblivious of the look on Nelson's face. "What I would like, though, is a copy of the Sentence."

"It's not ready," Nelson told him. "You'll have to wait."

"How long?"

Nelson shrugged carelessly. The contempt had now turned to insolence. "About two weeks," he said and walked out of the room and disappeared.

We were downstairs again and standing by the pickup when O'D remembered something. "There's a clerk Caetano and I sometimes had dealings with," he told us, "perhaps she'll be able to make a copy of the Sentence for us."

For a small sum of money and the promise never to divulge her name, the clerk quickly made a copy of Jan Westh's Sentence for us. This was just as well, because from that day onwards - if he hadn't been before - Nelson became our enemy, obstructing us and lying to us at every turn.

We saw little of Nelson while we waited for the deadline of the 24th July to arrive and at his sawmill, Westh carried on working as if he didn't have a care in the world.

Then, almost exactly a month after Caetano had died, Grumpy disappeared.

He disappeared right after he had eaten his breakfast of boiled mackerel and rice and left us with no clues as to what might have happened to him.

Although we loved all our animals, Grumpy was very special to us. For one thing, he had been given to us by Caetano and then, when we had seen what a detrimental effect Miss Sydney's bullying had had on him psychologically, we had developed a very soft and protective spot for him.

When evening came and Grumpy was still missing, we began to worry. This wasn't a cat that wandered far from the house.

The next morning we started a serious search for him in the bush and grass surrounding the house and the sawmill, calling his name and loudly shaking a box of Friskies, his favourite food. When we got no reply, we wondered fearfully if he'd been caught in a trap like Black Kitty ... or ... snatched by a worker or one of the local people like Mitzi had been snatched.

As the days passed with still no sign of Grumpy, wild thoughts made their way into my head. Grumpy was pure white, one of the reasons Caetano had chosen him as a gift for us. A white cat for white people. Had he been taken by a witch doctor, to kill and to use as muti in some horrible spell against us?

Although I had stopped talking to God since Caetano had died, I prayed a little prayer for Grumpy. "Oh, God," I said, "if Grumpy's still alive, please bring him back to us. Caetano gave him to us and he's the only link we still have with Caetano."

On the fifth day of Grumpy's disappearance, Fernand came to work drunk and obnoxious. O'D fired him on the spot and then, when Fernand threatened to kill him, sent a worker to call the local police. By the time Mario and another policeman arrived, riding down the track on the police motorbike, Fernand was long gone So after a brief conversation with O'D, the police drove off back to Macate.

Fernand's drunken behaviour, strange to tell, had some fortunate results. The unknown people who had taken Grumpy must have mistakenly thought we had called the police to investigate our cat's disappearance and lost their nerve because a mere half an hour after the police had gone, who should come walking unsteadily down the forest track but ... Grumpy!

Yellow eyes staring and filled with horror, as if he'd been in hell itself, he ran straight into the house, straight into the bathroom and hid under the bath.

It took a long time for O'D to coax him to come out from his hiding place and when he eventually crept out fearfully, we saw that his white fur was a grayish colour and that there was some kind of black stuff like soot oozing out of the corners of his eyes, out of his nostrils and out of his ears.

"What is it?" I asked O'D.

"It looks like charcoal dust," he told me. "I think whoever took him has been keeping him in a sack used for charcoal."

O'D's guess turned out to be right. Poor Grumpy's long sojourn in a charcoal sack had so choked him up with the black dust that it had affected his lungs. Unable to breathe properly, he wasn't able to eat or drink either. If we didn't get him to a Vet soon, he was going to die.

Across the border, Dr. Mafara examined Grumpy and x-rayed his lungs. Yes, there were specks of charcoal and charcoal dust in them.

"Is he going to live?" I asked.

"Cats are tougher than we think they are," he said. "Leave him with us. We'll nebulise him and try to get as much of this stuff out of him as we can."

While Dr. Mafara, Blessing and Brenda nebulised and looked after Grumpy, another rather traumatic event occurred.

One evening, while I was sitting on the sofa in the sitting room and waiting for O'D to return from Chimoio, I heard the sound of an approaching vehicle - a vehicle that didn't sound like O'D's red Toyota at all.

Since Samsone Joao's attack, I spent my evenings alone surrounded by an array of weapons to protect myself, just in case he came back as Biasse had suggested he might. While nine cats and a dog lay on the carpet to keep me company, a fiercesomely sharp panga lay on the sofa next to me. As well as the panga, there was also a heavy black torch that would give someone a painful whack on the head and a long stick made out of pau ferro. I had also invested in a new and powerful pepper spray.

During these solitary evenings, I often thought about Samsone Joao and even found myself actually wishing that he would, indeed, come back. And this time, I promised myself grimly, I would be ready for him. Oh, how ready, to mete out some of the treatment he had given me. "Come," I told him, "yes, come and see what's going to happen to YOU!"

The sound of the strange vehicle came nearer and then, all at once, there were two of them, racing down the forest track in the black night straight towards my house!

My bravado evaporated in the face of reality and filled with fear, I leapt to my feet. Bandits! Not Samsone Joao, not one man ... but several. Bandits! Infected by my fear, nine cats and a dog all leapt to their feet and milled around, growling. I looked around for my pepper spray. My spray ... where was my spray? Oh, no! I had left it in the bedroom!

Heart thudding with terror, I ran down the corridor, dog Bandit running close to me for her protection, not mine. In the bedroom, I grabbed the spraycan and ran towards the front door, Bandit still running close to me and getting under my feet. They needn't think I was going to be a pushover, oh no, I was going to fight! I was going to blast them with pepper, blast their faces, and then hit them very very hard on their heads with the black torch!

I ran outside and up to the vehicles. They were now parked outside my bedroom window. I was going to attack my attackers - surprise them by attacking them first! A man clambered out of the vehicle nearest to me ... a man with white hair, spectacles and a big fuzz of white enveloping his face.

"Hello, Val."

I skidded to a halt. Relief flooded through me and suddenly the awful, terrible stress I hadn't realised I was under took over and made me unravel in a totally bizarre way. "Fuck you, Murray!" I yelled. "Fuck you, Murray Dawson! I thought you were bandits ... you know I was attacked ... you know our partner's just been killed ... and you come in here, driving so fast ..."

Bursting into tears, I turned away from him and ran back into the house. At the table in the sitting room, I poured Ultra Mel into a tall glass and drank it all down in one go. I filled the glass again and then I sank down on the sofa and in between sobs and sniffs, sipped at the milk.

Murray walked slowly into the sitting room. He was followed by his brother Rob, also white haired, bespectacled and with a face covered in white fuzz and Tim, a well-built and dark-haired young man who was Rob's son. All three sat down and looked warily at me.

"We're sorry if we frightened you, Val," Murray began, "but we had to come in the dark because we're in trouble and we didn't want anyone to see us coming here."

349

"Trouble," I repeated and gulped down some more milk to steady my shattered nerves. "What kind of trouble?"

"We've got our foreman with us outside. He's been tortured by the CIO … he's in a pretty bad way … he escaped across the border and now they're looking for him."

"Oh," I said.

"Well," Murray went on, "we were sitting around, wracking our brains for a place where he could hide up safely until the heat's off and then I hit on the idea of bringing him here to you and O'D. You're the only people I know who're living in the middle of nowhere, the back of beyond. They'll never find him here."

The thought of giving refuge to a torture victim who was being hunted down by the dreaded Zimbabwean Central Intelligence Organisation was daunting, especially in view of all our own troubles piling up on us. What if the CIO picked up a clue and came down to the Nhamacoa? Killing people was nothing to them and their hideous tentacles stretched far across their border into neighbouring African countries with impunity. "I don't know if we can help, Murray," I said. "This has been such a terrible year for us, I don't know if we can cope with the CIO on our backs as well."

"Please, Val," Rob broke in. "If you help us out, we'll owe you a big, big favour."

We hid Ian, the Dawson's foreman, in the small laundry room under the house. He slept on one of our camp beds and ate the food Murray brought to him once a week and which Biasse, sworn to secrecy, cooked for him.

The Zimbabweans had caught him when some of the farm equipment Murray was smuggling across the border into Mozambique had got stuck in the mud during some heavy rains. At the police station, they had tortured him for information about Murray, beating him on the soles of his feet. He had escaped across the border when Murray had paid a large amount of money to a certain policeman to look the other way … and now the CIO were hunting for him.

While Murray's foreman languished morosely in our small laundry room, reading old copies of 'Fair Lady' and 'Femina' to relieve his boredom and Grumpy languished in a small cage, being nebulised every now and then by Dr. Mafara at his Mutare surgery, the deadline set in Westh's Sentence came and went and there was no word from the Dane.

He did not return our pine. He did not pay us our money.

"The Court needs six million meticais to execute the sentence," Nelson told O'D. And so on the 8th August, 2002, O'D paid IPAJ the money and we waited for Westh's arrest. Waited, in vain.

CHAPTER TWENTY EIGHT

BIASSE TAKES OFF HIS APRON

By the end of August, Grumpy was well enough to be brought home. We collected him from Dr. Mafara and although he still had black charcoal dust coming out of the corners of his eyes, his lungs were working again and he was able to breathe and eat at the same time.

And at the beginning of September, Westh was still free!

While the Dane was enjoying himself, O'D and I fumed with angry frustration. An unwilling participant in Mozambique's corrupt system of justice in the first place, O'D now found himself embroiled in a court case peopled by some extremely unsavoury characters.

Nelson became elusive, difficult to get hold of and we wondered what game he was playing.

When O'D did manage to pin him down, he gave us excuses that were highly unlikely. "Yes," he told O'D, "Judge Magaia signed the execution of Westh's sentence at the beginning of August. Unfortunately, the Messenger of the Court hasn't been able to find Westh to serve him with the papers. He's tried several times."

Then, when this excuse wore thin, Nelson told O'D that the Messenger of the Court was now sick ... too sick to see Westh.

Doing some investigating of his own, O'D discovered that Judge Magaia had not executed Westh's sentence after all and that Nelson had been telling us a pack of lies.

Furious at this discovery, we made a mistake. We turned to our friends for advice.

"Why don't you speak to a journalist at Chimoio Radio about the stalled court case?" Jinho suggested.

Forgetting that African government officials can't take even the slightest of criticisms, this seemed a good idea to us.

The journalist listened with interest to what O'D had to tell him and as it was necessary, of course, to hear the other side of the story as well, he made an appointment to speak to Judge Magaia on the 11th September.

At the meeting, the Judge erupted with fury when he heard why the journalist had come to see him.

Angrily, he told the journalist that *we* were troublemakers! That he did not recognise O'D as Caetano Martins' legal partner and stated that Caetano had brought the case against Westh in his private capacity and not as a representative of our Company. This was particularly bizarre, as the Judge in his own handwriting in Westh's Sentence had on every occasion written Caetano's name followed by the word 'representing' our company. At the end of his diatribe against us, he threatened *us* with court action if we should have any further thoughts of publicising the case!

It was Magaia's opinion, it seemed, that the case against Westh was as dead as our partner, Caetano.

Alone in the Nhamacoa and without a telephone to keep up with these events, I was completely unprepared for what was to happen next - in the afternoon of the very day the journalist had his meeting with Judge Magaia.

Biasse was down by the river, taking his usual afternoon bath and I was in kitchen making a salad when I heard the car. Thinking it was a customer I didn't go outside for a look. Frank, no doubt, would come and call me when he needed me.

About half an hour later, I heard the sound of voices approaching and so I went outside. I was just in time to see the Administrator of Gondola, accompanied by an entourage of 5 people, about to climb into a government pickup parked outside my bedroom window.

As the Administrator had never paid us a visit in all our years in the Nhamacoa and as it was usual for government officials to send you a letter informing you of their intention to visit your business, his omission to do so was ominous. And so was the fact that he had made his visit on a Wednesday, a day when everyone knew that O'D would be in town.

"Boa tarde," I greeted him.

He turned towards me.

"My husband isn't here," I told him, "but could I offer you something to drink? A coffee? Or some ..."

The Administrator's hatchet face turned harsh with dislike. "Oh, I can't be bothered to speak to her," he brusquely told his entourage, "her Portuguese is too bad," and rudely turning his back on me, he climbed into the pickup.

His entourage followed, he said something about me which set them all off laughing and then, as they drove away, he leaned across

353

the driver and waved his hand mockingly at me – just like a baby waves his hand - but in a gesture of extreme contempt.

I sat down on the verandah and waited for Frank.

When he came, I said "Well, Frank, what was that all about?"

"It is not good, Madam," Frank told me.

Chilled by his words, I said. "Tell me."

"The Administrator called us all together," Frank began "and then he started off by saying that you were bad people and that everyone in the area of Chikuvu hated you."

"Go on," I said, feeling anger beginning to stir inside me and replace the chill.

"He also told us he was going to give your second class planks away to the people and that he was going to make you buy us clothes and shoes."

"What a cheek!" I exclaimed.

"Yes, Madam, but that is nothing," Frank went on. "Then he asked if we had any complaints against you ... and the two sons of Biasse spoke up. They told him that the boss treated the workers badly, that he hit us, beat us ..."

"What?" I exclaimed, stunned by the lie.

O'D had employed Biasse's two sons as temporary grasscutters, as a favour to him. They had been working in Zimbabwe as labourers on a farm but had lost their jobs when War Vets had invaded it.

"Yes, Madam," Frank said, and added "then the Administrator told us that he was going to put it on the radio that the boss beats the workers."

"Did our other workers also complain about us?" I asked.

"No, Madam."

While I waited for O'D to return from Chimoio, I puzzled over the Administrator's visit. He had been out to make trouble, but why?

In the evening when O'D told me that he'd had another meeting with the journalist from Chimoio Radio and that Judge Magaia had called us 'troublemakers' and threatened us if we publicised the court case, it all became quite clear to me.

The Aministrator's visit was no coincidence. *They* were out to make trouble and to make us look bad!

The Administrator's visit had some consequences even he would not have foreseen and the following day a particularly nasty incident occurred.

At the morning roll call, our workers told O'D what Biasse's sons had said to the Administrator. This caused a terrible uproar. Biasse's sons screamed hysterically at our workers, threatening to kill them for relaying their words to O'D. Then, when O'D fired them for their threats, they demanded to be paid instantly, there and then.

Since Samsone Joao's attack, we no longer kept much money in the house and so he told them they would have to wait for their money until the following day.

They didn't like this. Getting hold of some large empty plastic containers and planting themselves in front of our house, they proceeded to give us the same treatment they had seen the War Vets give the Zimbabwean white farmer when they had invaded the farm on which they'd been working.

Hour after hour, they banged and drummed on the containers, yelling and shouting and singing.

I closed all the curtains in the rooms to shut out the ugly sight they made.

Biasse came up the back stairs into the kitchen, silent and with his face set and wooden like a small brown mask.

"Tell your sons to go away, Biasse," I ordered.

Without a word, he turned his straight little back on me and returned to the cook hut.

"Biasse!" I called after his back. "Tell your sons to go!"

The drumming and screaming went on all day. I couldn't understand why Biasse did nothing to control his sons and he refused to explain himself.

O'D ignored them but whenever he walked over to the house from the workshop, Manuel, the older of Biasse's sons, tried his best to provoke him. Dancing around O'D, he stuck his face insolently right into O'D's face over and over again, wanting O'D to hit him, wanting an excuse to go to the police, to be on the radio, to suck up to the Administrator …

Peering through the gap in the sitting room curtains, I whispered "Don't hit him, O'D, don't play into his hands …" even though I myself wanted to resort to violence, to tweak Manuel's nose and pull it out until it was as long as the lying Pinocchio's nose.

Unable to break through O'D's control, they started shouting something at Biasse.

I walked down the back stairs. Azelia was leaning out of the cook hut window, a shocked expression on her face.

355

"What are they shouting, Azelia?"

"Dona, they are telling Biasse that if he doesn't stop working for you, they are going to beat him! Their own father!"

Now it was my turn to be shocked. What kind of children were these? Had Biasse's sons lost their minds? The madness in Zimbabwe was obviously infectious.

Finally, just to put a stop to everything, I called Biasse to come and speak to me and when he came, I said "Take off your apron, Biasse."

Biasse gave me a bitter look. "Thank you, Madam," he said and untied his khaki apron and handed it to me. Before I could say another word, he turned on his heel and disappeared down the stairs. Through the gap in the curtains, I saw the would-be War Vets stop their drumming. Biasse had joined them. They turned away from the house and walked down the forest track together ... two sons, with the father they had threatened to hit ... and then, they turned the corner and vanished from sight.

I had not, of course, fired Biasse. I had only intended to put an end to the ugly scene that was being played out in front of my house. However, it seemed he thought I had told him to go - permanently - and that's just what he did.

O'D wrote a letter of complaint about the Administrator's behaviour to the Governor, and Dona Louisa (the Governor's secretary) came down to see us, bringing the Administrator with her.

While we all sat on the verandah, the Gondola Administrator put on a performance that filled me with wonder. Was this the same harsh, rough, rude man who had come to the Nhamacoa to make trouble for us? How he had changed! Now his face was amiable, his voice soft and gentle in its reasonableness. Surrounded by the little entourage of sycophants who had accompanied him on his first visit to us, he denied everything. His sycophants backed him up. The Senhora's Portuguese was so bad she had misunderstood things!

To Dona Louisa's credit, she wasn't taken in. No doubt she was used to the masks African government officials put on and take off to fool people.

Knowing that he would never apologise, she did it for him, in his name. "On behalf of the Administrator," she said, "I am very sorry."

September melted into October and still the Chimoio Judiciary did nothing to execute Westh's Sentence.

356

We consulted our friends again.

"Get another lawyer," Jinho advised us.

"Who?" we asked, angry that we were being forced deeper and deeper into the murky mire of what passes for Mozambican 'justice'.

"There's one called Pawindiwa," he told us. "I don't know how good he is but he can't be worse than Nelson!"

Without an alternative, O'D paid Pawindiwa a visit.

The lawyer agreed to take on the case and set out his conditions – an upfront payment of 30 million meticais – about 1,000 pounds sterling!

Naturally, O'D balked at this outrageous demand and Pawindiwa finally settled for 10 million.

O'D's letter to Nelson dispensing with his 'services' brought a letter in reply which clearly indicated the total insanity of the Chimoio judiciary.

Furious at being fired, Nelson told O'D that any claim he had to the court case was as illegitimate as his claim to be Caetano's partner! That Caetano had taken legal action against Westh in his private capacity and not as a representative of our company and that he, Nelson, had been acting on behalf of Caetano and not on behalf of our company.

That said, he now demanded payment for his services from us, claiming 20% of the money Westh was supposed to pay back to us but had not paid back - the sum of 135 million meticais, amounting to about 4,000 pounds!

Ending the letter off with a threat, he gave us his bank account number at BIM Bank and told us that if the money wasn't paid into the account within FIVE DAYS, he was going to take action against us.

Naturally, we ignored Nelson's letter and his demented demands.

Now, O'D embarked on a long series of meetings with our new lawyer. At first, when Pawindiwa told O'D he had had talks with Magaia and would be able to bring the Westh case to an end by 10th November, we were hopeful that we were at last getting somewhere. However, time dragged on and nothing happened. And then one day, towards the end of the year, Pawindiwa took us by surprise. He disappeared out of our lives without saying anything to us.

He was now working on something terribly important down in Beira, his receptionist told us and no one knew when he'd be back.

In the end, O'D went to see the Procurator about the lack of action and at first the Procurator was friendly. However, after the man had spoken to Judge Magaia about the case, his tone changed and he became as angry and threatening as the Judge.

He told O'D that O'D was 'confused in the brain' and that if he wasn't careful, Judge Magaia would be well within his rights to take O'D to court for besmirching and maligning Magaia's name!

Thwarted on every side to see justice being done in Mozambique, there was nothing left for us to do but to give up the unequal struggle.

Westh had won. The thieving Dane from squeaky-clean Denmark had got away with his crime because Caetano had died. How fortuitous for Westh …

CHAPTER TWENTY NINE

MOZAMBIQUE UNMASKED

The year 2003 began with Missy's death.

She was a sweet little cat, with a pointed face and the greenest of eyes. Despite being the last of Miss Sydney's kittens to be born and the smallest in size, Missy wasn't a pushover. No doubt this was due to Miss Sydney's fighting feminist genes that she had passed on to her daughter. Missy knew her rights as any of the other cats that tried to bully her had soon found out! Quite often, when I placed a bowl of milk on the kitchen floor and Spike, Raji and Jasper crowded around to drink, Missy would wade in there and using her furry grey elbows in a most unladylike manner, would jab and shove at her brothers until she had pushed them out of the way and taken the bowl over for herself.

Like Raji, she wasn't a very domesticated cat, spending a lot of her time during the day sleeping in the long tall yellow grass not far from the water tank and this may have been the cause of her death.

The problem with Missy's health started with some invisible mites that lived either in the ground or in the long tall yellow grass. At first, there was just a small bald spot on the back of her neck where she had scratched at the itch, but then, as the days went by, the bald spot grew larger and she scratched so much at it that a strip of skin came loose and hung flapping away. This loose piece of skin terrified her. She thought it was some kind of alien creature that had attached itself to her and she ran around the house like a mad thing, trying to get away from it. Eventually, we managed to catch her and hold her just long enough for O'D to carefully cut off the flapping skin but then she went and hid herself on the roof of our house and while she was up there, there was a heavy rainstorm and she got soaked to the skin.

Mr. Matola, the Vet in Chimoio wasn't up to much with animals unless they were farm animals and by this time, there were no longer any good Vets left in Mutare. Missy developed a high fever and then pneumonia set in.

Knowing there was nothing we could do and not wanting Missy to drag herself off into the bush to die alone, I put her gently onto a large comfortable cushion on the floor next to our bed and listened to her struggling to breathe. She was thirsty, I knew, but couldn't drink the water I had placed in front of her.

"Oh, little Missy, I'm so sorry we can't help you," I told her and stroked her gently on her little head. Ill as she was, she still managed a purr at my touch. "But all the Vets have run away."

Animal lovers will know how sad and painful it is to watch their beloved pets dying before their eyes and being helpless to do anything for them. We couldn't even put Missy to sleep to spare her from her agonizing death.

The end came one dark and early morning at four o'clock. I heard Missy struggle off the cushion and when I turned on the light, there she was, trying to force herself through the mosquito net in order to get under the bed. She opened her mouth wide in a last desperate effort to gasp for a breath and then with a loud despairing shriek, she drowned in the liquid that was filling her lungs.

The beginning of the year also brought another bolt from the blue. More trouble boiled up for us with another government official, this time in the Forestry Department.

Rungo had it in for us, it seemed, and now he showed his hand. With Caetano gone, he set out to bring us to our knees in the most callous of ways.

Sending a team of no less than six Forest Rangers to check out our felled logs in the forest, Rungo decided we'd broken a new law. It appeared that we now needed a document from the Forestry Department to transport our felled timber the short distance from the forest to our sawmill and as we had neglected to obtain this document, Forestry were going to confiscate all our logs!

Horrified by the sight of the Forest Rangers gleefully painting the letters DPA all over our timber, O'D appealed to Bertuzzi for help. Bertuzzi had formed the Association of Foresters and he, in his capacity as Secretary and another forester called Nunes who was the President of the Association made an appointment with the Provincial Director of Agriculture to talk about our problem with Rungo.

When the Provincial Director agreed that Rungo was out of order and overturned his decision to confiscate all our logs, Rungo was furious.

Foiled in his attempt to get hold of our logs, he now delayed with the issuing of licences for our sawn timber at the sawmill and unable to sell any timber without these licences, our business ground to a standstill.

Customers who made the long trip down to us to buy wood went back to Chimoio empty-handed and what little money we had left, began to dribble away.

Then, one day when O'D went into the Forestry Department for another attempt to get Rungo to see sense, he was told some grim news by Rungo's deputy, Abdullah.

"Rungo's not here," Abdullah told O'D, with something of a smirk. "He's gone to Germany."

Germany! O'D felt a sinking feeling in his stomach. "When will he be back?"

"Oh, in about three months' time," Abdullah replied carelessly. "And he didn't leave any instructions about your licences with me, so it's no use asking me to help."

The blow was enormous. How were we going to survive for three months without being able to sell our wood?

As if all of this wasn't enough, in July, one month after the anniversary of Caetano's death, Miss Sydney disappeared.

By this time I had replaced Biasse with a young Zimbabwean refugee called Lloyd. Lloyd had once been a waiter at Meikles Hotel in Harare and although he couldn't cook, he helped around the house. There was something wrong with Azelia - asthma, she said the doctor had told her - and she was becoming terribly, terribly thin.

At lunchtime, Lloyd told me, young boys slipped onto our land and rummaged around in the hole we had dug for our garbage. When he saw them at it, he shouted at them and tried to catch them but they were too fast for him, first pulling faces and sticking their tongues out at him before running away through the trees.

On the morning of Miss Sydney's disappearance, I saw her wandering off in the direction of the bushes near the rubbish hole. I called her name and she stopped for a second and looked over her shoulder at me. "Come," I called. "Come here." But with a last wilful look at me with her green eyes, she darted away into the undergrowth.

When Miss Sydney didn't put in an appearance for her supper or her breakfast of boiled mackerel and rice the following day, we started looking for her and calling her name. Our searches turned up no sign of her or even a hint of what had happened to her until about ten days later on a Sunday, when O'D and I heard the sound of voices down by the rubbish pit. The boys were on our land again. They started to run when they saw O'D but he caught one of them and the boy confessed. They were the children of the prophetess who lived across the river and they had killed my little Miss Sydney. Killed and eaten her.

Rungo returned from Germany and O'D drove off to the Forestry Department to pay him a visit.

Nothing had changed. Rungo still appeared to have some mysterious problem with us and while our licences continued to lie unsigned, the worst finally happened and our money ran out.

Without money, we weren't able to pay the wages. And without their wages, our workers weren't able to buy any food. Our food supplies also began to run out and when one day, I used the same tea bag over and over again for cups of tea that grew progressively paler and paler, I knew we had sunk to a new low. Panic began to rise up in me. We had been through hard times before but never like this. We were going to starve!

Then, our fuel ran out.

Without fuel, we weren't able to use the diesel generator. And without the generator, we weren't able to pump water up from the borehole. A few days later, the water tank ran dry.

WE WERE NOW WITHOUT WATER! WITHOUT WATER TO BATH ... WITHOUT WATER FOR COOKING ... WITHOUT WATER TO **DRINK**!

Who could we go to for help? Family and friends in Zimbabwe who might have been able to give us some support had all fled the country or were in situations as bad as ours. We were caught tight in the vice-like grip of Mozambican corruption and there was no one to turn to for rescue.

The terrible stress we'd been living under for so long now started to affect us in different ways.

During the day, O'D kept his mind and hands occupied by repairing our equipment. In the evenings after work, he read books and I could only imagine how he must have been feeling because he never spoke to me. And so, I lived in a silent world with only my own thoughts for company. I didn't even have Biasse to talk to anymore and I had stopped talking to God after Caetano had died.

Caetano's death preyed on my mind. Some weeks after the funeral, O'D had bumped into a nurse he knew and for a while they had spoken about Caetano and how he had died. "It's the opinion of the Chimoio medical profession" the nurse had told O'D "that Caetano was over-medicated."

Although the nurse's words confirmed what most of us suspected, that Caetano had been killed by the incompetence of a doctor (a not uncommon occurrence in Africa) dying in the middle of the trial seemed too much of a coincidence to me, especially when I took into account how Westh had benefitted from our tragedy.

The timing of Caetano's death also worked on my mind. If he had died before the trial had begun or after the trial had ended and the Sentence had been passed, I would have let it go. But Caetano had been alive on the day the Sentence was supposed to have been passed, only to find that it had been delayed, put off because Judge Magaia had suddenly become ill ...

How neatly everything had fallen into place, just as neatly as it had done when Samsone Joao had come to murder me.

"Do you think Caetano died because of witchcraft, Jinho?" I asked him one day.

He thought for a moment. "It's possible, Vaal."

"He was afraid of Westh's workers. He thought they had gone to a feiticeiro about him."

Jinho looked dubious.

"Well, it wouldn't have been Westh, would it? He's from Europe."

"But living with a Mozambican woman now. Haven't you heard? His wife left him and went back to Denmark."

"Oh, did she now? I wonder why she left him?" I mused.

"It's something we will never know," Jinho told me.

In the night, the forest drums took over my sleep and began to torment me. Invading the bedroom with their loud booming sound, they pounded in my head, making me dream strange dreams.

I dreamed of a worker arriving back from Gondola where Caetano had last worked felling panga panga, and telling me that he had found a letter from Caetano on the front seat of the blue Gaz. "Give it to me," I demanded, but the worker had fallen into a trance and a spirit had taken him over, babbling away in a woman's high tinkling voice and talking Chitewa, a language I didn't understand. "Who killed Caetano?" I asked the spirit, "Who?" but she just went on babbling away. Ignored, I started shouting at her, "Who killed Caetano? Who killed Caetano?" until the eerie sound of someone blowing an animal horn sounded in my ear and startled me awake.

One morning, I woke up with fingers that were completely numb and thumbs that I couldn't bend.

Then, another morning, I woke up to find myself covered in a red rash.

Spiralling down into a pit of the deepest and blackest depression I had ever known, I was overwhelmed by a sense of complete and utter hopelessness.

O'D had liked Mozambique so much, had put our money and the years of our lives into the country and Mozambique had returned the compliment by taking everything … everything … from us.

One afternoon in the spare bedroom, the room I used as a study, I sat in frozen despair in front of my old manual Facit typewriter and tried to make sense of what was happening to us.

It all seemed to have started when Westh had stolen our pine and Caetano had decided to take him to court. Caetano had been so afraid of witchcraft that he had run from one witch doctor to another to protect himself. Had O'D and I, too, become entangled in the witchcraft that bedevilled Mozambique? Or … had we somehow already become entangled perhaps, before we had even *arrived* in the country?

Thinking back over the years, I remembered the plank that had flown off the roof at Arrojela, flown straight at O'D, to hit him a glancing blow on his wrist. This hint of the supernatural had become overt in Mossel Bay, when my mother and I had had that chilling ghostly experience after my father's death. And then, of course, it had finally manifested itself openly and brazenly in Nora Swete, laughing at us … mocking with its blank white eyes … because it knew what lay in store for us while we were completely oblivious of our future.

We had come, O'D and I, into enemy territory - witchcraft country - two lapsed Christians, and it … whatever it was … hated us.

Kirby Jennings had warned me to be careful but I hadn't really taken him seriously. Words from the Gospel of John came into my mind. "The thief comes to steal, to kill and to destroy," Jesus had said. Yes, that was exactly what had happened to us. Westh had *stolen* from us, Caetano had been *killed* and now the Mozambican government officials were doing their best to *destroy* us. Who was this 'thief'? I wondered.

All of a sudden, I had a tremendous sense of evil swirling all around me, evil so strong that it almost took my breath away and made me feel weak and faint. Help … we needed help … special help … and if we didn't get it soon, something really, REALLY bad might well be going to happen to us.

I raised my useless hands and placing my numb fingers on the keyboard of my typewriter, I began to write a letter. A letter to Achim, the German Missionary, asking for help.

Achim wasn't at home when O'D drove up to Moyo Mukuru's gates and so he handed my letter to Achim's guard to give to him.

I waited for Achim's answer expectantly but when three weeks went by without a response from him, I knew I had once again been let down. I had made a desperate plea for help and Achim had ignored it! Was this the way a Pastor, one of God's very own special people, should behave? Full of wishy-washy talk about 'love conquering evil' and no concrete help?

While I harboured bitter thoughts about Achim, unbeknown to me, Achim was going through some trials and tribulations of his own.

Living in a country where everyone was always kandonga-ing across the border, Achim had been unable to resist temptation and had attempted some kandongas of his own. Unfortunately, as Pastors are supposed to keep to the straight and narrow, God was not with Achim on the morning he set off to smuggle purchases for his Mission out of Zimbabwe and into Mozambique. Caught by the Zimbabweans, he experienced the unthinkable and found himself under arrest!

Left in the dark about Achim's problems, my depression deepened.

O'D solved our financial problems temporarily by selling our Nissan 20 ton lorry and then, when a Danish Aid Agency put in an order for planks and beams, O'D didn't say no. He loaded the planks into the open back of the red Toyota and drove off very early in the morning for Chimoio. Government officials were notoriously late risers and he was certain there would be no one up and about at five in the morning to catch him selling his wood without a licence from Rungo.

Then, one afternoon, O'D discovered that a woman had moved onto sawmill land down by the Nhamacoa River and had started to clear it in order to open a machamba. She moved off after he spoke to her, only to reappear some weeks later and this time started clearing land just on the other side of some trees very close to the back of our house! When O'D again went to speak to her, accompanied by the local Frelimo Secretary of the area, she refused to budge, now claiming, untruthfully, that the land had been sold to her by an employee of the old Magalhaes sawmill.

A few days later, when Lloyd returned from a visit to the ramshackle banca (bar) just down the track from us, he arrived back in a state of agitation and with a warning.

"Maam, I met that woman who has moved onto your land and we have to be very careful of her," he told me fearfully.

"Why, Lloyd?" I asked.

"Because she is a … witch woman! She was there, at the banca, telling everyone she was a witch!"

"Oh, she was probably just telling you that to scare you, Lloyd," I told him.

"No, Maam!" Lloyd's eyes filled with the fear of witchcraft that held all Africans captive. "I am certain that she *is* a witch!"

Oh, how charming, oh how delightful, to hear that on top of everything else that was happening to us we now had a witch as a close neighbour as well! Was evil closing in on us? After all, there was still quite a lot of empty land in the Nhamacoa that the woman could have occupied, so why had she deliberately chosen to move onto sawmill land? And so near to our house?

It was difficult to ignore the presence of the witch woman, if, indeed, that was what she was. Separated from us only by a footpath and a thin band of trees, she and her son's two wives began to clear the land, chopping down every tree which her son then began to turn into charcoal for sale in Chimoio. Soon, several huts of poles and grass went up and goats blared their blaring sound, while babies played in the dust with the chickens.

An enemy had arrived right on our doorstep.

Then, one morning, we discovered that Mogsie had disappeared during the night!

Sure that she couldn't have gone far, we began to search for her. Since Dr. Mafara's departure for New York, poor little Mogsie had come down with an infection and had lost her hearing. Her deafness had also made her lose her sense of direction and when she wanted to walk anywhere, she went around and around in an endless tight little circle. It was a pitiful sight but without a Vet to consult and examine her, we had no idea how we could help her.

Although we looked all over the place for Mogsie, we never found her, or even a trace of her. Lloyd told us he had seen a giant owl in the big old mango tree next to the spare bedroom on the night she disappeared and so we could only come to the conclusion that she had somehow managed to wander outside and had been taken by the owl.

"I want my cat!" O'D said. He was terribly upset. He and Mogsie had had a special kind of relationship.

I didn't know what to say. Death was stalking us. Something was picking us off, one by one. We needed help, but where to get it?

And then I remembered something.

Once, when O'D had driven across the border without me, he had given a lift to two people. They had told him that they were South African Missionaries based in Chimoio and had given him a small yellow card with their names, their address and their telephone number. Colin and Betsie were their names and they were Afrikaaners from the Rhema Church in Alberton, near Johannesburg.

"Call them. Please," I told O'D.

Although Colin and Betsie didn't know us, they made the journey down to the Nhamacoa almost immediately. They knew all about witchcraft, it seemed, having had some rather bad experiences with it themselves when they had first arrived in Mozambique.

"Is your house clean?" Colin asked me, when he sat down in the sitting room. He was a stocky middle-aged man, deeply tanned, and with a head of curly black hair.

"Uh ..." I said, taken aback by the question. I looked at the great spiderweb the golden orb had woven across the ceiling and the mud nests the wasps had made in the grass above our heads and in the folds of the curtains. "It's as clean as I can get a house, in a place like this."

Colin shook his head at my lack of understanding. "No, that's not what I meant. Have you searched your house to make sure somebody hasn't left something from a witch doctor in one of your rooms?"

"I don't think there's anything like that here," I said slowly, remembering the witchy object Seven had found in his hut.

"You must make sure," Betsie told me. Small and slim, she had great big blue eyes and long silky brown hair.

"I will," I assured her, and began to tell them about the things that were happening to us.

"Do you have a Bible?" Colin asked, when at last I stopped talking.

"Yes," I said, and went to get it from the bedroom.

When I handed it to Colin, he examined it and then looked at me with disapproval. "It's never been opened," he said accusingly.

"I do ... er ... look inside it," I told him, embarrassed.

"The pages are still all stuck together," he went on, "as if it's brand new ... "

Unable to defend myself, I kept silent. As well as never reading the Bible I had bought to replace the one I had given to Steven, I had also given up my short forays into my father's little Bible when Caetano had died.

Colin gave my Bible back to me. "Turn to Psalm 91," he told me, "and read it out aloud. It's a psalm of protection."

I read out the psalm and then Colin and Betsie held out their hands to us. We took their hands and joined together, stood in a small circle in the middle of the sitting room. Colin began to pray for us and while he spoke, sudden tears welled up out of my eyes and embarrassingly began to pour down my face and fall in great big drops onto the carpet like a rainstorm. The more I tried to stop them, the more they fell. They were the tears of the terrible despairing grief and fear that had been wrenching at my heart for so long, mixed with an enormous sense of relief. We were safe now, I knew. I had felt the power of Colin's words. When he stopped praying and we all said 'Amen', I hurried from the room to mop myself up.

When I came back, O'D was making tea and coffee.

"Four sugars please," Betsie told O'D, unashamed of her excessive sugar intake.

Colin took a sip of his coffee. "Foreigners never think they're being affected by witchcraft," he told us. "They all just think they're having a run of terrible luck. They can't understand it. Betsie and I were just the same when we first came here. Awful things happened to us and it was only when it occurred to us that it might be witchcraft and we started praying for protection, that things got better."

Before they left for the drive back to Chimoio, Colin promised to give me some Rhema cassettes. They would help us a lot, he told me, in turning our circumstances around.

Colin and Betsie's prayers had an almost immediate affect on our lives. For some reason known only to himself and to God, Rungo suddenly signed our licences and on the 6th November, almost a year from the time we had applied for them, we were at last allowed to start operating again.

We did notice something peculiar, though, with the licence for the logs in Gondola. In all the years we'd been dealing with the Forestry Department, the licences had always expired on the 31st December of every year. This licence, however, expired on the **30**th December, 2003. One day less than usual.

"I wonder why he did this?" O'D mused, suspecting foul play.

We were soon to find out.

The fifty three days Rungo had given us weren't nearly long enough to pull our panga panga logs and transport them down to the sawmill even with the help of one of Pedro of Lofor's lorries but O'D did his best. Knowing that the Forestry Department was going to claim our logs as 'abandoned timber' if we didn't manage to bring them all to the sawmill by the 30th, he galvanised our workers into working overtime. Then, when the deadline ran out and he only had one more lorryload left at Gondola, he decided to take the risk and bring them down to us.

Achim and his wife, Patricia, had invited us over to their house at midnight to see in the New Year and by ten o'clock, I was dressed up and waiting for O'D to come back from Gondola. When the minutes ticked by and the Old Year turned into the New Year without any sign of him, I took off my party clothes and got into bed. By now I knew the signs of trouble. A non-appearance on O'D's part always meant disaster!

O'D finally arrived home, tired and dirty. Rungo had, as we had suspected, cunningly set a trap for O'D and O'D had obliged by falling right into it.

"They were waiting for me in Gondola," O'D told me, wearily sinking down onto the edge of the bed. "They waited until I had loaded the last of our logs onto Pedro of Lofor's lorry and then they arrested the lorry. They confiscated our wood, they confiscated Pedro's lorry and then they fined us two thousand U.S. dollars."

I sat up slowly. The terrible feeling of despair that had been overwhelming me for almost a year began to dissipate ...

"A smirking Forestry Fiscal gave me something of an explanation," O'D went on. "Rungo hates you," he told me. "He hates you because you don't pay bribes."

... and another emotion, a stronger emotion began to take me over ...

I shot out of bed, filled with fury and a really bad, bad feeling that I had never in my life felt before. The same emotion the

369

Mozambican government officials had been showering on us ever since Caetano had died. A terrible feeling of hatred. A blazing, all consuming hatred. I gave a scream. "That comes to over FOUR AND A HALF THOUSAND U.S. DOLLARS!"

"Don't shout at me," O'D said.

"I'm not shouting at YOU", I yelled, falling back into bed. "I'm shouting at RUNGO ... RUNGO, that ... that ... oh, that unutterable ... SWINE!"

This time, Bertuzzi and the Forestry Association got nowhere with Rungo. Shocked by the ferocity of his action for what was, after all, a tiny misdemeanour, they did their best for us. The wood had been cut down legally, all the licence fees had been paid and we had merely been transporting our own logs down to our very own sawmill, not to a customer or another part of the country, they argued. After all, what was one DAY?

Rungo was obdurate. Our wood was his, and so was our money!

"You mustn't be bitter," Colin told me, when he handed over a plastic carrier bag full of Rhema tapes.

"I'm NOT bitter!" I said, grittily. "I'm angry! ANGRY!"

"You must forgive people who do bad things to you," Betsie told me.

Forgiveness was the last thing I felt like doing when I was still raw and bleeding from all the wounds the Mozambicans were inflicting on us!

"You know," Colin went on thoughtfully with more advice, "I think it would be best if you put all this behind you and just forgot about it. You're only going to get into more trouble if you try to fight the system. Remember what happened to Carlos Cardoso."

I did, indeed. Carlos Cardoso was a Mozambican journalist who had been investigating corruption in the BPD bank. He had been gunned down in a street in Maputo. Nympine Chissano, President Chissano's stepson, was alleged to have ordered the murders.

Although it went against the grain, I knew Colin was talking sense. We weren't in Carlos Cardoso's league but we had obviously ruffled some feathers and made people angry with us.

The next afternoon, I emptied out Colin's carrier bag and examined the cassettes he'd chosen for me. "God is looking for you," I read on the side of one tape. Another was entitled "When I am weak, He is strong."

I chose a tape called "Doing the word of Jesus" and slipped it into my cassette recorder, unaware that this small action was going to change my life - and O'D's life - completely.

The tape was electrifying. Rooted to my chair for almost an hour, I listened to an American pastor called Charles Capps talking about God in a way I had never heard anyone talk before. "Talk to the mountain (the problem) in your life," he told us, "and if you *believe* what you *say*, you can move it out of your life."

"God is waiting to help you," Don Caywood told me in another tape. "Don't keep Him waiting till tomorrow. Go to Him now!"

There was nothing negative about the Rhema tapes. Everything was possible through God. There was no need to be a victim, passively accepting the kicks and blows of life. With God's help, we could change our circumstances around completely and become victors. "If God be for you," Don Caywood quoted from the Bible, "who can be against you?"

Colin's cassettes gave a terrific boost to my wilting spirits and galvanized me into action. Things were so bad I didn't even have an old tea bag now to dunk into a cup of boiling water.

Walking down the forest track one morning after I had finished listening to the last cassette, I looked for a suitably private spot where I could be alone and unheard. According to the Rhemas, I had to talk to God aloud (as I unwittingly used to do before Caetano's death) and this time I didn't want anyone else to hear me.

I stopped just past the entrance gate and standing under the leafy trees, looked up into the blue, blue sky. "We need help, God," I said.

I didn't ask God for revenge or even for justice. Those were not the things we needed. Rungo had brought us to our knees and we were now beyond the point of being just broke. He had not only taken what little money we had left but had put us into debt.

"We're running out of food," I told God, and timidly made my request. "We need … ten million meticais."

Always be specific when you ask God for things, the Rhema tapes had told me, and that way you'll know for sure that He was the one who answered your prayers.

Not sure whether God *was* going to answer me - after all, I had turned my back on Him for more than a year now – I slowly walked back to the house.

The next day, something quite out of the ordinary occurred. Thanks to Rungo and the long year during which he hadn't allowed us to sell our wood, our customers had all deserted us for other sawmills but in the afternoon, a pickup drove down the track and Mr. Chuabo, who hadn't been down to the sawmill to buy timber for about three years, climbed out of it. "I need some wood," he told O'D and handed over … yes, TEN MILLION METICAIS!

After Chuabo had driven off, I walked along the track back to the shady spot where I had asked God for help. Sunshine, brighter than bright, danced around me and dazzled my eyes. I was thrilled and filled with a sense of awe. A nonentity of a woman living in the back of beyond, I had prayed to God and the very next afternoon He had answered me by giving me exactly what I had asked Him for!

I was in the middle of thanking God when another feeling flooded through me. Along with the awe, came … fear. Taken aback, I fell silent and in that instant I realised that I had glimpsed the true nature and power of God. This wasn't the mythical, cosy and one-sided God of love that some Western people had dreamed up to make themselves feel good. This was the real God, a God not only of love but One who had other sides as well. A God of judgment, not a God to be taken lightly or to turn your back on. Struck by what had happened, I realised I had just experienced the Biblical fear of God.

The ten million didn't last long and in the weeks that followed, I made several more requests for money.

Standing once again under the shade of the leafy trees just past the entrance, I asked God for another ten million meticais. Again Mr. Chuabo paid us a visit the very next afternoon. This time, however, he gave O'D not ten but eleven million meticais.

For some days, I pondered on the difference in the amount I had asked for and the amount I had received. What was God telling me? Was he telling me not to limit Him and that I could ask for more?

Back under the leafy trees at my special spot, I decided to ask God for more, much more. This time, I decided to ask him for … fifty million meticais.

A day later, Mr. Chibante, who owned a large and busy carpentry shop in Chimoio, drove his lorry down to us. He needed wood he told O'D, a great deal of wood!

At the end of summer, when the leaves were beginning to turn coppery-brown, Azelia died.

One morning, when I went into the laundry room to take washing out of the washing machine, I was struck by the terrible change in her tall, willowy figure. With her back towards me, she was sitting down and ironing with the heavy charcoal iron. Her once strong shoulders had shrunk into skeletal thinness and I could see that handling the iron was an effort for her.

An infinite sadness gripped me. Azelia had worked for me for eight years and now, I knew, she too was about to die. Although she had always insisted she was suffering from asthma, I'd had the idea that this wasn't true and that her 'asthma' was, in fact, AIDS. There was nothing I could do for her but there was one last little thing I could give to her.

I put a hand on the back of one of her painfully thin shoulders. "Azelia," I said, trying to keep my voice steady and not to let her know that I knew, "how would you like to go on holiday for a month, with full pay?"

She didn't turn around. "I would like that Dona," she told me in a muffled voice. "When can I go?"

A tear rolled down my face and I quickly turned away from her in case she looked around and saw I was crying for her. Oh, Azelia. Oh, poor, once lovely, strong, Azelia. The last of the three people I had become so fond of and who had made my life in the Nhamacoa so much easier. I opened the door of the washing machine and started pulling clothes out into a plastic basket. "Today, when you're finished."

Azelia took more than a month's holiday. One day, Lloyd met her on the forest track and she told him she wasn't going to come back to work. A few weeks after this meeting, she died.

After Azelia's death, Lloyd brought a young woman called Joaquina to work for me and she couldn't have been more different to Azelia. Small, lean and a real woman of the bush, Joaquina's only possessions were the dirty skimpy top and capulana she was wearing. Discovering she knew absolutely nothing about anything, I had to begin from scratch and gave her some of my old clothes, a bar of soap and some lessons on hygiene. Unable to read and write or even count to more than ten, she made Lloyd and me laugh when she told us she had been six years old when her son had been born.

Lloyd left for better things in Chimoio and a tall old cook called Domingo arrived out of the blue, looking for a job. Unable to believe my luck, I employed him. He had worked in Zimbabwe, he

373

told me, for the Colcom meat company and before that, for a Jewish couple in Bulawayo.

Joaquina and Domingo had been working for me for a couple of months when I found the strange little bottle. One morning, handing out ingredients to Domingo for a special recipe for lunch, I reached up to the spice rack for the oregano and noticed a tiny glass bottle wedged between the cinnamon and the nutmeg.

"Is this yours, Domingo?" I asked, showing him the little bottle. It was filled with something that looked like a yellowish oil.

"No, Madam," he said.

I pulled out the tiny wooden stopper and sniffed the bottle's contents. There was no smell. I held it out to Domingo to sniff. "What do you think it is?"

"I don't know, Madam."

I got the same reaction when I questioned Joaquina and when I asked the only other person who had access to the house, he looked blank as well.

"Did you leave this in my spice rack?" I asked O'D.

"Never seen it before," he told me.

There was only one conclusion to come to. Hidden in my spice rack, the tiny bottle was the very thing Colin had warned me to look out for - a fetish from a witch doctor!

I carried the bottle to the rubbish pit and threw it in. Who, I wondered, wanted to harm us? Could it be ... the witch woman? Had she talked Joaquina into hiding the fetish in my kitchen? We'd had a lot of trouble from her and her family and we had caught her son's two wives cutting down some of our small trees. They were stealing our planks in the dead of night, I was sure, why else had they built their huts so close to us? They were like one of the mountains the Rhema tapes had talked about. I had to get rid of them. I had to get them out of our lives.

The next day, in the afternoon, using my newfound knowledge from Colins' cassettes, I decided to take on the witch woman.

Standing underneath the avocado trees, I stared in the direction of her hut, not far from the back of our house and hidden only by a thin band of tall grass and forest. "Witch woman!" I said loudly and authoritively, "in the name of Jesus of Nazareth, I order you to leave sawmill land! Leave and go back to the place you came from! Leave right now!"

Back in the house, I sat down on the sofa and wondered what affect my words were having on the woman. Was she suddenly feeling an irresistible urge to return to her last place of residence? Was she already throwing her possessions into a capulana, tying it into a bundle …

A horrible and frightening sound broke into my thoughts. Startled, I looked up and saw an ancient, white-haired and wrinkled old woman stomping past the east-facing sitting room window. Making the sounds a rabid dog would make, she growled and snarled and snapped in awful inhuman fury.

What was *this*? I ducked down out of sight. Hopefully, she wouldn't see me.

The animal sounds grew fainter and fainter and when I was sure the woman was gone, I went outside. Jonah, Alfixa's son, was standing by the carpenter's bench, sharpening some chainsaw teeth. I walked over to him.

"Did you see that old woman, Jonah?" I asked.

He nodded his head.

"Where did she come from?"

"Here," Jonah pointed his finger at a spot on the ground, just in front of his feet.

"What?" Taken aback, I stared down at the spot. Was he telling me that the old woman had materialized out of the ground in front of him?

"I didn't see where she came from," he explained. "I was working and when I looked up, she was just here." Again he pointed at the spot in front of him.

"Oh, I see. Do you know her?"

"No, I have never seen her before."

Shaken, I walked slowly back to the house. Weird. How very, very weird. No sooner had I ordered the witch woman to leave, than a strange and very angry old crone who bore no resemblance whatsoever to the witch woman who lived near my house, had come stomping past my window and making horrible demonic animal sounds. This was no coincidence, I was sure. What was going on here? Was this a REAL witch woman and not the other?

In the kitchen, I lit a match and turned on the gas under the kettle. I needed a cup of tea to revive myself. What a fright the old woman had given me! In future, I told myself, I would leave these

things up to God. He knew much more about what was going on than
I did.

CHAPTER THIRTY

GOD'S RADIO STATION
And I will give you shepherds according to My heart who
will feed you with knowledge and understanding

I came across Transworld Radio by chance, or so I thought.

Although Colin's tapes had been a real help, I knew that there
was something missing. I needed something more than the Rhema
sermons, helpful as they were.

One evening, tired of the dreary news on the BBC World
Service and horrified by the awful things I was hearing on SWRadio
Africa, the independent Zimbabwean radio station broadcasting out of
London, I slowly turned the dial on my shortwave radio, searching for
music and something to lighten my mood. I was halfway up the
shortwave one waveband when my attention was caught by some
words spoken by a very English voice, a voice which seemed to be
speaking directly to me from out of my radio.

"You've just been through a terrible time, haven't you?" I
heard the calm and gentle voice of Dick Saunders say. "A terrible
time of trouble and darkness such as you've never experienced before
and which you thought would never end. If you would just put your
trust in God, He'll help you ... He won't let you down ... People will
let you down ... but God never will."

I slowly sank down into a chair to listen. God ...

"You probably think you've found us by accident, don't you?"
the English voice went on, "But you didn't, you know. It was God
who directed your hand, God who directed that dial you were turning
on your radio."

Astonished, I listened to this man on the radio who seemed to
know all about my circumstances and then, when he was finished
talking, a Canadian called Dr. Lutzer who had a dry and witty sense of
humour began to talk about God. He was followed by others; Chuck
Swindoll, David Jeremiah and the wonderful Dr. J. Vernon McGee,
who was taking us on something he called his Bible Bus with his
twangy Texas accent. Just when I needed it, I had found Transworld
Radio - God's radio station!

From then on, I listened every evening and every morning to Dick Saunders and the other Pastors. Apart from Dick Saunders, who was English and from Hailsham, there were Pastors from Canada, America, Australia, South Africa and Zimbabwe. Transworld Radio was an in-depth Bible teaching station, I discovered, where passages were often explained, sentence by sentence.

Like a thirsty man stumbling into an oasis, I drank in their teachings.

My Bible took on a battered look, I underlined sentences, made notes in the margins and on the inside of the covers, the gold lettering on the front cover wore off.

Why had it taken so long to find this radio station?

Something I had once read in a book about Buddhism flitted into my mind. "When the pupil is ready, the Guru will appear." Obviously, I had been a tough nut to crack, to soften up!

Full of enthusiasm for a book I had ignored for years, I embarked on an intensive period of learning that was to last for years and was infinitely satisfying. Armed with my new knowledge, I discovered to my surprise how Biblically illiterate most of the world was. Even western Christians seemed to fall into this category. No wonder everyone crumbled when faced with a disaster.

On the BBC World Service, I caught an episode of 'West Way', the BBC's attempt at a soap opera. Here, astonishingly, I heard the 'Roman Catholic priest' tell a lapsed member of his congregation that, "Jesus kissed the feet of lepers."

"He never did that!" I told the BBC sternly. "Do your homework!"

Another time, a Canadian Professor of Philosophy excitedly told the BBC that he had solved the puzzle of Jesus' walk across the stormy waters of Galilee. "He wasn't walking on water," the Professor told the world, "he was walking on ice - because the water had frozen over!"

I glared at the radio. "Get real!" I told the Professor. "Can't you read? The disciples' fishing boat 'was in the middle of the sea, *tossed by the waves* for the wind was contrary' when they had seen Jesus walking towards them." How had the Professor come up with the ice? And how absurd!

Eve did not eat an apple, you know, and Jesus was not visited by three wise men but by wise men who gave him *three* gifts. Mary Magdalene wasn't a prostitute and according to the prophet Isaiah, about seven hundred years before Jesus was born, God did not sit over a flat earth but above the *circle* of the earth.

"There is no such thing as evil," a man said on NPR, the American radio station I had found on the World Space Satellite Radio Allan Schwarz had brought to us from Johannesburg.

"Oh, yes there is," I contradicted him. "You just close your eyes to it because you don't want to see it."

Isolated as I was in a tiny patch of forest in the middle of nowhere, God had taken the trouble to give me teachers of his own choice. He had invited me to join His vast congregation of unseen radio listeners who, I discovered, lived in countries all over the world. I had become a member of Transworld Radio. I had become part of God's invisible Church.

CHAPTER THIRTY ONE

THE NHAMACOA FILM CLUB
2009

When Afonso hung the DVD from the lowest branch of the mango tree in front of the shop, the word went out. "It's Kapfupi! The Notorious Kapfupi! They're showing 'What goes around, comes around' on Saturday!"

Late in the afternoon, they began to arrive, when the sun glowed low and rosy on the horizon. They came over the hills and down through the valleys, crossing rivers until they reached the footpath that wound up through the shady trees and led them up the final hill to the dazzling white shop with the green doors and green windows.

Climbing the steps up onto the shop verandah, they sat down on the dark panga panga benches Carlito, the carpenter, had made for them and waited in noisy, chattering anticipation. Old and young, men and women, these were the subsistence farmers who had destroyed the Nhamacoa forest, hacking and chopping at it and burning until thirty thousand hectares had gone up in smoke in the form of charcoal.

They enjoyed Kapfupi, the Shona films about the ragged Zimbabwean who was always up to tricks and trying to outsmart his neighbour. Another favourite were the bushmen in the South African film 'The Gods must be Crazy' and its sequel. Then, there were all the action films. Although these films were American and in a language they couldn't understand, the people liked them because there wasn't a lot of boring incomprehensible talk. Van Damme, Dolph Lundgren, Chuck Norris, they enjoyed them all but there was one whom they admired above all the others and that was ... Arnold SCHWARZENEGGER!

Schwarzenegger was unstoppable in his fight against villains. In the film 'Eraser', despite being spiked in the hand by roofing nails, blown up in a gas explosion, knifed right through a leg, sucked out of an aeroplane with a parachute that failed to open, not to mention being shot in the shoulder and attacked by crocodiles in a zoo, their battered bloodstained hero only swayed unsteadily on his feet for a few seconds. And when he fought his last great battle, the Nhamacoa film club got so carried away that they stood up on their benches and screamed and shouted and shook their fists in their support for him. He was their hero. Someone who made them dream. He was a man who fought for justice and always beat the bad guys.

Most of the American action films, I noticed, were filled with villains who were Chinese or who looked Chinese.

"Do you think the people are getting the idea that the Chinese are the bad guys of the world, Douglas?" I asked. Douglas operated the DVD player and television O'D had set up on one of the verandah walls for the film shows.

"They *are* the bad guys of the world," Douglas said grimly.

Like Lloyd, Douglas was another Zimbabwean economic refugee working for us. He had once been a chef at the luxurious Leopard Rock Hotel in the Vumba until Mugabe's destruction of the country had led to the demise of the very lucrative Zimbabwean tourist industry.

Not only did Douglas dislike the Chinese for the support they were giving Mugabe in the form of money and arms but he also had a personal beef with them. This had taken root when he had been forced to buy a tube of Chinese toothpaste at the Mutare market when the country had been going through a particularly tough time and the shops had been empty of Colgate.

"It had a picture of a cat on the tube," Douglas had told me, "and it was called 'Le Miaow' or something. It had a very funny taste and, even worse, it had a terrible numbing effect on my taste buds! I couldn't taste anything for hours after brushing my teeth with that zhing zhong stuff!"

For a cook, the loss of sensation in his taste buds was, naturally enough, not something to be taken lightly! Eschewing fresh breath and dental hygiene, a disgruntled Douglas had thrown his 'Le Maiow' toothpaste into a dustbin.

"My best friend also brushed his teeth with this 'Le Miaow'," Douglas had continued with a shudder, "and in his case, all the skin on the inside of his mouth peeled off in little bits and pieces!"

"Shows you what they think of us," I had told Douglas.

We made sure we never bought Chinese DVDs. These were also of the 'zhing zhong' quality, as the Zimbabweans had taken to calling the shoddy goods the Chinese thought were fit for Africa. We kept their products out of our shop as well. We didn't want our customers coming down with strange illnesses or complaining that the article they had bought the day before had broken or stopped working.

I had come up with the idea of the shop when Idalina Fiosse Gavumende, the large, fat and new Chefe do Posto in Macate had closed down our business in 2006. We had got on well with Sainete and fairly well with his replacement, Musapata, but Idalina, who had trained as a nurse in Cuba, had something against us before she had even set her eyes on us.

After the battering we had received from the Mozambican government officials in 2002 and 2003, we had managed to struggle back onto our feet, selling the remains of the panga panga from Gondola and buying new timber licences with the money to begin operating again.

Then, deciding to have something of a clean up, O'D had sent our tractor driver Fernandinho off down the forest track with several trailer loads of offcuts for the people now living around us. Not only was this wood given to them for nothing, but word had also been sent out that they could come to the sawmill and under our foreman Naison's supervisory one good eye, take away as much as they could carry of more free offcuts in the form of thin beams. It had taken them three whole days to demolish this huge pile and soon afterwards all the huts around us had boasted doors and windows, tables and benches.

Then, at the end of 2005, Idalina had paid us a visit, accompanied by the new Administrator of Gondola, a woman even larger than herself.

Tramping around the sawmill with her entourage, Idalina had asked O'D for the (naturally) free donation of some doors and windows for a small maternity house she was planning on building in Macate and O'D had told Luis Raoul our carpenter to get busy on this. When the work was finished, O'D had driven off to Macate to deliver the doors and windows and although the new nurse who had taken Mario's place had thanked him for the gift, there had been no word of gratitude from Idalina, although the doors and windows had come to a considerable sum of money.

Trouble had started when more people had decided to move onto sawmill land. Emboldened by the witch woman's success, Isaac had enlarged his machamba on the other side of the Nhamacoa River by moving across the river and helping himself to half of a piece of sawmill land next to the bit she had taken. Then Maqui, who had worked for us as a scout, had moved onto another part of sawmill land, in the north. Despite O'D's attempts to remove them, they had refused to budge.

Driving down to visit us one weekend, Teofilo Mendonca had been visibly shaken by these land grabs. "You'd better get the Land Registry Department to mark out your boundaries all over again," he had warned O'D. "Quickly!"

Our request to the Land Registry Department had coincided with our request for a new felling licence for 2006 and when Idalina had sent word to O'D to attend a meeting, she had given him the impression that the meeting had concerned his new timber licence. Before the Forestry Department would give us permission to carry on with our business, we now had to get permission from Mr. Maforga, the very important and traditional tribal chief of a huge area stretching from the Nhamacoa right down to Inchope.

Accompanied by Naison and Afonso, O'D had driven off to the meeting place and had been surprised to find not Mr. Maforga but a large and rather belligerent crowd of the people now living around us. The mood of the crowd had lightened momentarily when someone had produced a chair for O'D to sit on – a chair with a rickety leg – and which had immediately toppled over. The sight of O'D on his back on the ground with his legs in the air had delighted the crowd and they had roared with laughter.

Then the true nature of the meeting had been revealed. O'D had been tricked into coming to a 'People's Court' where accusations were going to be leveled at him by the population.

"He never gives us any wood," someone in the crowd had complained to Idalina. "He burns it instead!" There had been growls of angry agreement.

"He never gives us any lifts in his car!" an ancient old woman had screamed.

Their voices rose in a babble. "He won't fix the road! He won't give us wood for school desks! He hasn't given us a clinic!"

Taken aback by Idalina's trickery and the peoples' hostility, O'D had said nothing in his defence. It had been obvious that the new Chefe do Posto had not been out to create harmony.

A week later, when Marcelino had arrived from the Land Registry Department to mark out our boundaries, the people's mood had turned even uglier. Already whipped up against O'D by Idalina's communist Cultural Revolutionary type Peoples' Court, they had followed along behind Marcelino and his GPS machine, making a

383

threatening buzzing sound just like a swarm of angry bees. The land was theirs! We were trying to take it away from them!

"They are very dangerous," Idalina had warned O'D. "You must be careful of them."

It had soon become clear to us what Idalina had been up to. She had been using us as a political football in order to curry favour with the people and had played a game that might well have ended disastrously for us. The people were, indeed, dangerous. In Chimoio about a year later, they rioted and burnt a member of a gang of thieves to death by putting a tyre around his neck and setting it alight. Even a policeman had been killed.

Now, thanks to Idalina, when O'D had driven past Lica on his way home in the evenings, angry words and abuse had been hurled at him along the way. Abuse such as "Boer! Go back home to your own country, Boer!" and once, someone had even chopped down a tree on the forest track to block his way. Naison and Afonso had also been reviled as traitors to their race. "Filhos do branco!" people had insulted them, accusing them of being "Sons of the white man!"

Kashangamu's son had been caught pulling out my little panga panga seedlings on our southern boundary.

An enormous fire had been started up suspiciously close to the Maqui family's hut and thousands of O'D's precious little teak seedlings had been burnt.

On our western boundary, there had been more arson. Isaac's brothers had set the long dry yellow grass on our side of the boundary alight and had succeeded in incinerating eight hundred and forty one of my panga panga saplings.

"They want you to go," Jose, one of our night guards, had told me, "because they want the last of the trees and to make machambas on sawmill land."

And then, when Idalina had reluctantly put her signature on the document Mr. Maforga had finally signed and O'D had handed it in to the Forestry Department, he had discovered that the new Head of Forestry had given him a licence to cut in the very same area as another forester.

At last, O'D had given up the unequal fight. A minor government official trained in Cuba, with the aid of the subsistence farmers living around us, had closed us down.

"Let's go," I had said to O'D. "Let's leave Mozambique. What are we doing living here among people who are always telling us how much they hate us?"

"Where will we go?" O'D had asked.

"Back to England," I had told him. "To a place where people keep to the rules and there's justice."

My suggestion hadn't gone down well. O'D had been born out of his century and living a cramped, constricted life in a cold, grey, drizzly country would never do for him. He needed challenges to overcome and he loved the wide open spaces of Africa, its colour, its warmth and its people, crazy as they often were. He was also not going to take failure lying down, especially a failure caused by other people.

We had lost a small fortune in Mozambique and to leave the Nhamacoa where we had spent 12 years of our lives, planted thousands of indigenous trees, put in a dam, not to mention the expensive borehole, and renovated three houses the Mozambicans had destroyed during the war, would cause us to lose even more.

I had heaved a sigh. "They're not going to let us stay here now that we haven't got a business anymore," I had told O'D.

The expression on his face had turned stubborn and it had been obvious what he intended to do. Never a quitter, he was going to grind it out and unfortunately for me this meant that I was going to have to grind it out as well. Oh, how I hated all this grinding it out!

"Don't worry," he had told me, "I'll think of something."

For a while, we got by and made a little money by hiring out our chainsaw operators, our chainsaws, tractors and trailers to all those Mozambican foresters who had no equipment of their own but were now allowed to fell timber for all the Chinese who were flooding into the country.

And then, when Marcelino had told us we had to have another meeting with the people and the Chefe do Posto to re-do our boundaries all over again because our papers had been lost, an idea had popped into my head.

It had happened when I had gone along to this meeting to give O'D some moral support and had been sitting next to Mr. Penembe.

During our long wait for Idalina (Mozambican government officials are notoriously unpunctual and she was no exception) we didn't talk much and the people had been on their best behaviour this

385

time. No doubt this had been something to do with Mr. Penembe's presence - another of my ideas!

Dignified and white-haired, Mr. Penembe was a longtime friend of O'D's. His mother had been a Mozambican woman, his father a Greek and his real name was Ernesto Hazakis. Well-respected and a journalist, he had taken on the pseudonym of Penembe, the Mozambican name for that giant rock lizard, the leguaan, in order to write his articles. I had invited him as a witness and for our protection. Everyone knew Frelimo were scared of him, because of what they had done to him during the civil war.

Mr. Penembe had been living with a Bulgarian woman at that time and Frelimo hadn't liked that. So, they had burst into his house one night and had given him such a terrible beating that he still bore the scars today on his face and body. Then, they had sent him off to one of their camps in Gorongosa to be 're-educated'. Torn away from the Bulgarian woman, he had never seen her again. She had been told to get out of Mozambique and although she had borne him a child, not surprisingly, she had never returned.

Idalina had arrived almost an hour late for the meeting, giving no apologies for our long wait. Loathing had bubbled up in me. She had used the people against us, playing the racist angle, the land angle and had ruined our business. What she had done hadn't helped the people either. Over the years, many of the people at the meeting had come to us for jobs when their harvests had failed. Now, she had taken away this safety net.

After Idalina had lowered her bulk down onto a chair, which unfortunately didn't have a rickety leg to topple her over, a thought had struck me. You fought fire with fire. Yes … The people were the key. We must do what Idalina had done, but with a difference. While she had used them destructively, creating disharmony, we would do the opposite, repairing the damage and paying back bad with good.

For years, the people living around us had been ignored and neglected by the government. Sometimes, when I had met Aid Agency workers at a social event in Chimoio, I had tried to persuade them to come down to the Nhamacoa to do something for the people but even they had overlooked their needs. Without a second look, flashy cars bearing the UNICEF logo had shot past the poorly thatched school where the children perched on poles and wrote in their exercise books using their laps for desks. The Missionaries, too, had been surprisingly blind to their existence, brushing off my suggestions of spiritual help and preferring to minister from the comfort of their homes to people in the towns.

We couldn't give them a school but we could do something to save their money and the long, tiring trips they had to make to shop in Chimoio. We could also do something to brighten up their unutterably bleak and dreary lives, to give them nice things and some entertainment ... to make them laugh ... to give them dreams ... a little knowledge of the world outside the Nhamacoa ... yes, we would do something to help them, and in doing so, help ourselves too!

When there had been a lull in the conversation, I had opened my mouth.

"A shop," I had told the people. "We're going to build a shop for you."

There had been a buzz of interest and a flicker of excitement had come into their eyes. Take that, Idalina!

"Promising to build a shop," Mr. Alberto had carefully written down on the pad of paper he'd been using to record the minutes of the meeting.

O'D had given me an incredulous look.

"And as well as this," I had continued, "we're going to have a television and show films at the shop. Free films!"

At a signal from Mr. Alberto, applause had burst out and O'D had given me a glare.

"And now," I had gone on rashly, "Senhor Pixley is going to buy everyone a Coke or a Fanta!"

"I'd rather have a beer!" a voice had piped up in the back row.

It had taken a while to get O'D to come around to my idea. "I'm not doing anything for that destructive rabble, that bunch of environmental terrorists," he had grouched.

"But you have to," I had told him, "I made a promise and as a Christian I can't break it."

The opening of the shop in May 2009 had been a great event and had gone off very successfully.

We had invited forty people to the inaugural lunch and Mr. Penembe had helped out with the cooking, drinking lashings of red wine at ten in the morning while he had stood over Douglas and Carlito the gardener and given instructions on how to barbecue chicken, making Carlito turn hot chicken drumsticks over the coals with his fingers! Teofilo Mendonca and his wife Bernadette had arrived suitably late as was the custom of government officials and

Idalina, although invited, had been a poor loser and had failed to turn up at all.

Mr. Maforga had fasted for a week in order to prepare himself to perform the traditional 'spirit' ceremony at the shop and had brought about three hundred and fifty of the population with him - all, of course, expecting to eat!

Dressed in a khaki uniform adorned with a brilliantly coloured sash across his chest and with his old-fashioned Colonial type khaki cap on his head, Mr. Maforga had looked more like the president of an African country than a real African president.

After he had poured some red wine onto the ground for the spirit, he had told the listening population not to burn our trees, that forests were important and the heritage of future generations of Mozambicans.

He had also warned them not to steal from us and had threatened that if they did, he would cut off their noses before handing them over to the police and they would go to jail with two holes in their faces. The listening population had roared with laughter at the picture he had conjured up.

Afterwards, we had been severely tested when almost four hundred people had converged on our kitchen, all expecting to eat. Somehow, we had managed to give almost everyone a little rice, a little sadza, a piece of chicken, some goat stew. We had cut Douglas' delicious sweet bread rolls into quarters and Mr. Alberto had ladled out mahewu, the innocuous maize and sugar drink and douro, the not at all innocuous maize beer.

There had been a lot of jollification on the verandah of the shop afterwards. The people had watched music DVDs on the television and had drunk Mozambican alcoholic drinks called 'Dynamite', 'Knockout', 'Buffalo Gin' and 'Temptation'. Mr. And Mrs. Maforga had both downed several 'Knockouts' and had become very merry, giving a dancing demonstration that had finished with Mr. Maforga having to use his walking stick to help him get back up from his knees. On his feet again, he had given us a salute and two or three bows.

The war between the people and ourselves had at last ended.

And as for the drums, which had disturbed my sleep for so many years, they've grown weak and faint, overpowered by the television on the shop verandah and Arnold Schwarzenegger. They're losing their power, just like the green and red ghost that wandered around at night for so many years down by the Nhamacoa River.

"The sawmill ghost isn't around that much anymore," Afonso told O'D the other day. "Since the shop opened, people have only seen it a couple of times and it doesn't frighten them anymore."

Well, you know what I think? I think that the red and green Nhamacoa ghost's increasingly rare appearances may have had something to do with the fact that the people have chopped down all the trees along the banks of the Nhamacoa River, including those around the lovely fairytale pool our workers once used to bathe in. It was probably some kind of insect that glowed in the night and is becoming extinct because its habitat has been destroyed.

On the other hand ...

Afonso and the people may well be right and there is a ghost – a ghost that is beginning to vanish, along with all the other old things that once held sway here in the Nhamacoa.

EPILOGUE

THE NIGHT THE BANDITS CAME

By 2010, the once large and beautiful Nhamacoa forest had virtually disappeared. All that remained were small areas of trees dotted around, here and there.

We had managed to save about 28 hectares around our house and as the population destroyed their habitat, machamba by machamba, all sorts of animals, birds and reptiles started fleeing into our trees for refuge.

The baboons were gone, though. Unlike the other animals that had found sanctuary with us, they had been trapped in the local cemetery and had been killed by the locals and their dogs.

Some of the other monkeys had been luckier and soon our trees began to teem and heave with Vervets.

The shy Samango monkeys were no trouble at all, as they kept to the treetops but the Vervets became a real menace. They weren't monkeys in my garden anymore but had become monkeys on my verandah, monkeys in my laundry room and monkeys in our outdoor kitchen. If we weren't careful, they would soon be monkeys in our house and maybe I would even catch them bouncing on our bed! We were going to have to do something about them, but what? It was all very well saving a bit of forest and some animals but there were obviously some negative consequences to this!

The solutions people were proposing weren't helpful. "Hunters," Idalina told the population, "to kill them all." Others suggested poisoning the Vervets or selling them to the Chinese.

"We're going to have to get help," I told O'D. Killing the animals was a sickening thought, especially as the problem was a man-made problem.

And so we decided to turn O'D's films of the forest and its inhabitants into a video blog and to put them onto the Internet. Perhaps we could raise interest this way, enough interest to raise funds to protect what little was left of the Nhamacoa and to transport the Vervets to Gorongosa. Perhaps also to raise funds to reforest and to give the animals now living in this cramped space more room.

But first, we needed someone to help us to edit O'D's films ...

We found Lee Shoniwa in a room at the International School, working on a documentary for a Danish Aid Agency. He was a young Zimbabwean refugee, thin as a rake and living on a shoestring and he desperately needed all the money he could get.

Bored with his bread and butter work, his eyes lit up with enthusiasm when he saw our films. The beauty of our little forest and its creatures enchanted him.

"How long will it take to edit them and put them onto the Internet?" I asked.

Lee was overly optimistic. "About a week," he told us, "if I really concentrate on it."

It was May when Nora Swete paid us a visit. We hadn't seen her since 1996. She came marching past our house and when she saw O'D, she asked him for some money. He gave her a little and she left.

After Nora Swete had gone, I went for my usual walk down the forest track with Bandit and when I got to our entrance, I saw evidence of her handiwork. Salt and charcoal, used in witchcraft, were scattered over the two large concrete flower tubs Naison had made and the nostrils and ears of the two wooden guards carved into the gate posts were filled with cooked sadza. Was this a fetish? I wondered, as I cleaned away her mess and if it was, what did it mean?

We began to have problems after Nora Swete's visit.

During a trip to Tete, someone stole O'D's car keys and after a Mozambican electrician had worked on the pickup so he could start it without the key, it developed a fault no one could fix. Every now and then and without any warning at all, the pickup would suddenly stop dead and all the lights would go out.

Then, Lee found himself caught up in the middle of a food riot and had to flee for his life with bullets and stones whizzing around his head.

The Internet went down for three weeks.

O'D had three freak car accidents and was lucky to escape unharmed.

Lee had his scary encounter with the Black Mamba.

And then, to cap it all, there was the terrifying bandit attack on 4th December …

They attacked Douglas first, before coming to us.

He was sound asleep when the double doors of his room whispered open. Torchlight shining in his face woke him up and thinking it was O'D, he mumbled, "What is it, Boss?"

391

Then he saw them, all seven of them, standing around him, and his blood turned to ice in his veins.

They were violent, kicking a chair and breaking it. Then they dragged him up onto his feet and ripping off his clothes, they half-strangled him with a piece of his T-shirt which they had torn into strips.

Naked, gagged, blind-folded and with his arms and legs too tightly tied up with electrical cable, Douglas found himself roughly manhandled down to the Nhamacoa River. There, they threw him down on the ground and left the seventh bandit to guard him while they walked up to our house.

After what seemed like an interminable time, during which Douglas had been certain he was going to be killed, he heard someone shouting the name "Zito! Zito!"

His captor moved off and as soon as Douglas was sure he was alone, he began the struggle to free himself. Managing to slip off the gag, the blindfold and the cable from his legs, he struggled to his feet and, numb with pins and needles, hobbled off to the nearest house.

This turned out to be the witch woman's house and knocking on the door, he called out for help. Although alone and fearful, she opened the door and peered out. With his back to her, so she wouldn't see his full and shameful nakedness, he spoke to her over his shoulder.

"Bandits," he told her, "they've got guns and one of them is dressed in police uniform. Please cut this cable binding my arms."

The only thing she had was a large old blunt kitchen knife and she sawed through the cable with difficulty. Once he was free, she ran for her life and hid herself in the banana trees, terrified she would be next on the bandits' list.

Douglas walked back up the path to his room in the shop to put on some clothes. His heart heavy with his dreadful experience and unaware that we had been the bandits' real target, he set off to tell us what had happened to him.

Reaching our house, he stumbled up to O'D and Lee who were standing outside anxiously calling for me and when he heard that the bandits had also attacked us and I was missing, the shock was too much for him and he collapsed onto the ground in a dead faint.

The bandits had left shortly after I had made my escape. Clutching their loot, they had asked, "Where is the Senhora?"

"I don't know," O'D had said.

Deciding to forget about me, they left by the front door and noticing O'D's red Toyota parked nearby, went over to it. While one of them slashed its tyres with his machete, another, eager for blood, wanted to disable O'D as well and in a most unpleasant manner.

"Shoot him in the foot! Let's shoot him in the foot!" he urged the leader.

But the leader ignored the suggestion and they finally walked off, with a few mocking parting words for O'D.

"Why don't you get yourself a better car?" they laughed, cocky with success.

For a while, O'D and Lee stood and watched the bandits disappear down the track.

"If we had a phone, we could get them caught," O'D said, "but they've taken them all."

"They didn't find mine," Lee told him. "It was under my pillow."

Without his own phone, the only number O'D could remember was the number of his old friend Teofilo Mendonca and as luck would have it, Mendonca just happened to be in Catandica when he received O'D's sms.

Mendonca alerted Lt. Col. Tomo, the Head of the Protection Police and Wilson in Gondola, and scrambling for cars, drivers, petrol and armed police, they hit the road.

In the meantime, O'D and Lee started looking for me. They were worried that the seventh bandit had met me in the dark and had killed me.

"Val!" they called. "Val!" and then, when I didn't answer, they became desperate. "Vaaal! VAAAAAL!"

When I heard them calling, I raised my head warily. Was this a trick? Were the bandits searching for me and forcing O'D to call me? No way was I going to come out of hiding, only to be caught again and dragged off by those hideous creatures! I would only leave my hideout at dawn, when the bandits would be gone.

When the first tinge of light touched the sky, I walked out of the forest and past the still empty shop. Now I heard other voices calling me, also with a touch of desperation.

"Vaaaal!" Lee shouted. "Madam!" Douglas shouted.

"I'm here!" I shouted back.

Inside the house, I went into the bathroom and turned on the taps. I needed a bath to wash off the mud. I was covered in scratches

393

and my ribs hurt where Red-shirt had held me while he'd been dragging me around.

Clean and dressed again, I walked back into the kitchen on feet that were full of thorns and threw my torn and bedraggled capulana into the dustbin.

"Tea? Coffee?" I called out to O'D, Douglas and Lee.

They were sitting in silence at the table in the middle of the mess the bandits had made of the sitting room, each thinking their own thoughts. The offer of coffee revived them.

When I placed the cups down on the table, Douglas was the first to break the silence. "I was sure they were going to kill me," he said. He chose a cup and drank down some coffee. "I was praying and praying all the time."

"I was praying too," I said. "I'm sure God saved us. Those people were definitely killers."

"It was spiritual warfare," Lee said quietly. He was off to Theological College in 2011 and was convinced the devil was trying to take him out.

And then Douglas opened his mouth and said the words that were to have fatal consequences for him a few weeks later. "This has only made my faith in God stronger," he told us, not knowing that what he had said was like a challenge.

There was the sound of cars racing down the forest track and then several pickups came to a screeching halt outside the house. The police. About thirty of them, and bristling with rifles! Followed closely by Mendonca and his friend Luis.

Inside the house, Tomo looked around our ransacked sitting room and a speculative gleam came into his eyes. "I've seen this before," he murmured thoughtfully. "It looks just like the modus operandi of the bandits who attacked the Chinese sawmill at Tembwe in November. They shot one of the Chinese in the leg and then sprayed the windows with AK-47 bullets."

Mendonca, who was an expert when it came to human nature, exchanged a look with Tomo. "The first thing the bandits are going to do is to go to a bar and spend some of that money they've stolen," he said, "but if the police go looking for them, they'll go underground."

Turning to Douglas, he asked "Do you think you would recognise any of the bandits if you saw them again?"

Douglas nodded his head. "I think so."

"Then Douglas must come with me and we'll go looking for them," Mendonca told Tomo.

Wilson gave Lee a hard look. "And I'm taking HIM back to Gondola for questioning," he told us.

My heart sank. This was just like the Mozambican police, to take the easy way out and try to pin the crime on a foreigner. "Lee's a friend of ours," I said, "he didn't have anything to do with this."

Wilson ignored me. "Vamos!" he said, with a last look around the room. "Let's go!"

After the police left, we had a surprise visit from Kashangamu's son.

"We saw the bandits' car yesterday," he told O'D. "It was dark blue and," he handed over a scrap of paper, "this is the registration number."

'AAM 201 MC", O'D read out. Puzzled, he looked up. "Are you sure this number is right?"

"I'm sure," Kashangamu's son told him.

Now a new problem arose. How were we going to get this information to Teofilo? Wilson had whisked Lee off to Gondola police station, taking away our only access to a phone!

I grasped at a straw. "The shop phone! Perhaps the bandits didn't take it."

Sure enough, the bandits hadn't seen the shop phone and although it was practically out of credit, it got us through to Mendonca.

"Look for a dark blue car, Teofilo!" O'D shouted, "Registration number AAM 201 MC!"

"What?" Teofilo shouted back. "Are you sure about that number?"

"Yes!" O'D shouted, just as the phone went dead. We had run out of credit.

In Chimoio, Mendonca and Douglas trawled the streets, stopping off at every bar for a beer. They were sitting at Soalpo, drinking their twelfth beer and still surprisingly stone-cold sober when Teofilo gave a sudden start. A voice out of nowhere had spoken to him and had given him a message. "The car is at Fepom!" the voice told him.

Putting his unfinished beer down on the bar table, he stood up. "Come on!" he told Douglas. "I know where the car is! It's at Fepom!"

It didn't take long to find the car. As they drove into Fepom, there it was! Up in the air at the carwash, being cleaned of the mud it had picked up on the road down to the forest.

"Look! Look!" Douglas pointed excitedly at the dark blue Toyota Mark II. "There it is! There!"

Mendonca slapped his pointing finger down. "I see it but we don't want anyone to know that we're looking for it."

Pretending he also wanted his car washed, Mendonca parked his car right behind the bandits' Toyota, blocking its exit. "Now," he murmured to Douglas and raised his cell phone to his lips. "The car is at Fepom," he told Tomo. "At the car wash."

Tomo's men were on standby and within minutes the inhabitants of Fepom were startled by the appearance of the Rapid Intervention Force who surrounded the area and secured it. Arrests were made and then when it was all over, Mendonca and Douglas drove back to our house.

Sitting at the table under the big old mango tree, they drank even more beers while they described what had happened. Mendonca was euphoric at the part he had played in the arrests. "You'll get all your things back now," he told me with a beaming smile. "You"ll see!"

By the end of the week, five of the bandits were in jail, as well as a policeman called Tinga and his nephew. Yes, the Mozambican police had lived up to their reputation of eating at the same table with bandits and had been involved in the attacks, renting guns, ammunition and police uniforms out to our attackers. Far from doing their duty to protect us, they were hand in glove with criminals and murderers.

Although there were still some bandits evading capture, including the extremely dangerous leader, I was in high spirits. Only a few days had gone by since the attack and they were getting picked up. Teofilo was right. Any minute now, we were going to get our things back!

Douglas was in the kitchen making pancakes when I gave him the news. "It's only a matter of time now before they get the rest of them, Douglas," I told him.

Douglas gave a grim smile. He was still simmering over his treatment by the bandits and the wounds they had left on his arms with their too-tight cable.

"I hope they go to jail for the rest of their lives!" he said.

396

And then I opened my mouth and uttered the words that were also to send out a challenge.

"Yes!" I said, thumping a fist into the open palm of my other hand and giving a gleeful laugh. "That'll teach them to mess with us Christians!"

Two weeks after the attack, I discovered just how much the bandits had learned from 'messing with us Christians.'

It was about 7 o'clock on the night Douglas, Antonio our dayguard and a young girl gathered around O'D outside our house and spoke to him in lowered and urgent voices.

Wondering what they were talking about, I walked outside and joined them. "What's going on?" I asked.

No one answered me and then after a long pause, O'D said, "We didn't want to frighten you but we've had a message that some people have been looking for us in Macate. Six men, driving two of those Toyota Mark IIs and a motor cycle. Nobody told them where we live. This young girl's sister memorised the registration number of one of the cars. AAI 209 MP. It seems that some kind of revenge attack is being planned."

The news filled me with terror. My legs turned to jelly and I had a hard time to keep from falling. "We must hide – right away – in the forest!" I cried.

Everyone looked at me with dubious expressions on their faces.

"I think I'll phone Murray and ask him what he thinks," O'D said.

While O'D looked for network to make his phone call, I ran back into the house on rubbery legs. In the bedroom, I threw off my clothes and rummaged around in the cupboard for something more suitable for a fugitive running for their life. Black jeans, black top, black cardigan. Into my shoulder bag went our passports and grabbing my pepper spray, I ran outside again.

Everyone was still standing where I had left them.

"I managed to get hold of Murray," O'D told me.

"And what did he say?" I asked.

"He said, 'Get the hell out of there right away, O'D and come to us here in Gondola!"

I looked at Douglas. "And what about you, Douglas?"

"I'll be alright, Madam. They're not after me and if they come, I know where to hide."

The drive out of the forest and along the dirt road to Chimoio was terrifying. An eerie air of menace hung over the countryside, hideous danger lurking behind every tree, every bush and every bend in the road. Everytime the lights of a car appeared in front of us or behind us, my heart gave a lurch of fear. Was this them? Were we going to be rammed? Hacked at with a machete or gunned down? The only weapon we had to defend ourselves was the little pepper spray I was clutching so tightly in my hand and our pickup, so battered by freak accidents, was in no shape to outrun the bandits' speedy Mark IIs.

At last we drove onto tar and the road to Gondola. Just another sixteen kilometres to Murray's house and safety, but anything could still happen. Then, just a few kilometres from Murray's turnoff, without warning, the pick-up's lights went out and the car engine died on us. The Tete electrician's handiwork had brought us to a standstill at a most inopportune moment!

"Oh, no! Now what?" I panicked.

"It's alright," O'D assured me. "We're not far from Murray's house. We can walk it."

And then, for no reason at all, the pickup's lights came back on again, the engine started up and we were back on our way!

At Murray's house, Murray and his sister, Dal, were waiting for us with worried looks on their faces. I fell into a chair in their tiny sitting room and closed my eyes. Was this never going to end? It was all like a weird and hideous dream, almost impossible to believe it was happening to us in real life. Bandits had come uninvited into our lives, they had attacked and robbed us and then had got caught by a clever government official because they had been stupid enough to drive a flashy car in a poor rural area and now - incredibly – MORE of them were coming with revenge in mind! They were all mad. Mad. But then this was Mozambique … Africa …where everyone seemed to be out of their minds …

Cars pulled up outside Murray's house. Mendonca and Tomo. They looked worried too. "Don't go back to live in your house until the new year," Tomo warned O'D. "YOU can go back during the day," he added, "but Valeria must on no account go back there."

Although the revenge bandits' car was sighted several times in Chimoio and each sighting was reported to Tomo, the police never did anything about it. And although with the help of Jinho, we traced it to Albas garage in Maputo, this was never investigated. The last sighting

398

occurred on 21st December, and after that it was never seen in Chimoio again.

At the beginning of January, O'D and I went home and the first thing he did was to make bars for our bedroom windows and a big metal door to block off the corridor and keep the bedrooms and bathroom safe from AK-47 bullets. Sadly, life in the forest would never be the same again.

Soon after we arrived back home, Douglas went off to Zimbabwe for a week. He had looked after our house and animals well while we were in hiding. On his own and lonely, he had filled the empty hours by baking cakes for O'D to take to us in Gondola, cakes so scrumptious that Murray who had a sweet tooth ate one whole cake all by himself, all in one go and almost threw up as a result.

On my first morning home, Douglas said, "We are all scattered now, Madam."

"No we're not," I told him. "We're back now."

"The bandits have scattered us," he repeated, as if he hadn't heard me.

Douglas' words were prophetic. He didn't return from Zimbabwe after his week off and we began to get a little anxious. The bandits had stolen his wallet and his Identity Card and so he had taken the kandonga route into Zimbabwe. He had laughed when I had worried about him travelling without an Identity Card.

"I'll be fine, Madam," he had assured me.

But he had not been fine.

He'd been attacked by Zimbabwean soldiers as he'd been crossing the border and they had beaten him up so brutally, he had ended up in Chimanimani Hospital for two weeks.

About two months later, he sent us an sms. All it said was "My health is too unpleasant to come back to work. You'd better get another cook."

I remembered him sitting at the table drinking coffee after the bandit attack and telling us that the attack had only increased his faith in God. Now, that faith had been challenged by a second attack and I could only hope it hadn't been destroyed.

As for the bandits, twelve of them, as well as some policemen, were arrested. The terrible leader's wife turned out to be just as evil. She was jailed for stealing children.

Although some of the bandits had been caught the very same day of the attack, not one of our things was found by the police. And although the bandits were sentenced to twelve years in jail for attacking the Chinese sawmill at Tembwe, O'D's statement to the CID 'disappeared' and our case against them was buried and never came to court.

We had all played our part in their capture but we had been let down by those who were supposed to protect us and to give us justice.

And as for Nora Swete ? Her visit to us after an absence of fourteen years was, I'm sure, no coincidence. As Lee had said, we had been through a spiritual war but we had survived.

Now, I hope it's time for a little rest, a little peace and quiet.

Lightning Source UK Ltd.
Milton Keynes UK
UKHW010623141019

351570UK00002B/421/P